Language and Social Justice in Context

Scott Saft

Language and Social Justice in Context

Hawai‘i as a Case Study

palgrave
macmillan

Scott Saft
College of Hawaiian Language
University of Hawaii at Hilo
Hilo, HI, USA

ISBN 978-3-030-91250-5 ISBN 978-3-030-91251-2 (eBook)
https://doi.org/10.1007/978-3-030-91251-2

This Palgrave Macmillan imprint is published by the registered company Springer Nature Switzerland AG
The registered company address is: Gewerbestrasse 11, 6330 Cham, Switzerland

Acknowledgements

There are many people who generously provided assistance throughout the process of researching, writing, and preparing this book. First of all, I thank wholeheartedly the students, faculty, and friends of the Ka Haka ʻUla o Keʻelikōlani College of Hawaiian Language at the University of Hawaiʻi at Hilo. In particular, I am indebted to Jainine Abraham, Lito Arkangel, Jake Unger, Faʻfaleaʻi (Fale) Samau, and Sarah Juran for their valuable contributions. I could not have collected parts of the data and interpreted some of the language materials without their help. Additionally, much appreciation goes to Iota, Pila, and Yumiko, friends and colleagues who continuously offered important insights and sometimes added much needed levity to the process.

This book would not have been possible without certain key people from Palgrave Macmillan and Springer Nature. I am grateful to Cathy Scott for giving me the opportunity in the first place to submit a book proposal to Palgrave Macmillan. Alice Green played a role in keeping me on the path toward completion, and I must express the utmost of gratitude to Redhu Ruthroyoni for helping turn a sloppy manuscript into an actual book. I also give a huge "thank you" to Timothy Reagan from the University of Maine for reading a draft of the manuscript and providing his endorsement.

In terms of helping me understand how language is used in Hawai'i, I give special recognition to the former mayor of Hawai'i County, Billy Kenoi, who proudly displayed his local roots throughout his entire political career by using Pidgin and mixing multiple languages in the public domain. Unfortunately, for all us, Bruddah Billy lost his battle with leukemia in 2021, but it is easy to see that his strength and indomitable spirit live on in many multilingual people born and raised in Hawai'i.

I also want to express my gratitude to Zena for her patience as I finished the last pages of the manuscript, even as beautiful sites, delicious food, and happy conversations beckoned. I also thank Miiko, Ryan, and Bree for taking care of Shadow and allowing me to make my final edits without interruption.

As he has done for his entire life, my son Sebi served as a constant source of amazement and inspiration throughout the writing process. Whether it be through sports or linguistics, there is truly nothing happier and more meaningful in life than getting to share your interests and passions with your own child.

Finally, I want to acknowledge the people of Hawai'i who have for generations endured injustices as they saw their land and their language taken from them. My time in Hawai'i has allowed me to bear witness to some incredible acts of courage and also of aloha on the part of many of them. This includes the peaceful protectors who, through the philosophies of *Aloha 'Āina* and *Kapu Aloha*, engage daily in a struggle to maintain the beauty and the sacredness of Hawaiian lands. More than anything else, though, I have been awed by those who have fought and are still fighting for the survival of the Indigenous Hawaiian language. There are too many of such people to list them all here, but I acknowledge especially those with whom I have worked the closest: Pila Wilson, Kauanoe Kamanā, Larry Kimura, Iota Cabral, Hiapo Perreira, Kekoa Harman, Lei Kapono, Keiki Kawai'ae'a, Kananinohea Māka'imoku, Lehua Miller, Makalapua Alencastre, and Noelani Iokepa-Guerrero. Through their steadfast devotion to their language and culture, they have taught me so much more than any textbook about the importance of saving languages to empower next generations of speakers with indigenous linguistic and cultural resources. *E ola mau ka ʻŌlelo Hawaiʻi*!

Contents

1
Introduction

As I set out to research and write a book on language and social justice during the COVID-19 pandemic, I was reminded daily through my consumption of the media of the importance of dialogue about social justice. The COVID-19 pandemic further exposed the dangers of deep-seated inequalities in wealth and access to health care throughout the United States as economically challenged people of color proved to be the most likely to succumb to the virus. This includes indigenous people in the United States, particularly members of the Navajo community, who became sick and died at an alarming rate (Gifford, 2020). Moreover, the availability of vaccines, what should have been an event to celebrate, revealed inequalities in the distribution of resources not just in the United States but also across the world as poorer countries remained ravaged by the virus while extra vaccine dosages sat in American storage facilities. And as if COVID-19 was not enough, the pandemic overlapped with the murders of African Americans at the hands of the police in separate incidents, with the most well-known being the asphyxiation of George Floyd in Minneapolis. These slayings fixed a spotlight on the discrepancy between the experiences of people of color and those of

S. Saft, *Language and Social Justice in Context*,
https://doi.org/10.1007/978-3-030-91251-2_1

white Americans and led to protests and subsequent government responses that magnified a racial divide in the United States.

To be certain, the pandemic and the killings of African Americans point to a dialogue that must extend beyond language. Nonetheless, there is a close link between language and social justice that must not be ignored. The languages chosen by people and the manner in which they speak those languages can serve as a direct source of discrimination, a point underscored by several books recently published with justice in their titles. *Linguistic Diversity and Social Justice: An Introduction to Applied Sociolinguistics* by Ingrid Piller (2016) highlights the extent to which speakers of minority languages suffer linguistic discrimination in public domains of society such as business, education, health care, law, and government. Piller notes that there can be a "linguistic disadvantage" in society that should be recognized "as a form of structural disadvantage … that warrants a sustained public debate as to how it can be best mitigated" (Piller, 2016: 3). *Linguistics in Pursuit of Justice* by John Baugh (2018) describes the role of language in linguistic profiling, housing discrimination, and linguistic harassment, which includes the usage of unwanted language toward people, an act that can comprise sexual harassment. Another recent book, *Linguistic Legitimacy and Social Justice* by Timothy Reagan (2019), offers a critique of the ideology of "linguistic legitimacy," often used to stigmatize languages such as African American English, Spanglish, Sign Language, and Yiddish as inferior to English and other dominant languages. As Reagan (2019: 30) notes, this ideology is "potentially destructive and oppressive" since it results in discrimination that negatively affects speakers of those languages.

While negative perceptions about the language of "others" can be a source of discrimination, arguably the greatest linguistic injustice is for speakers to witness the endangerment and even death of their languages. This is, in fact, a regular occurrence for many minority and/or indigenous languages. The linguist Michael Krauss found in 1992 that 80% of Native North American languages spoken at that time were in danger of being lost (Krauss, 1992). He likewise noted that for Australia the percentage of moribund Aboriginal languages was even worse at 90%. One update of Krauss's numbers indicated that, as of 2010, 75% of the languages in use in 1950 in Australia, Canada, and the United States were now extinct or moribund (Lewis & Simons, 2010). While there may be multiple causes of "language endangerment" and "language death" (see Mufwene, 2004), the loss of a language is often the direct result of intentional efforts on the part of settler colonists to prevent native groups from speaking their own languages. As Roche (2020) asserts, "speakers and signers of indigenous and minoritized languages have repeatedly explained that their languages are endangered due to failures of social justice—the oppression, marginalization, stigmatization, exclusion, deprivation, and so on—that take place in the context of imperial, colonial, and nationalist domination" (Roche, 2020: 164; also see Davis 2017; Jacob, 2013; Mac Ionnarachtaigh, 2013; Taff et al., 2018). Roche (2020: 168) emphasizes that such "language deprivation" "enforces a condition of what Stauffer (2015: 2) calls ethical loneliness on users of endangered languages," which in turn causes debilitating damage to indigenous communities throughout the world, where rates of poverty and suicide far exceed other communities.

Language, however, is not merely a source of social injustice. It can also serve as a crucial resource for combatting discrimination and oppression. Baugh (2018) serves as a strong advocate for the use of linguistics toward the advancement of justice, noting not only how Franz Boas' (1911) early work on language and culture debunked myths of racial superiority but also how more recent areas such as forensic linguistics allow language specialists to affect justice directly. Similarly, Avineri et al. (2019a) introduce their edited volume by emphasizing the contributions to social justice of sociolinguists such as Gumperz (1982), Heath (1983), Hymes (1962), Labov (1966), and Wolfram (1974) through research documenting the role of language in the construction of social hierarchies, linguistic and racial differences, and social inequalities. They then present a set of chapters exploring how language may be used to alleviate injustices in fields such as education, health, and law and policy.

Language also becomes a resource for social justice through educational initiatives such as the SKILLS program developed by Mary Bucholtz and her colleagues in an effort to promote "sociolinguistic justice" (Bucholtz et al., 2014; Bucholtz et al., 2015; 2016, 2017, 2018). Implemented in K-12 classrooms to foster "self-determination for linguistically subordinated individuals and groups in sociopolitical struggles over language" (Bucholtz et al., 2014: 145), instructors work together with the students on a range of topics to aid in understanding of "their full linguistic repertoires" and their exploration of "academic research and critical perspectives on language to create opportunities for youth to share and create their own linguistic and cultural knowledge" (Bucholtz et al., 2018: 10). Moreover, language is also at the center of "language revitalization" movements aimed at increasing the number of speakers of indigenous languages (Grenoble & Whaley, 2006; Hinton et al., 2018; Olko & Sallabank, 2021). By offering indigenous communities the opportunity to reconnect with ancestral knowledge and culture through language, programs of language revitalization are helping people regain the confidence and well-being to counter the oppressive forces that brought distress to their families and communities.

Recognizing that language can function both as a source of injustice and as a resource for justice, this book builds on prior research by exploring the intersection of language and social justice in a specific part of the world, Hawai'i. Hawai'i consists of an isolated chain of islands situated in the Pacific Ocean, but it nonetheless is marked by significant cultural and linguistic diversity that includes the Indigenous Hawaiian language, a creole language known by the name of Pidgin, and also several other languages such as Chinese, Japanese, Portuguese, Ilokano, and Tagalog that began arriving with immigrants as early as the mid 1800s. While such diversity can have an enriching effect since it provides residents and visitors alike with different cultural experiences and contact with various ways of speaking, it also can lead to hierarchies within society that leave speakers of certain languages feeling the heavy burden of discrimination and injustice. This burden is especially heavy in Hawai'i for the Native Hawaiian population that has seen systematic degradation and near-eradication of its language, and it also is felt acutely by immigrants and their children compelled to give up their home languages due to an American educational system that prioritizes English. Placing a focus on Hawaiian, Pidgin, and immigrant languages, this book emphasizes that speakers of these languages need to be accorded space in society to develop, learn, and transmit them to future generations. I do this largely by placing a focus on the analysis of language practices in context in both spoken and written discourse. The analysis also examines the phenomenon of language mixing, a frequent occurrence in Hawaiian society (Saft, 2019; Saft et al., 2018). The focus on language practices in context will make it possible to uncover some of the obstacles that prevent access to languages and services and it will also highlight the creativity and linguistic skills of people raised and living in a multilingual society such as Hawai'i.

Definitions of social justice sometimes center on the idea of equality, but the approach to language and social justice adopted in this book goes beyond the pursuit of equal treatment at an official level. Here, it is noteworthy that a local constitutional declaration in 1978 made both Hawaiian and English official languages of the state, thus putting the two languages on equal footing at a governmental level. However, this declaration did little in terms of giving residents the rights and the means to employ Hawaiian in official sectors of society such as education and the judicial system. In order to make inroads in terms of using Hawaiian, programs and schools had to be created that promoted Hawaiian and mostly excluded other languages, especially the dominant language of English. Still, even with these programs and even with voices of support from within the government, Hawaiian speakers still face obstacles in terms of gaining the right to employ Hawaiian in the public sphere.

Equity is another concept commonly used to explain social justice, and it typically refers to the idea that people should readily have access to the resources necessary to live as healthily and happily as possible. Without questioning that this should be the case for all people in Hawai'i, this book departs slightly from the concept of equity in that it considers the possibility of "group-differentiated" rights in terms of language in society. More specifically, I suggest that Hawaiian, as the indigenous language spoken in the islands long before speakers of English and other languages arrived, deserves preferential status in terms of language rights in all official domains. In addition, I propose that Pidgin, as another language native to Hawai'i, be granted rights that would enable speakers to feel comfortable speaking Pidgin, especially in the domain of education since that is where educators and administrators typically discourage students from speaking Pidgin even though it may be the language they speak at home. Finally, I claim that even with preferred status given to Hawaiian and Pidgin, it is also possible to create an educational system that offers speakers of immigrant languages opportunities to learn and develop their ancestral languages. All of this, I suggest, could be done in a way that does not detract from the learning and usage of English in society.

While the approach adopted here is tailored to focus on Hawai'i, I follow previous language researchers in maintaining a "strong" view of the role of language in social justice (Avineri et al., 2019b; Baugh, 2018; Bucholtz et al., 2014; Bucholtz et al., 2016, 2017; Piller, 2016). In this view, the support and maintenance of diverse ways of speaking in a society are not just "fair" and "humane" but also essential to the health and well-being of its members. Part of this strong view is criticism of the expectation that children will avoid their home language in school to learn a dominant language such as English. Such an educational practice commonly detaches people from perhaps their most natural resources, their languages. This adherence to what has been called a "monolingual mindset" (Clyne, 2005, 2008; Hajet & Slaughter, 2015) privileges speakers of the dominant language but also prevents all people, including speakers of majority languages, from reaping the full social, mental, and physical benefits of multilingualism.

While a monolingual mindset may not inhibit people from using a minority language in the home, it does result in the promotion of a national language such as English at the expense of other languages that are often rendered more or less invisible in public. This situation has been termed by May (2014) "untrammeled public monolingualism" that benefits speakers of the dominant language and disadvantages those who speak other languages and may not be deemed as proficient in the dominant language. Even in places that officially recognize more than one language—with Hawai'i being one example, "the endorsement of widespread formal multilingualism remains extremely rare" with the actuality being "that one language variety … still dominates in terms of its widespread use in the public domain." (May, 2014: 372). In contrast to this "untrammeled public monolingualism," this book explores the possibility of working toward a "public multilingualism" (May, 2014) and in fact argues that "public multilingualism" is the path to a healthier and therefore better society. I proceed in this chapter by first providing further information about the Hawaiian context in the next section, I then briefly relate the Hawaiian situation to the greater American context, and I follow that by outlining the basic argument as to why it is so crucial to adopt a social justice perspective toward language. After that, I describe the methods of analysis to be used and finally conclude with a brief description of the book's organization and remaining chapters.

1.1 The Hawaiian Context

Prior to the arrival of Westerners in the late 1700s, Hawai'i prospered as a Hawaiian-speaking society, with variations of the language spoken across the islands (Wilson, 1998a, 1998b). Contact with the West, including the arrival of American missionaries in 1820, led to an increased presence of English speakers in Hawai'i. The beginning of sugar plantations in the 1830s, influenced by American business interests, not only bolstered the position of the English language in the islands but also resulted in the importation of workers from Asia, Europe, and other Pacific Islands to perform the hard labor of farming the plantations. In addition to bringing in further linguistic diversity, the arrival of this mix of languages resulted in the creation of the creole language known today as Pidgin. Linguistic pluralism in Hawai'i has been further sustained in the mid-1900s as the local economy became dependent on a tourism industry that continues to bring in workers and visitors from around the globe.

Hawai'i is an interesting case study because at the same time that linguistic diversity grew within society, English rose to prominence as the dominant public language in education, business, and politics. This rise was aided by several important events, such as the overthrow of the Hawaiian Kingdom in 1893 by a group of American businessmen with the help of the American military, the legislative decree in 1896 of English as the only acceptable language of education, the annexation process of Hawai'i as a United States territory that began in 1898, and the declaration of Hawai'i as the 50th state in 1959. In linguistic terms, the decree of 1896 was especially important because it ushered in an era when children were punished in school for speaking the Indigenous Hawaiian language, which subsequently prompted parents to forego teaching their native language to their children in favor of English and ultimately left the Indigenous Hawaiian language in a state of severe endangerment.

Despite the ascent of English and the decline of Hawaiian, many people in Hawai'i, sometimes as a part of a defiance toward the English status quo, maintain pockets of multilingualism in their decision to "in practice do their own thing, or rather, things" (Bickerton, 1998: 54). Indeed, the 2016 statistical report "Detailed Languages Spoken at Home in the State of Hawaii" (Statistical Report, 2016) shows that 25.4% of Hawai'i's population speaks a language other than English at home. Moreover, a local newspaper, the Star Advertiser, reported in 2016 that "Hawaii has the highest proportion of non-English speakers among other states in the nation" (Hawai'i Leads Country, 2016). The same newspaper article notes that the Ilokano-speaking population in Hawai'i has tripled since the 1980s with Tagalog and Ilokano standing as the most common languages spoken after English. The statistical report also lists Japanese directly after Tagalog and Ilokano and includes Spanish, Hawaiian, Chinese, Korean, and Samoan as languages spoken in homes in Hawai'i.

The fact that Hawaiian makes that list is a credit to language activists, who undertook in the 1980s and 1990s an intense process of language revitalization that led gradually to the establishment of a pathway through which people in Hawai'i can be educated primarily in Hawaiian, beginning from preschool through the undergraduate and even the Ph.D. level of graduate school. This movement grew from grassroots endeavors in the 1960s and 1970s, often referred to as the Hawaiian Renaissance (Kanahele, 1982), to bring back Hawaiian cultural activities such as lei making, music, dance, and navigation techniques. These activities paved the way for the declaration in 1978 of Hawaiian as an official language of the state (with English) and the construction of the first Hawaiian medium preschool in 1984. These efforts resulted in the re-establishment of Hawaiian as a medium of education, something which had not existed since the nineteenth century.

Furthermore, it is possible to walk into the local libraries and bookstores and find literature written in the local creole language that began developing over 150 years ago due to contact with the outside world. That same creole language, referred to locally as Pidgin, is also still regularly heard outside of the bookstores on the streets, in the malls, on the playgrounds, and in the homes and family gatherings of many of the residents. In fact, it has been estimated that nearly half of the population in Hawai'i, about 500,000, speak Pidgin (Sakoda & Siegel, 2003).

Besides Hawaiian, Pidgin, and English, there are places outside of the home where other languages flourish as a primary means of communication. The tourist industry, which brings in tourists from all over the world but especially from Japan, has created at least one area, namely Waikīkī, where Japanese serves as a major source of communication in the plethora of hotels, stores, and restaurants that mark Waikīkī as the center of tourism. Hawai'i also has a Chinatown with markets, restaurants, and stores run by Chinese-speaking vendors, and farmers and other vendors speaking Ilokano and Tagalog stand out in some of the farmers' markets that are popular across the islands. Hawai'i also has a number of churches that cater to speakers of specific languages that include, Samoan, Ilokano, and Korean.

In addition to the development of an educational pathway through Hawaiian, Hawai'i has an established system of higher education that, while treating English as the default official language, includes opportunities to learn multiple languages. The University of Hawai'i (UH) system consists of three university campuses, two on the island of O'ahu and one on the island of Hawai'i, and seven community colleges, four on O'ahu and one each on the islands of Hawai'i, Maui,[1] and Kaua'i. In addition, many of the campuses offer distance learning and outreach programs that service the community. The biggest campus, UH Mānoa on O'ahu, included 25 languages in their list of courses for fall of 2019, Arabic, Cambodian, Chamorro, Filipino, French, German, Greek, Hawaiian, Hindi, Ilokano, Italian, Japanese, Korean, Latin, Mandarin, Māori, Portuguese, Russian, Samoan, Sanskrit, Spanish, Tahitian, Thai, Tongan, and Vietnamese. The other campuses and outreach programs do not offer this number of languages but they do offer the opportunity, depending on the campus and the program, to study languages such as Hawaiian, Japanese, Korean, Mandarin, and Spanish. Hawai'i also has three other 4-year colleges, all on O'ahu, that provide courses in various languages.

[1]Maui College also offers some 4-year programs.

At the community level, adult education courses offer the possibility of studying some languages, and there are also opportunities for younger members of society to receive education in their languages and through their cultures. One example is the Le Fetūao Samoan language Center that was established in 2008 to provide free language courses for children from preschool to high school. The Samoan program has received outside funding and has received attention from outside of Hawai'i (Hanneman, 2015). There are also programs outside of the regular school systems for kids to learn Japanese, Mandarin, and Korean, and there is also a program designed to teach Tokelauan language and culture (Reeves, 2018).

Outside of education, in 2006 Hawai'i became, according to the website, the first state in the nation to pass a language access law in 2006 to ensure that individuals with limited English proficiency have meaningful access to state-funded services in Hawai'i.[2] This law created the Office of Language Access (OLA) and served as an impetus for the creation of services designed to serve a multilingual society. The state offers, free of charge, court interpretation services for nearly fifty languages and currently makes it possible for the written version of the driver's test to be given in 14 languages.

Finally, any discussion emphasizing the plurality of languages in Hawai'i would not be complete without mention of the frequency with which people in the islands tend to mix languages. Although code-switching was once viewed as a type of negative interference due to the inability of speakers to maintain one linguistic system, it should be viewed as a credit not just to the knowledge of multiple languages held by individual residents of Hawai'i but also to their creative abilities. As Saft et al. (2018) observe, the mixing of languages such as Hawaiian, Pidgin, and English occurs in the social media and public domains such as politics (also see Saft, 2019).

However, even with the recognition of individual linguistic abilities and even with the availability of language services and also attempts to promote languages through education, many people in Hawai'i still

[2]https://health.hawaii.gov/ola/about-us/.

suffer in ways that relate to linguistic and cultural differences. Despite the availability of educational pathways in Hawaiian, the increase in demand to learn the language has resulted in a shortage of qualified teachers, which means that the supply is not yet meeting the demand. According to a report from the Hawai'i State Teachers Association (Teacher Shortage Crisis, 2019), 43% of Hawaiian immersion classrooms are taught by teachers who are not fully qualified or licensed to do so. One reason for this shortage is the lack of materials and the extra work of creating a curriculum through Hawaiian. One teacher, Leimomi Kaaihili Leong, is quoted as saying that "There are very few curricula, assessment, planning, classroom materials that are rooted in Hawaiian immersion education or even just any native language immersion education. Hawaiian immersion is not a translated education of English medium education. Therefore, it is not just an issue of translating everything" (Teacher Shortage Crisis, 2019). The same article also notes that a lack of pay compensation makes it difficult for teachers already strapped with a full schedule to find the time to develop vital curricular materials.

The lack of available teachers was highlighted in a lawsuit against the state by the parent of two schoolchildren on Lāna'i, a small island off of Maui that is included as a part of Maui County, for not providing education through Hawaiian. The school's inability to offer this option was a result of the lack of available teachers. The state supreme court ultimately ruled that Hawai'i's state constitution, in which Hawaiian has been declared as one of two official languages of the state, requires "reasonable access" to Hawaiian immersion. While this was a "success" for the status of the Hawaiian language in the state and suggested that more financial resources and other incentives need to be invested toward Hawaiian immersion, the ruling in and of itself did nothing to improve the availability of resources to provide such education.

Some may ask if the two schoolchildren might have been served just as well in the regular English classes, but according to Poai (2019), the two children had moved from Pā'ia Elementary School's Hawaiian language immersion program to Lāna'i and had no option outside of Lāna'i Elementary School, where one of the children was asked to repeat kindergarten because she could not read or write English. The other child was "reprimanded for responding to written assignments in the Hawaiian language." As Poai (2019) explains, the principal offered the assistance of the school psychologist, but no services were offered to assist with needs related to the Hawaiian language. Especially given that the children were reprimanded for merely trying to speak their ancestral language, the lack of support harkens back to an earlier time when Hawaiians were regularly punished for speaking Hawaiian and raises questions related to social justice.

The case of these two children conjures up some of the injustices of the recent past faced by speakers of Hawaiian, but it also brings to the surface a rather clear record in Hawai'i of discrimination against speakers of languages other than English, including not just Hawaiian but also Pidgin. Even as Pidgin grew into a creole in the early 1900s, it was already defamed as "the jargon of the plantations" and the "pidgin English of the streets" (Tamura, 1996: 435) by those favoring English as the primary language of education, politics, and business. Moreover, there have been official attempts to ban Pidgin from being used in the classroom (Higgins, 2010; Lockwood & Saft, 2016; Tamura, 1996) and there was a lawsuit brought in 1987 by two local Hawai'i employees of the National Weather Service for discrimination on the basis that their speech was not standard English (Lippi-Green, 1994; Lockwood & Saft, 2016; Matsuda, 1991; Sato, 1991, 1993; Tamura, 1996).

To be sure, recent language activism (Sakoda Siegel, 2003; Da Pidgin Coup, 2008; Higgins, 2010, 2021a, 2021b; Saft, 2019) has helped raise the status of Pidgin within Hawai'i to the extent that it has been recognized since 2015 by the U.S. Census Bureau as an official language in the Hawaiian Islands (Laddaran, 2015). Still, recent analyses suggest that the prestige of Pidgin in Hawai'i is mostly "covert" in that it serves as a signal of a local identity that separates people born and raised in Hawai'i from those with the category of "haole," which is still associated with acts of colonization such as buying land and appropriating culture (Furukawa, 2018). Overt prestige still lies with English as the language most highly regarded at the official, public levels of society. As Furukawa (2018: 41) reports, the covert/overt distinction in prestige means that "the local people of Hawai'i have an interesting love/hate relationship with the language of their local culture." Although it is still passed down to future generations, many locals, in a kind of "linguistic schizophrenia"

(Furukawa, 2018; Higgins, 2010; Kachru, 1977; Yokota, 2008), are still ashamed to admit to outsiders that they speak this stigmatized language.

And even supposing that we guardedly suggest that the status of Pidgin in Hawai'i is on the rise, there are still other languages that face significant levels of discrimination. Discrimination seems especially prevalent for a group of people, frequently referred to in public discourse as "Micronesian," that represent the most recent group to arrive in Hawai'i in significant numbers. Although the category "Micronesian" actually consists of a diverse group of people from areas in the Pacific who possess different cultures and speak different languages, they are connected via the 1986 Compact of Free Association (COFA) that has allowed them to migrate to the United States without visas to pursue economic opportunity, better education, and health care. The COFA agreement was reached after recognition of the degree to which these islands in the Pacific were negatively affected by the nuclear testing program engaged by the United States, which has made parts of these islands uninhabitable and caused sickness to the residents. Grouped together in Hawai'i under the category of "Micronesian," not only have the children been forced to try to assimilate through English as a second language programs that rarely offer support in their first languages but they have also faced significant discrimination and even violence due to cultural and linguistic differences (Saft, 2019; Talmy, 2006). Only recently have bilingual services in health care, housing, and the judiciary been offered to speakers of these languages, but these services have not been effective in alleviating the life-altering stigma attached to this latest group of arrivals.

There is evidence that this linguistic and cultural stigma is related to the general health of the people. It has been suggested, for instance, that "Micronesians" in Hawai'i suffer from "a high burden of certain cancers, diabetes, heart disease, skin infections, and chronic infectious diseases" (Hagiwara et al., 2016: 485), and they also face severe poverty and homelessness in Hawai'i (Weiner, 2016). This state of affairs is at least partly derived from linguistic obstacles that have made it more difficult for them to gain access to health care and to find solutions to problems such as homelessness.

Moreover, statistics show that health problems afflict not just people in the "Micronesian" category but also those in the more general category of "Pacific Islanders," including Native Hawaiians. Stafford (2010) notes that "some groups of Native Hawaiians and Pacific Islanders now represent some of the highest instances of general health disparate rates in the nation" (Stafford, 2010: 786–787). This is closely connected to "socioeconomic disparities" in which "almost 18% of Native Hawaiians and Pacific Islanders live below the poverty threshold compared with about 12% in the general population" (Stafford, 2010: 787). The high poverty rate also directly connects to the likelihood of being uninsured and thus unable to seek and receive medical treatment. Indeed, Morisako et al. list "cultural competency" and "local language skills and communication" as impediments to gaining access to necessary health care (Morisako et al., 2017: 39). Likewise, a report published in 2013 from the John Burns School of Medicine at the University of Hawai'i at Mānoa notes, "similar to Blacks across the nation, Hawaiians are dying at younger ages, with dramatic differences starting in the mid-life range" (Look et al., 2013: 7; also see Panapasa et al., 2010; Ka'opua, 2011). This includes a higher rate of death from diabetes, heart disease, and also cancer compared to the overall state population (page 9). While such a result certainly derives from many factors, one of the key points to be underscored in this book is that there is a close relationship between language and mental and physical health and that strengthening language access is a crucial strategy for improving the health and life spans of all people in Hawai'i.

Also related to the topic of social justice is the fact that Pacific Islanders are subject to higher incarceration rates in Hawai'i. An ACLU-Hawaii video (Policing and Communities of Color in Hawai'i Webinar, 2020) reports that in 2018 40% of the people incarcerated were Native Hawaiian even though only 20% of the population identified as Native Hawaiian.[3] This statistic is consistent with another report from the Prison Policy Initiative, which used 2010 census information to indicate that 39% of the prison population was in the category of Native

[3]https://www.youtube.com/watch?v=vc_1BxDdJDc&feature=youtu.be&fbclid=IwAR0UGw-WrdASCI-fiStbMlw4XORCxk9S3bUQHtx05XrPQ1kihO4OVATCMaU.

Hawaiian/Pacific Islander despite statistics showing that only 10% of the population placed themselves in this category (also see Sonoda, 2008).[4] High rates of incarceration for people of color in the United States are an issue that encompasses more than language (Mauer and King 2007; Nellis 2016), but one of the suggestions in this book, through the direct connection between language and well-being, is that such a discrepancy in the percentages may not exist had a higher value been placed on learning Hawaiian and other ancestral languages of the Pacific Islanders.

Finally, before moving to the section, there is one final point to recognize about the Hawaiian context, namely the long and deep history of fighting for social justice in Hawai‘i. This includes Native Hawaiians such as Robert Wilcox and Joseph Nāwahī who fought for the rights of Native Hawaiians before, during, and after the overthrow of the Hawaiian Kingdom in 1893, the strikes by the immigrant plantation workers in the early 1900s to secure better working conditions and wages, and the various struggles engaged in by Native Hawaiians in the 1960s and 1970s over sovereignty, land, housing, water, and nuclear testing on the island of Kaho‘olawe, to name just a few of the many issues requiring social justice (see Goodyear-Ka‘ōpua et al., 2014; Silva, 2004). Moreover, the existence of a strong spirit of social justice in Hawai‘i has never been on display as much as it has recently in the dispute over attempts to build a telescope on the sacred mountain of Mauna Kea. A large portion of the Native Hawaiian community, led partly by a group of young speakers of Hawaiian, stood aligned in non-violent protest of the telescope and in the rights of Native Hawaiians to self-determination of their own lands (Casumbal-Salazar, 2017). As part of protecting the land on Mauna Kea, these protectors created a base of operations at a lower level of the mountain consisting of, among other services, free food, free health care, and free education with instruction in Hawaiian history, politics, and the Hawaiian language. Although this book focuses specifically on language in Hawai‘i, I have received much inspiration from the people, both young and old, who work to protect sacred lands as part of the continued fight for justice in Hawai‘i.

---

[4] https://www.prisonpolicy.org/profiles/HI.html.

1.2 The Greater US Context

Since the overthrow of the Hawaiian Kingdom in 1893, Hawai'i has fallen under the rule of the United States, a period marked by annexation as a territory in 1898 and the declaration of statehood in 1959. Even though Hawai'i has developed its own unique linguistic trajectory in the past 120 plus years, it has received tremendous influence from the United States and it is therefore important to remember the degree to which the United States has engaged in a sometimes brutal campaign to suppress multilingualism and forcibly construct a monolingual mindset. This campaign includes a program of "residential schools" that took Native American children from their parents and placed them in boarding schools to teach them English and assimilate them into American culture. This program, represented by the phrase "Kill the Indian, save the man," prevented children from speaking their mother tongues and resulted directly in the endangerment and extermination of numerous Native American languages. By stripping Native Americans of their languages and cultures, these schools have left Native American communities with a legacy of poverty and high suicide rates (Chrisjohn et al., 2006).

As the United States was endeavoring to stifle Native American languages, the "educated" sector of society was engaged in efforts to reign in another source of multilingualism in the United States, namely the increase in immigration from Europe. After reportedly seeing negative academic performance from immigrants still speaking their first languages in the home, the child psychologist Goodenough (1926: 393) wrote that "this might be considered evidence that the use of a foreign language in the home is one of the chief factors in producing mental retardation as measured by intelligence tests" (also quoted in Hakuta, 1989). Otto Jespersen (1922: 148), a linguist known for his work in historical linguistics, demonstrated the prevailing "limited-capacity model" of the brain when he stated about bilingual children that "the child in question hardly learns either of the two languages as perfectly as he would have done if he had limited himself to one … the brain effort required to master the two language instead of one certainly diminishes the child's power of learning other things." These views were supported at approximately the same time in history by the top position in the United States as the president, Theodore Roosevelt, declared that "we have room for but one language in this country, and that is the English language, for we intend to see that the crucible turns our people out as Americans, of American nationality, and not as dwellers in a polyglot boarding-house" (quoted in Piller, 2016: 39).

Lest we think that this "monolingual mindset" is merely the product of out-of-date political and educational philosophies, we still see similar opinions on public display in the United States. Piller (2016), for example, describes the backlash from a high school valedictorian's decision in Newman, California, in 2012 to give his graduation speech in Spanish instead of English. After noting that this event received criticism from the Fox news commentator Bill O'Reilly, Piller (2016: 42–43) writes:

> Editorials in many media outlets across the country followed suit and widely decried the speech as evidence of rudeness and lack of respect for the United States. On many of these media websites, the territorial principle as a self-evident reason why the choice of Spanish at a US high school graduation speech was 'wrong.' For instance, commentators argued that 'Bill O'Reilly is 100% correct. this is America not Mexico. He should of given his speech in english not Spanish' or that 'In America we speak English and to conduct the valedictorian speech in Spanish is wrong.' Another comment, which received the highest number of likes in the debate ... read, "This was a flagrant insult to the United States of America which is an English speaking nation."

The territorial principle here referred to by Piller is the belief that a language such as English is tied to a place like the United States, and this tie is so strong "that English constitutes an important cohesive device for the melting pot nation and that using English and English only is essential for social cohesion" (Piller, 2016: 39). This is a belief repeated by Donald Trump during his 2016 presidential campaign in his reaction to the usage of Spanish by another politician, Jeb Bush. Trump proclaimed that "this is a country where we speak English. It's English. You have to speak English" (Diez, 2019; Goldmacher, 2016). The same idea has been supported at the political level through interest groups such as

ProEnglish, which promotes legislature to make English the official language of the United States and also takes the position that Puerto Rico must adopt English as its official language if it is to be considered for statehood.[5] As Stephen Guschov (2018) emphasizes on their website, "ProEnglish Board of Directors Chair Dr. Rosalie Porter has stated that 'any legislative attempt by the island to become the 51st state must stipulate that English become its primary official language of the government, courts, and school system.'".

It may be tempting to rationalize "ProEnglish" as a political agenda of a minority that ultimately has little effect on social life and social structures, but statistics indicate that the monolingual mindset in the United States directly influences aspects of the educational system, in particular the teaching of languages other than English. Here, it is worth quoting at length from Reagan and Osborn (2019: 74), who describe a decline in U.S. foreign language education:

> There is a growing shortage of well-qualified foreign language teachers (U.S. Department of Education, 2016), budgetary limitations increasingly threaten foreign language education programs (especially at the elementary and middle school levels) (Skorton & Altschuler, 2012), student enrollments in foreign languages at all levels are declining, sometimes precipitously (Pufahl & Rhodes, 2011), the percentage of universities that require foreign language study continues to decline (Skorton & Altschuler, 2012), offerings in many less common languages (including, for instance, Arabic, Hebrew, Japanese, and Russian) are being reduced or eliminated altogether (Skorton & Altschuler, 2012), and program articulation remains a major concern (see Pufahl & Rhodes, 2011: 267). At the K-12 level, only 18.5% of students in the United States study of a foreign language—and even in Wisconsin, the state with the highest percentage of students enrolled in a foreign language course, only slightly more than 30% of all students study a language other than English (Phillip & Abbot, 2011). Finally, although roughly 18% of the U.S. population report speaking a second language (in comparison to 26% of Canadians and 54% Europeans), less than 1% of American adults are proficient in the language that they studied in a U.S. classroom. (Friedman, 2015)

[5] http://proenglish.org/.

These statistics are striking and according to Reagan and Osborn (2019: 83) serve as evidence of the "normative monolingualism of U.S. society" (Reagan & Osborne, 2019: 83). To be sure, there have been attempts to promote the study of languages in the United States; for instance, Reagan and Osborn (2019) observe that the American Academy of Arts and Sciences released a report in 2013 urging increased foreign language learning in the United States. Likewise, as Salomone (2010: 232) notes, people in the United States frequently "admire multilingual skills in other peoples" and "give lip service to supporting language learning among native-born Americans." Nonetheless, the reality seems to suggest that the United States ultimately "clings to English monolingualism in practice" (Salomone, 2010: 232) and leads to the conclusion that "the United States is ideologically, if not empirically, profoundly monolingual, and relatively few Anglo-Americans honestly believe that foreign languages are really necessary for the marketplace" (Osborne & Reagan, 2019: 81). As this book endeavors to show through a focus on languages in Hawai'i, the monolingual mindset is a hurdle not just to getting more people to study foreign languages but more generally to gaining benefits from studying and speaking languages that are key to achieving linguistic justice.

1.3 Language as Key to Social Justice

Those who follow and promote a monolingual mindset fail to understand that learning and comprehending more than one language, whether it is foreign language, an immigrant language, or an indigenous language has tremendous cognitive benefits for individuals and communities and therefore holds a crucial key to improving people's lives, the lives of speakers of minority and majority languages included. As a part of making the case for a social justice approach to language, I lay out in more detail the link between language and well-being in the next three subsections.

1.3.1 Language and the Brain

Attitudes about bilingualism in academia began to change after Peal and Lambert (1962) reported results showing that French–English bilingual children outperformed monolingual children on verbal and non-verbal intelligence tests. Such a result led the authors to suggest "that the bilingual child had 'mental flexibility, a superiority in concept formation and a more diverse set of mental abilities'" (reported in Edwards, 1994: 69). Subsequent research yielded several studies showing similar higher scores for bilinguals, which led to the coining of the term "bilingual advantage" and to the bilingual advantage hypothesis. Once thought of being a detrimental attribute, bilingualism came to be recognized for the cognitive benefits that it provided for people. Antoniou and Wright (2017: 2) summarize these advantages when they write, "the evidence now suggests that experience with two languages confers a general 'bilingual advantage,' with improvement in executive function (Bialystok et al., 2007), metalinguistic awareness (Cummins 1978), cognitive flexibility, creative thinking, and perhaps even several years' delay in the onset of dementia." In terms of dementia, comparative research between monolinguals and bilinguals has yielded findings demonstrating a difference of approximately four to five years in the onset of dementia, including Alzheimer's disease (Bialystok et al., 2007; Craik et al., 2010; Kim et al., 2019; Woumans et al., 2015). Moreover, there is evidence that the effect of delaying cognitive decline was found in both individuals who acquired a second language as a child and in those who acquired it as an adult (Bak et al., 2014), and there has been research suggesting that protection from aging is even greater for speakers of more than two languages, with the biggest advantage given to individuals who speak four or more languages (Kavé et al., 2008; also see Van den Noort et al., 2019 for further discussion).

In general, these benefits are attributed to the fact that the presence of two or more languages modifies brain structure and results in a functional neuroplasticity (Bialystok et al., 2012; Kim et al., 2019), which in turn leads to the enhanced abilities and the advantages just noted. As Kim et al. (2019: 2) write, "experience-dependent brain activity provokes the formation of neural connections and structures in order to respond to the demands of managing multiple elements of numerous language systems, such as phonology, semantics, syntax, and grammar" (also see Costa et al., 2014). This research on brain structure challenges the so-called two solitudes approach (Cummins, 2008) that tended to view bilingualism in the brain in terms of the possession of two separate competences, a notion that fostered a belief in interference in which competence in one language hinders the development of second and third languages (see Grosjean, 2010). Instead, functional neuroplasticity suggests that speakers who study multiple languages build on an already developing linguistic competence, a process which adds to their cognitive and creative abilities. Some researchers have employed the term "multi-competence" to capture the capacity of people who are bilingual and multilingual to deploy and even mix multiple languages in written and spoken communication (Cook, 1991, 2007; Li, 2011).

To be sure, not all research has yielded such a definitive correlation between bilingualism and cognitive prowess. Clare et al. (2016) noted a failure to see an advantage in delay in Alzheimer's onset in Welsh-English bilinguals as compared to English bilinguals, and Fuller-Thomson (2015) found contradictory results in a review of the effects of bilingualism on the delay of dementia. In general, this research does not deny the possibility of positive effects of bilingualism on brain function but instead indicates the necessity of continued research that explores the various factors that may be involved in determining how learning multiple languages at different ages affects the human brain. Thus, even though Van den Noort et al. (2019: 29) conclude in their review of the literature that "we found some evidence for a protective effect of bilingualism again cognitive decline in aging," they soon thereafter also note that "lifelong bilingualism is a complex individual process, and many factors seem to influence this and need to be investigated further…" Even Bialystok, one of the researchers most responsible for promoting the idea of a "bilingual advantage," has adopted a cautious approach in recent work suggesting that "the intention is not (necessarily) to recommend that everyone become bilingual as a bulwark against cognitive decline and dementia but rather to use the evidence from bilingualism to gain deeper understanding of how cognitive reserve works and find accessible means of making protective experiences more widely available" (Sullivan & Bialystok, 2017: 4).

Still, even though some findings have not been definitive, the existence of a prevalence of research pointing to a link between learning multiple languages and cognitive advantages and enhanced brain health should, at the very least, prompt an overall reconsideration of the tendency to adhere to a monolingual mindset. It should encourage everyone, speakers of both majority and minority languages, as well as policy makers, educators, parents, and young people alike, to take a much deeper look at the institutional structures and personal decisions that devalue the learning of languages and embrace the possibility that an emphasis on language learning may be critical to the maintenance of brain health and the preservation of brain functions for longer durations of our lives.

1.3.2 Language and the Well-Being of Indigenous Populations

In addition to the cognitive advantages just discussed, language specialists concerned about language endangerment observe a close tie between learning ancestral languages and the well-being of people and their communities. Well-being is not a very specific concept, but it is an appropriate way to consider the role of indigenous languages given that indigenous groups have suffered due to a loss of language and culture that affects both mental and physical health and that leads to issues concerning self-identity, self-autonomy, resilience, as well as an overall sense of happiness. Reyhner (2010: 142) provides an apt synopsis of the benefits of ancestral languages when he writes that "the native use of the native tongue is like therapy, specific native words express love and caring. Knowing the language presents one with a strong self-identity, a culture with which to identify, and a sense of wellness." Sivak et al. (2019: 2) similarly note that "traditional languages are a key element of Indigenous peoples' identity, cultural expression, autonomy, and spiritual and intellectual sovereignty," and Grenoble (2021: 17–18) speaks of a general well-being when she writes that "people who actively participate in language revitalization report a better mindset and higher levels of self-esteem than before."

Well-being includes the ability to overcome processes such as colonization and cultural appropriation that are responsible for the economic and spiritual hardships faced by many indigenous groups throughout the world. These are the processes that have throughout history separated indigenous people against their wills from their families, lands, cultural practices, and languages. Sivak et al. (2019: 2) aptly summarize the challenges in terms of achieving well-being.

> Pervasive racism, marginalization, family disconnectedness, community dysfunction, and social disadvantage constitute chronic causes of stress among Aboriginal communities and have ongoing effects on the mental health and wellbeing of individuals. In particular, it is the loss of land, culture, and identity that have been highlighted by Indigenous people as fundamental causes of ill health.

Speaking and learning indigenous learning languages can thus serve an important role in "healing the negative effects of colonialism that have disrupted many indigenous homes and communities". (Reyhner, 2010: 139).

In findings focusing on specific aspects of well-being, Hallet et al. (2007) build on earlier work (Chandler & Lalonde, 1998) to show a link between indigenous language knowledge and a decrease in suicide. Employing indigenous language knowledge as an indication of cultural continuity within communities, they apply a factor analysis to census data in districts in British Columbia and yield results showing that communities with higher levels of language knowledge have fewer suicides. In their words (Hallet et al., 2007: 11):

> High language knowledge bands averaged 13.00 suicides per 100,000 (well below the provincial averages for both Aboriginal and non-Aboriginal youth), while those with lower language bands had more than 6 times the number of suicides (96.59 per 100,000).

Based on these findings, they conclude very straightforwardly: "altogether these results demonstrate that Indigenous language use, as a marker of cultural persistence, is a strong predictor of health and well-being in Canada's Aboriginal communities" (Hallet et al., 2007: 14).

This conclusion was supported by later work in Canada by Ball and Moselle (2013: 31), who found that "First Nations adults with intermediate or advanced proficiency in the language make up a 'lower proportion' of those with suicidal thoughts or attempts" (also quoted in McIvor, 2013: 126). High suicide rates are a serious problem in many indigenous communities—see, for example, Boyden's (2016) description of the community effects of suicide on a northern Ontario Cree reserve of Attawapiskat and also the book-length research by ChrisJohn et al. (2006) on suicide by Native Americans in Canada—and these findings indicate that language programs that reconnect people with language, culture, and land may be an important step toward restoring individual and community well-being and reducing the tendency toward suicide (Walsh, 2018).

A connection has also been made between indigenous languages and lower incidence of diabetes in native communities (Hallett et al., 2007; Hovey et al., 2014; Oster et al., 2014; Sivak et al. 2019). Oster et al. (2014), for instance, use language prevalence as a measure for cultural continuity among Cree and Blackfoot in Alberta, Canada, and find that "our quantitative results … suggest that some First Nations in Alberta have been better able to preserve their culture (as measured by Indigenous language knowledge) and consequently are relatively protected from diabetes" (Oster et al., 2014). Although not focused specifically on language, Hovey et al. (2014) report research in a Kahnawake (Mohawk) community that recognized diabetes as symptomatic of years of oppressive social conditions derived from colonialism. They further suggest that the fostering of a Kahnawa:kenro:non identity through the indigenous language and culture is a means of dealing with the historical trauma that resulted in high rates of diabetes.

Some research on the connection between indigenous languages and well-being has emphasized how learning and speaking an ancestral language can promote general feelings of happiness. Sivak et al. (2019) conducted interviews in Australia with sixteen Barngarla community members ranging from ages 15 to 50, with many interviewees describing connections to spirituality and happiness. In the words of one respondent: "You're looking at us and seeing us happy, and it's because we're genuinely happy. You know, when we're learning our language and talking it. It is coming from a place where it's making you happy" (Sivak et al., 2019: 11). Similarly, Biddle and Swee (2012) use a cross-sectional survey of the Australian indigenous population to show a positive relationship between indigenous languages and happiness, "which correlates to mental health and wellness" (Sivak et al., 2019: 12). Their data indicate an increase in happiness when the respondents are connected to their languages, cultures, and lands. In general, Sivak et al. (2019) find that happiness for aboriginal people derives from many things related to the revival of native languages, including forging reconnections to community, reconnections to one self, and also connections to the land, leading to the conclusion that "aboriginal health means not just the physical well-being of an individual but refers to the social, emotional and cultural well-being of the whole Community in which each individual is able to achieve their full potential as a human being thereby bringing about the total well-being of their Community" (Sivak et al., 2019: 12; NACCHO, 2011).

Speaking indigenous language is often referred to as a sign of resiliency, which in turn has been understood as a sign of well-being (Fleming & Ledogar, 2008; Gracey and King, 2009; Liebenberg et al., 2015; McGuire 2010; Wood et al., 2020). Noting that resilience is "what keeps people strong in the face of adversity and stress," King et al. (2009: 82) emphasize that "it has many indigenous facets: spiritual connections, cultural and historical continuity, and the ties with family, community, and the land." In research on Inuit youth, Liebenberg et al. (2015) report on the case of an at-risk Inuit youth, referred to by the pseudonym of John, who through activities that include learning Inuktitut at school was able to form "the foundation of a resilience processes that surround him" (Liebenberg et al., 2015: 113). In emphasizing the importance of resilience in indigenous communities, Roche (2017), in fact, discusses the possibility of a "resilience linguistics" through which patterns of resilience in a community may be studied and applied to promote language maintenance and revitalization.

Whether we frame the effects of learning indigenous ancestral languages in terms of well-being, happiness, resilience, or a decrease in suicide and sickness, research is showing clear patterns of healing in indigenous communities. As Taff et al. (2018: 863) assert, "if we are concerned about the physical and emotional health of indigenous peoples, then it is important to recognize that language can heal. Proliferation of language continuity efforts (revitalization, perpetuation, transmission, restoration) can heal traumas and can strengthen individual and their language communities." This positive relationship between learning an ancestral language and individual and community health seemingly leads to only one conclusion; energy and resources should be put into ensuring that indigenous communities are freely able to learn and teach their ancestral languages. Furthermore, if we add into the mix findings from the previous section about the potential cognitive advantages of bilingualism, this should strengthen our conviction about how crucial language is to a social justice perspective that is concerned with the health and well-being of all people.

1.3.3 Educational Structures and Multilingualism

If society is to consider seriously a social justice approach to language, it follows that we need educational structures that provide easy access for people, starting at a young age, to multiple languages. Although the United States has, as referred to earlier, followed an assimilationist agenda through much of twentieth century, expecting Native Americans and immigrants alike to learn English without concern for other languages they know, bilingual educational programs emerged in the 1960s. Thomas and Collier (2012) observe that Coral Way Elementary, which began in 1963 in Dade County, Florida, was the first documented two-way bilingual school. According to Thomas and Collier (2012), Coral Way was populated by Cuban students speaking Spanish as well as native English speakers from the community and consisted of a half day (50:50 ratio) of instruction in each language. The success of Coral Way —Thomas and Collier note that "the Cuban students excelled, reaching grade-level curricular mastery in both English and Spanish" and that "the native English-speaking students also performed at and above grade level in English" (Thomas & Collier, 2012: 9)—led to the spread of similar programs in other parts of the United States. Thomas and Collier count 56 programs in 13 states by 1968. They also note that "in addition to Spanish–English programs, funding went to bilingual schools teaching through English and Sioux, Pomo, Keresan, Navajo, Cherokee, Chinese, Cantonese, Japanese, Portuguese, or French" (Thomas & Collier, 2012: 10).

These programs, termed two-way programs and also known as dual language programs, served first language speakers of two different languages, usually English and one other language, granting students the opportunity to develop proficiency in both. At the same time, another type of bilingual education, often termed one-way immersion, started in Canada in 1963 as a way for English speakers "to acquire the curriculum through French and English" (Thomas & Collier, 2012: 10). These programs, according to Thomas and Collier (2012: 10), "continue to demonstrate students' high academic achievement, at or above grade level, when tested in both languages," and they also came to been adopted in U.S. elementary schools often at a 90:10 ratio, with 90% of the instructional time in the minority, non-English language.

As Tedick (2015) observes, though, there has been a split in terms of the educational opportunities for majority language and minority language students. For majority language students, which in the U.S. context typically means students growing up with English as their first language, bilingual education usually provides an opportunity to add more languages to their repertoire. However, for minority language students, which here means students entering school with a language other than English as their first language, bilingual education often was another way of enforcing the need to learn English. As Tedick (2015) and others have noted (Ovando, 2003; Wright, 2012), the 1960s, sparked by Martin Luther King and the Civil Rights Movement, saw the government pass the 1968 Bilingual Education Act (BEA), which, despite containing "ambiguity and unclear goals" (Wright, 2012: 600), prompted states to develop bilingual education programs to "address the unique linguistic and educational needs of limited English proficient students" (Wright, 2012: 601). Calls for such programs increased after the U.S. Supreme Court decision in Lau v. Nichols in 1974 led to the Equal Educational Opportunities Act of 1974 stipulating that schools "take appropriate action to overcome language barriers that impede equal participation by its students in instructional programs" (Wright, 2012:

601). In short, schools were tasked, ready or not, with the implementation of programs that would assist limited English students with their progress in school.

As Tedick (2015) notes following Baker and Jones (1998), the response to the need for bilingual education of minority language students can be divided into "weak" and "strong" forms of bilingual education. The weak form is largely represented by "transitional bilingual education" (TBE) that pulls students out of their regular courses to receive special instruction in English. This is considered weak because the concern is not the maintenance of the student's first language. As Tedick (2015: 12) writes, the "primary goal is not for students to become bilingual and biliterate, but rather for students to function in mainstream, English medium classes; thus they utilize students' L1 only as a temporary bridge to classes taught in English only." As Tedick also observes, these TBE programs are often referred to as subtractive because they promote the loss of the students' first language as they attempt to gain proficiency in English. Cummins (2007: 223) emphasizes that the students' first languages are often purposely avoided in these programs with a focus on "instructional use of the target language (TL) to the exclusion of students' L1, with the goal of enabling learners to think in the TL with minimal interference from L1." Since the main objective is transitioning students back into mainstream English classes, TBE programs "regard students' L1 (and by implication, the knowledge encoded therein) as an impediment to the learning of L2" (Cummins, 2007: 232) and thus serve as a way of "destroying through monolingual English instruction the linguistic gifts that children from non-English backgrounds bring to our schools" (Tedick, 2015: 10 referencing the words of Ovanda, 2003). Despite criticism from linguists and language specialists, subtractive programs continue to be popular given that they can be administered with limited resources and without hiring significant numbers of new teachers.

In contrast to the weak forms represented by TBE programs, there are strong forms of bilingual education that function, at least in theory, as additive programs that help students maintain their first languages and thus work toward bilingualism. These include programs labeled as developmental bilingual education (often referred to by the acronym

DBE), maintenance bilingual education, and also enrichment bilingual education. Also in this category of additive programs would be the two-way (aka, dual language) and one-way immersion programs that were mentioned above. Finally, another related approach is known now as indigenous immersion because it focuses specifically on education through an indigenous language for revitalization purposes and for the promotion of self-determination by indigenous communities (Fortune & Tedick, 2008; May, 2013: Tedick, 2015; Tedick et al. (2011). Although two-way, one-way, and indigenous language represent three different types of immersion, Tedick et al. (2011) emphasize commonalities among the three and how they may work, sometimes in combination, to enrich the lives of people because they all place an emphasis on language learning and teaching in order to add languages to the lives of students and not to transfer them back into monolingual English education.

Proponents of strong forms of bilingual education advocate for approaches that allow students to spend more time learning through their first languages. Thomas and Collier (2012: 16) refer to their earlier work (Collier & Thomas, 2009) in which "they make the case that it takes an average of six years to reach grade-level academic achievement in the second language in a well-implemented program that uses the students' native language for instruction." This fits well with strong forms that begin early in elementary school and continue through at least junior high and possibly even through high school, and it also fits with the emerging belief "that social-emotional, cognitive, and linguistic processes are best developed in the two languages of the child across all curricular subjects, for as many as years as possible" (Thomas & Collier, 2012: 19).

Indeed, advocates of strong forms of bilingual education see the promotion of bilingualism as a key to enhancing student achievement in school. After 28 years of lifelong joint research that has analyzed 6.2 million students records, Thomas and Collier (2012, 2017) report that "along with fellow researchers across the world, we continue to find that the most powerful predictor of language minority student achievement in second language is nonstop development of students' L1 through the school curriculum" (Thomas & Collier, 2012: 91). In making this statement, they cite research from a variety of sources that "find patterns similar to those we have found" (Thomas & Collier, 2012: 91 citing the work of Dolson, 1985; Greene, 1998; Krashen & Biber 1988; Lindholm-Leary, 2001; Lindholm-Leary & Borsato, 2006; Lindholm-Leary & Genesee, 2010; Lindholm-Leary & Howard, 2008; Ramirez, 1992; Rolstad, Mahoney & Glass, 2005; Willig, 1985). Tedick (2015: 13) offers a similar summary focusing on two-way immersion: "A considerable body of research indicates that the TWI model is highly effective for minority-language learners (Lindholm-Leary, 2001; Lindholm-Leary & Genesee, 2010; Thomas & Collier, 2012). Studies have consistently shown that both minority-language and majority-language learners in these programmes do as well as or better than peers schooled only in English on standardized tests of achievement including in English (Lindholm-Leary, 2001; see Genesee & Lindholm-Leary, 2013, Thomas & Collier, 2012, for reviews)."

Results showing strong achievement by students in strong forms of bilingual education support the idea that students do not learn languages separately but instead that the development of first languages expedites the learning of subsequent languages. This is in fact the claim made by Cummins in his interdependence hypothesis that emphasizes that students do best when their prior knowledge in one language is actively engaged as they are educated in another different language. In Cummins' words (1981: 29):

> To the extent that instruction in Lx is effective in promoting proficiency in Lx, transfer of this proficiency to Ly will occur provided there is adequate exposure to Ly (either in school or environment) and adequate motivation to learn Ly.

Cummins (2009: 24) explains this with a specific example when he writes:

> In concrete terms, what this principle means is that in, for example, a Basque-Spanish bilingual program in the Basque Autonomous Community in Spain, Basque instruction that develops Basque reading and writing skills is not just developing Basque skills, it is also developing a deeper conceptual and linguistic proficiency that contributes significantly to the development of literacy in the majority language (Spanish).

Hence, while pronunciation, vocabulary, and grammatical structures may differ across languages, there exists "an underlying cognitive/academic proficiency that is common across languages. This common underlying proficiency makes possible the transfer of cognitive/academic literacy-related proficiency from one language to another" (Cummins, 2007: 232). Rather than treating the L1 of students as an impediment to learning another language, which is the case in weak forms of bilingual education that adopt a subtractive approach, educators desiring to promote mastery of a second language such as English should also work to develop students' first languages as a part of tapping into the language proficiency that has already been acquired by the students. This idea of an underlying common proficiency has been called by different names, a "common operating system" (Baker, 2001), "common underlying conceptual base" (Kecskes & Papp, 2000), and a "common underlying reservoir of literacy abilities" (Genesee et al., 2006), but the suggestion of all these terms is that students can learn two or even more languages at the same time and they will all work together toward the "development of the overall multilingual system, including the L1" (Cummins, 2007: 234).

In addition to enriching building students' linguistic proficiencies, research also shows that strong forms of bilingual education can have transformative effects, especially on the lives of younger people. Portes and Rumbaut (2001: 274), for instance, point out that children of immigrants are inescapably in a process of identity negotiation and claim that additive bilingual education, as opposed to "full assimilation," is a path that "is closely intertwined with preservation of fluent bilingualism and linked, in turn, with higher self-esteem, higher educational and occupational expectations, and higher academic achievement... Children who learn the language and culture of their new country without losing those of the old, have a much better understanding of their place in the world" (also quoted in Cummins, 2009: 28). Cummins (2009: 29–30) aptly sums up this connection between bilingual education and social justice:

> Effective education for minority or subordinated group students challenges coercive central goal of education within this framework is *empowerment*, understood as the *collaborative creation of power* (Cummins, 2001). Power is generated in teacher-student. interactions such that

> students (and teachers) feel more affirmed in their linguistic, cultural and intellectual identities, and more confident in their ability to succeed at school. By virtue of the fact that it incorporates students' home language as a medium of instruction, bilingual education goes some way to challenging coercive relations of power and affirming students' identity (emphasis in the original).

Inasmuch as bilingual education provides students, especially students who may be disadvantaged and face discrimination due to minority status, with the empowerment to succeed and achieve goals that they themselves have self-determined, then the link between bilingual education and social justice is readily apparent.

The same is very much true for indigenous immersion programs. Indigenous immersion programs may be administered in a variety of formats including one-way immersion, what May (2013) calls "total immersion," and also two-way immersion (usually with English in North America), but findings are showing that programs incorporating indigenous languages experienced not only enhanced "student motivation, self-esteem, and ethnic pride" (McCarty, 2011a: 12–13) but also improved academic achievement. McCarty (2009, 2011b), for example, discusses a Navajo program from kindergarten through eighth grade that used Navajo literacy materials to read first in Navajo and then in English and also taught "mathematics in both languages and studied science and social studies in Navajo, including Navajo clanship, history, social problems, government, and economic development" (McCarty, 2011a: 5). In terms of results:

> By the fourth grade, NI (Navajo immersion) students performed as well as on local tests of English as comparable students in mainstream English (ME) classes. Immersion students performed better on local assessments of English writing, and were 'way ahead' on standardized tests of mathematics, discriminatory as those tests are. (McCarty, 2009: 134, referencing the work of Holm & Holm, 1995: 150)

Based on such results, McCarty (2009: 135) asserts that "language revitalization and academic achievement, including proficiency in 'academic' English for high-level tasks, are not mutually incompatible goals."

Moreover, the Navajo program produced other results, namely increased trust between school leaders and among parents, staff, and students, and enhanced ability of the students to be active participants in their own education. The students, as McCarty notes, "came to value their Navajo-ness and to see themselves as capable of succeeding because of, not despite that Navajo-ness" (McCarty, 2009: 133).

Another example, reported by Morcom and Roy (2017), is the Ojibwe language immersion program at the *Mnidoo Mnising Anishinabke Kinoomaage Gamig* (MMAK) Early Learning Kindergarten in Canada. Like the Navajo program at Rock Point, the program starts out in Ojibwe and then gradually introduces English, and also like Rock Point, research results demonstrate positive effects of indigenous immersion. Not only do the results indicate "age-appropriate English language development by the end of the their second year," but also they show that "cognitive skill becomes one of the participants' strongest areas of developments" (Morcom & Roy, 2017: 74). This leads to the conclusion that "students in the MMAK demonstrate additive bilingualism, or robust language acquisition in both their first language (in this case, English) and the target language (Anishinaabemowin)" (Morcom & Roy, 2017a: 74–75).

The category of indigenous immersion is especially relevant to this study because of the success of the movement to revitalize the Hawaiian language. Lauded as one of the most successful cases of language revitalization in the world (Wilson and Kamanā, 2011), Hawaiian language education in Hawai'i has primarily employed a one-way immersion format, with English not introduced into the curriculum until the 5th grade in what is now a preschool through 12th grade system. From 5th grade, English is taught for one class period a day while the rest of the curriculum remains in Hawaiian. This approach has not only resulted in an increase in number of speakers as well as the reintroduction of intergenerational transmission, but it has also produced strong academic results. Wilson and Kamanā (2011: 49) note that students in one of the two Hawaiian medium high schools in Hawai'i, named Ke Kula o Nāwahīokalani'ōpu'u, "have higher academic outcomes on average than their Native Hawaiian peers enrolled in English-medium schools." The school also has a 100% high school graduation rate and 80% college attendance rate. As these percentages indicate, the school's focus on Hawaiian does not hinder students' ability to excel on English-based assessments. With a focus on literacy in Hawaiian from a young age (Galla & Wilson, 2019; Wilson & Kamanā, 2017), students develop strong overall linguistic skills in both languages (Wilson & Kamanā, 2011).

The above discussion mentions Hawaiian, Navajo, and Ojibwe immersion, but Morcom and Roy (2017) note other programs for Native American languages such as Inuktitut (Bougie et al., 2003; Louis & Taylor, 2001), Hualapai (Watahomigie & McCarty, 1994), Blackfoot (Kipp, 2000), Arapaho (Greymorning, 1997), Mohawk (Agbo, 2001; White, 2015), and Maliseet (Perley, 2011), among others (Demmert, 2001; Grenoble & Whaley, 2006; Morcom, 2017; Morcom & Roy, 2017b). Moreover, indigenous immersion education has played and is playing a major role in communities across the world, most notably for languages such as Māori, Sami, Welsh, and Hebrew, to name just a few (Baker & Jones, 1998; Fishman, 1991; May, 2013).

It is not only indigenous immersion programs that have been increasing. The United States has seen a rise in schools offering additive bilingual programs, especially at the beginning of the twenty-first century. Baker (2001) notes that there were approximately 200 such programs in the United States by the year 2000, but the Center for Applied Linguistics website (CAL) offers a directory of dual language and one-way immersion programs in the United States and houses a listing of nearly 900 programs, the majority of which are Spanish–English but also include Arabic, Japanese, Korean, Mandarin, French, German, and Russian programs. In particular, California seems to be a hotspot for bilingual education as the Los Angeles Unified School District alone lists 182 dual language programs for the district.[6] In fact, the Orange County website for dual language programs boasts that "Anaheim Elementary School District is the first Orange County school district to offer dual language programs in all 23 schools, beginning 2019–2020, including the first Korean dual language immersion program in an Orange County

[6]https://achieve.lausd.net/Page/7524#spn-content.

School District."[7] At a more national level, as Wright (2012: 610) asserts, two-way programs, because they do not require minority language speakers to be "pulled out" for special classes, "have successfully moved bilingual education from the realm of remedial education into the realm of enrichment education."

Given that additive bilingual education has produced positive results that extend beyond the classroom to well-being, and given the increase in availability of such programs, there is little excuse for not providing young people in the U.S. access to the type of education that will allow them to learn multiple languages. This, of course, does not mean that bilingual programs should be hastenly implemented as there have been concerns voiced about two-way and one-way programs. One such concern is the establishment of power hierarchies that favor majority language speakers and create unequal access for minority language speakers (Cervantes-Soon et al., 2017; de Jong & Bearse, 2012; Flores & Garcia, 2017; Flores and McAuliffe, 2020). Another concern is that ratios such as 50/50 and even 90/10 suggest a tendency to teach the languages in separation, a point which seemingly contradicts research showing that students learn second languages better when the first language is in play (Wiley & Garcia, 2016). Nonetheless, additive bilingual programs represent hope for minority and indigenous students looking to improve their lives through educational achievement and the attainment of higher self-esteem and better overall wellness, and they likewise offer cognitive advantages for majority students who may not have given much though to learning multiple languages. They provide an alternative to an untrammeled public monolingualism that on the surface seems to advantage some people, particularly, affluent majority language speakers, but in reality reinforces hierarchies that foster poverty, crime, and other hardships that ultimately have negative effects on all people within society. As will be discussed in this book, outside of progressive educational pathways available through the Hawaiian language, public education in Hawai'i does not offer much opportunity for speakers of languages other than English to develop their languages and thus reap the

[7] https://sites.uci.edu/bilingualteacher/dual-immersion-schools/.

benefits of bilingualism and multilingualism. Discussion will underscore the fact that this lack of additive bilingual education serves as impediment to linguistic justice in Hawaiian society.

1.4 Methodology

Despite an increase in research on the intersection between language and social justice, there is not one tried and true preferred method of investigation (see Barakos, 2020). As I began the research for this book, I knew that I needed a flexible approach to accomplish two main goals: (1) examine linguistic practices at the discourse level in order to elucidate both the difficulties faced by people in using and gaining access to language and also underscore the abilities of people in a multilingual society to organize discourse in creative and dynamic ways; and (2) consider the relationship of the languages to one another and to the language recognized to be dominant in Hawai'i, English.

There are concepts that have been used previously to describe the co-existence of languages in multilingual societies, including diglossia and territorial bilingualism. While such terms may apply to some phenomena in Hawai'i—for instance, the relationship between English and some languages, especially Pidgin, often appears to be diglossic in nature and there are likewise "territories" in Hawai'i where some languages are spoken more than others. Nonetheless, as I have argued elsewhere (Saft, 2019), terms such as diglossia and territorialism typically imply static relationships among languages and therefore do not go very far in terms of understanding the extent to which people in Hawai'i switch and even mix languages as part of their daily patterns and routines.

Ultimately, I decided to return to an area of inquiry, namely linguistic ethnography (Rampton, 2007; Ramptonet al., 2014; Rampton et al., 2004) that I have employed in previous work (Saft, 2019). Linguistic ethnography draws greatly on the work of researchers well-known in the areas of sociolinguistics, linguistic anthropology, and discourse analysis (i.e., Duranti, 1994; Goodwin, 2000; Gumperz, 1982; Hanks, 1996; Hymes, 1962, 1996) as a part of treating language practices as "actions that help construct the social and cultural worlds of the participants, not as actions that are result of already in-place features of society and culture" (Saft, 2019: 11). Linguistic ethnography analyzes language, in other words, as it is embedded in and constitutive of the ethnographic situation itself with meaning emerging "within specific social relations, interactional histories and institutional regimes, produced by agents with expectations and repertoires that have to be grasped ethnographically" (Rampton, 2007: 585). This dynamic, dialectic relationship between language usage and context should thus make it possible to gain insight into how language can, on the one hand, serve as a source of discrimination that reinforces social inequalities and, on the other hand, function as a resource for empowerment that facilitates well-being in individuals and communities.

Linguistic ethnography is attractive because of a flexibility that, rather than attempting to impose restrictions on techniques of analysis, welcomes the application of a combination of methods and approaches toward understanding language in culture and society. Rampton (2007: 585) explains this view when he writes that "linguistic ethnography is in itself neither a paradigm, a cohesive 'school', nor some kind of definitive synthesis. Instead, it is more accurately described as a site of encounter where a number of established lines of research interact, pushed together by circumstance, open to the recognition of new affinities, and sufficiently familiar with one another to treat differences with equanimity." Emboldened by such a statement, this book seeks to gain insights into language and social justice through a variety of methods. For instance, a critical discourse analysis of language usage in the media is used in two chapters in the book, in Chapter 3 to illustrate news discourse that discriminates against Hawaiian and again in Chapter 5 to demonstrate how reports in newspapers of immigrant languages such as Ilokano, Tagalog, Marshallese, and Chuukese do not match with educational practices. Chapter 4 employs a discourse analysis of both spoken and written texts as a part of investigating the place of Pidgin in society, and I also apply in Chapter 6 the concepts of translanguaging and translation to data that consist of language mixing. Moreover, Chapters 5 and 7 also make heavy use of the ethnography part of linguistic ethnography, including observations made by myself as well observations that come from the reports of other writers.

The ethnographic side of linguistic ethnography also enables consideration of the application of the findings of the analyses to the role of language policy and planning in facilitating and/or suppressing social justice. Language policy and planning has evolved as an area of research within linguistics, and, as researchers have noted, there is a close relationship between language policy and power that ethnographic description of language usage in society can help elucidate (McCarty, 2011b; Wright, 2016). As discussed earlier, it is clear that Hawai'i, by declaring Hawaiian and English as official languages of the state and by instituting policies that enable translation and interpretation in the court system, has made its own attempts at language policy and planning at an official, governmental level. Yet, as already noted and as will become clearer throughout the book, these official policies have done little to promote the acquisition of Hawaiian as well as that of immigrant languages. One of the desired outcomes of this book, therefore, is to use the analyses of data in various contexts together with ethnographic observations to further discussion of how language policy and planning in Hawai'i can function to advance linguistic justice in society.

It is also particularly the ethnographic side of linguistic ethnography that allows for the application of the findings of the study in terms of linguistic human rights. Linguistic human rights is a concept that has been developed by Skutnabb-Kangas (2018), who makes a distinction between "instrumental language rights" and "linguistic human rights." Instrumental rights refer to the right to use language to enrich one's life via their career, travel, etc., while linguistic human rights "are so fundamental that every individual has them because that individual is a human being, so inalienable that no state is allowed to violate them, and which are necessary for individuals and groups to live a dignified life" (Skutnabb-Kangas, 2018: 13). While not unconcerned about instrumental language rights since pursuit of language study for business and leisure can serve as a crucial way for people to enhance their linguistic abilities and thus gain the benefits of bilingualism, this book is primarily concerned with linguistic human rights as these are the rights most crucial in terms of social justice. As Skutnabb-Kangas and Dunbar (2010) assert, any attempt to deny speakers of indigenous and minority languages the right to speak and learn their languages constitutes a violation of basic linguistic human rights and should be deemed crimes against humanity. Using the analyses and discussion in this book, I hope to point out that more needs to be done in Hawaiian society to protect the linguistic human rights of the people in Hawai'i.

I also intend to apply the ideas about linguistic human rights of May (2011, 2014) and Kymlicka (1995, 2001, 2007) to consider the possibility of what has been called "group-based rights" or "group-differentiated rights." More specifically, through discussion and analysis that pays close attention to the Indigenous Hawaiian language, I suggest later in the book in the Conclusion that language policy in Hawai'i must prioritize rights for Hawaiian before other langues. At the same time, I maintain that Pidgin also be granted preferential status and that, particularly in education, more attention be given to speakers of immigrant languages to ensure that they, as emergent bilinguals, are able to develop their first languages as well as English. As noted earlier in this chapter, I argue that this is possible and, instead of detracting from the ability of immigrant students to master English, will only add to their ability to develop English proficiency and will make for a society that is, on the overall, stabler and healthier.

1.5 Organization of This Book

Following this introduction, this book consists of six chapters of analyses before arriving at the conclusion. Chapter 2 sets the stage for the chapters of analyses by offering a critical examination of the historical development of linguistic ecologies in Hawai'i through a focus on the two processes of American colonialism and resistance. Chapter 3 concentrates on the Hawaiian language and intends to show, first of all, how public discourse can function to impede the advancement of Hawaiian in society despite its status as an official language. The analysis then provides analyses of two linguistic practices, the usage of person categories and possessive forms, in the speech of elders and younger speakers of Hawaiian in order to demonstrate the unique cultural and linguistic perspective that Hawaiian adds to society. The attention in Chapter 4 turns to Pidgin with particular attention given to the usage of Pidgin in public domains to emphasize that it deserves to be treated as a viable public language in society. This chapter also includes interviews with Hawaiian-speaking advocates of Pidgin that shed light on the barriers that prevent more people from appreciating the place of Pidgin in Hawaiʻi. The topic of Chapter 5 is immigrant languages, but due to the large number of languages that have found their way to Hawaiʻi, this chapter is devoted to the discussion of two specific language groups in Hawaiʻi, those referred to by the categories of "Filipino" and "Micronesian." The discussion in this chapter considers the role of public education in Hawaiʻi in providing a subtractive language experience that leads to discrimination and makes it difficult to develop the bilingual skills of students. Chapter 6 adopts the perspective of translanguaging to discuss the common occurrence of language mixing in Hawaiian society. Through analyses in three different contexts, the chapter considers how the translanguaging skills of the participants contrast with the educational emphasis on English and it also underscores the tremendous creative linguistic skills possessed by people in Hawaiʻi. The focus of Chapter 7 differs from the other chapters as it provides a participant observational account of how the linguistics program at the University of Hawaiʻi at Hilo has been redesigned to contribute to the work of language revitalization in Hawaiʻi and also to contribute in other ways to the local community. Finally, Chapter 8, the Conclusion, is used as an opportunity not just to reflect on the analyses but also to consider, as a final activity, a social arrangement of languages that would promote linguistic justice in Hawaiʻi. More precisely, I use the Conclusion to argue briefly for the need for group-differentiated language rights that can promote the overall development of a healthier and more well-adjusted society.

Finally, I note that among the various sources employed in this book in order to understand the relationship between language and social justice in a Hawaiian context, an effort has been made to incorporate as much as possible the voices of people from Hawaiʻi. I mention this in light of criticisms concerning research on Hawaiʻi and the Native Hawaiians that is based primarily on the ideas of academics, government officials, and others who rely almost strictly on English language sources (Kameʻeleihiwa, 1992; Silva, 2004, 2017; Williams, 2011). As emphasized by these critics, there now exists a number of accounts from Native Hawaiian writers that document early experiences in dealing with changes to Hawaiian society due to the arrival of white Europeans and Americans. Many of these early sources are in the Hawaiian language through Hawaiian newspapers, poems, and music, but there is also a recent increase in written and spoken voices from Pidgin speakers and writers and speakers of some of the immigrant languages as well. Although certainly not enough to gain as complete of an understanding as necessary of language and social justice in Hawai'i, I have attempted to employ and rely on these sources whenever possible.

References

Agbo, S. A. (2001). Enhancing success in American Indian students: Participatory research at Akwesasne as part of the development of a culturally relevant curriculum. *Journal of American Indian Education, 40*(1), 31–56.

Antoniou, M., & Wright, S. (2017). Uncovering the mechanisms responsible for why language learning may promote healthy cognitive aging. *Frontiers in Psychology,* 8. Retrieved from https://www.ncbi.nlm.nih.gov/pmc/articles/PMC5736569/

Avineri, N., Graham, L. R., Johnson, E. J., Conley Riner, R., & Rosa, J. (Eds.). (2019a). *Language and social justice in practice.* Routledge.

Avineri, N., Graham, L. R., Johnson, E. J., Conley Riner, R., & Rosa, J. (2019b). Introduction: Reimagining language and social justice. In N. Avineri, L. R. Graham, E. J. Johnson, R. Conley Riner, & J. Rosa (Eds.), *Language and social justice in practice* (pp. 1–16). Routledge.

Bak, T. H., Nissan, J. J., Allerhand, M. M., & Deary, I. J. (2014). Does bilingualism influence cognitive aging? *Annals of Neurology, 75,* 959–963.

Baker, C. (2001). Foundations of Bilingual Education and Bilingualism Multilingual Matters Bristol, UK

Baker, C., & Jones, S. P. (1998). *Encyclopedia of bilingualism and bilingual education.* Multilingual Matters.

Ball, J., & Moselle, K. (2013). *Contributions of Culture and Language in Aboriginal Head Start in Urban and Northern Communities to Children's Health outcomes: A Review of Theory and Research.* Prepared for Division of Children, Seniors & Healthy Development, Health Promotion and Chronic Disease Prevention Branch.

Barakos, E. (2020). Linguistic and social justice: Toward a debate of intersections and disjuncture. *Journal of Sociolinguistics, 24*, 265–277.

Baugh, J. (2018). *Linguistics in pursuit of justice.* Cambridge University Press.

Bialystok, E., Craik, F. I. M., & Freedman, M. (2007). Bilingualism as a protection against the onset of symptoms of dementia. *Neuropsychologia, 45*, 459–464.

Bialystok, E., Craik, F. I. M., & Luk, G. (2012). Bilingualism: Consequences for Mind and Brain. *Trends in Cognitive Science, 16*(4), 240–250.

Biddle, N., & Swee, H. (2012). The relationship between wellbeing and indigenous land, language and culture in Australia. *Australian Geography, 43*, 215–232.

Boas, F. (1911). *The mind of primitive man.* The Macmillan Company.

Bougie, E., Wright, S. C., & Taylor, D. M. (2003). Early heritage-language education and the abrupt shift to a dominant-language classroom: Impact on the personal and collective esteem of inuit children in Arctic Québec. *International Journal of Bilingual Education and Bilingualism, 6*(5), 349–373.

Boyden, J. (2016). The true tragedy of Attawapiskat. *Maclean's.* Retrieved from https://www.macleans.ca/news/canada/attawapiskat-and-the-fallout-of-intergenerational-trauma/

Bucholtz, M., Castillas, D. I., & Lee, J. S. (2018). *Feeling it: Language, race, and affect in Latinx youth learning.* Routledge.

Bucholtz, M., Castillas, D. I., & Lee, J. S. (2017). Language and culture as sustenance. In D. Paris & H. S. Alim (Eds.), *Culturally sustaining pedagogies: Teaching and learning for justice in a changing world* (pp. 43–59). Teachers College Press.

Bucholtz, M., Castillas, D. I., & Lee, J. S. (2016). Beyond empowerment: Accompaniment and sociolinguistic justice in a youth research program. In R. Lawson & D. Sayers (Eds.), *Sociolinguistic research: Application and impact* (pp. 25–44). Routledge.

Bucholtz, M., Castillas, D. I., & Lee, J. S. (2015). Team collaboration and educational partnership in sociocultural linguistics. *American Speech, 90*(2), 230–245.

Bucholtz, M., Lopez, A., Mojarro, A., Skapoulli, E., Van der Stouwe, C., & Werner-Garcia, S. (2014). Sociolinguistic justice in schools: Student researchers as linguistic experts. *Language and Linguistics Compass, 8*(4), 144–157.

Casumbal-Salazar, I. (2017). A fictive kinship: Making "modernity", "ancient Hawaiians", and the telescopes on Mauna Kea. *Native American and Indigenous Studies, 4*(2), 1–30.

Cervantes-Soon, C. G., Dorner, L., & Palmer, D. (2017). Combating inequalities in two-way language immersion programs: Toward critical consciousness in bilingual education spaces. *Review of Research in Education, 41*(1), 403–427.

Chandler, M., & Lalonde, C. (1998). Cultural continuity as a Hedge against suicide in Canada's first nations. *Transcultural Psychiatry, 35*(2), 191–219.

Chrisjohn, R., Young, S., & Maraun, M. (2006). *The Circle Game: Shadows and Substance in the Indian Residential School Experience in Canada.* Theytus Books.

Clare, L., Whitaker, C. J., Mrtyr, A., Martin-Forbes, P. A., Bastable, A. J. M., Pye, K. L., Quinn, C., Thomas, E. M., Mueller Gathercole, V. C., & Hindle, J. V. (2016). Executive control in older welsh monolinguals and bilinguals. *Journal of Cognitive Psychology, 28*(4), 412–426.

Clyne, M. (2005). *Australia's Language Potential.* University of New South Wales Press.

Clyne, M. (2008). The monolingual mindset as an impediment to the development of plurlingual potential in Australia. *Sociolinguistic Studies, 2*(3), 347–366.

Collier, V.P., & Thomas, W.P. (2009). *Educating English Learners for a Transformed World.* urquerque: Dual Language Education of New Mexico-Fuente Press.

Cook, V. J. (1991). The poverty-of-the-stimulus argument and multi-competence. *Second Language Research, 7*(2), 103–117.

Cook, V. J. (2007). The nature of the L2 user. *Eurosla Yearbook, 7*(1), 205–220.

Costa, A., & Sebastian-Galles, N. (2014). How does the bilingual experience sculpt the brain? *National Review of Neuroscience, 15*, 336–345.

Coup, D. P. (2008). Pidgin and education: A position paper. *Educational Perspectives, 40*, 30–39.

Craik, F. I. M., Bialystok, E., & Freedman, M. (2010). Delaying the onset of Alzheimer disease. *Neurology, 75*, 1726–1729.

Cummins, J. (1978). Bilingualism and the development of metalinguistic awareness. *Journal of Cross Cultural Psychology, 9*, 131–149.

Cummins, J. (1981). The Role of Primary Language Development in Promoting Educational Success for Language Minority Students. In California State Department of Education (Ed.), *Schooling and Language Minority Students: A Theoretical Framework* (pp. 3–49). Los Angeles: California State University, Evaluation, Dissemination and Assessment Center.

Cummins, J. (2007). Rethinking monolingual instructional strategies in multilingual classrooms. *Canadian Journal of Applied Linguistics, 10*(2), 221–240.

Cummins, J. (2009). Fundamental psycholinguistic and sociological principles underlying educational success for linguistic minority students. In T. Skutnabb-Kangas, R. Phillipson, A. K. Mohanty, & M. Panda (Eds.), *Social justice through multilingual education* (pp. 19–35). Multilingual Matters.

Davis, J. (2017). Resisting rhetoric of language endangerment: Reclamation through indigenous language survivance. *Language Documentation and Description, 14*, 37–58.

de Jong, E., & Bearse, C. I. (2012). Dual language programs as a strand within a secondary school: Dilemmas of school organization and the TWI mission. *International Journal of Bilingual Education and Bilingualism, 17*(1), 15–31.

Demmert, W.G. (2001). *Improving Academic Performance among Native American Students: A Review of the Research Literature.* ERIC Number: ED463917. Retrieved from https://eric.ed.gov/?id=ED463917.

Diez, B. (2019). 'English Only': The Movement to Limit Spanish Speaking in US. *BBC.* Retrieved from https://www.bbc.com/news/world-us-canada-50550742.

Dolson, D. (1985). Bilingualism and Scholastic Performance: The Literature Revisited. *NABE Journal,* 10, 1, 1–35. (ERIC Document Reproduction Service No. EJ 367 966 and ED 291 257).

Duranti, A. (1994). *From grammar to politics: Linguistic anthropology in a Western samoan village.* University of Berkeley Press.

Edwards, J. (1994). *Multilingualism.* London and New York: Routledge.

Fishman, J. (1991). *Reversing language shift.* Multilingual Matters.

Fleming, J., & Ledogar, R. J. (2008). Resilience, an evolving concept: A review of the literature relevant to aboriginal research. *Pimatisiwin: A Journal of Aboriginal and Indigenous Community Health*, 6, 7–23.

Flores, N., & Garcia, O. (2017). A critical review of bilingual education in the United States: From basements and pride to boutiques and profit. *Annual Review of Applied Linguistics, 37*, 14–29.

Flores, N., & McAuliffe, L. (2020). 'In other schools you can plan it that way': A raciolinguistic perspective on dual language education. *International Journal of Bilingual Education and Bilingualism.* https://www.tandfonline.com/doi/abs/10.1080/13670050.2020.1760200?journalCode=rbeb20s

Fortune, T.W. & Tedick, D.J. (2008). *Pathways to Multilingualism: Evolving Perspectives on Immersion Education*. Multilingual Matters.

Friedman, A. (2015). America's Lacking Language Skills. *The Atlantic*. Retrieved from https://www.theatlantic.com/education/archive/2015/05/filling-americas-language-education-potholes/392876/

Fuller-Thomson, E. (2015). Emerging evidence contradicts the hypothesis that bilingualism delays dementia onset. A commentary on "age of dementia diagnosis in community dwelling bilingual and monolingual Hispanic Americans" by Lawton et al. *Cortex, 66*, 170–172.

Furukawa, G. (2018). Stylization and language ideologies in Pidgin comedic skits. *Discourse, Context and Media, 23*, 41–52.

Galla, C. K., & Wilson, W. H. (2019). Early and emergent literacy practices as a foundation for Hawaiian language medium education. In A. Sherris & J. K. Peyton (Eds.), *Teaching writing to children in indigenous languages* (pp. 25–43). Routledge.

Genesee, F., & Lindholm-Leary, K. (2013). Two case studies of content-based language education. *Journal of Immersion and Content-Based Language Education, 1*(1), 3–33.

Genesee F., Geva E., Dressler C., Kamil M. (2006). Synthesis: Cross-linguistic Relationships. In D. August, & D. Shanahan (Eds.), *Developing Literacy in Second-Language Learners* (pp. 153–174). Mahwah, NJ: Erlbaum; Washington, DC: Center for Applied Linguistics.

Goldmacher, S. (2016). Trump's English-only Campaign. *Politico*. Retrieved from https://www.politico.com/story/2016/09/donald-trumps-english-only-campaign-228559

Goodyear-Ka'ōpua, N., Hussey, I., & Wright, E. K. (Eds.). (2014). *A nation rising: Hawaiian movements for life, land, and sovereignty*. Duke University Press.

Gifford, S. (2020). Navajo Nation Coronavirus Rates Higher than 48 States: Records. *New York Daily News*. Retrieved from https://www.nydailynews.com/coronavirus/ny-coronavirus-navajo-nation-20200414-yy53wpkbcjb55psckvbosgbma4-story.html

Goodenough, F. (1926). Racial differences in the intelligence of school children. *Journal* of *Experimental Psychology, 9*, 388–397.

Goodwin, C. (2000). Action and embodiment within situated human interaction. *Journal of Pragmatics, 32*(10), 1489–1522.

Gracey, M., & King, M. (2009). Indigenous health part 1: Determinants and disease patters. *Lancet, 374*, 65–75.

Greene, J. (1998). *A meta-analysis of the effectiveness of bilingual education.* University of Texas-Austin.

Grenoble, L. (2021). Why revitalize? In J. Olko & J. Sallabank (Eds.), *Revitalizing endangered languages: A practical guide* (pp. 9–22). Cambridge University Press.

Grenoble, L., & Whaley, L. (2006). *Saving languages: An introduction to language revitalization.* Cambridge University Press.

Greymorning, S. (1997). Going beyond words: The Arapaho immersion program. In J. Reyhner (Ed.), *Teaching indigenous languages* (pp. 22–30). Northern Arizona University.

Grosjean, F. (2010). *"Bilingual" life and reality.* Harvard University Press.

Gumperz, J. (1982). *Discourse strategies.* Cambridge University Press.

Hagiwara, M. K. I., Miyamura, J., Yamada, S., & Sentell, T. (2016). Younger and sicker: Comparing micronesians to other ethnicities in Hawaii. *American Journal of Public Health, 106*(3), 485–491.

Hajet, J., & Slaughter, Y., (Eds.). (2015). *Challenging the monolingual mindset.* Multilingual Matters.

Hakuta, K. (1989). *Bilingualism and intelligence testing: An annotated bibliography.* Bilingual Research Group.

Hallett, D., Chandler, M. J., & Lalonde, C. E. (2007). Aboriginal language knowledge and youth suicide. *Cognitive Development, 22*, 392–399.

Hanks, W. (1996). *Language and communicative practices.* Westview Press.

Hanneman, M. (2015). Harvard Lauds Samoan language center. *Midweek.* Retrieved from https://www.midweek.com/harvard-lauds-samoan-language-center/

Hawaiʻi Leads Country. (2016). Hawaiʻi leads country in non-English speakers. *Star Advertiser.* Retrieved from https://www.staradvertiser.com/2016/05/23/breaking-news/hawaii-leads-country-in-non-english-speakers/

Heath, S. B. (1983). *Ways with words: Language, life, and work in communities and classrooms.* Cambridge University Press.

Higgins, C. (2010). Raising critical language awareness in Hawaiʻi at Da Pidgin coup. In B. Migge, I. Leglise, & A. Bartens (Eds.), *Creoles in education: An appraisal of current programs and projects* (pp. 31–54). John Benjamins.

Higgins, C. (2021a). Promoting Pidgin at the University of Hawaiʻi at Mānoa. In G. Clements & M. J. Petray (Eds.), *Linguistic discrimination in U.S. higher education: Power, prejudice, impacts, and remedies* (pp. 174–188). Routledge.

Higgins, C. (2021b). Engaging the public in sociolinguistics for social justice: Advocating for Pidgin speakers in Hawai'i. In D. S. Warriner & E. R. Miller (Eds.), *Extending applied linguistics for social impact* (pp. 13–34). Bloomsbury Academic.

Hinton, L., Huss, L., & Roche, G., (Eds.). (2018). *The Routledge handbook of language revitalization.* Routledge.

Holm, A., & Holm, W. (1995). Navajo language education: Retrospect and prospects. *Bilingual Research Journal, 19*(1), 141–167.

Hovey, R., Delormier, T., & McComber, A. (2014). Social-relational understandings of health and well-being from an indigenous perspective. *International Journal of Indigenous Health, 10*(1), 35–54.

Hymes, D. (1962). The ethnography of speaking. In T. Gladwin & W. C. Sturtevant (Eds.), *Anthropology and human behavior* (pp. 13–53). Anthropology Society of Washington.

Hymes, D. (1996). *Ethnography, linguistics, narrative inequality: Toward an understanding of voice.* Routledge.

Jacob, M. (2013). *Yakama rising: Indigenous cultural revitalization, activism, and healing.* University of Arizona Press.

Jespersen, O. (1922). *Language: It's nature, origin, and development.* Henry Holt & Company.

Kachru, B. B. (1977). Linguistic schizophrenia and language census: A note on the Indian situation. *Linguistics, 15*(186), 17–32.

Kame'eleihiwa, L. (1992). *Native land and foreign desires: Pehea lā e Pono ai.* Bishop Museum Press.

Kanahele, G. (1982). *Hawaiian renaissance.* Project WAIAHA.

Ka'opua, L. S., Braun, K. L., Browne, C., Mokuau, N., & Park, C. B. (2011). Why are native Hawaiians underrepresented in Hawai'i's older adult population? Exploring social and behavioral factors of longevity. *Journal of Aging Research.* Retrieved from https://www.hindawi.com/journals/jar/2011/701232/

Kavé, G., Nitza, E., Shorek, A., & Cohen-Mansfield, J. (2008). Multilingualism and cognitive state in the oldest old. *Psychology and Aging, 23*(1), 70–78. https://doi.org/10.1037/0882-7974.23.1.70

Kecskes, I., & Papp, T. (2000). *Foreign language and Mother Tongue.* Lawrence Erlbaum Associates Publishers.

Kim, S., Jeon, S. G., Nam, Y., Kim, H. S., Yoo, D., & Moon, M. (2019). Bilingualism for dementia: Neurological mechanisms associated with functional and structural changes in the brain. *Frontiers in Neuroscience, 13.* Retrieved from https://www.ncbi.nlm.nih.gov/pmc/articles/PMC6868000/pdf/fnins-13-01224.pdf

King, M., Smith, A., & Gracey, M. (2009). Indigenous health part 2: The underlying causes of the health gap. *The Lancet, 374*, 76–85.

Kipp, D. R. (2000). *Encouragement, guidance, insights, and lessons learned for Native language activists developing their own tribal language program.* Grotto Foundation.

Krashen, S., & Biber, D. (1988). *On course: Bilingual education's success in California.* California Association for Bilingual Education.

Krauss, M. (1992). The world's languages in crisis. *Language, 68*, 4–10.

Kymlicka, W. (1995). *Multicultural citizenship: A liberal theory of minority rights.* Clarendon Press.

Kymlicka, W. (2001). *Politics in the vernacular: Nationalism, multiculturalism, and citizenship*. Oxford University Press.

Kymlicka, W. (2007). *Multicultural Odysseys: Navigating the new international politics of diversity*. Oxford University Press.

Labov, W. (1966). *The social stratification of English in New York City.* Center for Applied Linguistics.

Laddaran, K. C. (2015). Pidgin English now an official language of Hawaii. *CNN.* Retrieved from https://www.cnn.com/2015/11/12/living/pidgin-english-hawaii/index.html

Lewis, P., & Simons, G. (2010). Assessing endangerment: Expanding Fishman's GIDS. *Revue Romaine De Linguistique, 55*(2), 103–120.

Li, W. (2011). Multilinguality, multimodality, and multicompetence: Code- and modeswitching by minority ethnic children in complementary schools. *The Modern Language Journal, 95*(3), 370–383.

Liebenberg, L., Ikeda, J., & Wood, M. (2015). "It's just part of my culture": Understanding language and land in the resilience process of aboriginal youth. In L. C. Theron, L. Liebenberg, & M. Ungar (Eds.), *Youth resilience and culture*. Springer.

Lindholm-Leary, K. (2001). *Dual language education*. Multilingual Matters.

Lindholm-Leary, K., & Borsato, G. (2006). Academic achievement. In F. Genesee, K. Lindholm-Leary, W. Saunders, & D. Christian (Eds.), *Educating English language learners* (pp. 157–179). Cambridge University Press.

Lindholm-Leary, K., & Genesee, F. (2010). Alternative educational programs for English learners. In *Improving education for English learners: Research-based approaches* (pp. 323–382). California Department of Education.

Lindholm-Leary, K., & Howard, E. (2008). Language and academic achievement in two-way immersion programs. In T. W. Fortune & D. J. Tedick (Eds.), *Pathways to bilingualism: Evolving perspectives on immersion education.* Multilingual Matters.

Lippi-Green, R. (1994). Accent, standard language ideology, and discriminatory pretext in the courts. *Language in Society, 23*(2), 163–198.

Lockwood, H., & Saft, S. (2016). Shifting language ideologies and the perceptions of Hawai'i Creole among educators at the university level in Hawai'i. *Linguistics and Education, 33*, 1–13.

Look, M. A., Trask-Batti, M. K., Agres, R., Mau, M. L., & Kaholokula, J. K. (2013). *Assessment and priorities for health & well-being in Native Hawaiians & other Pacific peoples*. Honolulu, HI: Center for Native and Pacific Health Disparities Research, John A. Burns School of Medicine, University of Hawai'i at Mānoa.

Louis, W., & Taylor, D. M. (2001). When the survival of a language is at stake: The future of Inuttitut in Arctic Quebec. *Journal of Language and Social Psychology, 20*(1–2), 111–143.

Mac Ionnrachtaigh, F. (2013). *Language, resistance and revival: Republican prisoners and the Irish language in the North of Ireland*. Pluto Press.

Matsuda, S. (2016). Drop-out or push-out? micronesian students in Honolulu. *Pass*. Retrieved from https://www.pass-usa.net/micronesian-students-honolulu

May, S. (2011). Language rights: The "Cinderella" human right. *Journal of Human Rights, 10*, 265–289.

May, S. (2013). Indigenous immersion education: International developments. *Journal of Immersion and Content-Based Language Education, 1*(1), 34–69.

May, S. (2014). Contesting public monolingualism and diglossia: Rethinking political theory and language policy for a multilingual world. *Language Policy, 13*, 371–393.

McCarty, T. L. (2009). Empowering indigenous languages—What can be learned from native American experiences? In T. Skutnabb-Kangas, R. Phillipson, A. K. Mohanty, & M. Panda (Eds.), *Social justice through multilingual education* (pp. 125–139). Multilingual Matters.

McCarty, T. L. (2011a). *The role of native languages and cultures in American Indian, Alaska native, and native Hawaiian student achievement*. Brief prepared for the promising practices and partnerships in Indian education (P3IE) program evaluation group, under a contract from the U.S. Department of Education Office of Indian education programs to Kauffman & Associates Inc. of Spokane.

McCarty, T. L. (2011b). *Ethnography and language policy*. Routledge.

McGuire, P. D. (2010). Exploring resilience and indigenous ways of knowing. *Pimatisiwin: A Journal of Aboriginal and Indigenous Community Health, 8,* 117–131.

McIvor, O. (2013). *Protective effects of language learning, use and culture on the health and well-being of indigenous people in Canada.* Retrieved from https://www.semanticscholar.org/paper/Protective-Effects-of-Language-Learning%2C-Use-and-on-McIvor/66b23f335bc571f735ce62124a5883da93994089

Morcom, L. A. (2017). Self-esteem and cultural identity in Aboriginal language immersion Kindergarteners. *Journal of Language, Identity & Education, 16*(6), 365–380.

Morcom, L. A., & Roy, S. (2017a). Learning through language: Academic success in an indigenous language immersion kindergarten. *Journal of American Indian Education, 56*(2), 57–80.

Morcom, L. A., & Roy, S. (2017b). Is early immersion effective for aboriginal language acquisition? A case study from an Anishinaabemowin Kindergarten. *International Journal of Bilingual Education and Bilingualism, 22*(5), 551–563.

Morisako, A. K., & Tauali'I, M., Ambrose, A. J. H., & Withy, K. (2017). Beyond the ability to pay: The health status of native Hawaiians and other Pacific Islanders in relationship to health insurance. *Hawai'i Journal of Medicine & Public Health, 76*(3), 36–41.

Mufwene, S. (2004). Language birth and death. *Annual Review of Anthropology, 33*, 201–222.

NACCHO (National Aboriginal Community Controlled Health Organisation). (2011). *Constitution for the National Aboriginal Community Controlled Health Organisation.* NACCHO.

Olko, J., & Sallabank, J. (2021). *Revitalizing endangered languages: A practical guide.* Cambridge University Press.

Oster, R. T., Grier, A., Lightning, R., Mayan, M. J., & Toth, E. L. (2014). Cultural continuity, traditional Indigenous language, and diabetes in Alberta first nations: A mixed methods study. *International Journal for Equity in Health, 13*(1). Retrieved from https://equityhealthj.biomedcentral.com/articles/10.1186/s12939-014-0092-4

Ovando, C. (2003). Bilingual education in the United States: Historical development and current issues. *Bilingual Research Journal, 27*(1), 1–24.

Panapasa, S. V., Mau, M. K., Williams, D. R., & McNally, J. W. (2010). Mortality patterns of Native Hawaiians across their lifespan: 1990–2000. *American Journal of Public Health, 100*(11), 2304–2310.

Peal, E., & Lambert, W. (1962). The relationship of bilingualism to intelligence. *Psychological Monographs: General and Applied, 76*(27), 1–23.

Phillip, J., & Abbot, M. (2011). *A decade of foreign language standards: Impact, influence, and future directions.* Report of Grant Project #P017A080037, Title VII, International Research Studies, U.S. Department of Education to the American Council on the Teaching of Foreign Languages.

Piller, I. (2016). *Linguistic diversity and social justice: An introduction to applied sociolinguistics.* Oxford University Press.

Poai, A. K. (2019). *Clarabal Hawai'i Supreme court oral arguments: Clarabal v. Department of education (2018).* Retrieved from https://blog.hawaii.edu/kahuliao/ka-moae/spring-2018/clarabal/

Policing and Communities of Color in Hawai'i Webinar. (2020). Retrieved from https://www.youtube.com/watch?v=vc_1BxDdJDc

Portes, A., & Rumbaut, R. (2001). *Legacies: The story of the immigrant second generation.* University of California Press.

Pufahl, I., & Rhodes, N. (2011). Foreign language instruction in U.S. schools: Results of a national survey of elementary and secondary schools. *Foreign Language Annals, 44*(2), 255–288.

Ramirez, J. D. (1992). Executive summary. *Bilingual Research Journal, 16*(1–2), 1–62.

Rampton, B. (2007). Neo-Hymesian linguistic ethnography in the UK. *Journal of Sociolinguistics, 11*(5), 584–607.

Rampton, B., Maybin, J., & Roberts, C. (2014). *Methodological foundations in linguistic ethnography* (Working papers in urban language & literacies)

Rampton, B., Tusting, K., Maybin, J., Barwell, R., Creese, A., & Lytra V. (2004). UK linguistic ethnography: A discussion paper. In *UK linguistic ethnography forum* (pp. 1–24).

Reagan, T. (2019). *Linguistic legitimacy and social justice.* Palgrave.

Reeves, R. (2018). *How a tight-knit Pacific Island community is saving its culture.* Honolulu Civil Beat. Retrieved from https://www.civilbeat.org/2018/08/a-tight-knit-pacific-island-community-works-to-save-its-culture/

Reeves, R. (2018). How a Tight-Knit Pacific Island Community is Saving its Culture. *Honolulu Civil Beat.* Retrieved from https://www.civilbeat.org/2018/08/a-tight-knit-pacific-island-community-works-to-save-its-culture/

Reyhner, J. (2010). Indigenous language immersion schools for strong indigenous identities. *Heritage Language Journal, 7*(2), 138–152.

Roche, G. (2017). Linguistic vitality, endangerment, and resilience. *Language Documentation & Conservation, 11*, 190–223.

Roche, G. (2020). Abandoning endangered languages: Ethical loneliness, language oppression, and social justice. *American Anthropologist, 122*(1), 164–169.

Rolstad, K., Mahoney, K., & Glass, G. V. (2005). The big picture: A meta-analysis of program effectiveness research on English language learners. *Educational Policy, 19*(4), 572–594.

Saft, S. (2019). *Exploring multilingual Hawai'i: Language use and language ideologies in a diverse society*. Lexington Books.

Saft, S., Tebow, G., & Santos, R. (2018). Hawai'i Creole in the public domain: Humor, emphasis, and heteroglossic language practice in university commencement speeches. *Pragmatics, 28*(3), 417–438.

Sakoda, K., & Siegel, J. (2003). *Pidgin grammar: An introduction to the Creole language of Hawai'i*. Bess Press.

Salomone, R. (2010). *True American: Language, identity, and the education of immigrant children*. Harvard University Press.

Sato, C. (1991). Sociolinguistic variation and language attitudes in Hawaii. In J. Cheshire (Ed.), *English around the world: Sociolinguistic perspectives* (pp. 647–663). Cambridge University Press.

Sato, C. (1993). Language change in a Creole continuum: Decreolization? In K. Hyltenstam & A. Viberg (Eds.), *Progression and regression in language: Sociocultural, neuropsychological and linguistic perspectives* (pp. 122–143). Cambridge University Press.

Silva, N. (2004). *Aloha betrayed: Native Hawaiian resistance to American colonialism*. Duke University Press.

Silva, N. (2017). *The power of the steel-tipped pen: Reconstructing native Hawaiian intellectual history*. Duke University Press.

Sivak, L., Westhead, S., Richards, E,. Atkinson, S., Richards, J., Dare, H., Zuckerman, G., Gee, G., Wright, M., Rosen, A., Walsh, M., Brown, N., & Brown, A. (2019). "Language breathes life"—Barngarla community perspectives on the wellbeing impacts of reclaiming a Dorman Australian aboriginal language. *International Journal of Environmental Research and Public Health, 16*. Retrieved from https://www.ncbi.nlm.nih.gov/pmc/articles/PMC6843244/

Skorton, D., & Altschuler, G. (2012). America's foreign language deficit. *Forbes*. Retrieved from https://www.forbes.com/sites/collegeprose/2012/08/27/americas-foreign-language-deficit/?sh=21e3b5f44ddc

Skutnabb-Kangas, T. (2018). Language rights and revitalization. In L. Hinton, L. Huss, & G. Roche (Eds.), *The Routledge handbook of language revitalization* (pp. 13–21). Routledge.

Skutnabb-Kangas, T., & Dunbar, R. (2010). Indigenous children's education as linguistic genocide and a crime against humanity? A global view. *Galdu Cala: Journal of Indigenous Peoples Rights, 1*. Retrieved from https://www.afn.ca/uploads/files/education2/indigenouschildrenseducation.pdf

Sonoda, H. (2008). A nation incarcerated. In C. Fujikane & J. Okamura (Eds.), *Asian settler colonialism: From local governance to the habits of everyday life in Hawai'i* (pp. 99–115). University of Hawai'i Press.

Stafford, S. (2010). Caught between "The rock" and a hard place: The native Hawaiian and Pacific Islander struggle for identity in public health. *American Journal of Public Health, 100*(5), 784–789.

Statistical Report. (2016). *Detailed language spoken at home in the state of Hawaii*. Retrieved from https://files.hawaii.gov/dbedt/census/acs/Report/Detailed_Language_March2016.pdf

Stauffer, J. (2015). *Ethical loneliness: The injustice of not being heard*. Columbia University Press.

Sullivan, M., & Bialystok, E. (2017). The importance of bilingualism for the aging brain: Current evidence and future research directions. In E. Bialystok & M. Sullivan (Eds.), *Growing old with two languages: Effects of bilingualism on cognitive aging*. John Benjamins.

Taff, A., Chee, M., Hall, J., Hall, M. Y. D., Martin, K. N., & Johnston, A. (2018). Indigenous language use impacts wellness. In K. Rehg & L. Campbell (Eds.), *The Oxford handbook of endangered languages* (pp. 862–883). Oxford University Press.

Talmy, S. (2006). The other *other*: Micronesians in a Hawai'i high school. In C. Park, R. Endo, & A. L. Goodwin (Eds.), *Asian and Pacific American education: Learning, socialization, and Identity* (pp. 19–49). Information Age Publishing.

Tamura, E. (1996). Power, status, and Hawai'i Creole English: An example of linguistic intolerance in American history. *Pacific Historical Review, 65*(3), 431–454.

Teacher Shortage Crisis. (2019). *Teacher shortage crisis forces principals to hire Hawaiian immersion teachers who don't speak Hawaiian*. Retrieved from https://www.hsta.org/news/recent-stories/teacher-shortage-crisis-forces-principals-to-hire-hawaiian-immersion-teachers-who-dont-speak-hawaiian/

Tedick, D. J. (2015). United States of America: The paradoxes and possibilities of bilingual education. In P. Mehisto & F. Genesee (Eds.), *Building Bilingual Education Systems: Forces, Mechanisms and Counterweights* (pp. 1–22). Cambridge: Cambridge University Press.

Tedick, D. J., Christian, D., & Fortune, T. W. (2011). *Immersion education: Practices, policies, possibilities*. Multilingual Matters.

Thomas, W., & Collier, V. (2012). *Dual Language education for a transformed world.* Future Press.

U.S. Department of Education. (2016). *Teacher shortage areas: Nationwide listing, 1990–1991 through 2016–2017*. Washington DC: U.S. Department of Education, Office of Postsecondary Education.

Van den Noort, M., Vermeire, K., Bosch, P., Staudte, H., Krajenbrink, T., Jaswetz, L., Struys, E., Yeo, S., Barisch, P., Perriard, B., Lee, S., & Lim, S. (2019). A systematic review on the possible relationship between bilingualism, cognitive decline, and the onset of dementia. *Behavioral Science, 9,* 7. Retrieved from https://www.mdpi.com/2076-328X/9/7/81

Walsh, M. (2018). Language is like food…: Links between language revitalization and health and well-being. In L. Hinton, L. Huss, & G. Roche (Eds.), *The Routledge Handbook of Language Revitalization* (pp. 5–12). New York: Routledge.

Watahomigie, L. J., & McCarty, T. L. (1994). Bilingual/bicultural education at peach springs: A Hualapai way of schooling. *Peabody Journal of Education, 69* (2), 26–42.

Weiner, A. (2016). America's real migrant crisis is the one you've never heard of. *Mother Jones.* https://www.motherjones.com/politics/2016/12/hawaii-micronesia-migration-homeless-climate-change/

White, L. (2015). *Free to be Mohawk: Indigenous education at the Akwesasne freedom school.* University of Oklahoma Press.

Wiley, T. G., & Garcia, O. (2016). Language policy and planning in language education: Legacies, consequences, and possibilities. *The Modern Language Journal, 100*, 48–63.

Williams Jr., R. (2011). 'Ike Mōakaaka, seeing a path forward: Historiography in Hawai'i. *Hūlili: Multidisciplinary research on Hawaiian well-being* (Vol. 7, pp. 67–90).

Willig, A. C. (1985). A meta-analysis of selected studies on the effectiveness of bilingual education. *Review of Educational Research, 55*(3), 269–317.

Wilson, W.H. (1998a). The sociopolitical context of establishing Hawaiian-medium education. *Language, Culture, and Curriculum, 11*(3), 325–338.

Wilson, W. H. (1998b). I ka 'ōlelo Hawai'I ke ola, 'Life is found in the Hawaiian language.' *International Journal of the Sociology of Language, 132,* 123–137.

Wilson, W. H., & Kamanā, K. (2011). Insights from indigenous language immersion in Hawai'i. In D. J. Tedick, D. Christian, & T. W. Fortune (Eds.), *Immersion education: Practices, policies, possibilities* (pp. 36–57). Multilingual Matters.

Wilson, W. H., & Kamanā, K. (2017). The Hakalama: The 'Aha Pūnana Leo's syllabic Hawaiian reading program. In C. J. McLachlan & A. W. Arrow (Eds.), *Literacy in the early years: Reflections on international research and practice* (pp. 133–150). Springer.

Wolfram, W. (1974). *Sociolinguistic aspects of assimilation: Puerto Rican English in New York city.* Center for Applied Linguistics.

Wood, M., Liebenberg, L., Ikeda, J., & Vincent, A. (2020). The role of educational spaces in supporting Inuit Youth Resilience. *Child Care in Practice, 26*(4), 390–415. https://doi.org/10.1080/13575279.2020.1765143

Woumans, E., Santens, P., Sieben, A., Versijpt, J., Stevens, M., & Duyck, W. (2015). Bilingualism delays clinical manifestation of Alzheimer's disease. *Bilingualism, 18,* 568–574.

Wright, W. E. (2012). Bilingual education. In W. C. Ritchie & T. Bhatia (Eds.), *Handbook of bilingualism and multilingualism.* Wiley-Blackwell.

Yokota, T. (2008). The 'Hawai'i Creole problem': Attitudes about Hawai'i Creole. *Educational Perspectives, 41*(1–2), 22–29.

2

American Colonialism, Resistance, and the Linguistic Landscape in Hawai'i

As suggested in Chapter 1, Hawai'i is a bit of a paradox from a linguistic perspective. On the one hand, Hawaiian society is pervaded by a monolingual mindset that has left English as the dominant language in public domains. On the other hand, society is marked by a multilingualism that includes an educational pathway through the Native Hawaiian language, the continued intergenerational transmission of a creole language such as Pidgin, a central role for an immigrant language, Japanese, in tourism, one of the main industries that sustains the economy, and the widespread usage of language mixing. In order to shed light on this linguistic situation, this chapter probes the sociolinguistic history of the Hawaiian Islands since the late 1700s with a focus on two basic processes, colonialism and resistance. These two processes have maintained a reflexive relationship throughout modern Hawaiian history, with American acts of colonialism breeding resistance and resistance in turn triggering further attempts to reinforce colonial domination, followed thereafter by more resistance (and so on and so forth). There is, of course, a risk of oversimplification in reducing the complex linguistic history of Hawai'i to these two seemingly opposing processes. As Roche

S. Saft, *Language and Social Justice in Context*,
https://doi.org/10.1007/978-3-030-91251-2_2

(2019: 490) notes in his discussion of the oppression of minority languages in Tibet, emphasis on "the bilateral relations of domination and resistance" provides "an incomplete picture of the mechanisms of language oppression." Accordingly, discussion in this chapter will show how colonialism in Hawai'i has been a multilayered process that not only oppressed the Native Hawaiians and the immigrant populations but also compelled both groups to police their own and each other's language usage according to an Americanization process dominated by English. Recognition of the complexity of colonialism will likewise make it possible to understand resistance not as a one-dimensional process (us against them), but rather as a dynamic process constituted by conflicting beliefs among the oppressed groups.

2.1 American Colonialism

Kameʻeleihiwa (1992: 20) offers a succinct appraisal of the starting point of the colonial period and also its devastating effects on the Native Hawaiian population in the following passage:

> The greatest distress began in 1778, upon contact with the Western world. For one hundred years after the arrival of the first white explorer, Captain Cook, foreign diseases carried off the Hawaiian people. From Cook's low estimate in 1779 of a population of 400,000 (compared with a modern estimate of 800,000), the Hawaiian population declined to 40,000 by the time of the overthrow of the Hawaiian government in 1893. The death toll from Cook's time onward was certainly far greater than those lives offered in sacrifice to the war God Kū. During those years, Hawaiians saw their society falling apart as their friends and loved ones died around them.

Captain Cook was a British sailor, but the major leader in the colonization of Hawaiʻi has been the United States. Even with the presence of Westerners, the Hawaiian Islands existed as a united and independent kingdom until a group of American businessmen with the backing of the American military imprisoned the last reigning Hawaiian monarch, Queen Liliʻuokalani, and ousted the Hawaiian government in 1893.

Other notable events of American origin not listed by Kame‘eleihiwa (1992) include the arrival of American missionaries in 1820 and the "great māhele" land division of 1848, which, among other outcomes, gave American businessmen easier access to Hawaiian land. This easier access to the land enabled the businessmen to expand the sugar plantation business that resulted in the importation of laborers from various other countries, thus creating a linguistic landscape that went well beyond Hawaiian and English.

Although American influence in Hawai‘i increased leading up to 1893, the overthrow of the Hawaiian Kingdom ushered in an era of even further hegemony. English had gradually achieved prominence by 1893, but a legislative act in 1896 made English the only acceptable language of education. After setting up a provisional government run by American businessmen after the overthrow, the U.S. official made a resolution to annex Hawai'i as an American territory in 1898 and then later confirmed statehood in 1959 as the 50th state. While these are just a few of the acts of American colonialism, they provide a sense of the transformative and destructive nature of the colonial process. Kame‘eleihiwa's (1992) statistics showing the drastic decrease in the population of Native Hawaiians, an effect of the diseases and trauma introduced by outsiders, are perhaps the greatest indicator of the destruction wrought by American colonization (also see Stannard, 1989).

Education was a crucial location for the United States to push its colonial agenda. Despite the existence of traditional Hawaiian approaches to education that predate Western contact (see Charlot, 2005), Benham (1998) notes that the centralized educational system established in 1840 under Hawaiian rule was strongly influenced by Americans who had begun gaining influence within the Hawaiian government. She states directly that "the idea and structure of Hawai‘i's schools were therefore an American invention" (Benham, 1998: 123), and she emphasizes the degree to which American participation in the construction of the early educational system took its toll on the Native Hawaiians over the course of time.

> The effect then of educational policy over time has largely kept the Native Hawaiian voice "less" in defining school policy and culturally relevant school activities. Although a few Hawaiian immersion schools have been

> recently developed and state curricular policy mandates the teaching of Hawaiian culture and history, actual practice reveals a need for more resource attention. Yet, for the most part, governmental control over school policy still obscures any meaningful attempts to reform the public schools in ways that embrace cultural plurality and educational parity for all children. (Benham, 1998: 138)

Benham's criticism of school policy has been echoed by Kana'iaupuni et al. (2005: 40), who point out that an emphasis on the transmission of knowledge and the taking of standardized tests has "alieniated many Native Hawaiian children whose cultural roots suggest an inclination toward experiential learning in authentic environments (Kawakami, 2004)." Not only has the adoption of American educational practices left "some Native Hawaiian children disengaged and distrustful of social institutions such as school" (Kana'iaupuni et al., 2005: 40), but this is part of a larger process of "nearly two centuries of systematic political, racial, and cultural marginalization" that "has left the Native Hawaiian people in a precarious position" (Thomas et al., 2012: 337).

American colonialism in the domain of education is closely tied to the demise of the Hawaiian language. Legislative act 57, the 1896 law passed by the provisional government created by the American businessmen that overthrew the Queen, stated that "the English language shall be the medium and basis of instruction in all public and private schools" and represented a culmination of the process of language shift that can be traced back to the arrival of the missionaries in 1820. To be sure, the missionaries are credited with teaching the Native Hawaiians how to write down their own language, which in turn resulted in a high literacy rate and the creation of not just numerous Hawaiian language newspapers but also of a tradition of Hawaiian literature that is still appreciated today (Schutz, 1994, 2020). However, it is noted that a mere 26 years later in 1846, "the Hawaiian legislature declared that all laws enacted were to be published in both Hawaiian and English" (Lucas, 2000: 3) and "by 1850 English had become the language of business, diplomacy, and to a considerable extent, of government itself" (from Wist, 1940 and quoted by Lucas, 2000: 3). Indeed, there is evidence that this language shift was a purposeful effect of American colonialism in the name of "helping" the Native Hawaiians. The 1896 biennial report of the president of the Board of Education to the legislature stated that "the gradual extinction of a Polynesian dialect may be regretted for sentimental reasons, but is certainly for the interest of the Hawaiians themselves" (quoted in Wilson & Kamanā, 2006: 154). The phrase "for the interest of the Hawaiians themselves" demonstrates the degree to which the Americans in charge had worked to take away the rights of self-determination from the Native Hawaiians.

Based on reports from Hawaiian elders who spoke Hawaiian, school teachers devoted particular efforts after passage of the 1896 law to preventing students from speaking Hawaiian, including verbal and physical punishment (Kamanā & Wilson, 2012; Lucas, 2000; Wilson & Kamanā, 2006). As Kamanā and Wilson (2012: 77) explain, "It was common for children caught speaking Hawaiian to be punished by being hit, to be held after school, by being forced to stand in the corner holding up heavy stones, and be psychologically humiliated." Emma Kapūnohu'ulaokalani Kauhi tells the story in her book written in Hawaiian (Kauhi, 2000: 24) of starting school in Kalapana on the Big Island of Hawai'i at a time when she was unable to speak English. In her words in Hawaiian:

> *I ka manawa kula, ua ho'opa'i 'ia au no ka 'ōlelo Hawai'i i loko o ka pā kula i ka manawa ho'omaha li'ili'i. Ma mua o ka pau 'ana o ke kula, ho'omaopopo maila ke kumu kula i nā haumāna, 'ōlelo maila "Ho'i 'oukou i ko 'oukou home, mai 'ōlelo Hawai'i 'ōlelo haole wale nō."* ("During school, I was punished for speaking Hawaiian in the schoolyard during recess. Before school ended for the day, the teacher told the students 'when you go home, don't speak Hawaiian, use only English.'")[1]

Similarly, Eliza Kauila Poaha Reyes remembers (Woodside et al., 2011: 15) nearly being kicked out of school for speaking Hawaiian with her sisters. Indeed, attempts to prevent Native Hawaiians from employing their language extended from the school to the home as "the Department of Education sent spokespersons into the homes of Hawaiians who knew

[1]Throughout this book, I use italics for Hawaiian words and texts. This is done not to mark Hawaiian as unusual or strange but instead to bring Hawaiian to the attention of the readers.

English to intimidate them into using English at home" (Kamanā & Wilson, 2012: 77).

Even prior to the 1896 law, it is apparent that some schools had instituted measures to prevent Hawaiian on school grounds. In a telling sign of the times, Kamehameha Schools, a private school system established in 1887 for Native Hawaiian children, chose English as the medium of education from the start. According to Wist (1940; quoted in Lucas, 2000: 7), the first headmaster William Oleson made sure that "strict rules were set to prevent the use of other than the accepted tongue [English] on the campus." According to Kimura (1983: 196), it was not just the children who were punished: "teachers who were native speakers of Hawaiian (many were in the first three decades of the Territory) were threated with dismissal for using Hawaiian in school" (Kimura, 1983: 196). This type of intense pressure, with the legislative act of 1896 being enforced to a degree that threatened physical punishment, led many Hawaiian-speaking parents to the agonizing decision not to pass the language down to their offspring. Eliza Kauila Poaha Reyes recalls how her mother cried when the family decided to stop speaking Hawaiian at home due to external pressure (Woodside et al., 2011: 15). Kimura (1983: 196) writes, in fact, that "the main loss of language came through the school system, which attacked the language at its most vulnerable and important point, the children from Hawaiian-speaking homes." He also continues to emphasize the strength of the English-only policy through the assertion that "Hawaiian would certainly have remained the first language of the majority of the native Hawaiian population and a likely number of locally-born non-Hawaiians if it were not for the rigorously pursued policy of the territorial administration to replace Hawaiian with English" (Kimura, 1983: 197).

With such a forceful language shift movement, many writers in the later 1900s were anticipating the extinction of the Hawaiian language. Writing in 1960, Aspinwall already attributes to Hawaiian the status of "foreign language," proclaiming that "in our Hawaiian schools and colleges today we have ruled that all languages but English are 'foreign'" (Aspinwall, 1960: 9). Although she tries to be positive by listing some Hawaiian language written resources, she nonetheless seems to assume the extinction of the spoken language and the "Latinization" of Hawaiian by noting that the emerging resources have "assured future students of favorable conditions for studying Hawaiian in its written form" (Aspinwall, 1960). Walch (1967: 363) likewise seems to announce the end of spoken Hawaiian when he states that "the Hawaiian language which developed, grew, and began to flourish in such a short time, died in an almost equally brief period." Even some writers that recognized the existence of speakers of Hawaiian expressed pessimism toward the survival of the language. Benton (1981) predicted that Hawaiian would be the first Polynesian language to go extinct, and others have offered the dire figures that by the early 1980s there were less than 50 children under the age of 18 who spoke Hawaiian fluently (Wilson & Kamanā, 2006).

2.2 American Colonialism and Foreign Labor

As the above discussion attempts to show, the effects of American colonialism on Native Hawaiians and the Indigenous Hawaiian language are undeniably immense and must not be understated. At the same time, though, we need to appreciate that American colonialism in Hawai'i extends beyond the decimation of the native population and the attempts to eradicate Hawaiian. When the "great māhele" land division facilitated the sugar plantation business, plantation owners realized that they needed laborers to do the hard work of planting and harvesting the sugar cane.[2] The plantations first looked to the Native Hawaiians, both women and men, to work in the fields (Takaki, 1983), but due to a diminished population from disease and sickness and also due to the lack of desire on the part of the Hawaiians to work the long hours for little pay, this plan was not feasible (Beechart, 1985: 59).[3] The plantation owners thus turned

[2]Takaki (1983: 18) reports that by 1890, "three out of four privately held acres were owned were owned by white Americans or their corporations.".

[3]Although both Takaki (1983) and Beechart (1985) make note of reports indicating that Native Hawaiians did serve as capable workers, Beechert describes a survey in 1848 showing that "Hawaiian commoners busily engaged in their traditional occupations and strongly disinclined to work for low wages." Beechart (1985: 37) also notes that a number of Native Hawaiians angered the "enterprising agriculturists" of the plantations by deciding "to produce their own crops for sale to the eager shippers from California."

to "the only viable solution (Beechart, 1985: 60)," namely the importation of laborers from outside of Hawai'i.[4] The first significant group came via ship from China in 1852 on five year contracts, and although more workers from China came between the years of 1852 and 1875, it was not until the Reciprocity Treaty of 1875, which allowed the Kingdom of Hawai'i to export its products to the United States without tariffs, that the sugarcane business accelerated. The increase in demand prompted plantation owners to step up their recruitment of immigrant laborers. In addition to the Chinese, the plantations tried workers from Pacific Island sources that included the New Hebrides and the Gilbert Islands, and they also recruited from places such as Norway, Germany, Sweden, Spain, Russia, Korea, and Puerto Rico, among others. While many of these attempts at recruitment ended in controversy or with unhappy workers who left Hawai'i after only a short stay, the steady arrival of laborers from Portugal, Japan, and the Philippines, together with the Chinese, came to constitute a large percentage of the plantation workforce throughout the Hawaiian Islands. In particular, Japan provided the largest pool of laborers, with about 180,000 Japanese arriving in Hawai'i between 1885 and 1924 (Tamura, 1993). According to Matsu et al. (2011), by 1920 the Japanese constituted 42.7 of the population of Hawai'i. This includes some 25,000 laborers from Okinawa, which, not unsimilar to what happened in Hawai'i, had existed as separate kingdom until it was taken over by Japan in 1879 (Higashionna et al., 2011).

The plantation workers were responsible for creating a thriving sugarcane business following the Reciprocity Treaty of 1875, making the plantations owners rich and powerful. Many immigrant laborers stayed in Hawai'i beyond their initial contracts, and although some continued working on the plantations, many others moved on to pursue other businesses in Hawai'i. As Takaki (1983: 141) reports, "most Chinese left the plantation as soon as they could," an occurrence which helped

[4] It is interesting to note, though, that the blame for the failure of the first plantation on Kaua'i was placed on the Native Hawaiian laborers. As reported in Beechart (1985: 22), the first manager of the 1835 Kaua'i plantation, William Hooper, lamented in true colonizer fashion that his failures stemmed from "the complete worthless of Sandwich Islanders as laborers on a farm ... Centuries, at least, will intervene, ere they will understand that it is part of their duty to serve their masters faithfully" (quoted in Beechart, 1985: 22).

motivate the search for immigrant labor from various other places as well. The importation of different groups of laborers, in fact, provided a kind of safeguard for the rich plantation owners, who, through a system of "differential wages based on nationality" (Takaki, 1983; 155), could bring in workers to replace those demanding higher wages and better conditions (also see Beechart, 1985, Chapters 6 and 7). In this way, the owners of the plantations could protect their own wealth and at the same time maintain, or at least attempt to maintain, control over the immigrants' ability to improve their life situations.

Indeed, the maintenance of power over the growing immigrant population was a central concern of the white businessmen and political leaders. In addition to controlling them through cheap wages, they also preserved social hierarchy through the usage of descriptive language that portrayed the workers as the "exotic" but "inferior" "other." Beechart (1985: 148) quotes the U.S. commissioner of labor in 1906 as placing all the laborers of Asian origin together through the following comment: "The Asiatic laborers are looked upon contempt by their white employers but they in turn reciprocate thoroughly the race contempt which the white class feels for them .... The second generation of Asiatics, therefore, however much in such a community they may conform to American business customs, remain alien in thought and sympathy." Through the explicit categories of "Asiatic laborers" and "white employers," this commentary creates a sharp hierarchy that places the "Asiatic laborers" as the "alien other" that stands in contrast to the gold standard of the "white employers." As Okamura (2014: 22) notes, this was part of "the haole view of themselves as genetically superior to nonwhites," a stance behind the movement to seek non-whites to perform the hard labor of the plantations. Based on reports from the Hawaiian Sugar Planters Association, established by the plantation owners to support their own goals, "Caucasians were 'constitutionally and temperamentally unfitted for labor' in a tropical climate, while Asians and 'brown' men were 'peculiarly adapted to the exactions of tropical labor,' and could serve as satisfactory and 'permanent' field workers" (Takaki, 1983: 66).

This notion of racial superiority served as rational for hegemonic control over not just the immigrant laborers but also the Native

Hawaiians, who were depicted by the white missionaries and businessmen as too childish and irresponsible to govern for themselves. Samuel Dole, one of the orchestrators of the overthrow in 1893 and the first governor of the territorial government that followed, referred to the Native Hawaiians as "irresponsible people" (quoted in Okihiro, 1991: 12; Saft, 2019: 39), and Reverend Sereno E. Bishop called them "babes in character and intellect" who "were not intrusted with rule, because in their childishness and general incapacity, they were totally unfit for such rule" (quoted in Fuchs, 1961: 34; Okihiro, 1991: 12; Saft, 2019: 39). Even the Hawaiian language was attacked as being "childish," "feeble," and "insipid," among other adjectives, by Westerners who visited the islands in the 1800s (see Saft, 2019; Schutz, 1994 for more examples and further discussion).

The use of language to disparage the various groups of non-whites was thus a general tactic employed toward colonialism. At the same time, the white businessmen had to contend with another by-product of the plantation system, that is, the transformation of Hawai'i into a multilingual society. Minnie Forsyth Grant, a visitor to Hawai'i in the late 1800s, wrote that "amongst the many dialects and languages which assailed one's ear on a walk through the plantations were English, Portuguese, German, Native, Japanese, Norwegian, Chinese …" (quoted in Takaki, 1983: 117). And not only were these languages heard, but speakers of these languages took measures to disseminate their languages within society. In addition to newspapers written in both Hawaiian and English, newspapers were published in Chinese, Portuguese, Japanese, Korean, Tagalog, and Ilocano (see Bastos, 2018; Chapin, 1984; Him, 2010 for further information). Moreover, some of the communities of foreign workers created language schools that children attended in addition to their regular public schools. For example, Takaki (1983: 117) reports that German families in Lihue on Maui created a German language school to the extent that "In 1888 eighty-one out of the eighty-six German children in the public school also attended the German language school." Similarly, the Korean community established Korean language schools, with Patterson reporting 10 such schools in 1932 with 520 students (Patterson, 2000). Him (2000) gives 1881 as the date for the first Chinese language school with an enrollment of 17 boys, and soon thereafter schooling in Chinese expanded with Chinese-Christian offering Chinese classes mostly in Cantonese but also in the Hakka dialect as well. Chinese language education grew further and seemed to reach a peak in 1934. According to Him (2000: 130), "Honolulu became a major center for Chinese-language schools in the United States. In 1934, there were 3,106 students in 12 schools in Honolulu."[5]

The most common language schools were devoted to Japanese. The first school was started in 1893 Kohala on the island of Hawai‘i, and the number of schools grew steadily to twenty-two in 1904 and to 163 by 1919 (Asato, 2006). It is estimated that over 20,000 Japanese Americans attended these schools in 1920 with approximately 98% of the Japanese-American students enrolled in public schools also attending Japanese language schools outside of the public schools (Asato, 2006; Takaki, 1983). Asato (2006) notes a further increase to 41,192 students in 1934.

Though proving to be a successful strategy for ensuring a multilingualism in Hawai‘i through intergenerational transmission of immigrant languages, the language schools were targeted by the territorial government for eradication. Declaring "that every German school was a blow at American democracy and part of the pan-German machine" (Wagner-Seavey, 1980: 128), German language education was the first to be shut down in 1918 due to fears generated from World War I. The Maui News (Friday, May 3, 1918), in an article reporting that the school closed down the German school in Lihue, Kaua‘i, wrote:

> And this brings us to the question of why *any* foreign language school should be allowed to exist in the United States. Why would it be unjust to require that *all* schools for the young should be all-American? Why should foreigners who have come to our country to make their home object to conforming with the customs and even the habits of mind of the land of their adoption? Why should they seek to perpetuate their own national peculiarities which must always be out of harmony with their new environment.

[5]Bastos (2018) notes that there were plans to support a Portuguese school in Hawai‘i, but these plans did not come to fruition.

The same article later emphasized a connection between abolishing the foreign language schools and safeguarding citizens by exclaiming outrightly that "we have been too lax" in allowing the schools to persist. At approximately the same time, as reported by Asato (2006: 30), Reverend Albert W. Palmer of Honolulu's prestigious Central Union Church proclaimed in a public speech not just that "these Islands must be 100 percent American" but also that "the first and most obvious step is the elimination of foreign language schools." At nearly the same time, The Maui News (Friday, June 28, 1918) reports the Star-Bulletin of Honolulu as stating that "The war has brought sharply home to the United States how the persistence of foreign languages in some localities has held back thorough Americanization of the immigrants. Hawaii has the problem in an acute form, and some day we may expect to see a territory-wide rule abolishing foreign language grade schools."

The biggest campaign to close the language schools, however, focused specifically on the Japanese language schools. As early as 1906, the Hawaiian Star featured the headline "Only English in Public Schools" for an article describing how "the Board of Education yesterday afternoon turned down an application from an Ewa Japanese for permission to use the school house there, after the regular school hours, for a Japanese school" (Hawaiian Star, 1906, February 9th). The article noted that the Board would not "allow use of the school except for regular English courses." Construed first as a general language school "issue" and then explicitly as "the Japanese language school problem," the schools drew attention from the United States government, which decided to dispatch a team in 1919 to investigate. The team produced a report that found the schools to be "centers of an influence which, if not distinctly anti-American, is certainly un-American," and concluding by stating it "feels no hesitancy in recommending as a first and important step in clearing away the obstacles from the path of the Territorial public-school system that all foreign-language schools be abolished" (from U.S. Department of the Interior, A Survey of Education in Hawaii, 1920: 134, quoted in Asato, 2006: 40). Shortly thereafter, another English newspaper, the Garden Isle (June 8th) offered in 1920 the headline "Language Schools Must Go," in an article describing the federal report and emphasizing how it "insists upon the complete abolition of the foreign language schools, declaring them to be un-American and a barrier to the successful teaching of English in the public schools and the promulgation of American principals, ideals and customs."

Even before the report came out in 1919, the territorial government began legal efforts to regulate schools, including attempts to pass bills that would require teachers to pass a certification test on knowledge of English, American history, and civics and another bill that would restrict the hours of operation of the schools (Asato, 2006). These initial attempts did not deter the operation of the schools, but the territorial government continued to author legislature that made it difficult for the schools to proceed. The schools still persisted and the student population managed to grow until the onset of World War II and the Japanese attack on Pearl Harbor resulted in a mandate that closed the schools. Through a sustained campaign of Americanization and by making use of the anti-Japanese paranoia that arose prior to World War II, the United States was successful in deterring multilingualism and manufacturing an English monolingualism in Hawai'i.

Despite success in the attempts to suppress immigrant languages, the American attempt to make English the primary language of Hawai'i still faced one major linguistic challenge that was an unintended result of the importation of immigrant laborers, namely the rise of the creole language known as Pidgin. The first pidgin that emerged in Hawai'i in the 1800s was a Hawaiian-based pidgin due to the strength of the Hawaiian language at the time (Bickerton, 1998; Bickerton & Wilson, 1987). Researchers differ in terms of their opinion about how English became the lexifier of Pidgin; some believe that an English-based pidgin emerged separately from Pidgin Hawaiian and others believe that there was a "gradual transition" "between the pidgins" (Bickerton, 1998: 57). Nonetheless, most agree that sometime in the early 1900s, a "novel creole language" emerged as a more or less stable language that is now known by the name of Pidgin (Bickerton, 1998: 57; also see Reinecke, 1969).

Unfortunately though for Pidgin and for Pidgin speakers as well, Pidgin was under intense scrutiny from the start. The timing of the development of Pidgin corresponded with the increase of white Americans from the mainland who were not wealthy and thus were not able to afford to send their children to private schools "which had for eighty or ninety years been providing education in English for the children of missionaries and of aristocratic Hawaiians" (Aspinwall, 1960: 7; also see Higgins, 2010). The children from the mainland United States spoke English, and the fact that these children had to attend public schools with children who spoke Pidgin was immediately deemed a "problem" (Aspinwall, 1960; Higgins, 2010; Lockwood & Saft, 2016). As Tamura (1994: 199) reports, a 1920 federal survey indicated that "only 2 to 3 percent of all students entering Hawai'i public school at ages six and seven, about one-third to one-half of whom were Japanese, spoke Standard English." Reinecke (1969) observed in the 1930s that the percentage of people in Hawai'i who spoke standard English was about 15 percent, with the greater majority speaking either "Pidgin English" or "Hawaii Creole English."[6]

Even though Pidgin speakers outnumbered standard English speakers, Pidgin's fate as a stigmatized language was sealed because, first of all, power still resided with the white elite as Hawai'i as remained a territory of the United States, and, second of all, Pidgin, instead of being treated as a language in its own right, was subjected to constant comparisons with English. This is apparent in the description offered by Aspinwall (1960: 8):

> It is characterized by a sharply reduced structure ("Check roll?" "Neva check.") by omission of various parts of speech, ("You like go show?" sometimes by un-English word order ("Big, yeh, da puka!", by new auxiliary verbs ("Look, stay raining!" "I been tell him no.") and also by a sharp reduction in phonetic structure.

Implicit in terms such as "reduced structure," "omission," "un-English," and "sharp reduction" is the judgment that Pidgin does not live up to the standard of English and thus stands as inferior by comparison.

---

[6]As Tamura (1994: 199) notes "Hawaii residents have commonly used the term 'Pidgin' to refer to the entire spectrum of languages spoken by plantation workers and their descendants." Reinecke (1969) was one of the first to note distinctions within this spectrum. In general, the label "Pidgin" is used here to refer to the "novel creole language," but, as discussed briefly in Chapter 3, which is devoted to Pidgin, there are still variations within the way Pidgin is spoken in the Hawaiian Islands.

Indeed, the educators of the 1920s were quick to label Pidgin as a "problem." Tamura (1994: 98) notes that "Superintendent Willard E. Givens in 1924 called the 'English problem' the 'most baffling of the academic difficulties" in Hawaii's schools." She also notes that another superintendent, Will Crawford, agreed with Givens in 1927 that "the need for 'better English' was the schools' most pressing problem" and that Crawford also complained that "the bane of Pidgin English [Hawaii Creole English] has eaten deeply into the vitals of our language" (Tamura, 1994: 198).

In an attempt to deal with this English problem, and in the process appease the incoming white Americans who "demanded education specifically for their children" (Higgins, 2010: 30), the educational leaders implemented a system of English standard schools beginning in 1924. Admission to the English standards schools was dependent on an oral test, and speakers with features of Pidgin in their language were denied entry and sent back to their regular, non-English standard schools. Such a practice created a segregated school system (Higgins, 2010; Romaine, 1999) that, while not eradicating Pidgin, succeeded in continued promotion of negative attitudes toward Pidgin that "managed to keep creole speakers in their 'place'" (Romaine, 1999: 289) and keep "negative attitudes toward Pidgin ... institutionalized along race and class boundaries" (Higgins, 2010: 33).

It is apparent, then, that this campaign to discredit Pidgin succeeded in controlling society's view of Pidgin. Eades et al. (2006) report that attitudes throughout the 1950s and 1960s remained acutely negative. Superintendent Lowell Jackson is reported to have called Pidgin the "plain misuse of English" in 1966, school principal Manuel Kwon labeled it "abominable English" in 1959, and Bill Ewing, editor of the Honolulu Star-Bulletin, called Pidgin "the most execrable language in the world" (see Eades et al., 2006 for further discussion of these quotations). The same newspaper, the Honolulu Star-Bulletin, also featured an editorial in 1962 with the title "Why not just grunt?", thus comparing Pidgin to the language of animals (da Pidgin Coup, 2008: 32). Such negative opinions pervaded society for the rest of the twentieth century. This includes the attempt in 1987 by the Curriculum Committee of the Hawai'i Board of Education to implement a policy to allow only standard

English in schools (Eades et al., 2006; Sakoda & Siegel, 2003; Tamura, 1996). Although the attempt did not work, the Board of Education eventually adopted a "softer statement which 'encouraged' the modeling of standard English by teachers and staff" (Eades et al., 2006: 155). Moreover, a poll by the newspaper the Honolulu Advertiser in 1995 found that "two thirds of Hawai'i's residents say standard English should be the only language used to teach in the classroom" (Eades et al., 2006: 155). And, Pidgin has also served as a scapegoat for below average performance by Hawai'i's children on standardized tests with State Board of Education Chairman, Mitsugi Nakashima, claiming that "if you speak Pidgin, you think Pidgin, you write Pidgin" (from the Honolulu Advertiser, September 29, 1999; quoted in da Pidgin Coup, 2008: 35; Siegel, 2008: 59).

Given that a large portion of society speaks Pidgin, an essential component of the movement to "keep Pidgin speakers in their place" was to convince the speakers themselves of the inferiority of their language. Furukawa (2018: 41) refers to this as a form of "linguistic schizophrenia" (see also Higgins, 2010; Kachru, 1977) because even though many people in Hawai'i continue to use Pidgin, many those same people express "extreme shame" when asked about their usage. As Furukawa (2018: 42) notes, "a large segment of Hawai'i's population still insists that Pidgin is to blame for many of the failures of the educational system." This is, it should be noted, one of the more insidious aspects of the colonial movement to oppress languages, that is, to get speakers of a language to believe that their languages are subordinate to the dominant language. Convinced of the inferiority of their languages, speakers will then police their own language usage and help the colonizers promote the dominant language.

Like Hawaiian and immigrant languages, Pidgin was the target of an American colonial agenda that attempted to instill an English monolingual mindset in the multi-ethnic population in Hawai'i. As was the case for many Native Hawaiians and the immigrant laborers, many speakers of Pidgin were compelled to believe that English was the "proper" language. However, unlike Hawaiian and immigrant languages, Pidgin speakers did not fully switch to English, adopting instead a form of bilingual diglossia with English spoken in public domains and Pidgin in private settings like the home. We see below, though, that Pidgin is implicated in another level of the colonialism in Hawai'i. Later, it will also be shown that Pidgin features prominently in patterns of resistance in Hawai'i.

2.3 Asian Settler Colonialism

The above discussion aligns speakers of Hawaiian, immigrant languages, and Pidgin together as victims of the American colonial process, which has at one point or another attempted to eradicate all languages in Hawai'i other than English from public space. However, the literature reminds us that we need to be careful of stating this alignment too strongly. In contrast to the Native Hawaiians, the immigrants were not dispossessed of their lands; immigrants could and often did (and continue to) return to Japan, China, Portugal, the Philippines, etc., to visit their homelands and experience their ancestral cultures. The same is true with language. Immigrants in Hawai'i may have been forced to adopt English, but Japanese, Chinese, Portuguese, and Filipino languages are still spoken by millions in different parts of the world. Needless to say, the same cannot be said of Hawaiian. Such observations lead to consideration of another layer of colonialism in Hawai'i, termed Asian settler colonialism (Fujikane, 2008; Saranillio, 2013, 2018).

Asian settler colonialism emphasizes that immigrants who found economic success in Hawaiian society have done so primarily by making use of the colonial structures put into place by the United States. By doing so, they have contributed to the reinforcement of those colonial structures and have thus played a role in the same settler colonialism that has detached and continues to separate the Native Hawaiian population from its land, culture, and language. To this point, Fujikane (2008: 7) asserts, "the early Asian settlers were both active agents in the making of their own histories and unwitting recruits swept into the service of empire," and she also adds that "all Asian settlers, including colonial administrators, artists, teachers, students, writers, journalists, scholars, and many others who do not see themselves as having a political role to play, support and engage in the U.S. colonization of Hawaiians."

Writers who discuss Asian settler colonialism emphasize that the problem is not that immigrants from Asia looked to provide a better life for their families. Nor do they deny that the Asian immigrants in Hawai'i were themselves victims of American colonialism. As Fujikane (2008: 6) notes, "the sugar planters established the plantation as an economic base for an American settler colony by exploiting the unstable political and economic conditions in Asian nations resulting from American, British, Spanish, and Japanese imperialism." Additionally, Ortega (2017) underscores the degree of degradation experienced by some of the immigrants when she writes that the so-called American dream for her Filipino ancestors "was a near slave-trade situation" in which they were forced to wear "slave tags with numbers, stripped of our names." Invocation of the concept of Asian settler colonialism is therefore not intended to let the United States. off the hook for its colonial agenda against immigrant populations in Hawai'i.

However, Asian settler colonialism becomes especially relevant when we consider that both Asian immigrants and white settlers alike have heralded the success of the immigrants in Hawai'i as an example of "multiculturalism" and "democracy." Such a picture of American democracy "in action" leaves no place for Native Hawaiians struggling with homelessness, unemployment, high incarceration rates, and health problems other than to depict them as "failures" unable to pick themselves up by their own bootstraps (Fujikane, 2008: 3–4). Referencing the ideas of the late Hawaiian activist and scholar Haunani-Kay Trask (1999, 2000), Fujikane (2008: 5) explains that "the celebration of the 'immigrant' success story—a story often used by Asian settler political representatives in Hawai'i—is an attempt to legitimate Asian settler political power made possible by U.S. settler colonialism." In Trask's even more powerful words (2000: 2):

> For our Native people, Asian success proves to be but the latest elaboration of foreign hegemony. The history of our colonization becomes a twice-fold tale, first of discovery and settlement by European and American businessmen and missionaries, then of the plantation Japanese, Chinese, and eventually Filipino rise to dominance in the islands. Some Hawaiians, the best educated and articulate, benefit from the triumph of

> the Democratic Party over the *haole* Republican Party. But as a people, Hawaiians remain a politically subordinated group suffering all the legacies of conquest: landlessness, disastrous health, diaspora, institutionalization in the military and prisons, poor educational attainment, and confinement to the service sector of employment.

In particular, Trask takes issue with the fact that many children of immigrants have claimed the identity of "local" in Hawai'i, which is meant to mark their intimate relationship to Hawai'i and separate them from outsiders who are labeled with other categories such as "haole." Yet, as Trask notes, the identity of "local" is conflated with "native," a category that can only apply to Native Hawaiians. As Trask (2000: 2) writes:

> Our Native people and territories have been overrun by non-Natives, including Asians. Calling themselves "local," the children of Asian settlers greatly outnumber us. They claim Hawai'i as their own, denying indigenous history, their long collaboration in our continued dispossession, and the benefits therefrom. Part of this denial is the substitution of the term "local" for immigrant, which is, itself, a particularly celebrated American gloss for "settler."

Trask's point about the category "local" in this passage is clear. As she reminds us, "the issues before 'locals' have merely to do with finding a comfortable fit in Hawai'i that guarantees a rising income, upward mobility, and the general accoutrements of a middle-class 'American' way of life" while Native Hawaiians deal with "indigenous land and cultural rights, and survival of a people" (Trask, 2000: 20).

However, despite the power of Trask's argument, the distinction between "local" and "Native Hawaiian" becomes complex when we return the discussion to language and consider the role of Pidgin. Pidgin lies at the intersection of the identity categories "Native Hawaiian" and "local" because people from both have grown up speaking Pidgin as their first language. As noted above, Pidgin's development into a creole in the early 1900s overlapped with the U.S. territorial government's English campaign, but it is important to point out that this was also a period when the Hawaiian language was banned from education and when Hawaiian speakers were punished for trying to speak their native language. Accordingly, many Native Hawaiians stopped transmitting Hawaiian to their children, who in turn grew up speaking Pidgin since that was the language spoken by a significant portion of the immigrant children around them. Even as Hawaiian language revitalization grows, many people of Native Hawaiian blood still speak Pidgin in their homes. Kimura (1983: 195) addresses the Hawaiian-Pidgin connection very directly when he states that "Hawaiian remained the normal vernacular of Hawai'i until between 1910–1920, when it was replaced by pidgin English." He even takes this a step further and writes that "Pidgin cuts Hawaiians off from their ancestral root and aesthetic culture, along with the adaptive tradition to technological society that is also their heritage" (Kimura, 1983: 200). Such a statement seems to bestow blame upon Pidgin for pushing Native Hawaiians away from their ancestral language. Moreover, given that Pidgin developed from the American colonizers desires to profit from Hawaiian lands, we may be encouraged to view the emergence of Pidgin as another colonial source of language oppression in Hawai'i.

Yet, before further pursuing the relationship between Pidgin and American colonialism, we need to expand the discussion to consider the role of resistance in the development of language ecologies in Hawai'i. As the next section demonstrates, resistance has played a much more prevalent role in the evolution of modern Hawaiian society than suggested in American historical narratives focusing on Hawai'i. Pidgin, it will be shown, has occupied a central role in the expression of resistance in Hawai'i.

2.4 Resistance

There has been a tendency from an American perspective to portray the Native Hawaiian population as passive accepters of the overthrow of their kingdom in 1893, with the native population supposedly viewing it as an inevitable outcome of the survival of the fittest (Osorio, 2006; Williams, 2009, 2011). As Williams (2009: 155) notes, the missionary newspaper

"The Friend" stated soon after the overthrow of the Hawaiian Kingdom that "The natives have shown no disposition to resist the new government...The news of the Revolution appears to have been received by the natives on the other islands without demonstration of feeling." This, however, was far from the truth. Reaction and resistance were swift and strong from the native population. The American narrative of the passive Native Hawaiians erases, for example, the attempt in January 1895 by Native Hawaiians, led by Robert William Kalanihiapo Wilcox, to oust the government set up by the U.S. businessmen immediately after and to restore Queen Lili'uokalani to power with a new constitution (Nakanaela, 1993; Williams, 2011). As Williams (2011: 80) reports, "Wilcox and over 300 others were arrested and tried before a military commission set up under martial law."

Moreover, as detailed by both Williams (2009) and Silva (2004), resistance from Native Hawaiians included the creation of a petition of mass opposition in 1897 to the impending annexation of Hawai'i by the United States in 1898. The petitions were collected by three groups of Native Hawaiians and were delivered to the Senate of the United States. In total, the petitions were 556 pages in length with 21,269 signatures (Silva, 2004). On display in the Bishop Museum in Honolulu, the petitions offered a story that, "contrary to every history book on the shelf," allows Native Hawaiians to learn "that their ancestors had, as James Kaulia put it, taken up the honorable field of struggle" (Silva, 2004: 9). The name James Kaulia, in fact, is invoked because he gave "a stirring speech" in 1897 urging the Native Hawaiian population to oppose annexation (Goodhue, 1998: 37). As reported in the September 11th version of the Hawaiian Language Newspaper Ke Aloha Aina, Kaulia's speech ended with the following declaration[7]:

[7]Texts in the Hawaiian newspapers were printed without two spelling conventions, the use of an *'okina* for a glottal stop and the use of a macron called *kahakō* for long vowels, that are frequently used today. When quoting from the newspapers, I will the text as it appeared without the spelling conventions but later in the book when transcribing more recent spoken materials, the two conventions will be employed to make them accessible for current Hawaiian speakers.

> *E HOOHOLOIA. O makou ka poe i akoakoa ma kekahi halawai makaainana nui i Malamaia ma ka la 6 o Sepatemaba, A.D. 1897, ma ke kulanakauhale o Honolulu, Mokupuni o Oahu, Ka Hawaii Pae Aina, no makou iho a no ka Lahui Kanaka Hawaii a me ka hapanui o ka poe e noho nei ma loko o keia Pae Aina ke kue loa aku nei i ka hoohuliia ana o Hawaii me Amerika Huipuia.*
>
> Let it be decided. We the people gathered at a certain large meeting of the citizenry that was held on September 6th, 1897, A.D. in the city of Honolulu, on the Island of Oahu in the Hawaiian Island Chain, for our ourselves and for the Hawaiian people and for the majority of the people living on the Island Chain strongly oppose the annexation of Hawai'i by the United States.

Of particular interest here is the usage of the first-person exclusive plural pronoun *makou,* which, in a Hawaiian pronimal system that includes a distinction between exclusive and inclusive pronouns and also between dual and plural forms, makes it clear that Kaulia is making a distinction between the people he is speaking for, namely the citizens of Hawai'i, and the people he is speaking to, which would be those in the government (and others) pushing for annexation. This is, in another words, a declaration directed to the Americans who put themselves in charge of the government. And, it should be emphasized that the Hawaiian term *kue* ("opposition") is used together with the intensifier *loa* ("very much"), indicating that it is meant to be a very strong opposition to annexation.

Also conveniently overlooked in the American narrative of colonization is the fact that the last two monarchs in Hawai'i, Queen Lili'uokalani and King Kalākaua, displayed staunch support to the native population as well as resistance to the growth of American power in Hawai'i. Queen Lili'uokolani, the ruling monarch in 1893 at the time of the overthrow, was convicted of treason and sentenced to hard labor after the 1895 coup attempt on the provisional American government. The Queen came to power only in 1891 after the death or her brother King Kalākaua, but in her short time as leader of the kingdom, she attempted to institute a new constitution that favored the native population. A new constitution was necessary because under severe pressure from a group of white businessmen, King Kalākaua had agreed in 1887 to a revised constitution, termed the Bayonet Constitution that gave significant power to the non-Hawaiian population. The Queen, though, after hearing the voices of her fellow Hawaiians and meeting with native leaders such as Samuel Nowlain and Joseph Nāwahī, decided to institute constitutional changes (Liliʻuokalani, 1990; Silva, 1998). Aware of the Queen's intention to change the constitution, the small group of businessmen hastened their decision to begin their coup. Immediately following the coup, Queen Lili'uokalani wrote a letter to the instigators in which she stated, "I. Liliuokalani, by the grace of God under the constitution of the Hawaiian kingdom Queen, do hereby solemnly protest again any and all acts done against myself and the constitutional government of the Hawaiian kingdom by certain persons claiming to have established a Provisional Government of and for this kingdom." It was in this same letter that she also temporarily yielded her authority "to avoid ... the loss of life ... until such time as the Government of the United States shall, upon the facts being presented to it, undo the action of its representative, and reinstate me in the authority which I claim as the constitutional sovereign of the Hawaiian Islands." Later, once it became clear that the United States began to support the provisional government with the intent to annex Hawaiʻi, she also wrote letters to American politicians and also to President William McKinley in 1897 in opposition to the annexation treaty.[8]

Queen Liliʻuokalani's predecessor on the throne, her brother King David Kalākaua, has often been depicted and even ridiculed as a weak monarch who gave in to the wishes of the American businessmen (see discussion in Ing, 2019). As just noted, his reign, which began in 1874 and concluded with his death in 1891, saw non-Hawaiians increase their power through the establishment of the Reciprocity Treaty in 1875 and the Bayonet Constitution in 1887. In reality, though, more recent historical descriptions from a Hawaiian perspective emphasize the role played by Kalākaua in promoting the Native Hawaiian population. Through the motto *Hoʻoulu Lāhui,* he was, as Ing (2019: 125) notes,

[8]Some letters and other anti-annexation documents are available at http://libweb.hawaii.edu/digicoll/annexation/annexation.php.

"staunchly devoted to the independence of Hawai'i and the vigorous endurance of his lāhuikanaka" and he also "fought for Hawai'i's independence to the end of his life" (Ing, 2019: 9). This sentiment is supported by Beamer (2014: 176), who writes that "branching out from the reigns of the previous *mō'ī* ("monarchs"), Kalākaua heightened the nation's cultural consciousness while pushing to insure a new level of Hawaiian independence" (also quoted in Ing, 2019: 7). Ing (2019: 82) similarly underscores that "neither Kalākaua nor Hawaiians simply surrendered their constitutional rights and civil liberties to those Davianna McGregor-Aegado calls the 'missionary-planter elites'" (see McGregor-Alegado, 1979: xiii).

Traditional Western narratives also ignore the influence yielded by the Hawaiian Kingdom across the globe prior to the 1893 overthrow. As Gonschor (2020: 35) explains, "Hawai'i was unique in the nineteenth century world order as the only non-Western country to be recognized as a fully independent state with which Western nations had equal treaty relations." The equal international treaties entered into included those with France, the United Kingdom, Denmark, Sweden, Norway, Hamburg, Belgium, Spain, Netherlands, Luxemburg, Switzerland, Russia, Germany, Portugal, and also the United States. Moreover, Hawai'i was the first and, for several decades, the only non-Western state to be recognized as a coequal member of a group of states referred to as the Family of Nations (Gonschor, 2020). Gonschor (2020: 20) further notes that "by early 1887, Hawai'i maintained 103 legations and consulates worldwide, an impressive number given the comparatively small size of the country." As stated by Fernandez Asensio, the Hawaiian Kingdom "commanded such respect because it was a stable constitutional monarchy based on ethnic and religious pluralism, state-funded universal education, popular representation and a very liberal franchise, in a time when these virtues were uncommon even in the West" (Asensio, 2010: 10).

Even though the Hawaiian Kingdom achieved this international recognition following the arrival of the missionaries in 1820, scholarship adopting a Hawaiian perspective has been clear that Native Hawaiians remained the architects of their own kingdom. As Silva (2004: 9–10) writes, "The Kanaka Maoli created their nation in their own ways" that included "strategic accommodation to the Western ideas of nationhood and government, combined with an insistence on the value of Kanaka cultural identity." Gonschor (2020: 29) concurs with this sentiment when he writes that by the mid-1850s, "Hawai'i's constitutional system was a perfect example of hybridity, combining a foundation of classical Hawaiian political institutions with elements selectively appropriated from the Western constitutional systems considered to be the most progressive."

A further indication of the degree to which the Hawaiian Kingdom was an advanced society is the existence of a striving network of newspapers, both in English and in Hawaiian. As Chapin (1984) explains, the first Hawaiian language newspapers, beginning in 1834 with *Ka Lama Hawaii*, were created and run by the missionaries largely for the promotion of Christianity. These papers gradually came to include voices attempting to guide Hawai'i toward U.S. annexation of Hawai'i (Chapin, 1984). The missionaries, for example, established *Ka Nupepa Kuokoa* in 1861, which originally expressed opposition to the "heathenizing tendencies" of the Hawaiian monarchy (Chapin, 1984: 53).

It did not take long, however, for Native Hawaiians to launch their own newspapers, which consistently presented ideas in opposition to those in the press initiated by non-Hawaiians. 1861 marked the beginning of the first Hawaiian language newspaper, *Ka Hoku o Ka Pakipika*, to be edited solely by Native Hawaiians, and it was notable because of the originator, David Kalākaua, who was later to become King Kalākaua. *Ka Hoku o Ka Pakipika* "considered itself a voice for the 'common people' and encouraged the expression of Hawaiian culture and the use of the Hawaiian language" (Chapin, 1984: 68). One editor of the *Ka Hoku o Ka Pakapika*, S.D. Keolanui, accused one of the editors of the *Ka Nupepa Kuokoa* of being "rich and well-situated" and *Ka Nupepa Kuokoa* itself "of being the voice of *haole* business men" (Chapin, 1984: 68). The following passage from an 1861 publication shows the tone of resistance that pervaded some of the columns of the paper.

Ka Hoku o Ka Pakipika, October 3rd, 1861

1 *Ua hoolahaia aku e kekahi poe kue, "He Nupepa lapuwale Ka Hoku o Ka Pakipika."*
2 *Aka, ea! Eia na pepa imua o ko kakou maka, a me ka pepa hoi i oleloia he pepa a*
3 *hemolele, oi ka Nupepa Kuokoa; a pehea, ua oiaio anei ia mau olelo?*

"It has been said by some people in the opposition that "Ka Hoku Pakipika is an awful newspaper." But, hey, here is the paper now before our eyes, and with the paper that is said to be so perfect, that Nupepa Kuokoa; so what do you think? Are those words true?"

4 *O ka makemake o ka poe nana i hapai i keia Nupepa Hoku o ka Pakipika, eia no ia, o ka*
5 *hoonaauao i ka Lahuikanaka Hawaii, a he poe kanaka Hawaii no ka poe nana i hapai, a*
6 *eia no lakou ke hooikaika Hawaii nei, e holo pono keia Nupepa i waena o kakou*

"What the people who have conceived of this *Nupepa Hoku o ka Pakipika* want, it is this, the education of the Hawaiian people, and for those Hawaiian people, they are the ones trying to improve Hawai'i, it is the desire that this newspaper works well among them."

7 *O keia pepa, aole ia na kekahi haole, aole hoi na ka mea hookahi; aka, na kanaka*
8 *Hawaii maoli, a no ka ike ana, aole i hoopukaia i pepa kupono i ka makemake o na*
9 *kanaka Hawaii, a no ka lawa ole o ka makemake ma ko kakou mau pepa mua i hoolahaia*
10 *iho nei; a no ka ka hilinai ana hoi i ko kakou ano naauao, no laila ke kumu o ka hapai*
11 *ana o keia pepa e hoolaha aku i waena o kakou*

"This paper, it is not for some haole, it is not for just one person; but, it is for the true Hawaiian people, and it is due to the fact, that until now there has not been a paper that fits with the needs and wants of the Hawaiian people, that there has been enough what is wanted in the papers produced prior to this, that we should believe in our own education, these are the reasons that this paper has been created and distributed amongst ourselves."

12 *O ka Ahahui hoopuka i keia Nupepa, he poe kanaka maoli hoi, aole lakou i manao e*
13 *kukulu i keia Nupepa i mea imi waiwai, a i mea e puka ai no lakou; aka, eia wale no ko*
14 *lakou waiwai, o ka hoolaha aku i Nupepa ku kaawale, pili ole i kela aoao hoomana keia*
15 *aoao hoomana, a pili ole i ke kanaka hookahi; aka i na mea a pau. No laila, o ka waiwai*
16 *puka o ia Ahahui, eia no ia, o ka laha o ka ike i waena o na kanaka maoli, a e ku mai*
17 *iluna me ka olelo iho, ko kakou Nupepa ponoi keia*

> "The association that produced this Newspaper, it is a group of true Hawaiians, they did not decide to produce this paper to attain wealth, nor to serve just themselves; but here is the worth of their product, to extend a Nupepa that stands by itself, that is not attached to one religion or another, that is not attached to one specific people; but for everyone. So, this is the worthiness of this organization, the circulation of knowledge throughout the true people of the land, so they stand proud by saying this is our own Newspaper."

Of particular interest in this passage is that the writer names the missionary sponsored newspaper, *Ka Nupepa Kuokoa*, in lines 1–3 in addressing a direct challenge to that paper. The writer subsequently expresses in lines 4–6 that the paper, *Ka Hoku o Ka Pakipika,* is for the Hawaiian people and then reinforces this in lines 7–11 by stating that is not for some haole person (*aole ia na kekahi haole*). The writer then further emphasizes the same point in lines 12–17, namely, that the newspaper has been produced by Native Hawaiians not to gain wealth but instead for the *kanaka maoli*, which literally means the "real people" but serves as a reference to the Native Hawaiians. The passage then ends in line 17 with the phrase *ko kakou Nupepa ponoi keia* which uses the plural inclusive pronoun *kakou* that expresses to the reader, inclusively, that "this is our Newspaper (capital "N" included in the Hawaiian original)."

Among the many statements in the newspaper *Ka Hoku o Ka Pakipika* that supported the Native Hawaiians and showed resistance to the haoles, there were expressions of support for the Hawaiian language. The next passage, also from 1861, demonstrates an awareness of differences in not just languages but also cultural ways of speaking.

From November 14, 1861, Ka Hoku o Ka Pakipika

1 *Eia hou kekahi mea hoomaopopo hou aku i ke ano o ka launa ana me na alii. Mai*
2 *noho a pane kuaaka, kikoho, a kikoala hoi, e hoomaopopo i na hopuna olelo me ke*
3 *akahele, mai olelo hoohalikelike me na haole hoohepa o ka leo, ma ke ano kahuli e*
4 *like me ka haole kamailio ana*

> "Here is something else to remember about how to meet and talk with the ali'i. Do not just respond with random sounds and interrupt them, think about and choose your words carefully, do not speak like haoles with indistinct speech, and do not change your voice like the way haoles do."

5 *Ua kaulana o G.L. Kapeau i ka hana e like me keia, a penei no kana olelo. "'O kera*
6 *kanaka no e noho ana ma ke kochihanai.' 'A na rike hoi ke kahi a kera wahi manu me*
7 *ke Kohahe o kai. Penei no ka pololei. Ua like kela wahi manu me ke Koa'e o kai. A pela*
8 *ke ano nui o ka kekahi poe no e hana nei, o ka hookāpekepeke i ka hui olelo kanaka a*
9 *hoawiliwili pu me ka olelo haole. Mai hana peia, o loaa no kou hoohenehene ia mai e*
10 *ka poe e noho ana*

> "G.L. Kapeau is famous for doing things like this, this is something he said. 'That person standing with the kochihanai.' 'And it is like that bird with the Kohahe bird of the sea.' Here is the correct version. 'That bird is like the Koae of the sea.' And that is often how some people speak, by putting their words together vaguely and to mix with English. Do not do that or else you will you be made fun of by the people there."

This passage begins with advice on how to speak with people in the status of *alii*, which refers to Native Hawaiians at the level of chief or above. The writer then specifically mentions the term *haole* twice as a part of advising readers not to do some negative speaking acts, such as speaking indistinctly and changing voice, that are performed by haoles. Next, in lines 5–10, the writer offers the name G. L. Kapeau as a specific example of someone who is "famous" for doing these negative acts. The writer subsequently provides two sentences in lines 6–7 with alternate spellings, particularly the use of the letter "r," to signify that they are examples of strange Hawaiian that has been influenced by English. The writer also gives the "correct" version in line 7, and having done that, the writer next advises readers not to speak in such a way that includes a mixture with English as it will result in being ridiculed. This passage from 1861 then suggests that the Native Hawaiians saw English as a possible problem for the Hawaiian language, and it likewise shows that at least some Native Hawaiians were keeping an eye on their language. This is also apparent in the next passage from the newspaper, *Ke Aloha Aina*, another newspaper that was established by Native Hawaiians for Native Hawaiians. It is taken from the year 1896, after the overthrow of the Hawaiian Kingdom and the same year that the English-only law in education was passed.

August 1, 1896, Ke Aloha Aina

1 *I ko makou heluhelu ana iho i ka moolelo o ko kakou mau kula i keia wa, ua ike ihola*

2 *makou, ua uhi aku ia kapa eleele ma luna o ko kakou mau kula ma ka olelo Hawaii*

3 *ponoi, a ua huliamahi ae nei ka lawelawe ia ana o na kula a pau ma ka ʻolelo haole wale*

4 *no a ua nele loa ke aʻo ia ana ma ka olelo Makuahine*

"When we read the story of our schools nowadays, we see that a black blanket has been drawn over our very own Hawaiian language schools, and that all of the schools have given way to English only, leaving us without any teaching in our Mother language."

5 *A o ka hua o keia aupuni hou i makana mai ai i na kanaka Hawaii, oia ke ka makeloa*

6 *ana i ko kakou mau kula Hawaii, a hoolilo ae la i na kula haole auhuhu nana e pepehi i*

7 *ko kakou mau kula ponoi, a i keia la, ehia ?? o na kula olelo Hawaii mai Hawaii a Kauai*

8 *e kamau ana, me ke kunewanewa o kona ola ana*

"The great gift that the new government has given the Hawaiian people, it is death to our Hawaiian schools, with the English schools providing the poison for our own schools. How many Hawaiian language schools from Hawaiʻi to Kauai can last like this just barely hanging on?"

9 *Ke hoomanao nei makou i ko makou wa kamalii, o na kula Hawaii ka hapanui i loko o ka*
10 *aina nei, ua piha a ku mawaho na haumana o na halekula ia manawa, a ua oi pookela*
11 *loa aku ka hohonu o ka naauao o na keiki i ia wa mamua o keia wa*

> "We recall the time of our youth, when the majority of the Hawaiian schools on this land were full of students inside and outside of the school grounds, this was the time when the depths of education for the kids far exceeded that of the current time."

At the beginning of this article in line 1, the writer employs the first-person exclusive plural pronoun *makou* to refer to a group of people around her/him that does not include the audience of readers. Yet, the writer quickly shifts at the end of line 1 to the first-person inclusive plural pronoun *kakou* to discuss the dilemma of the schools by addressing the collectivity of Native Hawaiians. In doing so, the writer laments in lines 1–4 that the English-only status has woven a "black blanket" (*kapa eleele*) around the Hawaiian language, which is described first in line 2 as the "own language of Hawai'i" (*olelo Hawaii ponoi*) and the "mother language in line 4" (*olelo Makuahine*). The writer next in lines 5–8 demonstrates a critical perspective toward the new government (*aupuni hou*) for providing the "poison" (*auhuhu*) to "destroy our Hawaiian language schools" (*pepehi i ko kakou mau kula*). The writer then ends in lines 9–11 by proclaiming that the Hawaiian schools of previous times provided far better education than the current English schools.

Even though 1896 marked the end of education through the medium of Hawaiian, the Hawaiian language newspapers persisted in calling for the re-establishment of schools through the medium of Hawaiian. The passage below shows one such call from another newspaper, *Ka Puuhonua o na Hawaii*, that was run by Native Hawaiians. This article appeared in 1917, more than twenty years after the banning of Hawaiian schools.

January 26, 1917, Ka Puuhonua o na Hawaii

1 *I ikeia no ke kanaka no kekahi lahui ma kana olelo. Ina e nalowale ana ka olelo*
2 *makuahine o kekahi lahui, e nalo hia aku ana no ia lahui. I keia la, ua nalohia aku ko*
3 *kakou kuokoa, a i ka pau ana o ka kakou olelo makuahine, o ka pau ana no ia o ka lahui*
4 *Hawaii*

> "It should be known that for a group of people who have their own language, if the mother tongue of that group dies, then the people themselves also cease to exist. Today, our independence has been taken away, and if our mother tongue is also lost, then we will cease to exist."

5 *Ma na ano no nae a pau a kakou e nana aku ai, eia no ka mana hapanui iloko o ko kakou*
6 *mau lima. Ua lilo mau ia kakou ka hapanui o na wahaolelo i ka Ahaolelo. A eia i keia*
7 *poe ka mana e hana i mau kula Hawaii no kakou. No keaha la i hana oleia ai? Ua*
8 *hapaiia mai i kekahi mau kau a na na kanaka Hawaii no i pepehi*

> "No matter which way we look at it, the majority of the power still lies in our hands. We have a majority in the legislature. And these are the people with the power to make Hawaiian schools for us. Why would it not be done? The idea has been raised in several sessions but it has been the Hawaiians who have struck down the idea."

9 *I keia la, ke hepa mai nei ka oleloia ana o ka kakou olelo makuahine. Aole keiki 15*
10 *makahiki e hiki ke kamailio pololei i ka olelo makuahine o keia aina. A no keaha ke*
11 *kumu i hiki ole ai? No ka mea, aole a'o ia i ka olelo pololei. A i ka hala ana i na la*
12 *pokole wale no o ka pau no ia, a mai uwe aku kakou no ka mea, na kakou no i nanamaka*

> "Today, our mother language is not spoken correctly. There are no children of age 15 that can speak the mother language correctly. And why is that? Because they are not taught the correct way. And in a short time, it will be lost, and so we cannot complain if we just watch it happen."

13 *E na kanaka Hawaii, pehea no hoi e koho kakou i poe e hele i ka Ahaolelo e kokua mai ia*
14 *kakou? Malia paha o olelo mai kekahi, aole e hiki e a'oia ka olelo Hawaii ma na kula*
15 *aupuni. Ae aole no he kula aupuni a na Kepani ma Hawaii nei e a'o nei i ka olelo lahui o*
16 *ko lakou aina, aka, ke ku nei ia mau kula, a ke a'oia nei na keiki Kepani e ike i ka olelo a*
17 *kona makuahine. Ina ua hiki ole i ka Ahaolelo e ala no hoi kakou na kanaka Hawaii a e*
18 *kukulu no hoi i kula no na kakou*

> "To the Native Hawaiians, how do we choose such people to represent us at the legislature? Maybe they will just say that the Hawaiian language cannot be taught in the public schools. Yes but even though the Japanese do not teach their language in the public schools, their children are still taught their mother language. If the legislature cannot do it, then we the Native Hawaiians need to wake up and create a school for ourselves."

This passage begins in lines 1–2 with the very straightforward assessment that if a language dies so does its people, which leads to the suggestion in lines 3–4 that the Hawaiian language and the Native Hawaiians are approaching such a dire situation. The writer next notes in lines 5–8 that they, the Native Hawaiians, have a majority in the legislature and therefore should have the power to make Hawaiian schools. However, the writer also points out that it has been the Native Hawaiians who have not pursued the schools. This does not, though, deter the writer and, after noting in lines 9–12 that the language is not being learned correctly by the younger generation, he/she uses the phrase *E na kanaka Hawaii* ("to the Native Hawaiians") in line 13 to specifically address the Native Hawaiians in an attempt to inspire them in lines 13–18 to create a school for themselves. In making this call, the writer points out that the Japanese have managed to create schools to pass on the Japanese language to their children, thus suggesting that the Native Hawaiians do the same. The passage ends with the strong statement to the Native Hawaiians that "we" (using the inclusive pronoun *kakou*) should wake up and create a school for ourselves.

While this attempt in the newspaper in 1917 did not result in the type of school that the writer was hoping for, there nonetheless continued to be voices advocating for Hawaiian medium schools. The following article appeared in 1936 in the newspaper *Ke Alakai o Hawaii*, with the title *Hanini ke Aloha i ka Olelo Hawaii* ("Pour some Aloha on the Hawaiian Language").

Ke Alakai o Hawaii, 1936

E oluolu mai oe i kekahi wahi kaawale o kau Nupepa ao, ko'u manao i kakau ai—nona ke ae la ma luna—"Hanini ke Aloha I ka Olelo Hawaii,"—hiki ole ke kaohi iho. Ua like no ko'u manao me ko Mr. Geo. Kalaauhoano, e kalahea nei ma na paemoku o Hawaii nei. O ke alahele wale no e hooko ia ai, oia no ko kakou pupukahi, o ka manaoio i na manao e hiki ai ke kukulu ma luna o keia ninau ka Olelo Hawaii, e holomua ai. Hookahi wale no alahele e hiki ai ke kukulu hou ia ka Olelo Hawaii, e noi ia ka ahaolelo e wehe hou ia ke kula Olelo Hawaii e like me na halekula o na keiki Kepani e a'o ia mai nei, a o na keiki Pake hoi, aia no lakou ma na home e a'o ia ai e na makua. No ke aha mai ke kumu? No ka minamina no i ka olelo o ka aina hanau

> "Please spare me some space in your newspaper, the thoughts I am sharing—in the title above—"Pour some aloha on the Hawaiian Language"—are thoughts I cannot suppress. My ideas are similar to those of Mr. Geo. Kalaauhoano, that resound throughout the Hawaiian Island chain. The only way to accomplish this is for all of us to come together and have faith we can do something concerning the question of the Hawaiian language. There is only one way that we can rebuild the Hawaiian language, that is to ask the legislature to open Hawaiian language schools like the schools that exist for the Japanese children, and for the Chinese, their languages are learned through their parents. Why is this happening? Because they place great value on the language of their homelands."

In much the same way the writer of the 1917 article made reference to the Japanese language schools, this author uses the existence of schools for Japanese and Chinese children to question why the same cannot be done for the Hawaiian language. This passage ends by noting that the Japanese and Chinese are trying to teach their children because they value the language of their homelands, thus insinuating that the Native Hawaiians should do the same. Like the 1917 article, this passage reads as a call to the Native Hawaiians to take action, in this case to ask the legislature to open Hawaiian schools, to preserve the Hawaiian language.

The selection of these passages from Hawaiian language newspapers that span from 1861 to 1936 is important because they dispel the belief that the Native Hawaiians willingly and passively relinquished their language and switched to English. While it may be true, as some of the newspaper passages suggest, that Hawaiian medium schools suffered from a lack of support from some Native Hawaiians in the legislature, it is simply just not true that the collective Native Hawaiian population readily chose English over Hawaiian.

Indeed, there are those who believe that the strength of the Hawaiian language in the years leading up to the 1896 law was far greater than typically reported. Kimura (1983: 195) writes that even though "84 percent of the nation's 8,770 school children were instructed through the medium of English, and only 15 percent received their education in Hawaiian, the vast majority of the children had Hawaiian as their dominant tongue." Kimura even makes the point that the strength of the Hawaiian language had pervaded the families of the wealthy white plantation owners: "Children of pure English and American ethnic parentage made up less that 5 percent of the entire school enrollment at the time and even in this group it is certain that some of them spoke Hawaiian. There are in fact haole plantation families with a history of children growing up speaking Hawaiian before English during the monarchical period" (underlined emphasis in original) (Kimura, 1983: 195). This information strongly suggests a need to view the 1896 legislature banning Hawaiian in a new light. Instead of legislature that followed naturally from a desire to speak English, this legislature should be understood as an explicit colonial attempt to quell the power of the Hawaiian language. Kimura (1983: 195–196) in fact emphasizes that:

> Hawaiian was still the dominant language in terms of numbers of speakers at the time of American annexation in 1898, despite official legislative policy replacing Hawaiian with English. Since Hawaiian was the language understood by the majority of the electorate and citizens of the new territory, it was the language used by politicians, including non-Hawaiians. The language was also used in the legislature, and a provision of the Organic Act requiring debates in the legislature to be in English resulted in the need for interpreters for the Territorial House and Senate (until 1907) just to comply with the law for those legislators not fluent in English... At the beginning of the territorial period, English speakers in government not fluent in Hawaiian were often closed out of political discussion.

Based on these observations of the strength of the Hawaiian language in the late 1800s and early 1900s, it is possible to see how some, such as Kimura, have concluded that "Hawaiian would certainly have remained the first language of the majority of the native Hawaiian population and a likely number of locally-born non-Hawaiians if it were not for the rigorously pursued policy of the territorial administration to replace Hawaiian with English."

Furthermore, although the number of Hawaiian speakers did decrease over time, reports suggest that the Hawaiian language persisted and even flourished at least in some social contexts for a considerable time in the 1900s. According to Kimura (1983: 196), "resistance to English usage was steadfast in Hawaiian churches, where reading and writing Hawaiian language was incorporated into the Sunday school curriculum. It has only been in the past two decades that English services have predominated in many Hawaiian churches, and this has occurred primary because most native-speaking Hawaiian ministers have died." Kimura (1983: 196) adds shortly thereafter that "there are still congregations that conduct their services entirely in Hawaiian. Like the churches, Hawaiian benevolent organizations strictly maintain the Hawaiian language." One page later, Kimura (1983: 197) notes in detail some of these organizations:

> A Hawaiian Language League based on the Gaelic League was organized in the 1930s, and a Hawaiian language school was also organized. In 1950s, Lalani Hawaiian Village was created for the purpose of teaching

> Hawaiian language and culture. Ulu Mau Village created in the 1960s with a similar goal. Both attempts met with an early demise. The 1970s saw the creation of the ‘Ahahui ‘Ōlelo Hawai‘i, an organization established through assistance from the Kamehameha Schools to promote the Hawaiian language. This group is still actively pursuing its goal.

No information is given regarding the demise of some of the organizations included, but this list does suggest the lengths to which Hawaiian speakers went to protect and promote their language. Punishments and other means intended to prevent the usage of Hawaiian were not fully successful in preventing continued usage of the language. As Kimura (1983: 197) writes at that time, “the most important response … was the refusal of many parents and grandparents to speak English to their children in spite of discouragement by teachers. In many cases families refused to allow children to speak English to them at all, because they believed that Hawaiians should speak to one another in their own language.”

By offering evidence that attests to the perseverance of Native Hawaiians in speaking their language, I do not intend to take agency away American colonialism for the endangerment of Hawaiian. If anything, these pockets of resistance speak to the tenacity of the colonial agenda that had to contend with the strong will of much of the native population. Still, above anything else, these stories of resistance speak to the resolve of the Native Hawaiians in their struggle to fight colonialism, something that has received little recognition in the literature. In fact, John Reinecke, who spoke of a relatively rapid decline of Hawaiian in his 1935 dissertation, later amended his view:

> I have quite a bit of corroborative evidence for the wide-spread use and importance of Hawaiian at least through the 1910s. For example, the transcripts of interviews from the Kona Oral History project show how widely Hawaiian was spoken by other nationalities in what was one of the strongholds of Hawaiian. And Larry Kimura found there were some individual (Natives) no older than I who were more at home if Hawaiian than in Pidgin. (Reinecke, 1987: 74)

Charlot (2005: 680) supports Reinecke's amendments by stating that "this is true also of a number of older Hawaiians with whom myself have spoken," and also by concluding that "in fact, the evidence for the predominant use of Hawaiian by Hawaiians and the majority of the non-Hawaiian population through the nineteenth century and even into the twentieth century is overwhelming."

Another important reason for recognizing resistance among Native Hawaiians in the face of American colonialism is that it allows us to view the Hawaiian language revitalization movement in the 1980s not as a sudden occurrence but rather as an extension of earlier appeals from Hawaiian speakers to preserve their language. Often, as I stated in Chapter 1, the revitalization movement is viewed as an outgrowth of a period known in the 1960s and 1970s as the Hawaiian Renaissance, which saw a resurgence in interest in Hawaiian cultural activities such as music, dance, lei making, and voyaging. This was also the time when the Hawaiian sovereignty movement gained momentum with activism struggling on behalf of access to land and water. Yet, the Hawaiian Renaissance as well as the revitalization movement would not have been possible without the resilience of the Native Hawaiians who had struggled, at the risk punishment, to speak their native tongue and practice their cultural traditions. This is not to underestimate the amount of adversity encountered by those who initiated the Hawaiian language revitalization movement—Chapter 3 will describe how the movement still has to grapple with the monolingual mindset that prevents even further gains in society. On the contrary, the focus in this section on resistance throughout history on the part of the Native population is meant to underscore a pattern of resiliency that not only contrasts with Western narratives of Hawaiian history but also continues to the present day.

2.5 Resistance by Non-Hawaiians

Resistance to the attempts by the American elite to impose their will on Hawai'i was not only demonstrated by the Native Hawaiians. The immigrant laborers, especially those from Asia, often endeavored to resist the low wages and poor conditions of the sugar planation owners.

As Takaki (1983) notes, the plantations were a "contested terrain,"[9] where "planters tried to extract from laborers as much work as possible and where laborers struggled to acquire greater control over their work and a greater share of plantation earnings. It was also a place where bosses and workers sometimes engaged in violent confrontations" (1983: 127). Although there are reports of strikes and confrontations since the mid-1850s,[10] the occurrence of strikes increased after the Organic Act of 1900 established Hawai'i as an officially territory of the United States, which officially ended the labor contract system and which gave the laborers more freedom to protest. This was followed by strikes and demonstrations by Japanese workers on Maui, Kaua'i, and also O'ahu. As Takaki (1983) also notes, some of the strikes included interethnic cooperation involving Japanese, Chinese, and Portuguese laborers.

Even though the strikes of 1900 yielded some gains for the laborers (Takaki, 1983), they led to more intense strikes, most notably the "Great Strike" of 1909, another strike in 1920, and the Filipino Strike and Hanapēpē Massacre of 1924. The "Great Strike" of 1909 involved seven thousand laborers across several plantations (Takaki, 1983). As Takaki (1983) observes, unlike earlier strikes that were sometimes spontaneous occurrences, this strike was organized in advance, lasted for a comparatively long time of 4 months, resulted in the imprisonment of several Japanese leaders, and was supported by Japanese language newspapers that "repeatedly called attention to the need for wage increases for Japanese plantation workers" (1983: 153). Although the "Great Strike" of 1909 ended with many of the objectives of the laborers being met and with the return of its leaders from prison, the 1920 strike represented another attempt to achieve better working conditions. Japanese laborers were also involved, but this strike brought Japanese and Filipino workers together, thus providing a new direction for the labor movement that

[9]Takaki (1983) credits the term "contested terrain" to Edwards (1979).

[10]The earliest strike on record occurred in 1841 at the Kōloa plantation and was initiated by Hawaiian laborers. It started only 6 years after the founding of the first sugar plantation (see Takaki, 1983 and "History of Labor in Hawai'i" at https://www.hawaii.edu/uhwo/clear/home/HawaiiLaborHistory.html). Takaki (1983) also notes the year 1866 when a group of Chinese laborers on the same Kōloa farm refused to obey orders and even rushed their luna (overseer) with knives.

involved interethnic unity (Takaki, 1983). Lasting about 6 months, the strike, like the 1909 strike, was a highly organized strike based on a grassroots movement requiring planning across plantations as well as across the islands. The 1920 strike preceded an even larger and more violent strike in 1924 in which around 13,000 Filipino laborers went on strike again seeking better wages and conditions ("Labor strikes").[11] The strike turned violent and deadly when some of the Filipino strikers tried to prevent scabs in Hanapēpē on Kauaʻi from doing the plantation work. The dispatch of police to help the scabs resulted in twenty deaths, sixteen Filipino laborers and 4 police officers. Additionally, over one hundred Filipinos were arrested with sixty of them given four-year jail sentences ("History of Labor in Hawaiʻi").

The immigrant laborers also pushed back against the attempts by American-led government to close the language schools that allowed them to transmit their ancestral languages to children. As noted earlier in this chapter, the language schools created by speakers of Japanese, Chinese, Korean, and German came under increasing scrutiny with the rise of Americanism in the early 1900s and were eventually shut down completely with the onset of World War II. Yet, it is important to note that the Japanese immigrants, in particular, remained steadfast in their desire to educate children in the Japanese even with mounting criticism from the American leaders. After the government attempted to establish regulations in 1922 that would close kindergartens and the first two grades of Japanese language schools, the Japanese community resisted by filing suit in the Territorial Circuit Court that questioned the constitutionality of such regulations. This suit moved its way up the court system until it reached the Supreme Court in 1927, where judgment was made in favor of the foreign language schools. The Supreme Court, in short, found the attempts by the Hawaiian territorial government to curtail the schools unconstitutional and infringing on the rights of the parents and children. This decision, deriving from the Japanese community's willingness to resist the territorial government, allowed the Japanese languages to flourish, with enrollment in Japanese language schools

[11]Retrieved from https://sites.google.com/a/hawaii.edu/ndnp-hawaii/Home/subject-and-topic-guides/labor-strikes.

increasing from 26, 768 in 1926 to 33, 607 in 1928 (Niyekawa-Howard, 1974) and then to 41,192 in 1934 (Asato, 2006).

Moreover, Kam (2006) and Him (2000) note that following the conclusion of World War II, it was the Chinese community in Hawai‘i that pushed to remove the ban on foreign language schools. Through a process that included the support of Honolulu's *Chung Wah Chung Kung Hui* (Chinese Labor Association), litigation initiated by a Chinese language school, two parents, and three children (Kam, 2006), and also a petition that garnered between 30,000 and 50,000 signatures of supporters of various ethnicities, proponents of the schools helped prompt the territorial legislature to pass a law in 1949 that removed some of the crippling restrictions on the foreign language schools. Both Chinese and Japanese language schools reopened and enrollment gradually increased, although it never reached the peak amounts prior to World War II. Crediting this success to the persistence of the Chinese community, Kam (2006: 144) concludes that "Chinese Americans triumphed over forces determined to eliminate traces of their heritage, and beyond that the heritage of all Americans." The fact that the number of heritage language schools in present-day Hawai‘i is significantly smaller than it was in the 1900s suggests a gradual move toward monolingualism, but the resistance demonstrated by the immigrant laborers and their families in protecting rights to learn their ancestral languages continues today and potentially provides a blueprint of sorts for establishing additional language schools in the future.

2.6 Pidgin as Resistance

Mention of the immigrants' struggle against the linguistic hegemony of the American territorial government in Hawai‘i leads the discussion back to Pidgin. As mentioned earlier, the American elite, largely due to a fear that Pidgin was developing quickly into the common language of society, established a set of English standard schools beginning in 1924. In addition to requiring students to pass an oral test as a part of disallowing admission to students showing signs of Pidgin in their speech, this emphasis on so-called standard English also led to scrutiny of the speech of the teachers. As Tamura (1993: 49) further notes, the educator Benjamin Wist, who was president of the Territorial Normal and Training School, "began a systematic effort in the mid 1920s to change the speaking habits of aspiring teachers, from Hawaii Creole to standard English." According to Tamura (1993: 49):

> He required them to give five-minute extemporaneous speeches before a seven-member board. Those who passed had no further language examinations, but those who failed had to work on their oral English and repeat the test. In 1925, twenty-four students failed to graduate from the Normal School because of their inability to express themselves orally in standard English, and courses in 'corrective speech, public speaking, dramatics and parliamentary procedure' were added to the curriculum.

With this system in place, there were, by 1937, ten schools that were populated mostly by White Americans that created linguistic and racial division by keeping Pidgin speakers out (Tamura, 1994).[12]

According to Hughes (1993), the Portuguese community was one of the first to resist the English standard schools as they worried that if their children failed the oral test, they would be left to attend the non-English standard schools with predominantly children of Asian ancestry. Although Portuguese and non-Caucasian students were permitted entrance to the schools if they were able to pass the English tests, Tamura (1993) notes in fact that over years an increasing number of Japanese and other Asian students managed to enroll, and the schools also met with immediate resistance from leaders of the local Chinese and Japanese communities, with Dai Yen Chang, president of the Hawaiian Chinese Civic Association, noting that the schools "encouraged 'race prejudice' and were 'a step backward' in the process of acculturation" (quoted in Tamura, 1993: 55). Japanese newspapers such as *Nippu Jiji* and *Hawaii Hochi* criticized the standard schools as "examples of a 'Nordic caste' that was 'utterly at variance with the ideals for which America stands'" (Tamura, 1993: 55). Hughes (1993: 77) also reports that "the opposition

[12]According to Hughes (1993: 69–70), a form of "select school" for English-speaking children only had been in existence in Central Grammar School from before 1920.

grew as a new generation of Asian-ancestry parents came into contact with the public schools in 1940s." Hughes (1993) notes that protests were launched by parents of children attending a school in Honolulu, Maemae Elementary School, that, when it became an English standard school, saw 75% of the students fail the English test to gain entrance. When faced with transfer of the children to a distant school, the parents held demonstrations in front of ʻIolani Palace, the place where the territorial legislature met.

In addition to this general opposition to the segregation represented by the standard schools, there is evidence that the schools fostered a desire within at least some students to view Pidgin as a sign of resistance. In an article in the Hawaiʻi Tribune Herald posted online on September 9, 2019, Rochelle delaCruz notes that as she has grown older many of her classmates from Hilo would ask her "how come your pidgin is so much better than ours?" In response, she reports her answer as "Because I went to English standard school." She explains later that "When you attend a haole school but live in a local neighborhood, you betta not forget how foʻ say dat, birfday, and shoeses, or else nobody goin play wit you. But I must have known this early on, because outside of school (and my mother's earshot), I spoke pidgin with a vengeance." In other words, for the fear of being labeled "haolefied" due to her attendance of a standard English school, delaCruz felt that she had to "prove" that she still belonged in her neighborhood through a pronounced usage of Pidgin.[13]

This fits with what others have suggested about Pidgin as a form of resistance to American colonialism. Roberts (2004: 342) quotes from the life history of girl born in Hawaiʻi who attended a English standard school, "When I was in Central Grammar I know we were taught to speak correct English both in and outside of school but when I returned to Maui, my old friends made fun of my English which embarrassed me. They said I was 'stuck up' and 'you think you Haole' so I had to use the pigeon English and I am having the hardest time breaking that habit (Life History, LJ-8 [local-born girl, born ca. 1912]." Roberts likewise offers "There were other social meanings linked to ASE and HCE.

[13]Retrieved from https://www.hawaiitribune-herald.com/2019/09/09/opinion/i-spoke-pidgin-with-a-vengeance/.

Throughout the 1930s and possibly as early as the 1920s, local-born male speakers of ASE were often teased as 'sissies.' This suggests that HCE had become a resource for performing masculine identity" (Roberts, 2004: 343). And finally Roberts (2004: 343) offers a report from one of the newspapers saying that "Kamehameha [School] boys speak pidgin English on the campus and in their dormitories. To speak correct English is 'sissy,' they say" (Honolulu Advertiser, 9 May 1943, p. 24). This is to say, then, that Pidgin, as a language tied directly to a local identify, served as a resource for resisting the expectation of the English standard schools and possibly other schools as well that the students learn and use standard English, which was in contrast to a local identity. In summary, the schools helped to contribute to the covert prestige of Pidgin in society that has helped sustain Pidgin as a mainstay in the community.

Partly because of opposition, the government began dismantling the English standard school system shortly after World War II, even though some schools persisted until the early 1960s. As Hughes (1993: 84) notes, toward the abolishment of the schools "strong community pressure was critical" which made it politically "impossible for the schools to continue." At the same time, Hughes (1993) also discusses another reason for the closing of the schools, which was the belief that speaking "proper" English should be an emphasis of all of the schools, not just those with the label of English standard schools. Indeed, Young (2002: 418) reports from an interview with a woman named Lei that did not attend an English standard school that "even at a non-English Standard school, Lei cannot escape the standard English ideology, as she encounters a teacher in her school, Mrs. Vicente, who is strict in her belief in proper usage." Here, then, in this discussion of the English standard schools, we have the two processes of American colonialism and resistance at work. As part of taking and maintaining power, the American presence in Hawai'i pushed English as the most important language in Hawai'i, which in turn helped facilitate Pidgin as the primary language to be deployed to mark resistance to the standard language ideology.

The connection of Pidgin to resistance, though, becomes more complex once we go beyond the standard schools. Although Pidgin has become known as a predominantly "private language" restricted to the home and on the playground, one public domain in which Pidgin is particularly prevalent is comedy (Ellis, 2020; Furukawa, 2007, 2018; Hisatake, 2018; Labrador, 2004; Mindness, 2006; Wong, 1999). Some writers, though, have been critical of the usage of Pidgin in comedy because of a fear that "even in this domain, the pidgin speaker is often portrayed as an ignorant buffoon" (Wong, 1999: 207). Similarly, writing about a well-known skit called "Room Service" with comedian Rap Reiplinger, in which a Pidgin-speaking worker in the service industry attempts to take the room service order of an English-speaking tourist, Furukawa (2018) notes a tendency to see the performance as casting a negative light on Pidgin:

> People say that skits like Reiplinger's *Room Service* cast Pidgin speakers in a bad light, making them appear to be as incompetent or giving, as one person online called it "a hilarious example of bad service" (Preece, 2011) ... One particularly negative image is seen through the skit's construction of Pidgin as an obstacle to career success... Since tourism is the most powerful industry in the state (Liu & Var, 1986: 196), it mirrors the situation that many local-Pidgin speakers fear finding themselves in, being subservient to white English speakers while at work and being unable to succeed due to Pidgin.

Yet, despite the possible negative interpretations, Furukawa's micro-analysis of the skit itself reveals a "network of pro-Pidgin meanings" that resonate with local audiences because of the contrasts created between "impatient" and "emotionless" English speakers and Pidgin speakers portrayed as "patient and being honest and emotional" (Furukawa, 2018: 49). Furukawa's analysis suggests that the meanings conveyed in the skits can be empowering to Pidgin speakers as they emphasize the contrast between English and Pidgin and thus reinforce the covert prestige of Pidgin within Hawaiian society.

Hisatake (2018) examines the same skit "Room Service" and views an even more direct connection of Pidgin to resistance. Speaking specifically about comedian Rap Reiplinger, she writes that "he restages Hawaiʻi's encounter with the tourist, exaggerating white desires and behavior—

camping it up, so to speak—in order to convey Native Hawaiian Hawai'i's local cultures as resistant to the settler colonial possession of the islands" (Hisatake, 2018: 29). In making this connection to resistance, Hisatake (2018: 29) notes that the usage of "Pidgin unseats the dominance of settler culture through theatrical exaggeration, failed seriousness, and the oppositional politics and humor of camp. This comedy illustrates Pidgin's linguistic and political closeness to Hawaiian language —*'ōlelo Hawai'i*—and demonstrates Pidgin's ties to Native Hawaiian expression that is resistant to tourism and settler colonialism."

Due the direct connection it makes between the Indigenous Hawaiian language and Pidgin, this last sentence from Hisatake may seem to be a bit of a stretch, especially in light of the suggestion made earlier that Pidgin served as a replacement for Hawaiian as part of the process of colonialism. Yet, as Nordstrom (2010, 2015) notes, consideration of the linguistic situation at the time, with Hawaiian medium schools effectively banned and with punishments doled out to students for speaking their native language, it is possible to see Pidgin as both a result of colonialism and as a source of resistance. This is perhaps what Nordstrom (2015: 318) means when she, making reference to the work of Cushman (2011) on Cherokee, writes that "Pidgin can be considered both a minority language—the language identified with the settler local culture—*and* an Indigenous linguistic resource adapted as an act of what Ellen Cushman calls 'cultural perseverance.'" While Kimura notes, as stated earlier, "Pidgin cuts Hawaiians off from their ancestral roots and aesthetic culture" (Kimura, 1983: 200), he also recognizes that Pidgin has served as "the language that has been used in an attempt to fill the eradication of Hawaiian," and not only has it functioned "well the primary role of any language in the base culture: the identification of a people as a unique and cohesive entity, with the continuity of basic family values" (Kimura, 1983: 198) but its development has also "assured the cultural survival of Hawaiians."

By assuring cultural survival, the use of Pidgin by Native Hawaiians was therefore an act of resistance to a colonial agenda that intended to strip the native population of their language and culture. Nordstrom (2015: 321) writes, "speaking Pidgin for a Hawaiian embodies a noteworthy linguistic resourcefulness in efforts of both survival and resistance in the face of the violence, including an agenda of linguicide, that resulted in loss of nationhood." Taking this a step further, Nordstrom (2015: 322) connects Pidgin to Hawaiian indigeneity when she asserts that "recasting speaking Pidgin as an act of Hawaiian cultural perseverance frames the language as an assertion of Indigenous identity that is part of a cultural continuum predating Western contact and continuing through the present."

To be sure, the Native Hawaiians were not the only group to use Pidgin as resistance, and it is here where the usage of Pidgin merges the Native Hawaiians together with the immigrant laborers and their children, who as noted earlier have been referred to as Asian settlers (Fujikane, 2008). Kimura (1983: 199), in fact, notes that the creolization of Pidgin "involved all Hawaiian children by 1920, as well as the children of the immigrant plantation workers" and served as "the perfect tool for local children to resist the campaign to force them to speak English." It was through Pidgin, then, that the children of Native Hawaiians found solidarity with the children of the immigrants, and it was through Pidgin that the identity of "local" emerged as an unstructured mixture of ethnicities and cultures. This merging of Native Hawaiians and the immigrant families seemingly points to an interesting paradox; how can Pidgin simultaneously function as a symbol of the American colonialism that resulted in a loss of language and identity and also as a source of indigeneity that represents resistance and the persistence of nativeness?

Yet, rather than seeing this a strange and incomprehensible paradox, it makes more sense to view Pidgin within the context of the multiple layers of American colonialism. These multiple layers explain how Pidgin has developed over a relatively short period as a language with various meanings and has taken on different roles due to the ebbs and flows of American colonialism. Due to the timing of the ban on Hawaiian in education and the creolization process, it is a language that simultaneously helped detach the Native Hawaiians from their native culture and also served as a source of resistance to the pressures of Americanism that allowed for the perpetuation of indigenous ways of existing in Hawai‘i. This is why Kimura (1983: 198–200) can both be critical of Pidgin's role in relation to Hawaiian and note that "Pidgin was originally a form of Hawaiian" and that it "assured the cultural survival of Hawaiians" and also "assured a Hawaiian identity." This is also why writers such as Nordstrom can see a link between Pidgin and indigeneity and why Ellis (2020), in a discussion of the poet Joe Balaz's poetry written in Pidgin (Balaz, 2019), notes first that "in Balaz's hands, Pidgin is more than a pan-ethnic non-elite 'local' language" and next that "Balaz presents Pidgin as an indigenous language, an epistemic, aesthetic, and activist decolonizing resource" (Ellis, 2020: 2–3).

The layers of the colonization process can also aid in seeing that Pidgin has a role in the revitalization of the Hawaiian language. Using the Hawaiian term *'Ōlelo Pa'i'ai*, which was used to refer to the developing pidgin before creolization, Wilson (2017) credits *'Ōlelo Pa'i'ai* for assisting in the movement to revitalize the Hawaiian language. As he writes, "arguably most significant in the widespread support of Hawaiian language revitalization is the historical impact of multiracial use in the 1800s of a unique form of Hawaiian called *'Ōlelo Pa'i'ai* ("Dry Pounded Taro Language"), this was a pidginized form of Hawaiian easily learned and use by people of diverse backgrounds" (Wilson, 2017: 232). Even though it is commonly recognized that the lexifier of Pidgin is now English (Sakoda & Siegel, 2003), Pidgin retains similarities to *'Ōlelo Pa'i'ai* that seem to be highlighted when Pidgin-speaking students learn Hawaiian. As Wilson (2017: 232) continues, "modern *'Ōlelo Pa'i'ai*, now called Hawai'i Creole English by linguists and Pidgin by the general population, has also played an important role in revitalizing Hawaiian. Hawaiian words used in Pidgin and similarities in structure between Hawaiian and Pidgin have provided Pidgin speakers with an advantage in rapid learning of Hawaiian. In turn, the revitalization of Hawaiian has strengthened the Hawaiian component of Pidgin."

However, despite the assistance provided by Pidgin in learning Hawaiian, it goes without saying that Pidgin is not Hawaiian and thus does not fully represent the indigenous culture and knowledge system that existed prior to the arrival of Westerners to Hawaiians. For many Native Hawaiian students of the Hawaiian language, it is impossible to re-engage with the cultural practices and lifestyles of their ancestors without going beyond Pidgin to the "true" Indigenous language of the land, Hawaiian. In that sense, Pidgin still carries with it, even though it allows for a connection to Hawaiian and indigeneity, the remnants of an American colonialism that nearly eradicated the Hawaiian language and culture.

2.7 Conclusion

By placing a focus on the two processes of colonialism and resistance, this chapter has offered an explanation for a current Hawaiian society that consists of a noticeable multilingual character but is also marked by a monolingual mindset with English as the focal point. This is not to say that colonialism and resistance represent the only processes at work or even the best explanation for language ecologies in Hawai'i. Still, a nuanced approach that recognizes multiple layers of colonialism makes it possible, on the one hand, to understand the sustained efforts on the part of the American colonizers to suppress multilingualism, efforts which led to the demise of Hawaiian, the demonization of Pidgin, and also the undermining of attempts to transmit immigrant languages to next generations. Not all languages were suppressed in the same way nor at the same period of history; the Americanization movement affected first and foremost the Native Hawaiians, but it also deeply affected the immigrant laborers soon after they were brought to Hawai'i. The complexity of the colonialism project lies in the way that many immigrant laborers were compelled, in order to improve their life situations in their new homes, to utilize the same power structures that originally oppressed them, which has been labeled as Asian settler colonialism and which has also had negative effects on the Native Hawaiians and their pursuit of cultural and linguistic survival. One of the power structures employed by both Asian and White settlers has been the monolingual mindset to be critical of the usage of languages other than English, leading to a situation in which the offspring of Asian and other immigrants have decided not to speak their ancestral languages and have found fault with the usage of Pidgin by themselves and others.

On the other hand, though, this chapter has emphasized that American colonialism has not, by any means, prevailed in making English the only prominent language in Hawai'i. By giving overdue recognition to resistance as a force that has throughout recent history consistently been there to oppose colonialism, it is possible to see how groups in Hawai'i, beginning with the Native Hawaiians, have used resistance to preserve spaces for their languages within the linguistic landscape of Hawai'i. As noted, Pidgin's place within and between the two larger processes is complex, but it is also undeniable that Pidgin has come to represent a language of resistance for Native Hawaiians and immigrants alike. Focusing specifically on Hawaiian, Pidgin, immigrant languages, and language mixing, the remainder of this book provides further examples of the relationship between language and resistance in Hawai'i.

References

Asato, N. (2006). *Teaching Mikadoism: The attack on Japanese language schools in Hawaii, California, and Washington*. University of Hawai'i Press.

Asensio, R. (2010). Language policy in the Kingdom of Hawai'i: A worldly English approach. *Second Language Studies, 28*(2), 1–48.

Aspinwall, D. B. (1960). Languages in Hawaii. *PMLA, 75*, 4, 2, 7–13.

Balaz, J. (2019). *Pidgin eye*. Ala Press.

Bastos, C. (2018). Portuguese in the cane: The racialization of labour in Hawaiian plantations. In S. Aboim, P. Granjo, & A. Ramos (Eds.), *Changing societies: Legacies and challenges* (pp. 65–96). Imprensa de Ciências Sociais.

Beamer, K. (2014). *No Mākou Ka Mana: Liberating the nation*. Kamehameha Schools Press.

Beechart, E. (1985). *Working in Hawai'i: A labor history*. University of Hawai'i Press.

Benham, M. K. P. (1998). The voice "less" Hawaiian: An analysis of educational policymaking, 1820–1960. *The Hawaiian Journal of History, 32*, 121–140.

Benton, R. (1981). *The flight of the Amokura: Oceanic languages and formal education in the South Pacific*. New Zealand Council for Educational Research.

Bickerton, D. (1998). Language and language contact. In M. Haas (Ed.), *Multicultural Hawai'i: The fabric of a multiethnic society* (pp. 53–64). Garland Publishing.

Bickerton, D., & Wilson, W. H. (1987). Pidgin Hawaiian. In G. Gilbert (Ed.), *Pidgin and Creole languages: Essays in memory of John E. Reinecke* (pp. 61–76). University of Hawai'i Press.

Chapin, H. G. (1984). Newspapers of Hawai'i 1834 to 1903: From "He Liona" to the Pacific cable. *The Hawaiian Journal of History, 18*, 47–86.

Charlot, J. (2005). *Classical Hawaiian education: Generations of culture.* The Pacific Institute.

Cushman, E. (2011). "We're taking the genius of Sequoyah into this century": The Cherokee syllabary, peoplehood, and perseverance. *Wicazo Sa Review, 26*(1), 67–83.

Da Pidgin Coup. (2008). Pidgin and education: A position paper. *Educational Perspectives, 41*(1–2), 30–39.

Eades, D., Jacobs, S., Hargrove, E., & Menacker, T. (2006). Pidgin, local identity, and schooling in Hawaii. In S. J. Nero (Ed.), *Dialects, Englishes, Creoles and education* (pp. 139–163). Lawrence Erlbaum Associates.

Edwards, R. (1979). *Contested terrain: The transformation of the workplace in the twentieth century.* Basic Books.

Ellis, J. (2020). Da decolonizing real: Liberating humour in Joe Balaz's Pidgin eye. *The Journal of Commonwealth Literature, 1*, 1–14.

Fuchs, L. (1961). *Hawaii Pono.* Harcourt, Brace, and World.

Fujikane, C. (2008). Introduction: Asian settler colonialism in the U.S. colony of Hawai'i. In C. Fujikane & J. Okamura (Eds.), *Asian settler colonialism: From local governance to the habits of everyday life in Hawai'i* (pp. 1–42). University of Hawai'i Press.

Furukawa, G. (2018). Stylization and language ideologies in Pidgin comedic skits. *Discourse, Context and Media, 23*, 41–52.

Furukawa, T. (2007). No flips in the pool: Discursive practice in Hawai'i Creole. *Pragmatics, 17*(3), 371–386.

Gonschor, L. (2020). *A power in the world: The Hawaiian Kingdom in Oceania.* University of Hawai'i Press.

Goodhue, K. P. (1998). We are who we were: From resistance to affirmation. *'Ōiwi: A native Hawaiian Journal, 1*, 36–39.

Higashionna, R., Ikehara, G., & Matsukawa, L. (2011). The Okinawans. In J. McDermott & N. N. Andrade (Eds.), *People and cultures of Hawai'i: The evolution of culture and ethnicity* (pp. 131–151). Honolulu: University of Hawai'i Press.

Higgins, C. (2010). Raising critical language awareness in Hawai'i at Da Pidgin coup. In B. Migge, I. Leglise, & A. Bartens (Eds.), *Creoles in education: An appraisal of current programs and projects* (pp. 31–54). John Benjamins.

Him, M. L. (2000). Transmitting the Chinese heritage: Chinese schools in the United States mainland and Hawaii. In T. A. See (Ed.), *Intercultural relations, cultural transformation, and identity: The ethnic Chinese* (pp. 124–158). Manila: Kaisa Para Sa Kaunlaran, Inc.

Him, M. L. (2010). The Chinese community press in Hawai'i, Chinese America: History & perspectives. *The Journal of the Chinese Historical Society of America,* 95–103.

Hisatake, K. (2018). Hawaiian hospitality and hostility: Camp in Rap Reiplinger's Pidgin comedy. *Amerasia Journal, 44*(3), 27–48.

Hughes, J. (1993). The demise of the English standard school system in Hawai'i. *The Hawaiian Journal of History, 27,* 65–89.

Ing, T. L. (2019). *Reclaiming Kalākaua: Nineteenth-century perspectives on a Hawaiian sovereign*. University of Hawai'i Press.

Kachru, B. B. (1977). Linguistic schizophrenia and language census: A note on the Indian situation. *Linguistics, 15*(186), 17–32.

Kam, R. T. (2006). Language and loyalty: Americanism and the regulation of foreign Language. *The Hawaiian Journal of History, 40,* 131–147.

Kamanā, K., & Wilson, W. H. (2012). *Nā Kai 'Ewalu: Beginning Hawaiian lessons*. Hale Kuamo'o.

Kame'eleihiwa, L. (1992). *Native land and foreign desires: Pehea lā e Pono ai.* Bishop Museum Press.

Kana'iaupuni, S. M., Malone, N., & Ishibashi, K. (2005). *Ka Huaka'i: 2005 Native Hawaiian educational assessment.* Kamehameha Schools Pauahi Publications.

Kauhi, E. K. (2000). *He Mo'olelo No Kapa'ahu: The story of Kapa'ahu.* Pili Productions.

Kawakami, A. J. (2004). Issues central to the inclusion of Hawaiian culture in k-12 education. *Hūlili: Multidisciplinary Research on Hawaiian Well-Being, 1* (1), 111–130.

Kimura, L. (1983). The Hawaiian language. In *Native Hawaiians study commission: Report on the culture, needs, and concerns of native Hawaiians* (pp. 173–224). Department of Interior.

Labrador, R. (2004). "We can laugh at ourselves": Hawai'i ethnic humor, local identity and the myth of multiculturalism. *Pragmatics, 14*(2–3), 291–316.

Lili'uokalani. (1990). *Hawai'i's Story: By Hawai'i's Queen*. Mutual Publishing.

Liu, J. C., & Var, T. (1986). Resident attitudes toward tourism impacts in Hawaii. *Annals of Tourism Research, 13*, 193–214.
Lockwood, H., & Saft, S. (2016). Shifting language ideologies and the perceptions of Hawai'i Creole among educators at the university level in Hawai'i. *Linguistics and Education, 33*, 1–13.
Lucas, P. N. (2000). E Ola Mau Kākou i ka 'Ōlelo Makuahine: Hawaiian language policy and the courts. *The Hawaiian Journal of History, 34,* 1–28.
Matsu, C., Takeshita, J., Izutsu, S., & Hishinuma, E. (2011). The Japanese. In J. McDermott & N. N. Andrade (Eds.), *People and cultures of Hawai'i: The evolution of culture and ethnicity* (pp. 107–130). University of Hawai'i Press.
McGregor-Alegado, D. (1979). *Hawaiian resistance, 1887–1889* (Unpublished Thesis for Master of Arts in Pacific Island Studies). University of Hawai'i.
Mindness, H. (2006). Humor in Hawai'i: Past and present. *The Hawaiian Journal of History, 40*, 177–199.
Nakanaela, T. (1993). *The biography of Hon. Robert William Wilcox.* Retrieved from http://ulukau.org/chd/Texts/wilcox-intro.pdf
Niyekawa-Howard, A. (1974). History of the Japanese language school. *Educational Perspectives, 13*, 6–14.
Nordstrom, G. (2010). Rhetoric and resistance in Hawai'i: How silenced voices speak out in a colonized context. In D. Baca & V. Villanueva (Eds.), *Rhetorics of the Americas: 114 BCE to 2012 CE* (pp. 117–141). Palgrave Macmillan.
Nordstrom, G. (2015). Pidgin as rhetorical sovereignty: Articulating indigenous and minority rhetorical practices with the language politics of place. *College English, 77*(4), 317–337.
Okamura, J. (2014). *From race to ethnicity: Interpreting Japanese American experiences in Hawai'i.* University of Hawai'i Press.
Okihiro, G. (1991). *Cane Fires: The anti-Japanese movement in Hawaii, 1865–1945.* University of Temple Press.
Only English in Public Schools. (1906). *The Hawaiian Star*, Page 3, February 9th.
Osorio, J. (2006). On being Hawaiian. *Hūlili: Multidisciplinary Research on Hawaiian Well-Being, 3,* 19–26.
Ortega, N. (2017). *Settler colonialism still defines power in Hawaii.* Honolulu Civil Beat. Retrieved from https://www.civilbeat.org/2017/11/settler-colonialism-still-defines-power-in-hawaii/

Patterson, W. (2000). *The Ilse: First-generation Korean immigrants in Hawai'i*. Honolulu: University of Hawai'i Press.

Preece, D. (2011). *Room service in paradise—Rap Reiplinger*. Retrieved from YouTube. https://www.youtube.com/watch?v=-nrE8zGG_P4.

Reinecke, J. (1969). *Language and dialect in Hawai'i: A sociolinguistic history to 1935*. University of Hawai'i Press.

Reinecke, J. (1987). Appendix (Pidgin Hawaiian). In G. G. Gilbert (Ed.), *Pidgin and Creole languages: Essays in memory of John E. Reinecke* (p. 74). University of Hawaii Press.

Roberts, S. (2004). The role of style and identity in the development of Hawaiian Creole. In G. Escure & A. Schwegler (Eds.), *Creoles, contact, and language change: Linguistic and social implications* (pp. 331–350). Benjamins.

Roche, G. (2019). Articulating language oppression: colonialism, coloniality and the erasure of Tibet's minority languages. *Patterns of Prejudice, 53*(5), 487–514.

Romaine, S. (1999). Changing attitudes to Hawai'i Creole English: Fo' find one good job, you gotta know how fo' talk like one haole. In J. Rickford & S. Romaine (Eds.), *Creole genesis, attitudes and discourse* (pp. 287–301). Benjamins.

Saft, S. (2019). *Exploring multilingual Hawai'i: Language use and language ideologies in a diverse society*. Lexington Books.

Sakoda, K., & Siegel, J. (2003). *Pidgin grammar: An introduction to the Creole language of Hawai'i*. Bess Press.

Saranillio, D. I. (2013). Why Asian settler colonialism matters: A thought piece of critiques, debates, and indigenous difference. *Settler Colonial Studies, 3*(3–4), 280–294.

Saranillio, D. I. (2018). *Unsustainable empire: Alternative histories of Hawai'i statehood*. Duke University Press.

Schutz, A. J. (1994). *The voices of Eden: A history of Hawaiian language studies*. University of Hawai'i Press.

Schutz, A. J. (2020). *Hawaiian language: Past, present, future*. University of Hawai'i Press.

Siegel, J. (2008). Pidgin in the classroom. *Educational Perspectives, 41*(1–2), 55–65.

Silva, N. (1998). Kanaka Maoli resistance to annexation. *'Ōiwi: A Native Hawaiian Journal, 1*(1), 40–75.

Silva, N. (2004). *Aloha betrayed: Native Hawaiian resistance to American colonialism*. Duke University Press.

Stannard, D. (1989). *Before the horror: The population of Hawaii on the eve of western contact.* University of Hawai'i Press.
Takaki, R. (1983). *Pau Hana: Plantation life and labor in Hawai'i, 1835–1920.* University of Hawai'i Press.
Tamura, E. (1993). The English-only effort, the anti-Japanese campaign, and language acquisition in the education of Japanese Americans in Hawai'i, 1915–1940. *History of Education Quarterly, 33*(1), 37–58.
Tamura, E. (1994). *Americanization, acculturation, and ethnic identity: The Nisei generation in Hawai'i.* University of Illinois Press.
Tamura, E. (1996). Power, status, and Hawai'i Creole English: An example of linguistic intolerance in American history. *Pacific Historical Review, 65*(3), 431–454.
Thomas, S. L., Kana'iaupuni, S. M., Balutski, B. J. N., & Freitas, A. K. (2012). Access and success for students from indigenous populations. In J. C. Smart & M. B. Paulsen (Eds.), *Higher education of theory and research* (pp. 335–367). Springer.
Trask, H. K. (1999). *From a native daughter: Colonialism and sovereignty in Hawai'i.* Latitude 20 Books.
Trask, H. K. (2000). Settlers of color and "immigrant" hegemony. *Amerasia Journal, 26*(2), 1–24.
U.S. Department of the Interior. (1920). *A Survey of Education in Hawaii. Bulletin, 1920, No. 16.* Available at https://files.eric.ed.gov/fulltext/ED543381.pdf
Walch, D. B. (1967). The historical development of the Hawaiian alphabet. *The Journal of the Polynesian Society, 76*(3), 353–366.
Wagner-Seavey, S. (1980). The effect of world war I on the German community in Hawaii. *Hawaiian Journal of History, 14,* 109–140.
Williams, R., Jr. (2009). "Aole Hoohui ia Hawaii": U.S. collegiate teams debate annexation of Hawai'i and independence prevails, 1893–1897. *The Hawaiian Journal of History, 43,* 153–179.
Williams Jr., R. (2011). 'Ike Mōakaaka, seeing a path forward: Historiography in Hawai'i. *Hūlili: Multidisciplinary Research on Hawaiian Well-being* (7), 67–90.
Wilson, W. H. (2017). Hawaiian language revitalization. In H. Sato & J. Bradshaw (Eds.), *Languages of the Pacific Islands: Introductory readings* (pp. 220–237). CreateSpace Independent Publishing Platform.

Wilson, W., & Kamanā, K. (2006). For the interest of the Hawaiians themselves: Reclaiming the benefits of Hawaiian-medium education. *Hūlili: Multidisciplinary Research on Hawaiian Well-Being, 3,* 153–182.
Wist, B. (1940). *A century of public education in Hawai'i, 1840–1940.* Hawaii Educational Review.
Wong, L. (1999). Language varieties and language policy: The appreciation of Pidgin. In T. Huebner & K. Davis (Eds.), *Sociopolitical perspectives on language policy and planning in the USA* (pp. 221–237). Benjamins.
Woodside, O. L. L., Reyes, E. K. P., & Kim Jr., M. K. (2011). Nā Hulu Kūpuna: Living and sharing Hawaiian wisdom. *Hūlili: Multidisciplinary Research on Hawaiian Well-Being, 7,* 9–23.
Young, M. (2002). Standard English and student bodies: Institutionalizing race and literacy in Hawai'i. *College English, 64*(4), 405–431.

3

Barriers to and Promises of a Strong Hawaiian Language

Hawaiian is the indigenous language of the Hawaiian Islands, and accordingly, it is the basic position of this book that Hawaiian, from the perspective of social justice, needs to be granted preferential status within society. The Hawaiian language is deeply connected to the Hawaiian culture and an essential part of a Hawaiian identity, and therefore preferential rights that enable Hawaiian to be learned and spoken freely in society should directly influence the well-being of the Native population, which should also have positive affects on society on the overall. This is especially critical because, as noted in the first two chapters, the Native Hawaiians have been detached from their language, land, and cultural practices and have therefore suffered greatly in terms of various measures of health and happiness.

The argument could be made that Hawaiian has already been granted privileges, which is true to a certain extent. Hawaiian was declared together with English as one of the official languages of the state in 1978, a declaration which then helped enable Hawaiian language educators to reestablish schooling through the medium of Hawaiian. However, despite noticeable and even remarkable advances in Hawaiian language revitalization, the Hawaiian language still struggles for acceptance in

S. Saft, *Language and Social Justice in Context*,
https://doi.org/10.1007/978-3-030-91251-2_3

many domains of society. This chapter proceeds by first describing some of the efforts by Hawaiian language educators to reestablish Hawaiian medium education, it then offers a critical discourse analysis of media reports that view the usage of the Hawaiian language in public domains as controversial, and lastly it provides a discourse analysis of the usage of person categories and possessive forms by old and young speakers in order to highlight the potential that Hawaiian revitalization has to help speakers make a reconnection between a Native Hawaiian identity and Hawaiian lands.

3.1 Rebuilding Structures for the Hawaiian Language in Society

Prior to the arrival of Captain Cook in 1778, Hawaiian was *the* language of the islands; it was the language through which business, politics, cultural practices, and education were conducted (Charlot, 2005; Wilson, 1998a, 1998b). As noted in Chapter 2, American colonialism disrupted all of these activities. The Hawaiian language was banned from the classroom in 1896, and intergenerational transmission of Hawaiian was, except for a few rare cases, suspended as Hawaiian speakers were compelled to make the gut-wrenching decision not to pass the language down to their offspring. The Hawaiian language revitalization movement focuses on the re-teaching of the language and the renormalization of the language in society.

Much of the literature on Hawaiian revitalization has centered particularly on the creation of a system of Hawaiian medium schools, a model Cowell has described as "based on a richly supported immersion school environment" (Cowell, 2012: 173; also see McCarty, 2008). Spurred by the Hawaiian Renaissance of the 1960s and 1970s and the 1978 declaration of Hawaiian as an official language, a group of educators and parents established the non-profit organization ʻAha Pūnana Leo in 1983, which was modeled after the Te Kōhanga Reo program in New Zealand to promote Māori (Wilson & Kamanā, 2001). The establishment of the ʻAha Pūnana Leo led to the next structure, the first Hawaiian medium preschool on Kaua'i in 1984 and later a set of similar preschools throughout the islands. As young children went through the 'Aha Pūnana Leo preschools, a need developed to continue schooling at the K-12 level. In order to make this happen, however, advocates had to work with state politicians to pass legislature in 1986 that removed the ban on the Hawaiian language in education that had been in place since 1896. The removal of the ban helped pave the way for the expansion of Hawaiian medium education across different levels of education. As Wilson and Kawai'ae'a (2007: 39) assert, what was emerging was an indigenous immersion model that "aims for Hawaiian dominance upon graduation from high school." Hawaiian language educators, however, did not stop at high school; Hawaiian medium education continues at the university level, both at the undergraduate and graduate level. Not only can students graduate with a B.A. from Hawaiian studies programs taught primarily through Hawaiian but they can also, in what has been termed a P-20 system, continue through the medium of Hawaiian at the M.A. and Ph.D. levels (Wilson & Kamanā, 2014).

Yet, while this system of schools is a certainly a central component of Hawaiian language revitalization, educators involved in the movement emphasize that the key to success is not the instruction itself. Instead, it is the establishment of a system of interrelated structures focused on revitalization that extend beyond the classroom and beyond the schools to the home and also to society in general. As Wilson and Kawai'ae'a (2007: 38–39) explain:

> The life of a language exists in the system of structures, not in the instruction of content. Second language teaching of an indigenous language must be connected to language revitalization structures and systems if they are to do more than simply give Indigenous students a slight glimpse of their ancestral tongues.

The 'Aha Pūnana Leo preschools thus represent one structure that was established early on, but the preschools only remain effective as part of a system that connects them with other structures, such as the ability to continue Hawaiian medium education at the K-12 levels and also through outreach programs that link the schools to caretakers and to the home. One such program in Ke Kula o Nāwahīokalani'opu'u, a charter school on the Big Island of Hawai'i, is called *Hui Kīpaepae* ("Family enrichment") and brings families of students in the school together once a week for cultural events that include Hawaiian language lessons for caretakers.

Another structure put into place is the relationship between the same school, Ke Kula o Nāwahīokalani'opu'u (Nāwahī for short), and the Hawaiian Language College at the University of Hawai'i at Hilo (Ka Haka 'Ula o Ke'elikōlani is the name of the college). Nāwahī serves as a laboratory school for Ka Haka 'Ula o Ke'elikōlani (Ka Haka 'Ula for short) which makes it easy to link students from both institutions together in various cultural activities carried out through Hawaiian. For example, advanced Hawaiian language students at the university make scheduled trips to Nāwahī to observe and participate in classes and other activities. This co-participation of Hawaiian learners is meant not just to further develop their Hawaiian abilities but also to foster a desire within younger speakers to become even more dedicated to Hawaiian revitalization. Accordingly, it is not surprising that many of the undergraduate students majoring in the Hawaiian language decide to enter the Kahuawaiola Teacher Training Program, another structure put into place within Ka Haka 'Ula, upon graduating with their B.A. The Kahuawaiola program trains speakers of Hawaiian specifically and grants them certification to become teachers at various levels of the Hawaiian medium school system.

Moreover, another aspect of the relationship between Nāwahī and Ka Haka 'Ula is an initiative that allows high school students to take some designated courses at the university for university credit. The courses typically are taught through Hawaiian and often put the high school students in classes with university students who are also students of the Hawaiian language. Like the visits of university students to Nāwahī, the idea of this initiative is to encourage the young students to consider a future path for themselves that has the Hawaiian language at the center. As Wilson and Kawai'ae'a (2007) note, "structures create identity and the interaction of human beings as part of a social group." By creating a system of related structures such as the preschools, K-12 education, weekly family enrichment programs (*Hui Kīpaepae*) and university programs at both the undergraduate and graduate level, the Hawaiian revitalization movement has put into place structures to facilitate interaction in the Hawaiian language across groups and also to encourage the development of an identity as a Hawaiian speaker. Wilson and Kawaiʻaeʻa (2007: 38) emphasize that the structures are designed to "develop, protect, nurture and enrich young adult and child fluency in Hawaiian along with the crucial disposition to use Hawaiian with Hawaiian speaking peers." "Crucial disposition" is a term used by Wilson and Kawaiʻaeʻa (2007) to refer to the need of participants in an indigenous language revitalization to transform their own consciousness to employ an indigenous minority language in the face of societal pressure to follow the masses and adopt the dominant language of English.[1]

There is evidence of the effectiveness of this system of structures effective. In an article published in 2007, Keiki Kawaiʻaeʻa, Alohalani Housman, and Makalapua Alencastre, all Hawaiian speakers who participated in the early years of Hawaiian language revitalization, describe how their children graduated from Hawaiian medium schools and then subsequently went on to enroll their own children in the Hawaiian medium educational structures now in place (Kawaiʻaeʻa et al., 2007). In short, this is now three straight generations of Hawaiian language speakers, grandparents, parents, and children, which suggests the restoration of intergenerational transmission in Hawaiian. In the nearly fifteen years since the publication of that article, the revitalization movement has witnessed the emergence of several other families with three generations of Hawaiian speakers.

Another piece of evidence is that the Hawaiian language has expanded to other social domains. One example is the media initiative ʻŌiwi TV, which has been spearheaded by Hawaiian speakers and employs several graduates from the Hawaiian Studies program at the University of Hawaiʻi. ʻŌiwi TV produces several types of media content, including short video clips of cultural events and also longer documentaries. Some of the content is in English, but many of the materials are produced with narration and interviews exclusively in Hawaiian.

---

[1]The term crucial disposition is similar to Fishman's (1991) notion of "ideological clarification."

‘Ōiwi TV and the reemergence of intergenerational transmission stand as proof that the educational-based system of structures has been effective in spawning a “crucial disposition” that has led Hawaiian speakers to the decision to commit themselves to making the Hawaiian language a central feature of their lives. This system of structures is largely responsible for an increase in the number of speakers; many sources report that there were less than 50 child speakers of Hawaiian in 1983, but the number of speakers has continued to grow with more recent estimates suggesting that as many 15,000 people use or understand Hawaiian (McCarty, 2008 based on personal communication with William Wilson), with some of them referred to as “new native speakers” who have begun acquiring Hawaiian as a first language (Brenzinger & Heinrich, 2013: 9). Given this growth, it is not surprising that the Hawaiian revitalization movement has garnered attention across the globe as possibly “the most dramatic success story … to date” (Lomawaina & McCarty, 2006: 138).

The success of Hawaiian revitalization should mostly be attributed to grassroots efforts that began with a small group of dedicated Hawaiian speaking activists willing to work within, and sometimes in spite of, the American-based system of government that still exists in Hawai‘i. Silva (2017: 2) sums up the current situation by noting that “a child can conceivably now receive an education from an Hawaiian immersion preschool in Pūnana Leo to a PhD in programs conducted in Hawaiian or which are Hawaiian centered, and spend her time in voyaging, lo‘i farming, hula, or other Hawaiian arts, and thus, while still surrounded by a hegemonic American culture, live a life that is substantially based in Hawaiian culture.” The inclusion of the phrase “still surrounded by a hegemonic culture” recognizes that this pathway to Hawaiian language and culture education still clashes with ideological beliefs that allow English and American culture to dominate society.

To be sure, credit may be given to some members of the government who, from the early 1980s, were open to the idea of reinstituting Hawaiian medium education and who helped push through laws that made it possible, but for the most part, despite being life-changing to many individuals and families, revitalization efforts have not yet led to far-reaching social changes. Wilson and Kamanā (2013: 115), two leaders in Hawaiian revitalization, remark that "Hawaiian has definitely grown stronger, yet we still have no neighborhood or community where Hawaiian is the language of the street." They nonetheless remain optimistic by emphasizing that Hawaiian language communities "will come someday. We continue to make advances in our efforts and open new *honua*, which is what we call places where Hawaiian is dominant" (Wilson & Kamanā, 2013: 115). The next section provides an analysis of language in the media in order to demonstrate how public discourse can serve as a barrier to further advancement of Hawaiian in society.

3.2 Media Discourse and Barriers to Growth

The interlocking system of educational structures has, in effect, created a bit of a "safe haven" in an otherwise English dominant society where young speakers of Hawaiian are able to employ the Hawaiian language and allow their Hawaiian identities to develop and their knowledge of Hawaiian cultural practices to grow. As discussed, these structures are also making inroads into society represented by the reemergence of intergenerational transmission and the media initiative ʻŌiwi TV.

ʻŌiwi TV has been very productive in terms of content and coverage, featuring longer documentaries as well as shorter clips that provide important information to and about the Hawaiian speaking community. ʻŌiwi TV maintains a presence on cable television and on the Internet, but even though there have been attempts to use Hawaiian in the mainstream media—for example, the television broadcasting company KGMB presented an early morning segment in Hawaiian and there has likewise been a newspaper column written in Hawaiian, generally the local mainstream media in Hawaiʻi stands outside of the structures that guarantee the freedom to employ the Hawaiian language. In this sense, the media is not much different from other public domains of Hawaiian society besides education in terms of linguistic freedom. Periodically, this lack of freedom becomes a topic reported in the local news in English when people try to employ Hawaiian in social domains that do not typically offer access to the language. This section engages in a critical discourse analysis of two broadcasts in the local mainstream television news that report on two separate occurrences, one in which a Hawaiian speaker attempted to use Hawaiian in court and another in which a member of the Hawaiian House of Representatives tried to speak Hawaiian on the floor of the House. The analysis shows how the media presentation of these occurrences seems to provide implicit support for the current linguistic ecology that denies speakers of Hawaiian access to their language in these public domains.

The first four excerpts of data focus on an occurrence in 2018 when a Hawaiian speaker's usage of Hawaiian in an appearance in court was not recognized. Excerpt (1) below is taken from a news broadcast shortly after the occurence in a segment entitled "Language Battle."[2] This story is the lead story of that day's broadcast and it begins as the two anchors, HD and MY, introduce the story.[3]

Excerpt (1): Language Battle

1	HD:	Good evening everybody and thank you for joining us tonight a UH
2		Maui assistant professor of Hawaiian Studies has a warrant out for his
3		arrest tonight after refusing to speak English in a court appearance today
4	MY:	Samuel Ka'eo told us today that he is fighting for his right speak his
5		native language (.) our Alexander Zane spoke with him tonight on what
6		he plans to do now

The first anchor in lines 1–2 names the subject of the story not by name but rather by his title as "A UH Maui assistant professor of Hawaiian Studies." While this renders Hawaiian language as relevant to the story,

[2]This clip is available at https://www.youtube.com/watch?v=STOHm2hB4J4.

[3]The transcription conventions largely follow those of conversation analysis:

(.) micropause; (( )) information inserted by the author to describe the context; [start of overlapping talk;] end of overlapping talk; = latched utterances that follow without the usual pause in between; * spate of until legible talk.

the action of this subject is not framed in line 3 as trying to speak Hawaiian but instead as "refusing to speak English" in an official activity, namely a court appearance. The choice of the verb "refuse" thus portrays this action in a negative light, which also makes it easier to understand why there is "a warrant out for his arrest." Here, we can suggest that the usage of the phrase "refusing to speak English" conveys a different message than it would have had the anchor stated the warrant for his arrest stemmed from his attempt to speak Hawaiian in public.

The second anchor adds more specific information in lines 4–6, including the name of the subject, Samuel Ka'eo, and highlighting in lines 4–5 that "he is fighting for his right to speak his native language." Again, however, we have to consider how this information is framed. It is framed as being "told" to them by Ka'eo, who has just been described performing a negative action of "refusing" that led to a "warrant for his arrest." Moreover, the Hawaiian language is still not mentioned explicitly. The language in question is attributed only to Ka'eo as "his native language." There is no mention that this native language is recognized as the native language of the islands and of the Native Hawaiian people themselves. Nor is it framed as an official language of the state. Rather, it is constructed as the native language of one individual who has done a negative act by refusing to speak English and is therefore about to be arrested.

In line 5, the second anchor, MY, notes that they are going to follow up on this story by naming another reporter, Alexander Zane, who has spoken with Samuel Ka'eo. Yet, before Zane begins speaking, the broadcast shows a brief clip from Ka'eo's court appearance and his interaction with the judge. This is shown below as Excerpt (2).[4]

[4]This particular broadcast did not actually show the full exchange shown in Excerpt (2). Instead, it stopped after line 11 and did not show the judge's response in lines 12–13. The clip with the judge's response, however, is informative and is available on Youtube (https://www.youtube.com/watch?v=gRFO5-48bGc&t=226s), and I have thus included lines 12–13 here.

Excerpt (2): Language Battle

7	Judge:	You know I'm going to give you another opportunity, Mr. Ka'eo to just
8		identify yourself just so the record is clear, I'm going to ask you (.) one
9		last time (.) is your name Samuel Ka'eo
10	SK:	Eia au ke kū nei i mua ou, 'o ia ke kanaka āu i kāhea mai nei. Ke kū nei
11		i mua ou e ka lunakānāwai (.) aloha
12	Judge:	Okay, the court is unable to get a definitive determination for the record
13		that the defendant seated here is Samuel Ka'eo

After making it clear in line 7 with the word "another" that the judge had previously given the defendant an opportunity to identify himself, the judge in line 9 puts forth, in English, a direct yes–no question, "is your name Samuel Ka'eo." Questions such as this are known, in the analysis of conversation, as first-pair parts that make it conditionally relevant that the next speaker provide the expected second-pair part. Indeed, we can see that the defendant Ka'eo in lines 10–11 provides a response, in Hawaiian. He states in lines 10–11 that *Eia au ke kū nei i mua ou* ("I am standing here in front of you") *'o ia ke kanaka āu i kāhea mai nei* ("the person you called") *ke kū nei i mua ou e ka lunakānāwai* (.) *aloha* ("I am standing here in front of you, judge (.) aloha"), a statement that seemingly serves as a response confirming that he is, in fact, Samuel Ka'eo. Yet, while this response seems to satisfy the conditional relevance of the first-pair part, the judge nonetheless concludes in lines 12–13 that the court has not received a "definitive determination," which is to say that the question has not been answered. The problem, of course, is that Ka'eo has answered the question in Hawaiian, not English, which leads to the lack of definitive determination of Ka'eo's presence and which also results in the warrant for his arrest.

Following the clip from court, the news broadcast continues with commentary from the selected reporter, shown below as AZ. It is also in this excerpt that we see the voice of Ka'eo himself outside of the courtroom. (SK in the transcript).

Excerpt (3): Language Battle

14	AZ:	It was this exchange that ultimately led to a warrant being issued for
15		Samuel Ka'eo's arrest. Ka'eo who speaks Hawaiian and English fluently
16		chose to address the judge in Hawaiian. Judge Blaine Kobayashi said the
17		the court was unable to determine if Ka'eo was present.
18	SK:	Um and so I was quite surprised at the very beginning he made an issue of
19		(.) somehow (.) my responses (.) because it was in Hawaiian um he had
20		a huge issue with that um he you know he pretended somehow that I
21		wasn't there today somehow I was invisible
22	AZ:	Ka'eo faces charges in connection with a protest last August. He had
23		requested a Hawaiian language interpreter but one was not available
24		so the court granted the state's motion to have the trial continue in English
25		Ka'eo says he feels he should be able to defend himself in Hawaiian
26		saying he believes he and others have the right to do so
27	SK:	I think I got to put this in context that here I am as a Hawaiian person
28		representing myself in a criminal issue due to um fighting on the behalf
29		of the rights of the Hawaiian people and using the Hawaiian language is
30		best way to express that this is a Hawaiian issue and that being taken
31		away from me
		((Camera cuts to a scene from the courtroom after the judge declared that the court was unable to determine Mr. Ka'eo's presence))
32	Audience1:	*hewa*
33	Audience2:	*hewa*
34	Audience3:	*hewa*
35	AZ:	A spokeperson for the Hawai'i judiciary told us there is no legal
36		requirement to provide Hawaiian language interpreters to court
37		participants who speak English but prefer to speak in Hawaiian

AZ begins speaking in line 14 to let the audience know that it was this exchange that led to the warrant for Ka'eo's arrest. AZ then makes it known in lines 15–16 that Ka'eo speaks both Hawaiian and English fluently and then employs the verb "chose" to indicate that Ka'eo made a willful decision to address the judge in Hawaiian. AZ next quotes the judge as noting that "the court" was unable to confirm Ka'eo's presence. These word choices by the reporter AZ thus formulates Ka'eo's action as a willful individual decision that caused a problem not just for the judge but for the collective court.

This formulation, it should be noted, contrasts with Ka'eo's description in lines 18–21, in which Ka'eo employs the pronoun "he" twice in stating that "he," the judge had a problem with Ka'eo's usage of Hawaiian. Ka'eo's voice thus invokes the Hawaiian language specifically as he explains that, to him, the judge's unwillingness to recognize Ka'eo's usage of Hawaiian rendered Ka'eo as "invisible."

Although Ka'eo explicitly frames this as an issue of the judge not acknowledging Ka'eo's usage of Hawaiian, the clip goes back to the reporter AZ who, instead of speaking directly to Ka'eo's right to speak Hawaiian, adds the information in line 22 that Ka'eo was in court for a protest that occurred last August, and he also states in lines 23–24 that Ka'eo had been granted a Hawaiian language interpreter but since one was not available, "the court granted the state's motion to have the trial continue in English." AZ then notes Ka'eo's belief that he and others should be able to defend themselves in Hawaiian, which is followed by an excerpt of the interview in which Ka'eo expresses clearly in lines 27–31 his belief that Hawaiian is the best way to speak to this issue given that it is an "Hawaiian issue." This is followed by a quick shift from the voice of Ka'eo back to the courtroom scene as at least three members of the audience can be heard yelling the Hawaiian word *hewa* ("wrong") in response to the judge's declaration that Ka'eo's presence cannot be determined. The excerpt then goes back to the voice of the reporter AZ who reads the statement in lines 35–37 from the Hawai'i judiciary that there is no legal requirement to provide interpreters for Hawaiian speakers who are capable of speaking English.

This excerpt is significant in that it allows Ka'eo to express that Hawaiian people should be allowed to use the Hawaiian language to speak to Hawaiian issues (lines 27–31), but it is also significant that the reporter, and the broadcast in general, do not take this opportunity to discuss the basic rights of Hawaiian speakers to employ Hawaiian in a public venue such as the court. Instead of doing so, the reporter offers an official voice from a spokesperson in lines 35–37 that seems to contradict Ka‘eo's assertion that he has the right to use Hawaiian. The official statement from the spokesperson, in fact, ends with a reminder that someone like Ka‘eo can speak English but prefers to speak Hawaiian. This statement speaks on the collective behalf of the Hawaiian judiciary and thus constructs Ka‘eo's action as a personal preference, not as somehow representing the voice, or even a voice, of the native people of the islands.

Shortly after the conclusion of Excerpt (3), the newsclip comes to an end, but not before the voices of both Ka'eo and the reporter are heard one last time. Excerpt (4) shows the conclusion of the newsclip.

Excerpt (4): Language Battle

38	SK:	(I) will continue to demand through my words that I be recognized
39		as a human being that we as Hawaiians have a ri- we just have a
40		human right to speak our own language
41	AZ:	A spokesperson for the judiciary says Ka'eo is not being singled out
42		Ka'eo told me he himself plans to turn himself into authorities and
43		plans to continue speaking in Hawaiian in future court hearings

Note here that Ka‘eo begins in lines 38–39 by using the first-person pronoun I to emphasize that "I will continue to demand ... that I be recognized as a human being," but he soon changes pronouns in line 39 to relate this to the collective category of "Hawaiians" and how "we just have a human right to speak our own language." Contrast this move by Ka'eo, though, to AZ's remarks in lines 41–43. He immediately in line 41 invokes once again the spokesperson for the judiciary to state that Ka‘eo is not being singled out, thus suggesting that this is not aimed at a specific individual. Yet, AZ does not speak at all to Ka‘eo's attempt to relate his experience to the human rights of Hawaiians as a collective category and instead concentrates only at the individual level in lines

42–43 by remaining focused on what Ka'eo plans to do, namely to continue to speak in Hawaiian in future hearings. Accordingly, even though the news story offers an opportunity to present and discuss the right of Native Hawaiians to speak their own language, it ends with a statement that makes Ka'eo out to be a defiant person who is going to disobey the official position of the government that is represented twice by the mention of the "spokesperson for the judiciary." The story fails to mention even once that the same government that the spokesperson represents has a constitutional declaration as of 1978 that Hawaiian is one of two official languages of the state of Hawai'i.

To be sure, reports of this rejection of Hawaiian in the court lit the fuse of controversy as activists within Hawai'i and throughout the world voiced support for Ka'eo and for the Hawaiian language. Due largely to this support, the warrant for the arrest of Ka'eo was eliminated and actions were undertaken in an attempt to ensure easier access to interpreters so Hawaiian could be employed in court.

Nonetheless, it still remains that the news report of Ka'eo's court appearance missed an opportunity to initiate a discussion concerning the right to use Hawaiian in public. Critical discourse analysts have made note of the usage in media discourse of the process of generalization, whereby single occurrences are treated as indicative of general tendencies. They point out that generalization can reinforce stereotypical beliefs about groups of people that can result in discrimination (Billig, 2008; Unvar & Rahimi, 2013; van Dijk, 1993, 1995). Yet, what we see in Excerpts (1)–(4) is a focus on the part of the media report on a specific occurrence and a reluctance to generalize to the larger issue of rights to speak Hawaiian. The next set of excerpts, Excerpts (5)–(8), show a similar reluctance on the part of the media to address the general issue of rights to speak Hawaiian. It focuses on a single occurrence that happened in 2014 on the floor of the State House of Representatives. Excerpt (5) begins as the two anchors of the news program introduce themselves and the story.[5]

[5]The clip is available at https://www.youtube.com/watch?v=AOw3LWDLYPU.

Excerpt (5): The Controversial Hanohano

1	YD:	Representative Faye Hanohano causes another big stir at the state capitol
2		and this time it wasn't what she said but how she said it, good evening, I
3		am Yunji De Nies
4	PA:	Thank you for joining us, I am Paula Akana. Hanohano spoke Hawaiian
5		and Hawaiian only during only one comment on the house floor and that
6		caused a ruckus. The representative has already been accused of being
7		rude and possibly racist. Now some wondered if she's within her right to
8		speak Hawaiian without translating, KITV4's Andrew Perreira joins us
9		with that answer

The first anchor YD leads with the title and name of the woman who is at the center of the story, Representative Faye Hanohano. YD then explains in line 1 that Hanohano "causes another big stir at the state capitol," which, first of all, presupposes that Hanohano had caused other "big stirs" and, second of all, directly states that she has done it again. The anchor then in line 2 provides information that the "big stir" derives, "this time," from "how she (Hanohano) said it," which leads to a further presupposition that previous big stirs were caused by "what she said." The second anchor YD then introduces herself in line 3 before the second anchor PA takes a turn in line 4 to introduce herself and then to offer the more specific information through line 5 that Hanohano spoke Hawaiian, adding in line 6 that this was the cause of the "ruckus." PA continues in lines 6–7 to note that "the representative has already been accused of being rude and possibly racist," and by doing so not only indicates that speaking Hawaiian can lead to a "ruckus" but also connects speaking Hawaiian to "being rude and possibly racist." In particular, her use of "already" in line 6 suggests that her most current action, namely speaking Hawaiian, is somehow an extension of her "being rude and possibly racist."

After setting the scene by portraying Hanohano in a negative light as someone who caused a "ruckus" by using Hawaiian, the second anchor PA sets up the next part of the story in lines 7–8 through the question of whether Hanohano is "within her right to speak Hawaiian without translating." This raises the expectation that the news story will include a discussion of Hawaiian speaking rights. The next excerpt shows the continuation of the story as the reporter AP provides, as promised in lines 8–9 of this excerpt, an answer to the question.

Excerpt (6): The Controversial Hanohano

10	AP:	Paula, yes, Hawai'i is the only state in the union with two official
11		languages. Representative Hanohano was using one of them. Like
12		most legislative bodies, the House of Representatives has its own
13		rules regarding conduct
14	GW:	They should be proud of the way that we speak, the way that we
15		dress, and the way that we behave
16	AP:	But when embattled representative of Puna spoke in her native language
17	JM:	Representative Hanohano
18	FH:	Mahalo ho'omalu 'ōlelo. Kāko'o loa. Makemake au i ka ha'i'ōlelo o
19		ka luna maka'āinana mai Kapolei mai e komo i loko o ka puke hale
20		no nā maka'āinana [mahalo
21	AP:	[it touched off a mini firestorm as vice speaker John
22		Mizuno presided over the chamber
23	JM:	Representative Hanohano could you please translate for the members
24		(1)
25	FH:	'A'ole au e makemake e unuhi mai I don't wanna translate mahalo
26	AP:	That exchange prompted a clearly frustrated Mizuno to bang the gavel
27	JM:	Recess, subject to the ca-call of the chair recess ((bangs gavel once))
28	AP:	After a short interval, Mizuno came back with this
29	JM:	Rule 60.1 provides members should conduct themselves in a respectful
30		manner

AP begins in line 10 by providing the answer of "yes" to the question posed by PA about whether Hanohano is within her rights by speaking Hawaiian, and he explains by noting through line 11 that Hawai'i has two official languages and that "Hanohano was using one of them." This seems to move the reporting to a general level since it moves from a specific occurrence of speaking Hawaiian to a discussion of official languages of the state and people's rights to speak them. However, AP does not pursue this angle and next shifts in lines 12–13 the focus of the discussion from Hawaiian speaking rights to the rules of conduct in the House of Representatives. The report then continues with a focus on the topic of rules of conduct in lines 14–15 by showing an interview with one of the representatives, Gene Ward, who speaks to these rules of conduct when he states that people "should be proud of the way that we speak, the way that we dress, and the way that we behave." The report then transitions to a brief clip of Hanohano on the floor of the House of Representatives that is introduced by AP in line 16 with "but when embattled representative Hanohano spoke in her native language." The fact that this utterance begins with the contrastive conjunction "but" suggests that AP is going to introduce content that contrasts with the just-mentioned proper rules of conduct. He begins offering this content by referring to Hanohano as "embattled" and by noting that she "spoke in her native language." By employing the category of "her native language," AP accomplishes a shift from the category of "official language" to a category that specifically refers to Hanohano. It is "her native language," and thus we are no longer speaking at the general level of official language for everyone in the state. Additionally, this shift sets up the possibility that the specific action of speaking "her native language" is in conflict with the code of conduct in terms of how the representatives speak, dress, and behave.

The story then shows a brief clip of Hanohano on the House floor engaging in the action in question, namely speaking in Hawaiian. This is shown in the transcript in lines 18–20 after Hanohano is prompted in line 17 by JM, the vice speaker, to take a turn. Hanohano first offers her thanks to the vice speaker with the Hawaiian term *mahalo* and then continues in Hawaiian through line 20.[6] As Hanohano is at the end of her utterance in line 20, AP begins a voice over with an utterance in lines

[6] A basic translation of Hanohano's Hawaiian statement would be "Thank you. I support this and would like to see the words from the representative from Kapolei entered officially into the House log."

21–22 that, from a grammatical standpoint, seems to finish his utterance in line 16, which stated "when when embattled representative of Puna spoke in her native language." He declares in 21 that "it touched off a mini firestorm," thus constructing Hanohano's action of speaking Hawaiian as very controversial. Line 23 goes back to the original clip on the floor of the House and Representatives and shows the vice speaker of the House JM asking for a translation, but, after a one-second pause, Hanohano responds in line 25 in Hawaiian saying that she does not want to translate. This time she does translate at the end of line with the English statement "I don't wanna translate." The reporter AP again offers narration in line 26 to attribute frustration to Mizuno as expressed through the pounding of his gavel. The clip on the screen then shows Mizuno calling for recess in line 27 and the viewers do indeed hear one loud pound of the gavel at the end of line 27. AP informs the viewers that the vice speaker took only a short break, and then the clips show JM in lines 29–30 as he invokes Rule 60.1 which provides that "members should conduct themselves in a respectful manner." He is not shown referring directly to Hanohano's action of speaking in Hawaiian and refusing to translate, but the implication is that this is the conduct in question. By speaking in Hawaiian and refusing to translate, Hanohano has violated the official rules of the House. This is the same code of conduct referred to by AP and GW earlier. Thus, even though there is an earlier mention of Hanohano having the right to speak in Hawaiian, the news story has worked through line 30 to focus specifically on Hanohano's action and the establishment of it as a violation of the code of conduct in this particular context, the floor of the House of Representatives. Like the story focusing on Ka'eo in Excerpts (1)–(4), the report has stayed at a very specific level and refused to generalize about the implications of these actions of speaking in Hawaiian.

Through these first 30 lines, the newsclip has moved from the general issue of whether people such as Hanohano have the right to speak Hawaiian to the problematization of one specific usage of Hawaiian by Hanohano in a political domain in Hawai'i. Still, though, the news report is not finished and continues in Excerpt (7) with another voice that returns to the general issue of rights to speak Hawaiian.

Excerpt (7): The Controversial Hanohano

31	AP:	Quickly, representative Gene Ward stood up and said there is precedent
32		here
33	GW:	Well, according to the constitution, there are two official languages,
34		English and Hawaiian, therefore no translation is needed, that was the
35		prevailing legal authority two or three years ago, so Mr. Speaker I think
36		you've ah you've sort of varied ah a little off course from that
37	AP:	Mizuno agreed that there is no issue with the language Hanohano spoke
		((AP next reads a translation of Hanohano's speech that also appears on the screen))
42	AP:	Ward points out he was not coming to Hanohano's defense across the
43		board she still faces possible penalties for allegedly berating HPU student
44		Aaron Jacobs during a hearing and lashing out at DLNR staff with
45		remarks described as abusive, racially discriminatory, and inappropriate
46	GW:	I wasn't defending what she was saying or some of the things that she has
47		said in the past because they were pretty reprehensible things
48	AP:	Today Mizuno said the exchange with Hanohano brings up an interesting
49		point whether the House should pay for a Hawaiian language interpreter
50		during floor and committee sessions, House Speaker Joe Suki will make
51		that final call

AP announces in lines 31–32 that representative Gene Ward stood up following Mizuno's remarks, and the story then cuts to Ward's comments in lines 33–36. Speaking on the House floor and addressing the Vice Speaker Mizuno, Ward points out that the state constitution lists Hawaiian and English as official languages, which according to him means that no translation is necessary. Ward then suggests in line 36 that the vice speaker may have "varied off course" in suggesting that

Hanohano had violated the code of conduct. Yet, even though this seems to once again raise the discussion to a more general level concerning the right to speak in Hawaiian in the public domain in Hawaiian society, the reporter AP turns the focus once again to Hanohano and her "problematic" behavior in lines 42–45. AP notes that Ward's comments about the right to speak Hawaiian were not, according to Ward, meant to defend Hanohano. AP then provides specific details about a student who Hanohano had "allegedly berated," describing Hanohano's remarks as "abusive, racially discriminatory, and inappropriate" in line 45. The story then moves to part of an interview with Ward in which he directly states that he was not defending Hanohano because some of what she said was "pretty reprehensible." Finally, the clip cuts back to AP who ends the story by stating in lines 48–51 that the House speaker Joe Suki will make a final decision about whether the House should pay for a Hawaiian language interpreter. Although GW had raised the possibility that Hanohano has the right to speak in Hawaiian without an interpreter, the rest of the clip failed to discuss or even mention this right again. In fact, rather than concentrate on this broader issue of rights to use Hawaiian, the clip engaged in the process of "narrowing" by moving to keep the focus specifically on Hanohano's "reprehensible" behavior. Indeed, the two times in this clip that this broader issue was raised, in lines 10–12 and 33–36, were followed directly by narrowing that focused specifically on Hanohano's violations. Not only does this process of narrowing miss an opportunity to develop a discussion about rights to speak Hawaiian, but it also suggests that speaking Hawaiian in a political venue may constitute a violation of a code of conduct and thus send a message that it may not be acceptable to speak Hawaiian in official domains.

The two news stories, from 2014 and 2018, are not by any means the only mentions of the Hawaiian language in the local news. Nonetheless, these two stories underscore a reluctance to have a public discourse that seriously considers an equal role for Hawaiian in public domains. As shown in this section, public discourse generally fails to address rights to employ the Hawaiian language that stems from its status as an official language, and, more than anything, problematizes its usage in the public domain when it causes communication difficulties for English speakers. Given that coverage in the mainstream news does not seem favorable to an open discussion that considers expanded usage of the Hawaiian language in public, it is understandable that advocates for the Hawaiian language have begun with educational structures such as schools and looked to build outward with other interlocking structures. Such a strategy has ensured the revitalization of the language by producing an increased number of speakers through its structures. At the same time, though, as these first seven excerpts show, Hawaiian still has a considerable fight remaining if it is to achieve equal access in public domains outside of education.

3.3 Why Make a Place for Hawaiian in Society?

The fact that Hawaiian is the Indigenous language of Hawaiʻi, together with the fact it is the ancestral language of a percentage of the population that has been disenfranchised from its language, culture, and land, should be reason enough to do everything possible to ensure linguistic justice to the language and its speakers. In order to emphasize just how crucial the Hawaiian is to the Native Hawaiian population, which has suffered high rates of homelessness, poverty, sickness, and incarceration, I demonstrate through an analysis of discourse the intimate relationship among the Hawaiian language, Native Hawaiians, and the land. The analysis will, I hope, help make the point that a strong Hawaiian language can have an empowering effect because it can help reestablish the connection between a Native Hawaiian identity and the land that was taken away through American colonialism.

The analysis will begin with a focus on spoken and written discourse by people referred to by many participants in the language revitalization movement as *mānaleo* ("native speakers"). These are people who spoke the language from their childhood and whose speech as served as the primary model for teaching the language to the children and adults in the educational structures mentioned above. The speech of the *mānaleo* remains available largely in two forms, through two sets of interviews conducted in the 1970s, one set by Larry Kimura and another set by

Clinton Kanahele.[7] Many of these interviews have been digitized and can be accessed through the Internet. The second form in which the speech of the *mānaleo* remains is through the archives of Hawaiian language newspapers that began in 1834 soon after the arrival of the American missionaries in 1820.[8] A large database of the newspapers also exists on the Internet. For this section, I employ data from the set of interviews by Larry Kimura and from the Hawaiian newspaper archive.

Kimura's database comes from his radio show entitled *Ka Leo Hawai'i* that began in 1972, a time when elder native speakers of Hawaiian were still alive but when intergenerational transmission had been largely cut off. In fact, one of the purposes of the radio show was to document the speech of the elder speakers as well their engagement in Hawaiian cultural practices while it was still possible. Typically, the show features an interview by the host Kimura with a main guest (or sometimes guests) and it is also common for Kimura to take telephone calls from the listening audience, many of whom want to interact with the guest of that particular show. All interaction is in Hawaiian. Excerpt (8) below is taken from one of the shows in 1972 and begins to demonstrate the connection among language, identity, and land. It features interaction between two *mānaleo*, Luisiana Ka'awa Noa (shown as Ka'awa in the excerpt) and Lucy Kanoho'inea Kamana'o Mikasobe (Lucy in the excerpt). Lucy was Kimura's main guest and Ka'awa was a caller. At the beginning of Excerpt (1), Ka'awa is talking about a place, Hālawa, with which she and Lucy are familiar.[9]

[7]Kimura's database is available at http://ulukau.org/kaniaina/, and Kanahele's at https://library.byuh.edu/archives/kanahele.html.

[8]The newspapers can be accessed at https://www.papakilodatabase.com and also http://nupepa.org/gsdl2.5/cgi-bin/nupepa?l=haw.

[9]For the excerpts of Hawaiian from the radio program, Ka Leo Hawai'i, I provide the Hawaiian first in italics, followed by a word-by-word gloss, and then a more natural English translation. For the word-by-gloss, the following abbreviations are used: D = directional marker, EP = emphatic particle, PAS = passive, PL = plural, PS = possessive, PST = Past tense marker, NOM = nominalizer, O = object marker, TM = topic marker, S = subject marker.

Excerpt (8): Ka Leo Hawai'i: Luisiana Ka'awa Noa (Ka'awa) and Lucy Kanoho'inea Kamana'o Mikasobe (Lucy)

1	Ka'awa:	*'Ae. Nānā i luna wau o, i luna wau o Hālawa. 'A' ole wau i hele i lalo* yes look D above I D above I of Hālawa not I PST go D down "Yes, I looked from above, I was above Hālawa. I did not go down."
2	Lucy:	*'Ō, 'ō, 'ō* Oh oh oh "Oh, oh, oh."
3	Ka'awa:	*Mai luna mai a nānā ihola wau i lalo* From above D and look D I down "From above I looked down."
4	Lucy:	*'Ae, 'ae* Yes yes "Yes, yes"
5	Ka'awa:	*Aloha nō* Aloha EP "It is too bad."
6	Lucy:	*Hn: Kēia manawa, 'a'ohe po'e o laila. Ua pau ka po'e i ta hā'ule nō* Hn: this time not people PS there PST done the people the fall EP
7		*[ho'i* EP "Now, there are no people there. All the people have gone and fallen"
8	Ka'awa:	*[Pa[u:* Done "done"
9	Lucy:	*[a hele.* and went "left"
10	Ka'awa:	*Pau ka po'e i [ka* Done the people the "the people have gone and"
11	Lucy:	*['Ē. he mea, he po'e hīpī 'o ia ko laila [i tēia manawa* Yeah ones people hippies it PS there this time "Yeah, only hippies, that is what is there at this time."

12	Ka'awa:		*[a po'e hīpī* Oh people hippies
13		*Aloha nō ka po'e hīpī* Aloha EP the people hippies "Oh, the hippies, those poor hippies."	
14		((laughter is heard from the three participants Lucy, Ka'awa, and the host LK))	

In lines 1 and 3 Ka'awa relates that she stood above in Hālawa, and as she uses the phrase *Aloha nō* in line 5 to begin to express that it is "too bad", Lucy enters to explain in line 6 that the people have all left. In doing so, she employs the verb *hā'ule*, which literally means to "fall down," but as Ka'awa begins in line 8 to repeat the word pau "done" in apparent agreement, Lucy offers in overlap what seems to be a possible correction with the term *hele*, which means "went" or "left." In other words, she seems to be expressing the idea through line 9 that all of the people have left Hālawa, something which Ka'awa begins to confirm in line 10. However, before Ka'awa can complete her utterance, Lucy overlaps in line 11 to offer agreement *'ē* and then to add the information that there are only hippies there now. The utterance of *po'e hīpī* ("the hippies") in line 11 prompts Ka'awa to provide an *a* ("oh") in line 12, which may be characterized as a type of change of state marker, before repeating the term *po'e hīpī* ("the hippies"). She then states in line 13 *aloha nō ka po'e hīpī* "those poor hippies," which prompts the two interactants and the host to laugh.

The laughter in line 14 derives directly from Ka'awa's expression of sympathy for the category of *hīpī* in lines 12–13, but it surely also derives from the implication of Lucy's utterances in line 6, *'a'ohe po'e o laila* ("there are no people there") and line 11 *he po'e hīpī, 'o ia ko laila i tēia manawa* ("the hippies are the ones there now"), that hippies would not fall into the more general category of *po'e* ("people"). Although this connection draws laughter, I would like to suggest that explication of the seeming contradiction in Lucy's two formulations, *'a'ohe po'e o laila* ("there are no people there") and *he po'e hīpī, 'o ia ko laila i tēia manawa* ("the hippies are the ones there now") holds a key to understanding a Hawaiian perspective on the relationship among Hawaiian identity, land,

and language. In order to explicate this point, there are two aspects of these contradictory formulations that need to be unpacked.

The first is that, as the Native Hawaiian population came in increasing contact with people from the outside in the 1800s, it was common for them to refer to themselves with terms such as *po'e* ("people") and *kanaka* ("person") that stand as generic terms for people and to add either descriptors to these words or to use separate category terms when referring to non-Hawaiians. We see an example of this in Excerpt (1); Lucy uses the term *po'e* in line 6 to state that there are no people there but then adds the descriptor *po'e hīpī* in line 11. We see another example in Excerpt (9), which is taken from a newspaper article in the year 1836, only two years after Hawaiian language newspaper publications began in Hawaiian in 1834.

Excerpt (9): From the newspaper Ke Kumu Hawai'i: O'ahu, March 30, 1836

1 *He makani ikaika kona mea e hiki ole ai, he makani huhu loa, aole e aa ka poe*
2 *hooholomoku ke puka ma waho, a olelo mai ka poe ike, o na kanaka maoli a me na*
3 *haole ho'i, aole loa e ola ka moku uuku i keia makani, e poho no*

"The strong wind was his reason for not arriving, it was a severe wind, the sailors did not dare venture out, and according to the people who have knowledge about these things, the real people and the haoles, they said that smaller boats will not survive the wind, they will be lost."

In reporting the arrival of a severe wind that is treacherous for small boats, the writers employ the general category *poe* in line 2 to state that *olelo mai ka poe ike* ("according to the people who know"). This seems to be a general reference to "people" of no specific ethnicity, but the writer then clarifies by including an appositional statement, *o na kanaka maoli a me na haole hoi* ("the real people and the haole") that divides the category of *poe* into the two more specific categories *kanaka maoli* ("real people") and *haole* ("white person"). I give the literal translation here of *kanaka maoli* as "real people," but it is clear that this category, which adds the descriptor *maoli* ("real") to the generic word for person *kanaka,* is meant to refer specifically to Native Hawaiians. The word *haole* has sometimes served as a derogatory reference for a white person (see Rohrer, 2010 for further discussion), but there is no evidence in this passage that it is either negative or positive—it seems to be just a basic description. In doing such descriptive work, it provides a glimpse of how at least some Hawaiian speakers of that time were constructing their reality as the presence of people in the category of *haole* increased in Hawai'i. This passage from the newspaper does seem to first employ *poe* in line 2 as a reference including both Native Hawaiians and white people, but it is clear that *kanaka maoli* is reserved for Native Hawaiians and separates them from *haole*.

Excerpt (10) shows a similar example from 1893, immediately after the overthrow of the Hawaiian Kingdom.

Excerpt (10): From the newspaper Hawai'i Holomua, June 10, 1893

1 *Ua hookohu ae nei ka Aha Kuka o ke Aupuni Kuikawa ia Mr. Menoca, he Pukiki, i*
2 *lala a i hoa no ia Aha. Ua lono ia mai ke upu nei lakou e wae i Kanaka Hawai'i kekahi*
3 *Ma ka hoomaopopo aku he mau hana keia no ke kii ana i na kokua o na Pukiki a me*
4 *na Kanaka maoli i ke Aupuni Kuikawa, oiai, ua ike ia ke kue ia o ka hoohui aina.*

"The advisory council of the provisional government appointed Mr. Menoca, a Portuguese, as a member of that council. It was also heard that the members are hoping to choose a Hawaiian person for the council. We should remember though that this is part of an effort to gain support from the Portuguese and the Native Hawaiians for the provisional government, particularly since we are seeing resistance to their idea of bringing Hawai'i into the United States."

In reporting in line 1 the appointment of a person referred to as Mr. Menoca to the advisory council (*aha kuka*) of the provisional government (*aupuni kuikawa*) set up by those who overthrew the government, the writer of the article adds at the end of line 1, as a kind of appositive, that Mr. Menoca is Portuguese (*he Pukiki*). The article then employs the category *Kanaka Hawai'i* in line 2 to note that the council is hoping to add a Native Hawaiian, and finally, it separately lists the categories of *Pukiki* ("Portuguese") and *Kanaka maoli* ("Native Hawaiian") in lines 3 and 4 respectively to suggest that the council, which may be controversial because it is an advisory council of the provisional government, is actively seeking the support of the Portuguese and the Native Hawaiians in lieu of resistance to the provisional government's plan to align with the United States.

It is arguable that the first category used in this passage, *Pukiki* is unnecessary since it is treated as parenthetical to the first main point, namely, the appointment of Mr. Mendoca. Yet, the categorizing of Mr. Mendoca as Portuguese is important to the main point of the passage, which is that the provisional government is trying to gain the favor of the larger group of Portuguese in Hawai'i by appointing him. Also relevant to the larger point made in the passage is the division between Native Hawaiians and the Portuguese. The writer first in line 2 employs the general term *kanaka* with the descriptor *Hawaii* attached to refer to the Native Hawaiians but then later in line 3 and makes a division between the "real people" (*Kanaka maoli*) and the "Portuguese" (*Pukiki*). This overt category division suggests not only a sense of identity on the part of the Hawaiians as different from other groups but it also shows that this division was also relevant for the historical and political development of Hawaiian society.

Nicholas (2008, 2018) uses the expression "language as cultural practice" to describe Hopi youth and their attempts to learn, understand, and maintain the Hopi language practices that articulate a Hopi identity, and it makes sense that this type of categorization practice on the part of the Native Hawaiians developed over time as a cultural practice in order to express and preserve a Native Hawaiian identity in lieu of a rapidly changing society. Put another way, by referring to themselves through terms such as *po'e, kanaka,* and *kanaka maoli* that constructed them as the "real people" in relation to "others" from the "outside," the Native Hawaiians were able to ensure that they had their own cultural practices for defining their social world. These categories grounded themselves to each other via a Native Hawaiian identity, and as I will now show, they also made it possible to ground the Native Hawaiians to their land.

If we return to Lucy's speech in Excerpt (8), we can see that she does more than just express a distinction between types of people. With the statement, *'a'ohe po'e o laila* ("there are no people there") in line 6, she links the people to the land grammatically through the usage of the possessive construction *o*. The *o* is a grammatical marker that literally expresses that the *po'e* ("people") belong to *laila*, which is a pronoun ("there") that replaces the place mentioned earlier, Hālawa. The people are, from the perspective of the Hawaiian grammar, "of Hālawa."

Possession is heavily emphasized in the Hawaiian grammar and expressions of possessive relationships occur commonly in spoken Hawaiian interaction through a variety of grammatical markers. Lucy in fact employs another marker in line 11 that links the hippies to place of Hālawa. In her statement *he po'e hīpī, 'o ia ko laila i tēia manawa* ("the hippies, that is what is there at this time"), she uses the *ko* possessive, which directly links to *laila* ("there"), the place doing the possessing. A more literal translation for this statement in line 11 is that "there (Hālawa) is doing the possessing of them, the hippies." These two possessive markers as used by Lucy thus articulate a relationship that it is quite different from a western perspective; it is not necessarily people that possess the land but rather it is the land that is grammatically constructed as the possessor of the people, both the generic *po'e* and the *po'e hippie*. The people, in this sense, do not have control of the land. Instead, they belong to the land.

We can further emphasize this connection between land and the person by noting another aspect of possessive constructions in Hawaiian, namely that each marker, in this case *o* and *ko*, has an alternative, *a* and *kā*. This is referred to as the *kino'ō* and *kino'ā* distinction or the *o*-class and the *a*-class that depends on the "nature of the possession of the word" (Kamanā & Wilson, 2012: 160). Typically when Hawaiian speakers choose to use a possessive form, they must make a decision between the *o*-class or the *a*-class. In terms of meaning, the *a*-class "implies a human or animal owner, initiator or creator of something or some action" (Kamanā & Wilson, 2012: 161). An example would be *ka mea'ai a Kimo* (Kimo's food) that uses the possessive *a* to indicate that "the food" (*ka mea'ai*) belongs to and is controlled by Kimo. The *o*-class typically articulates a relationship not marked by control on the part of the possessor. As Kimura (1983: 183) explains, *o*-class typically represents a more "intimate" relationship: "the use of the O-class possessive markers here contrasts with the use of A-class possessive markers used with ordinary material good possessed by a person, and even hired hands, and spouses, who are treated as A-class and less intimately bound with one than O-class possessed items." The belonging of a person to the land would represent this type of intimate relationship defined by the *o*-class.

It also should be noted that an intimate relationship in which people naturally belong to the land is aligned with creation stories about the Native Hawaiians that emphasize the ancestral and genealogical relationship between Native Hawaiians and the land. According to the creation story of the Native Hawaiians, Wākea and Papa, the sky father and sky mother, mated and gave birth to the islands. As Kame'eleihiwa (1992) explains, Wākea also mated with their first daughter, Ho'ohōkūkalani, and their first child, an unformed fetus named Hāloanaka, was buried in land that then produced the first taro plant. Wākea and Ho'ohōkūkalani had a second child, named Hāloa after the first child, who is said to have been the first Hawaiian chief and the ancestor of all the Native Hawaiians. As summarized by Kame'eleihiwa (1992: 24), "The kalo plant, which was the main staple of the people of old, is also elder brother of the Hawaiian race." The land and the taro plant that come from the land and provide for the people all, in other words, exist in a very intimate relationship. Trask (1999: 59) expresses this relationship succintly by writing that "in our geneaology, Papahānaumoku 'earth mother,' mated with Wākea, 'sky father,' from whence came our islands, or *moku*. Out of our beloved islands came the taro, our immediate progenitor, and from the taro, our chiefs and people." From this perspective, it is possible to gain insight into a Hawaiian perspective that does not consider the land as an object under the control of people.

Hence, we may go back and suggest that these *o*-class and *a*-class possessives present another instance of language as a cultural practice given that speakers of Hawaiian employ them frequently to express a specific type of relationship in the Hawaiian perspective. In particular, the usage of the *o*-class between people and land allows for the expression of an intimate relationship that can construct the person as naturally belonging to the land. In addition to the interview with Lucy in Excerpt (8), we see that possessive constructions are employed regularly in the radio show database to express this intimate relationship. The two short excerpts (11) and (12) below present examples. In both excerpts, LK refers to the host of the program, Larry Kimura.

Excerpt (11): Ka Leo Hawai'i: Interview with Rachel Nāhale'elua Mahuiki (RM)

1 RM: *'O wau, 'ai i ka manō*
TM I eat O the shark
"As for me, I eat shark."

2 LK: *'Ai 'oe i ka manō*
eat you O the shark
"You eat shark?"

3 RM: *A 'o ko'u kahu hānai. Well kēia po'e, he 'ohana Hashimoto a no,*
and TM my adopted family this people family and PS
4 *no Kona nō kēia po'e. He, he Kepanī hapa a Hawai'i. Hele 'o ia*
PS Kona EP this people TM TM Japanese half and Hawaiian go s/he
5 *e kīloi laina mamake i ka ulua*
throw line want O the ulua

"And my adopted family, well these people, it was the Hashimoto family and These people were from, from Kona. The family was half Japanese and Hawaiian. He would go put his line in the water wanting to catch ulua."

Excerpt (12): Ka Leo Hawai'i: Interview with Irene Isaac Peters (IP)

1 IP: *A kāne 'elua, 'o ia nō 'o William Kinimakako'olua Peters*
and husband two it EP S
"And my second husband was William Kinimakako'olua Peters."
2 LK: *'Ae*
yes
"yes"
3 IP: *No Kaua'i nō 'o ia*
PS Kaua'i EP he
"He is from Kaua'i."
4 LK: *'Ō, no Kaua'i 'o ia. 'Ae he hapa Hawai'i?*
O PS Kaua'i he yes half Hawai'i
"Oh, he is from Kaua'i. Is he part Hawaiian?"

5 IP: *He hapa Hawai'i*

half Hawai'i

"(He is) part Hawaiian."

The speakers in these excerpts use a different possessive marker, the marker *no*, to express a relationship between people and the land. In Excerpt (11), RM states *no Kona nō kēia po'e* ("these people are from Kona") in line 4 and in Excerpt (12), IP remarks *no Kaua'i nō 'o ia* ("he is from Kaua'i") in line 3, which LK then repeats in line 4. Like the *o* and *ko* possessives discussed earlier, *no* also has an *a*-class variant, *na*. Yet, given the intimate relationship between people and land in the Hawaiian perspective, *no*, the *o*-class variant, is used to indicate that the people belong to those places, Kona in Excerpt (11) and Kaua'i in Excerpt (12). And even though the English translations seem relatively innocuous with "these people are from Kona" and "He is from Kaua'i," the use of the *o*-class possessive in *no* indicates that this is a very intimate relationship that anchors people to their homelands. In fact, one of the actions accomplished early in most of the interviews on LK's radio show is to employ these possessive constructions to connect the interviewee to their homes, an action which typically provides the host LK and the listening audience with much information about the interviewee's family, mutual acquaintances they might have, and the surroundings in which the interviewee grew up. The usage of possessives to anchor people thus constructs and reinforces a Native Hawaiian identity that is constituted by an intimate relationship with the land.

Not only do these two excerpts provide examples anchoring a Hawaiian identity in the land, but they also make use of the cultural practice of employing person categories in support of the anchoring process. Directly after RM links her adopted family to the place of Kona in line 4 of Excerpt (11), she next employs the two categories *Kepanī hapa* ("part Japanese") and *Hawai'i* (Hawaiian) to describe the family. This is important first of all because it establishes that the topic in question, which is that RM eats shark, has origins in a practice by a Native Hawaiian person. After stating through line 5 that her adopted family from Kona went fishing for ulua, a common practice for Native

Hawaiians, she then went on to report, in a segment not included in the transcript, that they ended up catching and eating a shark. Eating a shark is an unusual practice and it was greeted with surprise from the host LK, but it all stemmed from a traditional Hawaiian fishing practice, fishing for ulua. RM's categories in Excerpt (11) diverge slightly from previous examples in her usage of the term *Kepanī hapa* ("half" or "part-Japanese") and in her assignment of multiple categories to a single family (Part Japanese and Hawaiian). Yet, in this divergence, RM's categorization still very much serves as a cultural practice for dealing with a changing society that came to feature the mixture of ethnicities over the year. The combination of *kepanī hapa* and *Hawai'i* does not make the practice of fishing for ulua any less Hawaiian nor does it diminish the importance of the practice of using possessives to constitute people as belonging to the land. It still works as a cultural practice that grounds the fishing for ulua to a Hawaiian family that is from a particular place, Kona.

Excerpt (12) shows a similar relationship with LK's question in line 4 *he hapa Hawai'i?* ("is he part Hawaiian") and IP's affirmative response in line 5 *he hapa Hawai'i* ("he is part Hawaiian"). Later in the interview, the host LK establishes that he is also *hapa haole* ("part haole"), but this does not take away from the fact that IP's second husband is anchored to a place through the possessive *no Kaua'i* ("from Kaua'i"). The inclusion of the modifier *hapa* represents the evolution of the cultural practice of employing person categories in a changing society.

The examples thus far have shown a specific example of possessives being used to construct people as belonging to the land, but possessive constructions do more than just anchor people to the land in the Hawaiian perspective. They also allow speakers of Hawaiian to attribute different characteristics and features to the land, thus demonstrating the dynamic view which speakers of Hawaiian adopt toward their lands. Excerpt (13) offers an example.

Excerpt (13): Ka Leo Hawai‘i: Interview with Abigail Kāka‘e Kaleihana (AKK)

1	AKK:	*Kēlā wahi he wahi nani kēla ma mua* That place place beautiful that before "That place, it was a beautiful place before"
2	LK:	*[‘Ae* Yes "Yes"
3	AKK:	*[Like pū ‘o ia me kīhāpai ‘o Ekena* Like also it with garden Eden "It is also like the Garden of Eden"
4	LK:	*A:[:* Ah "Ah"
5	AKK:	*[Nui nā mea ulu nui nui nā i‘a nā hua‘ai nā mea like ‘ole a pau* Many PL thing grow big many PL fish PL fruits PL thing various all
6		*nui kona nani* Many PS beautiful "A lot of things growing big, a lot of fish, fruits, many various things It has lots of beauty"

This excerpt begins as AKK in line 1 states that the place in question was a beautiful place before. With support from the host LK in line 2, AKK continues in line 3 to note that it is "like the Garden of Eden." AKK then adds further details concerning its beauty in line 5, including lots of things growing, plenty of fish, and numerous fruits, before using a *ko* possessive in the third person to state *nui kona nani* ("it possesses much beauty"). Through the usage of the possessive form, the land is formulated as not just being beautiful but as being the possessor of the beauty. The usage of the *o*-class of possessor shows how this relationship of the land to its beauty is expressed as an intimate relationship.

There are further examples of attributions of possession to place later in the same interview. Excerpt (14), slightly longer the previous excerpts, contains several examples of possessive forms and makes a further point about the relationship between people and the land.

Excerpt (14): Ka Leo Hawai‘i: Interview with Abigail Kāka‘e Kaleihana (AKK)

1 LK: *‘O kēia awāwa o Waimea ma ka pilikai ‘elua ona lae ea*
TM this harbor PS Waimea at the sea shore two PS points right
“As for this harbor of Waimea, it has two points by the shore, right”
2 AKK: *ea?*
right?
“right?”
3 LK: *‘O Waimea ‘elua ona lae ma kekahi ‘ao‘[ao (*) ‘ao‘ao ‘ae*
TM Waimea two PS points at one side side yes
“As for Waimea, there are two points on one side”
4 AKK: *[ō ‘ae ma kekahi ‘ao‘ao ‘ae ‘ae =*
Oh yes at one side yes yes
“Oh, yes, on one side, yes, yes”
5 LK: *= He inoa nō nō ko kēia mau lae ‘elua*
Name EP EP PS this PL points two
“Do these two points have names?”
6 AKK: *I ko‘u mana‘o he inoa nō (.) but ‘a‘ohe ke ‘ano nō ho‘i o ko kākou po‘e (.)*
In PS idea name EP no the type EP EP PS PS we people
7 *‘a‘ole lākou wala‘au nui i ka wā kahiko*
Not they speak a lot at the time old

“I think they had names (.) but no, the way of our people
“They did not do a lot of talking in the olden times”
8 LK: *‘ē*
Yes
“yes”
9 AKK: *‘Ano hūnā nō ke ‘ano o nā kūpuna o ka wā ma mua*
Bit hide EP the type PS PL elders PS the time at before
“The way they were was they tended to hide things before”
10 LK: *‘Ae*
Yes
“yes”
11 AKK: *Inā ‘oe nīele ‘ōlelo mai he aha kāu e nīele mai nei*
If you ask say D what PS ask D
“If you ask them, they would just say what are you being so nosy about?”

12 LK: *hehehe*
13 AKK: *No laila nele ihola ʻoe i ka ʻike a kekahi manawa hoʻolōlō ʻoe kohu mea lā*
So lack D you the info and sometimes lie still you as if
14 *E hiamoe ana a hoʻomaka kēia poʻe e walaʻau a i ka walaʻau ʻana*
Sleeping and begin this people to speak and the speak NOM
15 *lohe kou pepeiao*
Hear PS ears

"So sometimes you would not have any information but sometimes you could lie still as if you are sleeping and these people would start speaking and your ears would hear"

16 LK: *hm:*
Hm
"Hm"
17 AKK: *Manaʻo ʻia ua hiamoe ʻoe ʻaʻ ole e hoʻolohe ana ʻoe i kā lākou mea*
Think PAS PST sleep you not listening you O PS they thing
18 *e walaʻau ai (.) ʻae ʻo ia ka pilikia o nā kūpuna ʻaʻole lākou i hāhaʻi mai*

Speak yes it the problem PS PL elders not they PST say D

"It was though that went to sleep and were not listening to what they were saying (.) yes, that was the problem with the elders, they did not just tell"

19 LK: *hm pehea kēia āu i ʻōlelo mai nei ma mua ʻo ka lae ʻo ka lae o ka ʻīlio*
Hm how this PS PST say D at before S the point S the point PS the dog
"Hm, how did you say it before, it is the point of the dog"
20 AKK: *ee ʻo ka lae o ka ʻīlio ʻo ia kēlā ma ka ʻaoʻao pūpūkea*
Yes S the point PS the dog S that on the side Pūpūkea
"Yes the point of the dog, this is, that is on the Pūpūkea side"

21	LK:	*a:* Ah "ah"
22	AKK:	*'o ia kona inoa ka lae o ka 'īlio* S PS name the point PS the dog "That is its name, the point of the dog"

In the very first line of this excerpt, LK asks a question that contains two *o*-class possessives, the harbor (*awāwa*) is constructed as possessed by the place name of Waimea (*awāwa o Waimea*) and then the harbor itself possesses "two points" (*'elua ona lae*). The phrase *'elua ona lae* employs the third person *o* possessive *ona.* After AKK confirms in line 4 that there are indeed these two points on one side (*kekahi 'ao'ao*), LK employs a *ko* possessive in line 5 to ask if the two points have names (*he inoa nō ko kēia mau lae 'elua?*). This *ko* possessive expresses the name as belonging to the point (*lae*). AKK begins a rather lengthy response that extends from line 6–18 in order to account for why it is difficult for her to come up with a straightforward answer. She explains the tendency of the elder Native Hawaiians around her when she was younger not to divulge much information. Lines 6–18 do not feature possessive forms related to place, but they do consist of several examples of possessive constructions, thus showing how important they are in Hawaiian language expression. AS AKK begins her account in line 6, she uses two *ko* possessives in line 6; she first states that *i ko'u mana'o* (literally, "in my idea"), and then she also notes that *ke 'ano nō ho'i o ko kākou po'e* ("the way of our people"). Likewise, there are two *o* possessives in line 9 as she notes that *'ano hūnā nō ke 'ano o nā kūpuna o ka wā ma mua* ("the way of our elders of olden times was to keep things hidden"). With an *o* before *nā kūpuna* ("elders"), the elders are possessing their particular way (*ke 'ano*), and with the other *o* before *wā ma mua* ("olden times"), this time frame is constructed as the possessor of AKK's elders (*nā kūpuna*). AKK also employs an *a* possessive in line 17 as a part of stating *kā lākou mea e wala'au ai* (literally, "their thing to talk about"), and then, soon after AKK finishes her account in line 18, which ends without an answer to the question about the name of the point, LK employs an *o* possessive in line 19 to note that AKK had suggested before that the name of one of the points is *'o ka lae o ka 'īlio* (literally, "the point of the dog"). The *o* possessive in this phrase constructs the point as belonging to the dog. AKK confirms this in line 20 and then adds in line 22, through a *ko* possessive that is the name of the point (*'o ia kona inoa*). This *ko* possessive places the name as belonging to the point.

There thus appears to be a bit of a paradoxical relationship expressed in this excerpt; possessive markers construct the name of *'o ka lae o ka 'īlio* ("the point of the dog") as belonging to the point (*'o ia kona inoa* "the place's name"), but the name itself uses an *o* possessive to construct the point as belonging to the dog. Yet, I would argue that it is not in fact a paradox; characteristics such as names and beauty belong to places, but places can also be constructed as belonging to other things, including dogs (and also people). Instead, it indicates that the relationship between the land and living organisms is a reciprocal relationship; places possess features and characteristics that include living organisms such as people and animals and people and animals also possess places. Excerpt (15), which comes from the same interview with AKK, provides another example.

Excerpt (15): Ka Leo Hawai'i: Interview with Abigail Kāka'e Kaleihana (AKK)

1	LK:	*A 'o kēia kahuna 'o Hewahewa n- no no O'ahu 'o ia* And S this priest S Hewahewa PS PS O'ahu he "And this priest, Hewahewa, he is from O'ahu?"
2	AKK:	*No Kohala 'o ia* PS Kohala he "He is from Kohala."
3	LK:	*A::* Ah "Ah"
4	AKK:	*No Kohala kēlā kanaka (.5) no kou ' āina, no Hawai'i* PS Kohala that person PS your land PS Hawai'i "That person is from Kohala (.5) from your land, from Hawai'i"
5	LK:	*'Ae* Yes "yes"

6 AKK: *Kohala kona one hānau kēlā*
Kohala PS birth place that
"Kohala, that is his birth place"

After mentioning the priest by his name of Hewahewa in line, LK employs the *no* possessive in line 1 to ask if he is from the island of O'ahu. AKK responds in line 2 by stating, once again with a *no* possessive that he is from Kohala. After a short reaction from LK in line 3, AKK repeats the *no* possessive in line 4 to restate that "that person" (*kēlā kanaka*) is from Kohala, and following a short pause, she notes that he, the priest Hewahewa, is *no kou 'āina, no Hawai'i* ("from your land, from Hawai'i"). In this last phrase, she invokes the information that the host LK is from the Hawaiian island that is known by the name "Hawai'i," where Kohala is located. Hence, the priest Hewahewa is from the same island as the host LK. Note though, that this statement *no kou 'āina, no Hawai'i* at the end of line 4 is very rich in that it contains three separate possessives, two *no* and one *ko* (realized through the form *kou*). The *kou 'āina* part of this statement constructs LK as the possessor of the land (literally, it is "your land"), but the addition of the *no* at the beginning also makes the *'āina* as the possessor of the original referent, namely Hewahewa. In other words, Hewahewa is anchored to the same land that, according to the *ko* construction, is possessed by the host LK. After LK agrees in line 5, KK utters another possessive in line 6, *Kohala kona one hānau* ("Kohala is his birth place"), which frames the birthplace of Kohala as belonging to the priest Hewahewa. The possessive forms in this excerpt, then, seem to simultaneously anchor the participants in their places and also make them the possessors of the places as well.

Possession from a western perspective tends to be conceived as a one-way relationship. People possess something, such as land, not typically the other way around. However, these excerpts seem to suggest a view toward possession that is much more reciprocal. In the case of place, people are conceived of belonging to their land which also becomes a part of them, making it possible to employ grammatical markers to express possession as a two-way street. This fits with the Hawaiian view that does not treat land as a commodity owned by people. In the Hawaiian perspective, "the land is not viewed as a commodity; it is the foundation of their cultural and spiritual identity as Hawaiians ... The land is part of their 'ohana ('family') and they care for it as they do the other living members of their families" (McGregor et al., 2003: 107). Thus, people belong to their *'āina* ("land"), but the land also becomes part of them and their *'ohana* ("family"), which results in a reciprocal relationship from the view of belonging and possession.

With the onset of the American colonial agenda, Native Hawaiians were separated from their language and their land, occurrences that have been detrimental to the native population both mentally and physically. This separation from the land made it difficult to maintain this reciprcal relationship of belonging. However, the revitalization of the Hawaiian language brings with it usages of person categories such as *kanaka* and *kanaka maoli* for reasserting a Native Hawaiian identity and it also brings usage of possessive constructions that have the potential to reinforce and re-emphasize a Native Hawaiian identity that is grounded in a reciprocal relationship between people and the land. These aspects of the Hawaiian language represent cultural practices, I would argue, that, with increased usage, have healing power in that they allow Native Hawaiians to rediscover, re-explore, and reinforce through their language this crucial relationship between a Native Hawaiian identity and the land.

3.4 A New Generation of Hawaiians Speakers

As the last section of analysis for this chapter, I turn the focus to younger speakers of Hawaiian language in order to gain insight into whether they are using language, especially possessive constructions, in a way that is similar to the since deceased *mānaleo* who were documented on the radio shows and in the olden Hawaiian language newspapers. I do this because of a question about the "authenticity" of the speech of younger speakers of the language, many of whom grew up speaking primarily English and did not begin their study of Hawaiian until after English was already established as their primary language. This type of speaker fits the category of "new speakers," about which O Murchadha et al. (2018: 11) writes, "the circumstances through which new speakers acquire their new languages and the linguistic varieties that they practice can be considered deficient by native speakers and even by new speakers themselves."

Indeed, this category of "new speakers" is potentially relevant to the Hawaiian revitalization situation. NeSmith (2005, 2019) has made a distinction between Type-1 and Type-2 speakers, with Type-2 speakers using a language termed "neo-Hawaiian" that is qualitatively different from Type-1 speakers who learn the language traditionally in the home. Referring to the relatively small community of Hawaiian speakers from the island of Ni'ihau, which was able to maintain intergenerational transmission, NeSmith notes that although Type-1 speakers still exist in Hawai'i, the revitalization movement tends to center on the language of Type-2 speakers. In his words, (NeSmith, 2019: 94), "virtually every teacher in the classroom today teaching new learners is a Type-2. While Type-1s diminish in the era of revitalization, Type-2s have quickly risen in political influence and far outnumber Type-1s." Further exacerbating the divide between the two types, according to NeSmith, is that the Type-2 teachers "frequently create new words that are foreign to Type-1s, and Ni'ihau speakers find many, if not all of these new words strange" (NeSmith, 2019: 104). NeSmith is not alone in his concern; Higgins (2019) also notes that "most speakers of Hawaiian today qualify as *new speakers*" (emphasis in original) and she does so in reporting interviews with learners of Hawaiian in which many of them made a distinction between a form of language referred to as "university Hawaiian" and the language spoken by their ancestors.

These concerns posed by NeSmith (2005, 2019) and Higgins (2019) should be taken seriously and serve as a reminder that there were in the past and continue to be different ways of speaking Hawaiian. As these various ways of speaking (re)emerge through the revitalization movement, it will certainly behoove the leaders of the movement to make concerted efforts to be as inclusive as possible in their work. Nonetheless, I have in earlier research (Saft, 2019) suggested that the language of the so-called new speakers of Hawaiian seems to follow, in at least some respects, the cultural patterns exhibited in the speech of elders who spoke Hawaiian prior to the disruption of intergenerational transmission. Following the work of Wong (2006, 2011), who suggests that "indirection is the norm when it comes to pointing at grammatical agents (Wong, 2011: 153)" and that "overt indication of an individul ... can often engender feelings of discomfort..." (Wong, 2011: 159), I examined the speech of new speakers featured in short video clips on the website of the media initiative ʻŌiwi TV in terms of expressions of agency and concluded that the new speakers in the video clips "are employing similar types of indirection in their expression of agency as the traditional speakers, an observation which suggests that current speakers of Hawaiian are preserving, at least in the expression of agency, a traditional perspective in their speech" (Saft, 2019: 88–89). In this section, I engage in a similar activity, this time focusing on the expression of possession by young speakers of Hawaiian.

Like my previous research, I examined video clips made available on ʻŌiwi TV, and for this analysis concentrate on a set of Hawaiian language speech contests featuring students at the Hawaiian medium schools that were held in 2018 and 2019. More specifically, the analysis focuses on speeches made by students in grades 6–8, which typically covers ages 12–14. There is no data available concerning the length of time the participants in the speech contests had been attending Hawaiian medium schools, but it is now quite typical for students to begin at the pre-kindergarten level and continue in Hawaiian medium education through the junior and high school. On the one hand, it is possible that some of these participants were raised with parents who speak Hawaiian and thus may fall in the category of "new native speaker" (Brenzinger & Heinrich, 2013), and, on the other hand, it is possible that they receive most of their Hawaiian language input in classrooms taught primarily by Type-2 speakers mentioned by NeSmith (2019), which may indicate that they themselves fall into the category of Type-2. Either way, they are youth educated through Hawaiian and thus represent the next generation of Hawaiian speakers.

Speeches contests are not, to be sure, representative of the conversational ability of the young speakers given that prior to presentation, the participants have had the opportunity to receive assistance from teachers, parents, and other mentors, and then to practice and also memorize their speeches. Still, though, the speeches serve as examples of some of the linguistic structures and cultural ideas (many of the speeches consist of the participants explaining some aspect of what the Hawaiian language means to them) that are either being taught explicitly or at least emphasized as part of their education. The speeches may, in other words, be idealized versions of the actual competence of the students, but they still employ the language and cultural patterns that are constitutive of their educational experience.

The first observation based on the data is that the young participants employed the *ko* and *o* possessives on a regular basis in their speeches. Excerpt (16) provides an example.[10]

Excerpt (16): 2018 Speech Contest

1 *I ka wā kahiko loa, ua pililoa ko kākou kūpuna i kā kākou ʻōlelo aloha me he ipo lā*
2 *ʻAʻohe aʻu ipo akā ʻike no au i ke aloha ʻōlelo. A hōʻike nō au i ke aloha ʻōlelo*
3 *ma koʻu ʻohana a me ka hale no ka mea ʻōlelo Hawaiʻi mākou ma nā wahi*
4 *like ʻole a i nā manawa a pau. ʻōlelo Hawaiʻi pū mākou i kā mākou mau*
5 *ʻīlio. A ʻōlelo Hawaiʻi mākou ma nā kūʻono ʻeha o ko mākou hale.*

"In olden times, our elders had a close relationship with our beloved language, almost like lovers. I myself do not have a lover, but I know about love for language. And I show my love for the language in my family and at my house because we speak the language together in all places at all times. We also speak the language to our dog. And we speak the language in all four corners of our house."

In line 1, the speaker uses two *ko* possessives, one *o*-class form in *ko kākou kūpuna* ("our elders") and one *a*-class form in *kā kākou ʻōlelo* ("our language"), to express that "our elders" had a close relationship with "our language." She next employs in line 2 an *a*-class form of the *o* possessive when she utters *aʻu ipo* for "my lover," and she also provides another *kā* in line 4 as a part of noting that she and her family speak Hawaiian to "our dog." Finally, she provides one further *o* and *ko* possessive in line 5

[10]The speech contest from 2018 is available at http://oiwi.tv/oiwitv/la-kukahekahe-2018-mahele-1-2/ and the contest from 2019 can be found at https://www.youtube.com/watch?v=YnRUX6zZ85U&t=351s.

when she emphasizes that her family speaks Hawaiian in all four corners of their house, with the *o* possessive signifying that the four corners belong to the house and the *ko* possessive making it clear that it is "our house."

Excerpt (16) is representative of the speeches in the data in that it uses several *o*-class and *a*-class possessives according to the situation. It was, in fact, quite common for the young speech makers to refer to "my" or "our family" (*ko'u* or *ko mākou 'ōhana*), our language (*kā kākou 'ōlelo*), and our elders (*ko kākou kūpuna*) as they made impassioned speeches about preserving "our" Hawaiian language that was spoken by "our" elders so that they can speak in "our homes" with "our families." In addition, the possessive forms used in line 5 demonstrate that this presenter has a good handle on the complexity of possessive forms in Hawaiian as she combines an *o* and a *ko* possessive at the end of the excerpt to simultaneously attribute possession of the four corners to the house and possession of the house to her family. Yet, while the speaker's possessives do attribute possession of the four corners to the house, there is no place in her speech that she anchors people to the land. This may be a product of the particular topic of her presentation, but it is striking that in the content of the two speech contests examined for this analysis there were not many examples of possessives used to connect people to place and land. Excerpt (17) offers another example.

Excerpt (17): 2019 Speech Contest

1 *I kēia lā e pane ana au i ka nīnau inā ho'i mai 'o Kamehameha i kēia lā a 'ike 'o*
2 *ia i ka 'āina, ka lāhui, a me ka 'ōlelo pehea kona na'au a he aha kona mau*
3 *mana'o...Inā 'ike 'o ia i ka 'āina, e hūhu ana 'o ia no ka mea inā hiki iā mākou ke*
4 *'ike kekahi o nā kānaka Hawai'i, 'ike mākou i nā 'ōpala akā 'a'ole mākou kea*
5 *waiho mākou ma ka 'ao'ao 'a'ole mākou e kiloi. Aia ka 'ōpala ma 'ō a kiloi lākou*
6 *akā 'a'ole i hele i loko o ke kini 'ōpala a waiho lākou 'a'ole kēlā nā po'e haole*

7 *wale nō kēlā nā po'e Hawai'i, 'o kēlā mākou, 'a'ole maika'i kēlā, e hūhu loa ana*
8 *'o ia*

> "Today I am going to answer the question about if Kamehameha returned today and saw the land, the Hawaiian people, and the language, how would he feel in his heart and what would be some of his thoughts... If he saw the land, he would be angry because if we could look at some of the Hawaiian people, we would see the garbage but we do not care, we leave it on the side, we do not throw it away. The garbage over there and they just throw it there but it does not get inside of a garbage can, and they just leave it. That is not just the haole people but also the Hawaiian people, that's us, it is not good, he would be angry."

This speaker begins in the first two lines by explaining that she is going to answer the question concerning how King Kamehameha, the king who unified the islands, would feel if he returned and saw modern Hawai'i. In doing so she uses two *ko* possessives in line two to refer to "his feelings" (*kona na'au*) and "his ideas" (*kona mau mana'o*). She then speaks specifically about the land in lines 3–7 and how Kamehameha might be angry if he saw people just throwing garbage on the land. She does employ an *o* possessive in line six to link the inside to the garbage can (*i loko o ke kīni 'ōpala*), and she also distinguishes two categories of people, the Native Hawaiians (*nā kānaka Hawai'i* in line 4 and *ka po'e Hawai'i* in line 7) and the "haole" (*nā po'e haole* in line 6), but she does not use any possessives to anchor the people in the land. Given her usage of category terms to draw a distinction between the Native Hawaiians and the haole, this might have been an opportunity for her to employ possessive markers to emphasize in some way that the Native Hawaiians are the ones who are anchored to the land.

Yet, while speakers did not use many possessives in the content of their speeches to present the land as a possessor, there was one part of the speeches in which the young speech givers frequently demonstrate awareness of the traditional practice of attributing possession to the land, namely, the sometimes poetic beginnings of their speeches in which they greet the audience and introduce themselves. Excerpt (18) provides an example.

Excerpt (18): 2019 Speech Contest

1 *Mai ka ua kanilehua o Hilo a i ka moena pawehe o Ni'ihau, 'ano'ai me ke*
2 *aloha kākou*

"From the soft mistlike rain of Hilo to the spotted mats of Ni'ihau, warm greetings to us all."

With two *o* possessives in line 1, this speech giver attributes the "soft mistlike rain" (*ka ua kanilehua*) to Hilo, which is a town on the Big Island of Hawai'i, and then constructs "the spotted mats" (*moena pawehe*) as belonging to Ni'ihau, which, as mentioned above, is one of the islands that makes up Hawai'i. After constructing the two places of Hilo and Ni'ihau as possessors, the speech giver then offers the main greeting *'ano'ai me ke aloha kākou* ("warm greetings to us all") to the audience.

This type of organization, where a speech giver leads with poetic language that often attributes possession to places in Hawai'i, is a very common way to start formal speeches in Hawaiian and was present in some form or another in all of the presentations. The next four excerpts, all taken from the very beginning of the speeches, provide examples. The possessive markers and the lands they construct as possessors are underlined in each excerpt.

Excerpt (19): 2018 Speech Contest

1 *Mai ka mauna 'o Hualalai i ke kai malino o Kona, Welina mai me ke aloha*
2 *kākou*

"From the mountain named Hualalai to the calm seas of Kona, Warm greetings to us all."

Excerpt (20): 2019 Speech Contest

1 *'Auhea 'oukou e nā kama nā mamo a me nā mamaka kaua o Hawai'i nei, mai ka*
2 *mokupuni 'o Hawai'i a i ka moku 'o Ni'ihau. Welina mai me ke aloha kākou.*

"Listen all of you, the children, the descendants, the bearers of the fight of this place here in Hawai'i, from the island of Hawai'i to the island of Ni'ihau, warm greetings to us all."

Excerpt (21): 2018 Speech Contest

1 *Welina mai kākou e nā hoamakamaka o ka 'ōlelo mākuahine, na kūpuna, nā*
2 *mākua, a me nā keiki o nei 'āina 'o Hawai'i, aloha*

"Greetings to us all, close friends of the mother language, the elders, the parents, and the children of this land of Hawai'i, greetings."

Excerpt (22): 2018 Speech Contest

1 *Welina mai e nā pua a me nā kama o nei mau mokupuni 'O Hawai'i nei*
2 *No Keaukaha mai au*

"Greetings to the flowers and the children of these islands here of Hawai'i. I am from Keaukaha."

Excerpts (19)–(22) are all similar in that the *o* possessive is used attribute possession to the land. In (19) it is Kona, a place on the Big Island of Hawai'i, that possesses the calm seas (*kai malino*). Excerpts (20)–(22) are all similar in that they construct types of people as belonging specifically to Hawai'i. Excerpt (20) asks first that the listeners all listen (*'auhea 'oukou*) before specifying that she is referring specifically to the "children" (*nā kama*), the "descendants" (*nā mamo*), and the "bearers of the fight" (*mamaka kaua*) who belong to this place of Hawai'i (*Hawai'i nei*). Excerpt (21) uses *o* to construct "close friends of the mother tongue" (*nā hoamakamaka o ka 'ōlelo makuahine*), the "elders" (*nā kūpuna*), the "parents" (*nā mākua*), and the "children" (*nā keiki)* as belonging to "this land here of Hawai'i" (*nei 'āina 'o Hawai'i*). And, finally, Excerpt (22) works similarly by anchoring the flowers (*nā pua*) and the children (*nā kama*) to "these islands here of Hawai'i" (*nei mau mokupuni 'O Hawai'i nei*). Additionally, Excerpt (22) shows the speech giver employing the *no* possessive to anchor himself to the land of Keaukaha. These four excerpts suggest that the young speech givers are learning, at least in the poetic language at the beginning, to employ possessives to anchor people to land in Hawai‘i.

Moreover, this section of the analysis has focused primarily on possessives, but it is apparent that in the various Hawaiian language terminology to refer to the people about whom they are speaking, including *kama* ("children"), *mamo* ("descendants"), *mamaka kaua* ("bearers of the fight"), *hoamakamaka* ("close friends"), *kūpuna* ("elders"), *mākua* ("parents"), *keiki* ("children"), and *pua* ("flowers"), the young speakers are also demonstrating an ability to employ person categories that refer to Native Hawaiians. None of these person categories specific ethnicity in the terms themselves, but it is arguable that they all, like *kanaka* and *po‘e,* are used specifically in this case to refer to Native Hawaiians. Especially, given that these are Hawaiian speeches about Hawaiian topics, there is a strong reason to suggest that the speech givers are using possessive constructions to anchor these categories of Native Hawaiians to their Hawaiian lands.

Excerpt (23) provides one final example of a speech giver employing a person category as well as a *no* and an *o* possessive to construct herself as belonging to the land.

Excerpt (23): Speech Contest 2018

1 *Welina mai kākou. ‘O kēia ka wā no ka noelo huliau no ka ho‘ohuli mana‘o. Eia*
2 *au he wahine o ke kai mā‘oki‘oki no Kainalu ma ka Moku o Keawe a me ke kai*
3 *loaloa o Kaluawehe ma O‘ahu nei... Ola ka ‘ōlelo Hawai‘i ma ka ‘āina o ko‘u*
4 *mau kūpuna ma ku‘u kulaiwi nei*

"Greetings to us all. This is the time to seek a turning point for changing perspectives. Here I am a woman of the sea striped with colors from Kainalu on the Island of Keawe and the long seas of Kaluawehe here on O‘ahu... The Hawaiian language lives on the land of my elders on my homeland."

In line 1, she begins with the greeting *welina mai kākou* "greetings to us all." Then after stating that it is time to find a turning point in order to change perspectives, she employs in line 2 an *o* possessive directly followed by *no* to state she is a woman who belongs to "the sea striped with colors" (*wahine o ke kai mā'oki'oki*) and who is from the place called Kainalu on the Big Island, here referred to by its poetic name *Moku o Keawe*. Next, after adding the additive conjunction "and" (*a me*) at the end of line 2, she then further constructs herself as belonging to the long seas of Kaluawehe on the island of O'ahu. There is no explanation about how she belongs to two separate places, but then, at the end of line 3, she uses another *o* possessive to indicate a reciprocal relationship where it is not just places that possess people but also people that possess the land. She does this through line 4 by invoking the person category of *kūpuna* with the expression *ola ka 'ōlelo Hawai'i ma ka 'āina o ko'u mau kūpuna ma ku'u kulaiwi nei* ("the Hawaiian language lives in the land of my ancestors on my homeland") that, through the usage of one *o* possessive and one *ko* possessive, attributes the land to "my" (*ko'u*) "elders."

In this brief introduction to her speech, then, the speaker in Excerpt (23) has used possessive markers and a person category to express a relationship in which the land is both the possessor and the one being possessed. To be sure, the speech giver in Excerpt (23) may employ possessives in a more complex manner than some of the other speech contest participants, but the analysis in this section shows that the younger speakers are learning how to use Hawaiian possessives and person categories from a traditional perspective, at least in formal speeches. If younger speakers are encouraged to follow elder native speakers and employ possessives and person categories to anchor themselves, like their elders did, to the land, then there is hope that future generations of Hawaiian speakers will rediscover the ability to ground a Native Hawaiian identity in this reciprocal relationship between people and the land.

3.5 Conclusion

After showing how the Hawaiian revitalization movement has been growing through a set of interlocked educational structures, the analysis in this chapter then presented two news clips that demonstrated how difficult it has been for the Hawaiian language to gain equal access in public domains. The analysis next concentrated on the usage in context of two aspects of the Hawaiian language, person categories and possessives, in order to emphasize that the revitalization of Hawaiian has the potential to allow speakers to regain a deep connection among a Native Hawaiian identity, language, and land. This is, of course, not to say that language is the only way to experience this relationship as there are many Native Hawaiians not closely involved in the revitalization movement who currently live off of and work with the land. Still, one of the main points of the analysis is that the Hawaiian language consists of grammatical features, particularly possessives, that present "natural resources" for the construction and reinforcement of a relationship between humans and land that goes beyond the typical possessive relationship expressed from a western perspective. However, despite the gains made within society, Native Hawaiians will not be able to employ their language freely and fully until Hawaiian is granted more access in public domains of society. Should Native Hawaiians be allowed to employ the Indigenous Hawaiian language freely within society, they will surely be able, as the analyses in this chapter suggests, to continue to rediscover and to further explore their relationship with their homeland.

References

Billig, M. (2008). The language of critical discourse analysis: The case of nominalization. *Discourse & Society, 19*(6), 783–800.

Brenzinger, M., & Heinrich, P. (2013). The return of Hawaiian: Language networks of the revival movement. *Current Issues in Language Planning, 14* (2), 300–316.

Charlot, J. (2005). *Classical Hawaiian education: Generations of culture.* The Pacific Institute.

Cowell, A. (2012). The Hawaiian model of language revitalization: Problems of extension to mainland native America. *International Journal of the Sociology of Language, 218,* 167–193.

Fishman, J. (1991). *Reversing language shift.* Multilingual Matters.

Higgins, C. (2019). The dynamics of Hawaiian speakerhood in the family. *International Journal of the Sociology of Language, 255,* 45–72.

Kamanā, K., & Wilson, W. H. (2012). *Nā Kai 'Ewalu: Beginning Hawaiian lessons*. Hale Kuamo'o.

Kame'eleihiwa, L. (1992). *Native land and foreign desires: Pehea lā e Pono ai*. Bishop Museum Press.

Kawai'ae'a, K., Housman, A., & Alencastre, M. (2007). Pū'ā i ka 'ōlelo, ola ka 'ohana: Three generations of Hawaiian language revitalization. *Multidisciplinary Research on Hawaiian Well-Being, 4*, 183–237.

Kimura, L. (1983). The Hawaiian language. In *Native Hawaiians study commission: Report on the culture, needs, and concerns of native Hawaiians* (pp. 173–224). Department of Interior.

Lomawaina, K. T., & McCarty, T. (2006). *To remain an Indian: Lessons in demoncracy from a century of Native American education*. Teachers College Columbia University.

McCarty, T. L. (2008). Schools as strategic tools for indigenous language revitalization: lessons from native America. In N. Hornberger (Ed.), *Can schools save indigenous languages? Policy and practice on four continents* (pp. 161–179). Palgrave Macmillan.

McGregor, D. P., Morella, P., Matsuoka, J., Rodenhurst, R., Kong, N., & Spencer, M. (2003). An ecological model of Native Hawaiian well-being. *Pacific Health Dialog, 10*(2), 106–128.

O Murchadha, N. P., Hornsby, M., Smith-Christmas, C., & Moriarty, M. (2018). New speakers, familiar concepts. In C. Smith-Christmas, N. P. O. Murchadha, M. Hornsby, & M. Moriarty (Eds.), *New speakers of minority languages: Linguistic ideologies & practices* (pp. 1–22). Palgrave Macmillan.

NeSmith, K. (2005). Tutu's Hawaiian and the emergence of a Neo-Hawaiian language. *'Ōiwi, 3*, 68–76.

NeSmith, K. (2019). Take my word: Mahalo no i to'u matua tane. In R. Asensio (Ed.), *Old Kava in new gourds: Language revitalization and schooling in Hawaii* (pp. 93–112).

Nicholas, S. (2008). *Becoming "fully" Hopi: The role of the Hopi language in the contemporary lives of Hopi youth—A Hopi case study of language shift and vitality* (Unpublished dissertation). American Indian Studies.

Nicholas, S. (2018). Practicing living and being Hopi: Language and cultural practices of contemporary Hopi youth. In G. Wigglesworth, J. Simpson, & J. Vaughan (Eds.), *Language practices of indigenous children and youth* (pp. 303–336). Palgrave Macmillan.

Rohrer, J. (2010). *Haoles in Hawai'i*. University of Hawai'i Press.

Saft, S. (2019). *Exploring multilingual Hawai'i: Language use and language ideologies in a diverse society*. Lexington Books.
Silva, N. (2017). *The power of the steel-tipped pen: Reconstructing native Hawaiian intellectual history*. Duke University Press.
Trask, H. K. (1999). *From a native daughter: Colonialism and sovereignty in Hawai'i*. Latitude 20 Books.
Unvar, S., & Rahimi, A. (2013). A critical discourse analysis of discursive structures in a political text. *International Journal of Science and Advanced Technology, 3*(3), 12–20.
Van Dijk, T. (1993). Principles of critical discourse analysis. *Discourse & Society, 4*(2), 249–283.
Van Dijk, T. (1995). Aims of critical discourse analysis. *Japanese Discourse, 1*, 17–27.
Wilson, W. H. (1998a). The sociopolitical context of establishing Hawaiian-medium education. *Language, Culture, and Curriculum, 11*(3), 325–338.
Wilson, W. H. (1998b). I ka 'ōlelo Hawai'I ke ola, 'Life is found in the Hawaiian language.' *International Journal of the Sociology of Language, 132*, 123–137.
Wilson, W., & Kamanā, K. (2001). Mai loko mai o ka 'i'ini: Proceeding from a dream, the 'Aha Pūnana Leo connection in Hawaiian language revitalization. In L. Hinton & K. Hale (Eds.), *The green book of language revitalization in practice* (pp. 147–176). Academic Press.
Wilson, W., & Kamanā, K. (2013). E Paepae Hou 'ia Ka Pōhaku: Reset the stones of the Hawaiian house platform. In L. Hinton (Ed.), *Bringing our languages home: Language revitalization for families* (pp. 101–117). Heyday Books.
Wilson, W., & Kamanā, K. (2014). *Beyond P-20: Reviving a dying language*. YouTube Video. Accessed on June 12, 2018. https://www.youtube.com/watch?v=6Uhmj7jRvCA
Wilson, W. H., & Kawae'ae'a, K. (2007). I Kumu Lālā: Let there be sources; let there be branches: Teacher education in the college of Hawaiian language. *Journal of American Indian Education, 46*(3), 37–53.
Wong, L. (2006). *Kuhi aku, Kuhi mai, Kuhi hewa ē: He mau Loina Kuhikuhi 'Ākena no ka 'Ōlelo Hawai'i* (Unpublished Ph.D. Dissertation). University of Hawai'i at Mānoa.
Wong, L. (2011). Hawaiian methodologies of indirection. In K. Davis (Ed.), *Critical qualitative research in second language studies: Agency and advocacy* (pp. 151–170). Information Age Publishing.

4

Pidgin: Overcoming Social Stigma

In an article published in March 2021 in the Midweek Magazine in Hawai'i (Mossman, 2021), the interviewee Dr. Llewellyn Young, the superintendent of Hawai'i Catholic Schools, is quoted as saying: "I come from Kekaha, and there we speak the harshest pidgin you can imagine!... Whenever we were away, my parents would tell my brother and I, 'In the house, you speak pidgin. But outside, you need to speak good English.'" With his explanation and with his choice of the descriptor "harshest," this quotation reveals a lot about beliefs toward Pidgin among many people in Hawaiian society. First of all, the fact that Young, who grew up speaking Pidgin himself, employs "harshest" as his adjective, is evidence that, as Wong (1999): states, "some of the worst critics of Pidgin are Pidgin speakers themselves." Yokota (2008: 28) has likewise noted that people born and raised in Hawai'i have referred to Pidgin speakers as "acting stupid" and being "retarded sounding."

This quotation also reveals the related belief that Pidgin, while deemed to be acceptable in the home, is not appropriate for usage in public domains. Drager (2012: 64) suggests the pervasiveness of this idea when she writes, "today, Pidgin is largely viewed as a language to use at home

S. Saft, *Language and Social Justice in Context*,
https://doi.org/10.1007/978-3-030-91251-2_4

and with close friends." Young's parents, then, are surely not alone in terms of monitoring the language of their children, making sure that they understand the hierarchical relationship between Pidgin and English. Both of these assessments, that Pidgin is "harsh" and that it is not for usage outside of the home, have origins in, as noted in Chapter 2, a colonial history that saw Pidgin emerge as a creole at a time when the United States increased its efforts to make sure English was the dominant language of education and other domains in Hawaiian society.

While negative beliefs about Pidgin are present in this quotation from Young, I would suggest that there is also at least a small display of pride in revealing in a public news source that he comes from Kekaha, a place where Pidgin is not just "harsh" but is in fact "the harshest … you can find." This expression of pride derives from the covert prestige accorded to Pidgin in society as a language that came to represent "local" resistance to the attempts by the American-led government to impose English and an American (haole) identity. Tamura (1994), for instance, refers to earlier sociolinguistic work by John Reinecke (1969), to note that among Nisei, second generation Japanese immigrants, "to speak Standard English was to proclaim oneself an American and to associate oneself with the dominant haole culture" and it likewise "meant disassociating oneself from one's class and racial group" (Tamura, 1994: 202–203). Pidgin, on the other hand, came to be "a badge of identity," (Tamura, 1994: 202–203) and it served as such a badge not just for the Nisei but, in fact, "involved all Hawaiian children by 1920, as well as the children of the immigrant plantation workers" as "the perfect tool for local children to resist the campaign to force them to speak English" (Kimura, 1983: 199).

The notion of covert prestige certainly goes a long way in understanding how Pidgin has retained a fierce resiliency in Hawai'i in the face of a severe negative stigma since the early 1900s; several writers suggest that nearly half of the population of 1.3 million are speakers (Drager, 2012; Sakoda & Siegel, 2003). Yet, contrary to the popular belief that Pidgin is a so-called private language, recent research from a sociolinguistic and discourse analytic perspective is demonstrating that Pidgin "has become more visible in Hawai'i's public sphere" (Higgins, 2015: 145). Higgins (2015), for instance, finds Pidgin in several public places, including public signage, restaurant menus, political websites, and letters to the editor, which leads her to assert that "domain boundaries for Pidgin and English may be more flexible than previously thought" (Higgins, 2015: 159). In order to explain this finding, Higgins (2015) builds on the notion of covert prestige through an economic analogy and suggests that Pidgin is gaining in "capital" in Hawai'i's linguistic landscape. She also emphasizes that this increased visibility of Pidgin may have ties to resistance, suggesting that "Hawai'i may present a case of resistance to globalizing pressures to embrace a cosmopolitan identity in pace with the rest of the world" (Higgins, 2015: 160). In this sense, despite a longstanding negative stigma, Pidgin's history as a language of resistance provides it with "capital" in society that makes it attractive in the public domain as a resource that "celebrates the local without aligning it with a world beyond" (Higgins, 2015: 161).

In line with the work of Higgins, I have also tried in prior research to emphasize the role of Pidgin in public discourse, focusing largely on the usage of Pidgin by a local politician in Hilo, Hawai'i in his public speeches and in his interaction with residents as a part of engaging in local politics (Saft, 2019; Saft et al., 2018). His usage of Pidgin contrasts with English (which he often mixes in his speeches) and thus consists of an element of resistance, but I have also, in light of the tendency to denigrate Pidgin as an impoverished and deviant variant of English, used the analyses to underscore the degree to which Pidgin functions as a viable language with crucial resources for the accomplishment of political discussions. In this chapter, as part of adopting a social justice perspective that advocates for a greater acceptance of Pidgin in Hawaiian society, I offer two additional analyses of Pidgin in context. The first analysis focuses on a piece of Pidgin literature in a magazine in Hawai'i, and the second centers on the usage of spoken Pidgin in a speech made by a participant in a public meeting. Both of these uses also represent forms of resistance, and in doing so, they serve as examples of Pidgin as a language skillfully used to convey a range of ideas.

Following these two analyses, I present excerpts from interviews with speakers of Hawaiian who also are advocates of Pidgin. These interviews are meant to explore, among other things, the relationship of Pidgin to Hawaiian revitalization in light of the suggestion that the development of

Pidgin may be implicated in the endangerment of Hawaiian. After presentation of the interviews, I situate the findings of the chapter within a general discussion of Pidgin advocacy and the role of Pidgin in society.

Throughout this chapter, I am going to work under the assumption that Pidgin exists as a separate language in Hawai'i. I do this even while remaining aware that the borderline between Pidgin and other languages in Hawai'i, particularly English, is not always especially clear. In fact, recognizing the fluid boundaries between the two some people employ the term "Hawai'i English" to refer to a variety of English spoken in Hawai'i. Still, though, I agree with Drager (2012: 62) who writes about her work that "Hawai'i English and Pidgin are treated here as separate languages. However, it is important to recognize that in actual use the distinction between them is not always so cut and dry as this might imply. Neither Hawai'i English nor Pidgin are homogeneous; as would be expected with natural languages, there is a great deal of variation" (Drager, 2012: 62). Descriptions of the grammatical features of Pidgin are available in other sources (Saft, 2019; Sakoda & Siegel, 2003; Siegel, 2008) and will therefore not be repeated here. The analyses below will, though, point out features of Pidgin grammar that are relevant to the data.

4.1 An Example of Pidgin Literature

I begin with an analysis of written literature because of the suggestion that Pidgin faces challenges in terms of being recognized as a literary language (Romaine, 1994, 1995, 1996, 2005). Referring to her own work (Romaine, 1994), Romaine (2005: 102) writes that she "concluded that further elaboration of Pidgin as a written language presented problems that would not easily be overcome without careful consideration of issues surrounding standardization and the status of Pidgin as a literary variety." Concerning first of all the issue of standardization, she viewed the major obstacle to be "the fact that most local writers had not seen the need for breaking with the tradition of using a modified English orthography to represent pidgin" (Romaine, 2005: 102). Because of this lack of standardization, "creole writing systems based on the orthographies of their lexifiers often do creoles a disservice in suggesting that they are inferior and deficient versions of the languages to which they are lexically affiliated" (2005: 105), which leads to the assessment that Pidgin is "forced to be a literary dialect rather than a full-fledged literary language."

The second concern about Pidgin's status as a literary variety centers on, according to Romaine (2005), the fact that Pidgin lacks the usage of a range of "points of view" in terms of writing style. More specifically, she notes that literary works published in Pidgin lack a detached third person point of view that is typically found in more developed forms of writing. As she notes, languages such as Pidgin that did not have a tradition of literature typically begin appearing in written works through direct quotes that animate characters. In her words (Romaine, 1995: 109), "the pattern of using Hawai'i Creole English to animate the speech of characters, but reverting to standard English for the main story line is often the starting point from which many local dialects and minority languages get a foothold in literature." She also notes that the next step is usually a transition to "to the first person present tense" (Romaine, 1995: 105). As she writes, "from a comparative literary perspective, Hawai'i Creole English and other minority varieties often make their break-through in literature by appearing first in the form of quoted speech within the novel, and later in first person narration" (Romaine, 1995: 113). However, she also notes that the next move in the transition to a literary language, which is usage of the language through a detached third-person narration, is quite difficult. As Romaine (1995: 115) pointed out over twenty-five years ago, "the use of third person narrative in dialect is extremely restricted. As far as I know, there is none in Hawai'i Creole English."

As Romaine emphasizes, her purpose in pointing out the difficulties in recognizing Pidgin as a "full-fledged" literary language was not to criticize Pidgin as an inferior language. In her words, she had hoped that her analysis and discussion might "spur writers to reflect on issues concerning their choice of spelling and to think about moving beyond current narrative strategies in order to exploit more fully the potential of Pidgin as a literary language" (2005: 104). At the same time, she was also worried that Pidgin's evolution as a literary language might weaken its message as a "counterdiscourse" that could be used to challenge the status quo represented by English. As she writes (Romaine, 1995: 84), "the use of creole languages in literature displaces the more powerful colonial language, standard English, from its privileged place at the center of mainstream as well as literary discourse." Thus, rather than portray Pidgin as inferior to any other written language, her concern here was exploring how Pidgin could develop as a literary language without losing its effectiveness as an expression of resistance.

Yet, even as Romaine was putting these concerns in writing, Pidgin continued to be used in literature and in poetry, even though writers have yet to land upon a standard orthography (Balaz, 2019; Chock, 1978, 1990; Ellis, 2020; Lum, 1986, 1990; Tonouchi, 2001, 2009; Yamanaka, 2000, 2006). In fact, it has been suggested that the lack of standardization has been beneficial for Pidgin writers as it allows for increased flexibility as well as creativity; "Pidgin speakers have a free field to create lexicography and orthography" (Ellis, 2020: 7). Along such lines, the first analysis will show how one well-known Pidgin writer, Lee Tonouchi, who has referred to himself as "Da Pidgin Guerilla" for his advocacy of Pidgin, strategically employs orthography to create contrasts between Pidgin and English, which in turn imbues the content of the prose with a heightened sense of resistance.

The analysis focuses on a short story by Tonouchi entitled "Da Untold Story of Hawaiian Santa" that originally appeared in 2014 in the Honolulu Magazine and was published in the online version of the magazine in 2019.[1] The Honolulu Magazine publishes its content almost exclusively in English, although it has run feature stories on the Hawaiian language and has had other content in Pidgin published by Tonouchi. Accordingly, the very inclusion of an article in Pidgin represents a departure from the typical practice of the magazine. The first part of Tonouchi's work "Da Untold Story of Hawaiian Santa" is shown below.[2]

[1]Available at https://www.honolulumagazine.com/da-untold-story-of-hawaiian-santa-a-pidgin-story-by-lee-a-tonouchi/.

[2]Following my decision to italicize the Hawaiian texts in Chapter 2, I am likewise using italics in this chapter to mark Pidgin. With Pidgin, it is slightly more complex given the flexible boundaries with English, but the italics represents the fact that most of the written and spoken texts in the first two analyses are meant to be Pidgin.

Excerpt (1): Da Untold Story of Hawaiian Santa

1 *I admit. I losing it. Any moment now I might jus buckaloose! Maybe it's cuz dis gotta be*
2 *da stupidest tourist question eva posed to me during my 15 years driving dis trolley bus*
3 *Maybe it's cuz of dat crazy onreal magazine article I jus read about da future of Hawai'i*
4 *nei. Maybe it's cuz dat article finally made me realize dat da American Dream I been*
5 *chasing, while trying for maintain my unsteady and junk-paying job, must not apply to*
6 *Hawai'i people. I guess up till now I nevah notice da fine print where da ting says*
7 "American Dream only applicable in the continental United States. Offer not valid in
8 Hawai'i." *For some reason, us, we always no count, brah. Like how if get one fast-food*
9 *commercial on TV, half da time da Hawai'i price not going be what dey say, cuz dey*
10 *flash da disclaimer,* "Prices may be slightly higher in Hawai'i." *Or like when we mail*
11 *order stuff and dey charge us "international" shipping. Like what is dat? And even when*
12 *I call'em up for correck dem for let'em know dat da battle's not yet won and Native*
13 *Hawaiians still fighting for sovereignty, dey jus respond with one* "Excuse me?" *Like dey*
14 *no catch on to da joke das not one joke*

Although the original pidgin that emerged in Hawai'i in the 1800s consisted of a lexicon that borrowed largely from Hawaiian, the modern creole language of Pidgin borrows greatly from English (Sakoda & Siegel, 2003), which explains why the majority of the words in this passage resemble English. Still, there a couple of terms in this passage that are not recognizable as having origins in English, particularly *buckaloose* in line 1 and *Hawai'i nei* in lines 3–4. According to Sakoda and Siegel (2003: 15), *buckaloose* is a term made from English but "not found in English," and *Hawai'i nei* is a borrowed expression from Hawaiian meaning something akin to "here in Hawai'i."

While many of the words seem familiar to English, it is the structure that separates Pidgin from English. This is seen at the beginning in line 1 with *I admit. I losing it*, both of which may be considered full sentences in Pidgin. As Sakoda and Siegel (2003) note, Pidgin grammar does not require an object, especially "it," and, likewise, auxiliary verbs are not required either. In fact, Pidgin allows for sentences without verbs at all, an example of which is seen in line 8. *For some reason, us, we always no count, brah*. The main component of this sentence *we always no count* qualifies as an "equational sentence" (Sakoda & Siegel, 2003) that is "verbless" since Pidgin does not require any form of the be-verb in this construction.

There is, though, a danger in focusing only on aspects of Pidgin grammar that seem, at first glance anyway, to be simpler than English. Such an observation comes with the risk of reinforcing the discriminatory view of Pidgin as a simplified or even broken form of English. Hence, it should be emphasized that Pidgin is just as, if not more, complex than English in some of its constructions, a point which is evidenced by the negative forms in this excerpt. As Sakoda and Siegel (2003: 80) emphasize, Pidgin uses four negative markers, *nat*, *no*, *neva*, and *nomo* while English tends to only use "not" to make a negative form. Each of the four negative markers in Pidgin is used in its context with differentiated meanings. In Excerpt (1), we see the usage of *not* five times, once each in lines 5, 7, 9, 12, and 14, but we also see one usage of *nevah* in line 6 with I *nevah notice da fine print*. In Pidgin grammar, *nevah* is "used before the verb or auxiliary to indicate negative and past tense" (Sakoda & Siegel, 2003: 83), which explains its usage here. The marker *no* is used twice, in lines 8 in the equational sentence *we always no count, brah* and then in line 14 in *like dey no catch on to da joke das not one joke*. Without going into the specific grammar rule here, Pidgin, as a language native to many people in Hawai'i, has nuanced differences between these four negative markers that are unconsciously employed by first language speakers but difficult to grasp by those who did not grow up speaking it natively.

In addition to negatives, other noteworthy aspects of Pidgin grammar in this excerpt occur in line 8 with the usage of *get* in the clause *Like how if get one fast-food commercial on TV* and in line 12 with the usage of *for* in

And even when I call'em up for correck dem for let'em know dat da battle's not yet won. Although these appear as (incorrect) English forms when put down in writing, they are actually aspects of Pidgin influenced from languages on the plantation. According to Sakoda and Siegel (2003), *get* is due to influence from the Cantonese *yauh* which can mean both "have/has" and "there is/are" in Cantonese. Indeed, in line 8, it would be translated into English as "if there is a fast-food commercial on TV." *For* derives from Portuguese *para* (translated in English as "for") as in sentences such as *Carlos e home para fazer isso* "Charles is the man to do that." Pidgin thus borrowed from Portuguese and arrived at *for,* which is, of course, different from English "to." The fact that these components of grammar have a basis in developed languages such as Cantonese and Portuguese dispel the myth that Pidgin is just a broken form of English. Pidgin developed naturally as its own creole language due to influence of several languages, only one of which is English. Other languages having notable influence on the vocabulary and structure and Pidgin are Hawaiian, Cantonese, Portuguese, and Japanese.

In Chapter 2, I related the development of Pidgin in Hawai'i to the idea of resistance, and thus it is not surprising that this article, which appears in a magazine that typically publishes material in standard English, consists of content that expresses resistance to specific images of Hawai'i. This is made clear in Excerpt (1) as the writer explains after line 1 the reasons why he *might jus buckaloose*. He notes in line 2 that one reason is the *stupidest tourist question eva posed to me during my 15 years driving dis trolley bus,* framing himself as a bus trolley driver whose job it is to serve tourists. He then notes from line 3 that another reason is that the "American Dream" *must not apply to Hawai'i people.* As he states in line 8 about the people in Hawai'i, *we always no count, brah.* Explicating the reason, he notes the uselessness of his own chase of the American Dream in his *unsteady and junk-paying job* (line 5), and he likewise notes that many of the perks given to people on the mainland do not apply to people in Hawai'i.

In explaining how people in Hawai'i are left out, the author juxtaposes Pidgin with English by using quotation marks to adopt an official voice that is not that of the writer. The first example of this appears in lines 6–8 with *I guess up till now I nevah notice da fine print where da ting says*

"American Dream only applicable in the continental United States. Offer not valid in Hawai'i." *For some reason, us, we always no count, brah.* In the text, which does not include italics, the grammar difference is one aspect of the prose that separates Pidgin from English, but the difference is also made apparent by the writer through the usage of quotation marks that only surround the English.

The writer uses the same strategy of question marks to juxtapose Pidgin and English two more times in Excerpt (1), once in lines 8–10:

> *Like how if get one fast-food commercial on TV, half da time da Hawai'i price not going be what dey say, cuz dey flash da disclaimer,* "Prices may be slightly higher in Hawai'i."

And again at the end in lines 11–14:

> *And even when I call'em up for correck dem for let'em know dat da battle's not yet won and Native Hawaiians still fighting for sovereignty, dey jus respond with one* "Excuse me?" *Like dey no catch on to da joke das not one joke.*

In lines 8–10, the English disclaimer consists of a full sentence that employs quotation marks and a switch in grammar from Pidgin to English to represent a kind of official voice that might be seen in an advertisement. Lines 11–14 contain only the quoted "excuse me?" but this expression with a question mark is an artful usage in that it represents a lack of understanding of the world outside of Hawai'i of the situation in Hawai'i. The Native Hawaiians fight for sovereignty is invoked as a joke that is not really a joke. In order to display that the "excuse me?" is meant to represent a voice from outside of Hawai'i, the writer first sets up this expression as a response of a general third person other through the usage of the pronoun *dey* and also surrounds it with quotation marks, thus marking it as the response of an outsider.

It is relevant here that the writer has chosen an orthographic style that is, relatively speaking, quite similar to English. For example, his choice of spelling for *correck dem* in line 12 simultaneously makes it easy to recognize its correlation to "correct them" in English but also to see it as something different, that is, as Pidgin. This is an important observation because the author Tonouchi chose this orthographic strategy even though there has been one attempt to develop an orthography for Pidgin, termed the Odo orthography, that has been adopted by linguists but not as much by writers partly because of a belief that its phonetic focus makes Pidgin difficult to read (Odo, 1975, 1977; see Sakoda & Siegel, 2003 for discussion). Tonouchi is one writer who has mostly not employed the Odo orthography, but, as this first excerpt shows, this does not prevent him from employing available resources, such as spelling and quotation marks, in a very skillful and strategic way to make the contrast between Pidgin and English obvious to readers. As this first excerpt shows, the clear juxtaposition of Pidgin and English is critical to the sense of resistance in the Pidgin used by story-teller in response to the perceived view of Hawaiʻi by English speakers from the outside.

Although not shown in the transcript, the author reveals the content of what is labeled in the first paragraph as the "stupidest tourist question eva posed to me during my 15 years driving dis trolley bus" soon after the conclusion of Excerpt (1). The question from the tourists that draws his ire is "Do you folks have Christmas in Hawhyah?" with the author employing the spelling "Hawhyah" for Hawaiʻi to represent how people outside of Hawaiʻi, that is to say tourists, might mispronounce the name of the state. The spelling here is not done to represent Pidgin but it still a strategic part of the story. The author then proceeds in the next few paragraphs to explain how he intends to answer the question in a way that will discourage tourists from wanting to stay permanently in Hawaiʻi. More specifically, he refers to a belief in Hawaiʻi that taking rocks from the volcano will anger a particular Hawaiian god who will then seek revenge, but he also explains, all in Pidgin, that he was told by his friend *Braddah Mike* that this is just a superstition created by a park ranger at the volcano who was tired of people stealing from the land. He then describes how he was going to borrow from Braddah Mike to construct a response to this "stupidest" question about Christmas in Hawaiʻi. Excerpt (2) shows the beginning of his story in response. This excerpt of data consists of three shorter paragraphs, which explains why there is a space of separation between lines 3–4 and lines 10–11 and also why each chunk begins with quotation marks that represents the continuation of the author's story.

Excerpt (2): Da Untold Story of Hawaiian Santa

1 *"No werry," I begin. "All your questions going be answered during da course of my*
2 *myth-o-ma-logical tale." I scan my rearview mirror. I see all eyes stay transfixed on top*
3 *me. Well, on top da back of my bolo head, anyway*

4 *"You know how da Haole Santa lives in da North Pole? You tink das extreme? Das*
5 *nahting. Hawaiian Santa, brah, he live in ... da volcano. I know Malibu ova dea looking*
6 *at me like he no believe. Well, he can go check'em out den. See, cuz before time, back in*
7 *da ol' hanabatta dayz, one good Hawaiian man named um, Kalikimaka, yeah,*
8 *Kalikimaka. He wuz weary. He wuz tired of big multinational corporations bullying him*
9 *off his house on da beach so dey could make all their fancy hotels. So for get dem for*
10 *stop hassling him, he wen decide for hele on.*

11 *"Den later when Kalikimaka wen go move up da mountain, rich real estate developers*
12 *wen go muscle him out again so dey could build all their luxury homes wit da scenic*
13 *views. Kalikimaka wuz tired fighting so he wen decide for move again. Dis time to where*
14 *nobody would boddah him. Straight into da volcano*

15 *"When people saw da guy who wen jump in da volcano dey assumed he wen commit*
16 *suicide. Da story wuz even in da papah and had his obituary too. It said Kalikimaka wuz*
17 *one good-natured man. Always laughing and smiling. Das why all his friends called him*
18 uh, 'Mele' Kalikimaka, cuz he wuz always so happy.

Like Excerpt (1), the writer employs quotation marks as a resource throughout Excerpt (2), except that they do not indicate a break from Pidgin to English. In this excerpt, they separate the writer's story as told to the tourists on the trolley from his commentary to his readers. Thus, we can see that the writer explains in lines 1–3 that he is going to answer all of their questions through his tale that he describes in line 2 as "myth-o-ma-logical," an obvious play on the English term "mythological." This term "myth-o-ma-logical" is not itself Pidgin, but it highlights what the writer is doing through his usage of Pidgin, namely, he is being creative in his language usage as a part of his creativity in constructing this "tale."

He begins the actual story of the Hawaiian Santa in line 4 and continues through line 18, but notice that his usage of Pidgin does not change as he tells his story directly to the tourists. He uses terms recognizably a part of the Pidgin lexicon, including *Haole* in line 4, *hanabatta* in line 7, and *hele* in line 10. *Haole* and *hele* both derive from Hawaiian, and *hanabatta* is a mixture of the Japanese word for nose (*hana*) and a Pidgin pronunciation for the English word "butter." The mixture of "nose" and "butter" in *hanabatta* represents snot around the nose and serves as a reference to the times of young children. Pidgin is also apparent in the grammatical constructions, including forms used in Excerpt (1) such as the negative marker *no* that appears in line 1 (*no werry*) and line 6 (*like he no believe*) and *get* in line 9. In addition, the writer also employs the past tense marker *wen* three times in line 10 with *he wen decide for hele on*, in line 13 with *he wen decide for move again*, and in line 15 with *dey assumed he wen commit suicide*. The regular past tense in Pidgin is not formed through the appending of the bound morpheme "ed." Pidgin instead employs the free morpheme *wen*. This is another aspect of Pidgin grammar that sets Pidgin apart as a separate language from English (Sakoda & Siegel, 2003).

The writer's creativity is also demonstrated through his decision to give the name of "Kalikimaka" to the main character of his story. *Kalikimaka* is actually the transliteration of the term "Christmas" in Hawaiian, and is commonly combined with the term "Mele," also a transliterated term from English "merry." Put together, *Mele Kalikimaka* is the term used by both Hawaiian and Pidgin speakers to give Christmas wishes. Without explaining to his tourists the meaning of *Mele Kalikimaka*, the writer plays on this in lines 17–18 by saying *das why all his friends called him uh, 'Mele' Kalikimaka, cuz he wuz always so happy.*

This is thus a creative and playful beginning to the story, but also notice that the writer's story that he begins to tell to the tourists on his bus has a very serious and even critical message. It is important that the main character Kalikimaka is introduced in line 7 as *one good Hawaiian man* because he is to become a victim of outside forces. The writers tells the tourists (and the readers) in line 8 that *He wuz tired of big multinational corporations bullying him*, which prompted him to decide to *hele on* in order to *for get dem for stop hassling him* (lines 9–10). Kalikimaka moved *up da mountain* in line 11, but the "rich real estate developers" in line 12 *wen go muscle him out again so dey could build all their luxury homes*. Forced to move again, Kalikimaka tried in lines 13–14 to go to a place *where nobody would boddah him*, more specifically, *straight into da volcano*. In line 15, the writer employs the pronoun *dey* to indicate that the general population *assumed he wen commit suicide*, and then the writer suggests that this contrasts with the perception of him as *good-natured*, *laughing*, and *smiling*, which then leads to the reference "Mele Kalikimaka" to describe his *happy* nature. The writer does, however, add the filler *uh* followed by a comma in line 18, thus suggesting that this is being written as a bit of joke.

The passage shown in Excerpt (2) also reveals a complexity in the point of view adopted by the writer in relating this story about Kalikimaka. The writer started out in Excerpt (1) with a primarily first-person perspective as he described his adverse reaction to the *stupidest* question from the tourists. Excerpt (2) also begins with a first-person perspective in the first three lines as he launches into the story, but in providing the details in lines 4–18, he employs a third-person perspective represented by the many uses of the pronoun *he*. The writer is thus engaging in a very artful and complex literary process, telling a story in the third person as part of a larger first-person narrative about the writer's experience driving a trolley for tourists. All of this is done through Pidgin, and contrary to concerns raised by Romaine about point of view, it is accomplished creatively and effectively.

In this way, then, the writer has employed Pidgin through line 18 of this excerpt to construct a creative, playful tale that describes how a good-natured Hawaiian man lost his merry quality due to the multinational corporations and rich real estate developers who bullied him out of his home. Eventually, this bullying led the Hawaiian man to commit suicide. Following these paragraphs represented in Excerpt (2), the writer reveals that Kalikimaka had not committed suicide and had *started for come bitter and resentful* according to the writer. He became bitter to the extent that he sought ways to get back at the people who were moving to the islands, namely the tourists, for example, he enlisted the help of the *menehune*, short mischievous creatures, to steal things from the tourists and otherwise bother them in an attempt to discourage them from staying in Hawai'i. The writer then includes a passage where he situates Kalikimaka's work with the *menehune* in some modern political history in Hawai'i. This passage is shown below as Excerpt (3).

Excerpt (3): Da Untold Story of Hawaiian Santa

1 *"Cuz still had rich people buying Hawai'i up. So Kalikimaka decided for do what*
2 *da government couldn't do. Back in da '70 s Gov. George Ariyoshi wen go enact*
3 *da law where public jobs could only go to Local residents. Da tinking wuz das*
4 *going deter outsiders from moving ova hea. Cuz how dey can come one resident*
5 *if dey no more one job? And how dey can get one job if dey not one resident?*
6 *And for long time da law wen fly. And wuzn't until recently dat couple Florida*
7 *guys wen sue and so da ACLU wen complain cuz dey said das illegal*
8 *discriminations and da Hawai'i law wuz actually unconstitutional. Da ACLU*
9 *legal director revealed how* 'It sends the message that nonresidents are not
10 welcome.' *I thought wuz obvious from da beginning, brah, when dey made dat*
11 *law, but actually took da lawyers 27 years for figgah dat out. Go figgah.*

Delivered through Pidgin and with quotation marks to denote this as part of the story being told to the tourists on the trolley, the writer first notes in lines 1–2 that even despite Kalikimaka's work with the *menehune*, the rich people were still *buying Hawai'i up*, and then he suggests that Kalikimaka was going to continue to make life difficult for those coming to Hawai'i from the outside. This then leads the writer to invoke the name of George Ariyoshi, who served as governor of Hawai'i from 1974 to 1986, and explain in lines 2–3, again through Pidgin, that Ariyoshi *wen go enact da law where public jobs could only go to Local residents*. The writer then explains in lines 3–5 that Ariyoshi's law, since it made it difficult to get a job in Hawai'i, was supposed to deter outsiders from moving to Hawai'i. He then notes using the Pidgin past tense marker *wen* in line 6 that the *for long time da law wen fly*. However, it is then noted in lines 6–8 that recently a Florida couple *wen sue and so da ACLU wen complain cuz dey said das illegal discriminations*, which led to a claim that the Hawai'i law enacted by Ariyoshi was unconstitutional. The writer then in line 9 again employs punctuation as a resource to offer a direct quotation from the ACLU legal director. Using single quotations because double quotations have been used at the beginning to mark the entire block of text as part of spoken text to the trolley riders, the writers switches from Pidgin to an English grammar to state the law "sends the message that nonresidents are not welcome." The writer then switches back to Pidgin in lines 10–11 to conclude this block with sarcasm suggesting that it should been obvious from the time the law was made that nonresidents were unwelcome. Here, the switch from English to Pidgin enables the writer to emphasize this sense of sarcasm and even exasperation that it took lawyers 27 years to figure out something so obvious.

It is notable in Excerpt (3) that the writer uses a third-party point of view to add some commentary about political history in Hawai'i to this story. Not only does he do this through Pidgin, but he also does it in a strategic way that makes use of punctuation to juxtapose English as an official voice in the official statement from the ACLU director and to add sarcasm to the story by juxtaposing the one English statement with a return to Pidgin in the last two lines. It is thus interesting that even as English is employed to represent an "official" voice, the writer is employing primarily Pidgin to explain some recent political history in Hawai'i.

Following the explanation of some historical background in Excerpt (3), the writer continues to add to the story of how Kalikimaka attempted to deter the tourists from staying in Hawai'i. In one block of the story not reproduced here, the writer describes how Kalikimaka tried to start a rumor that the island was going to sink *if had too many people.* Still, none of Kalikimaka's attempts succeeded in preventing outsiders from moving to Hawai'i, and so, as shown in Excerpt (4), he also made an effort to compel the sun to increase the degree of heat delivered to the tourists.

Excerpt (4): Da Untold Story of Hawaiian Santa

1 *"And so, wuz back to da drawing board for Kalikimaka. So you know how Haole Santa*
2 *get his sleigh with his reindeer, Hawaiian Santa get his outrigger canoe pulled by his*
3 *nine wild pua 'a. But look Palm Beach ova dea. She saying but pigs no can walk on water*
4 *Das right. And what? Reindeer can fly in da air? See, same smell. So what Kalikimaka*
5 *wen use his magic canoe for do? He wen go far out to sea, den taking his magic lasso*
6 *Cuz Kalikimaka's uncle wuz one paniolo so he had da kine cowboy background, ah,*
7 *li'dat, ah. But using his magic lasso he wen go lasso ... da sun. I know Westport ova dea*
8 *saying, but wouldn't da sun burn da rope? Das true, true. But what Westport dunno is*
9 *Kalikimaka wen go catch da sun ... nighttime. Plus his rope wuz magic, so leave it alone*
10 *So anyway, what's da point in dat? Da point wuz he wen do dat for talk stories with da*
11 *sun for convince da sun for turn up da heat on da tourists. Das why, you no notice,*
12 *Japanee tourists, Haole tourists, Chinese tourists, dey always getting really bad sun*
13 *burn. Most people tink ah, stupid tourist, why dey jus nevah use sunscreen*
14 *Das cuz in actuality tourists is getting '15.2 degrees of extra' sun. I kid you not*

Invoking the usage by *Haole Santa* of a sleigh pulled by reindeer, the writer notes in lines 2–3 that Kalikimaka employed an outrigger canoe that was led by *nine wild pua'a* using the term *pua'a* which originates in Hawaiian for wild pigs. The writer then refers to one of the tourists on his trolley by the place from which she came, Palm Beach, and suggests that she may not believe *pigs no can walk on water*. Even though this doubt comes from the tourist "Palm Beach," it is nonetheless stated via a Pidgin grammar because it is expressed through the writer's perspective; it does not use any kind of punctuation that would suggest it is a direct quotation. The writer then responds to this doubt in lines 4 by first agreeing with *das right*, but then he points out the absurdity in the idea that reindeer can fly and suggests that it is the *same smell* as pigs walking on water. He continues at the end of line 4 through line 5 that Kalikimaka took his canoe far out to see and used his *magic lasso*. The writer adds in line 6 that Kalikimaka had a *cowboy background* in line 6 because his uncle was a *paniolo*, a term with origins in Hawaiian for a person working on a ranch, in other words, a cowboy.

Next, in line 7, the writer again uses punctuation, this time three periods in succession, to note that Kalikimaka *wen go lasso … da sun*. The three periods indicate a leadup to an important point of the story. He then in lines 7–8 attributes another idea to one of his tourists, whom he calls "Westport," that would add doubt to the plausibility of the story. Specifically, that *da sun burn da rope*. But the writer has a response to this doubt as well, namely, as expressed in line 9, *Kalikimaka wen go catch da sun … nighttime*. Once again, the writer employs the three periods in succession to introduce and emphasize an important aspect of the story, in this case it is an aspect that will satisfy the doubts of the tourists on his trolley. In doing so, the writer also adds humor to his story. Next, the writer continues through 11 to explain that he wanted to catch the sun to *talk stories* in attempt to convince the sun *for turn up da heat on da tourists*. He then employs person category terms *Japanee tourists*, *Haole tourists*, *Chinese tourists* in line 12 to attribute the bad sun burns of these tourists as a result of Kalikimaka's *talking story* with the sun and convincing it to *turn up da heat*. This block ends in line 14 with the writer explaining that the tourists are actually getting *"15.2 degrees of extra"* sun. He adds *I kid you not* at the very end as a reference to the doubts.

This particular excerpt of the story is interesting for several reasons. As noted previously, Pidgin is used by the writer to narrate the story from both a first-person and third-person perspective, but in the block of text in Excerpt (4), the writer adds what is arguably a further layer of complexity by using indirect quotations to block off chunks of English that could be attributed to other speakers. He does this by giving the names "Palm Beach" in line 3 and "Westport" in line 8 to tourists on his trolley and by suggesting that they are doubting some of the facts of the story, but notice that the writer does not use quotation marks and continues to use Pidgin to indicate that these are meant to describe what the two named tourists may be thinking. Due to its complexity, this type of indirect speech has been linked to Bahktin's noting of "voicing" (Bahktin, 1981, 1986) and also been referred to as "reported speech," "constructed dialogue" (Tannen, 1995), and ventriloquism (Cooren, 2012, 2013). The attention garnered by this action in linguistics suggests that it is an intricate process, but, as Excerpt (4) shows, the writer is able, through his creative use of Pidgin and punctuation, to accomplish this creatively as part of what is already a complex story.

Second, the writer also makes use of punctuation to add to the humor of the story, particularly the punchlines that are marked by the three periods in succession in lines 7 and 9. Humor has been used as a general source of criticism and resistance throughout history (MacKenzie et al., 2018; Sorensen, 2008; Weaver, 2010), and, as noted in Chapter 2, research on Pidgin in Hawai'i has shown that Pidgin is a regular component of stand-up comedy. To be sure, there has been concern that the usage of Pidgin in comedy may portray speakers of Pidgin in a negative light (Wong, 1999), but it is clear that the humor in this story by Tonouchi is meant to add to the sarcastic sense of the story and thus add to the critical stance adopted toward the perspective of the tourist. The humor plays on the farfetched quality of the stories created in mainstream American beliefs about Santa Claus. The tourists employ their own stories of an imagined man flying in a sleigh pulled by reindeer and so how can they question the writer's story about an outrigger canoe pulled by *nine wild pua'a*. By pointing out this hypocrisy, the writer is employing Pidgin to poke even more fun at the tourists who could have ludicrously asked in the first place whether there is a Christmas in Hawai'i.

After this portion of the story, the writer laments in the next block of text that the added heat and sunburn was also unsuccessful in dissuading outsiders as they continued to move to the islands. He then continues to relay one last technique employed by Kalikimaka, the dispersion of gas from the volcano that is known throughout Hawai'i as "vog" and which contains, according to the writer, all *kine chemical elements*. In another usage of humor, the writer notes that *in those fumes is one gas dat affecks all recent transplant people. It gives dem one sense of feeling unwelcome*. He then goes on to describe how the gas leads the transplanted residents to complain about the food, the people, the local culture, as part of a seemingly unhappy experience in Hawai'i, which again points hypocrisy among the *transplant people*. They move all the way to Hawai'i only to complain about their new place of residence.

Following description of this last attempt by Kalikimaka, the writer then starts to wrap up the story and also the article. Excerpt (5) contains two of the last three blocks of text that conclude the article. To save space, lines 5–9, in which the writer wonders whether *Braddah Mike* is going to upset with him for making up stories, have been omitted.

Excerpt (5): Da Untold Story of Hawaiian Santa

1 *"And so dat concludes da legend of Hawaiian Santa." Nobody says anyting as I pull into*
2 *Hanauma Bay. I dunno if it's cuz dey distracted by da view as we drive down around da*
3 *bend or if it's cuz dey retinking* "Oh, whereever shall we buy our retirement homes
4 now?"

10 *I park my trolley bus and make some quick-kine announcements. "No forget for bring*
11 *your valuables. Cuz we not liable. You nevah know when going get Menehune.*
12 *Remembah now, no walk too close togeddah. Make sure you spread out da weight." I*
13 *smile little bit to myself when I notice Omaha and Malibu, stepping gingerly off my*
14 *trolley bus. I give dem all one shaka for tell'em goodbye and I give'em one friendly*
15 *reminder, "Meet back in two hours. Have fun. Relax. Take deeeeeeep breaths. Let it all*
16 *in. And no forget, Mele Kalikimaka!"*

Using quotation marks in line 1 to indicate that it is a quotation of actual speech, the writer announces to his trolley-riding tourists that the "legend" of Hawaiian Santa is finished. He then uses the end of the quotation to note that his tourists do not say anything in response to the story, which he attributes either to the distraction of the view or to a rethinking of their plan to retire to Hawai'i after hearing his story. In lines 3–4, he once again employs quotation marks to give "voice" to the tourists, which is marked by a switch into English grammar and English writing conventions with "Oh, whereever shall we buy our retirement homes now?" The writer then reports in Pidgin his final *quick-kine announcements* in line 10, marking the actual announcements through quotation marks as actual quoted speech. He invokes through line 12 several of the attempts by Kalikimaka to deter outsiders by referring to the *menehune* and by advising them to distribute their weight. He then ends the quotation marks to make fun of the tourists by expressing his inner recognition in line 13 that two of the tourists, Omaha and Malibu, are walking gingerly, which suggests that they have taken the seriously the part of the story about needing to watch the distribution of their weight. The writer then ends the story with a final quotation directing the tourists to meet back in two hours, and the story ends in line 16 with the statement "Mele Kalikimaka" by the writer to the tourists as they leave to thus invoking the double meaning of "Mele Kalikimaka." It is a local way of wishing someone Merry Christmas but in this case it also as a reminder of the story told by the writer through the trolley driver character in order to discourage the tourists from moving to Hawai'i. It is appropriate, then, that he ends with a salient Pidgin grammatical construction, the negative marker *no*, to remind the tourists *And no foget, Mele Kalikimaka*!

Tonouchi's piece is a linguistically and orthographically complex story that employs humor to express strong criticism of the American settler colonial agenda to move to Hawai'i and take land from the native population. It follows a tradition of employing Pidgin to produce humor in a way that serves as a form of resistance to American colonialism, and in doing so, it underscores the degree to which Pidgin can function as not just a literary language but as an important language in Hawai'i. Although adopting an orthography similar to English, Tonouchi employed various written resources, including different spellings, punctuation (especially quotation marks), and Pidgin grammatical constructions, such as negative markers to juxtapose Pidgin with English in a way that enables the writer to ridicule the tourists for their hypocrisy, and therefore really underscore the story as a work of resistance.

Given that the piece is written in Pidgin with only a few marked sentences in English, it is unlikely that it will be understood well by tourists, the very people that it mocks. This then raises an interesting thought that harkens back to the discussion in Chapter 2 about the relationship between Pidgin and Native Hawaiians, namely that a piece of Pidgin literature can stand as a general criticism of the American colonial agenda to take land from the Native Hawaiians. Tonouchi's choice of the Hawaiian expression *Mele Kalikimaka* as the name of the main character and his direct criticism of tourists and outsiders usage of land in Hawai'i suggests that his Pidgin literature is meant to iterate the criticism against American colonialism that Native Hawaiians have been making since the 1800s. The second analysis, presented below, also shows a speaker employing Pidgin to criticize the handling of Hawaiian lands.

4.2 Spoken Testimony in Pidgin

The second analysis of this chapter shows a spoken public testimony made in Pidgin that was recorded and posted on Youtube. Although the usage of Pidgin occurs in a very different context and is delivered through a spoken mode of communication, it is similar to that of Tonouchi's example of Pidgin literature shown above in that it provides a perspective of resistance. The source of data is a testimony made by a local resident in his 60s in front of a group of board members from the Hawaiian Homelands Commission in a meeting that occurred in 2019 on the Big Island of Hawai'i.[3] The speaker, Skippy Ioane (SI in the transcripts), is a performer and an entertainer who is also a known activist. He was, for instance, one of the elders arrested for protesting the building of a

[3]Retrieved from https://www.youtube.com/watch?v=1Ns6K8ONIPI&t=336s.

telescope on Mauna Kea in 2018. Excerpt (6) shows the beginning of his testimony. It follows the testimony of another activist who had begun her comments with a Hawaiian chant.

Excerpt (6) Skippy Ioane Testimony

1 SI: *I no can chant but I can tell you dis Collette look my hair* ((takes off his hat)) *look*
2 *yours something wrong* ((laughter from the audience)) *ya know eh what I like talk*
3 *about (.) is (.) how come (.) for so long (.) alas (.) ya know if we had sh- if we*
4 *never have shit for ten years you would tink could be (.) one misunderstanding (.)*
5 *but if we never have shit for 200 years someting up (.) you know what I mean dis*
6 *ting neva- hi auntie* ((waves hand)) *dis ting nevah just occur (.) so here's my point*
7 *(.) I like you guyz create one committee (.) for fin out what kanakas took da bread*
8 *(.) okay (.) now 200 years da kanakas no can go on the land (.) how come (.) who*
9 *dey wen pay off for keep us on da waiting list*

The very beginning of the testimony in line 1, with *I no can chant but I can tell you dis* is marked not just by Pidgin pronunciations but also by the usage of the same Pidgin negative marker *no* that was employed commonly by Tonouchi in his story. Directly following this first remark in Pidgin, SI engages in an action that he does several times in his testimony, namely, he briefly moves away from his main point to directly address somebody present at the meeting. This action, what I will label here as a "narrative departure," occurs when he states through line 2 *Collette look my hair* ((takes off his hat)) *look yours something wrong.* Through this narrative departure, SI addresses somebody out of the range of the video camera named Collette and makes a joke about her hair looking different from his. As shown in line 2 of the transcript, this "departure" draws laughter from the audience.

Yet, rather than lead to a further sequence between SI and Collette, SI makes use of the fact that he has access to the floor to move in line 2 to initiate his testimony. He states *ya know eh what I like talk about (.) is (.) how come (.) for so long (.) alas (.)*. In addition to aspects of the Pidgin grammar such as *like talk about*, SI employs the term *alas*, which has the meaning of "nothing." It derives from the Hawaiian term *'ala'ala*, which literally means "ink sack of a squid" but which also came to mean "useless" or "good-for-nothing." This utterance in lines 2–3 is also noteworthy because it contains the question term "how come." This is a question embedded within a larger statement and, even though there is a short micropause at the end, SI does not allow room for any other participant to attempt an answer. Instead, he continues in line 4 and 5 to switch the reference from *alas* to *shit* to make the point that the Native Hawaiian population has received nothing for 200 hundred years. Then, as he states in lines 5–6 *you know what I mean dis ting neva-*, he cuts off at the end of the Pidgin negative *neva-* to perform another narrative departure. He smiles, waves his hand, and utters *hi auntie* in line 6 to someone out of the line of the video camera. Then, like he did in line 2, SI returns after this brief departure to his point as he states at the end of line 6 *dis ting nevah just occur (.) so here's my point*. Note here that unlike the moment following first narrative departure in lines 1–2, in which he just moves on to begin his main point, there is some repetition of the phrase *dis ting nevah* as SI moves back into his testimony. He then starts in line 7 to make a request that *I like you guyz create one committee (.) for fin out what kanakas took da bread*. In doing so, he employs the person category *kanakas*, which has its origins in Hawaiian as the general word for "person" but which also, as discussed in the analysis in Chapter 3, is often used to refer specifically to Hawaiian people. Here, it is used to suggest that there were some Native Hawaiians who may have been at fault. This becomes clear through line 9 as SI once again uses the term *kanakas* in line 8 to suggest that there were some Native Hawaiians who were paid to keep other Native Hawaiians on the waiting list for land for 200 years.

Within these eight lines of testimony, SI has engaged in two "narrative departures," but he still has begun his testimony by requesting that the committee to which he is speaking create a separate committee to investigate which Native Hawaiians may be involved in preventing other

Native Hawaiians from receiving the land that is due to them. This is all accomplished through a Pidgin grammar, even though SI is using a form of poetic license to add creativity to his own Pidgin with terms such as "bread" to refer to money. I am going to offer further discussion on his usage of narrative departures, but I first show the continuation of the testimony below as Excerpt (7).

Excerpt (7) Skippy Ioane Testimony

10	SI:	*For so long da kanaka get nuthin (.) dea some corruption in kanakaville kay (.)*
11		*ya know what I mean eh da kanaka took da money there some chicken shit*
12		*kanakas now ya know when Queen Lili'uokalani got overthrowed it started den*
13		*da haole was paying off da- da titas and da brudahs and dey wen overthrow da*
14		*queen (.) dey neva just use haoles or Japanese I mean bananas (.) dey been use*
15		*some kanakas so what I like you guyz look for now no fart around now get right*
16		*down to da boogie woogie find out who been sell us out*

Once again using the category *kanaka*, SI expresses in line 10 that the Native Hawaiians have received nothing and that there is corruption in, as he once again adds a level of creativity to his Pidgin expressions, *kanakaville*. He then repeats in line 11 that some Native Hawaiians took the money and that this is evidence of there being some *chicken shit kanakas*. He adds a new opinion in line 12 that it began when Queen Lili'uokalani, the reigning monarch in 1893, was overthrown, and that this occurred, as expressed in line 13, with the help of *da titas and brudahs* who were paid off by *da haole*. *Tita* and *brudah* are Pidgin terms literally meaning "sister" and "brother" that probably derive from the way these words may be pronounced in Hawaiian (*tita* and *bulala*). Here, like the term *kanaka*, they are used here to refer to Native Hawaiians. This is made clear in line 14 when SI notes that they did not just use *haole* or *Japanese* ("bananas" is a derogatory reference to the Japanese who are "white" on the inside and thus in cahoots with the haole). Then, using the Pidgin past marker *been* at the end of 14 (and again line 16), he repeats that they used *kanakas* in line 15 and he finally once again adds in some extra creativity in lines 15–16 to implore the committee to *no fart around now get right down to da boogie woogie find out who been sell us out*.

One of the noticeable aspects of these first two excerpts is that there is considerable amount of repetition in SI's testimony. He has expressed three times the idea that the Native Hawaiians have received nothing, he has also suggested at least twice that some Native Hawaiians have been paid off, and he twice requests the committee to investigate the matter. He is sometimes creative in repeating these ideas—for instance, he uses the terms *alas*, chicken shit, and *nuthin* to state that the Native Hawaiians have received nothing. At the same time, he has also repeated some of the same terms, for example, the term *kanaka*, which was employed five times. Excerpt (8), the continuation of his testimony, shows more repetition of both ideas and terminology.

Excerpt (8) Skippy Ioane Testimony

17	SI:	*How many people make on da waiting list? Give me an answa*
18	Woman:	*30,000*
19	SI:	*huh, 30,000?*
20	Woman:	**
21	SI:	*How come nobody know? Who wen pay somebody not to know (.) how come*
22		*we don't know how many kanakas died waiting, mo bettah go Vietnam you get*
23		*paid or go Afghanistan go die you get paid (.) but my point is why is nothing so*
24		*prevalent (.) How you Bob? You mighty quiet there I no see you long time (.)*
25		*you know what I mean why is nothing so prevalent (.) for our community (.)*

This excerpt begins with a question from SI in 17, *how many people make on the waiting list*, in which he uses the term *make*, which comes originally from the Hawaiian word *make* for "die," to ask how many people have died while waiting to receive land. Note here, that after the question, he makes it clear that he wants an answer with *give me an answa*. This extra request is likely necessary because SI has addressed people in the venue before in lines 1–2 and line 6 without waiting for a response (at least no response was audible in those cases). Following his request in line 1, he receives an answer in line 2 that the number is 30,000, which prompts him to repeat the number with some surprise in line 3, as indicated by his utterance of *huh*. This then prompts him to make a series of utterances from line 21 through line 24 that structurally take the appearance of questions. He asks *how come nobody know*, *who wen pay somebody not to know*, *how come we don't know how many kanakas died waiting*, and *why is nothing so prevalent*. Through these questions, he repeats points that he already made, namely that somebody has been paid off and that the Native Hawaiians have received nothing.

It is interesting to note that even though SI employs these utterances in lines 21–24 that are structurally questions with the interrogatives "how come," "who," and "why," he does not wait for nor does he seem to expect responses, at least at this point in his testimony. There are short micropauses in lines 21, 23, and 24, but these are not long enough to indicate that SI is expecting an answer. In this sense, they serve almost as rhetorical questions that enable SI to assert his belief that people should know how many Native Hawaiians died while on the waiting list, that some Native Hawaiians were paid to keep quiet, and that it is a problem that the Native Hawaiians have received nothing. It is certainly relevant that they take on a question structure, especially since such a structure may help SI prompt members of the audience to ask and consider the same types of questions. But at the same time, as research on discourse has demonstrated across the years, statements that take the form of interrogatives perform a variety of different actions that go beyond questioning, including asserting (Han, 2002; Schegloff, 1984). In this particular case, these "questions" enable SI to repeat some of the assertions that he made previously about someone among the Native Hawaiians getting paid to help leave the rest of the Native Hawaiian community with nothing.

Following these "questions," SI then performs another narrative departure in line 24 by addressing directly somebody named Bob and asking him how he is. It is not clear from the video if the addressee acknowledge this question in any form, but we do see that SI makes another statement to Bob—he uses the Pidgin negative marker *no* to state that *you mighty quiet there I no see you long time* before returning, following another micropause, to his testimony in line 25. He returns to his testimony by performing another repetition of the idea of nothing being prevalent through another question *you know what I mean why is nothing so prevalent (.) for our community* that does not seem to expect a response.

There may be a tendency to view a political testimony with so many repetitions and "departures" as somehow deficient or, at least, "strange" from a western approach that seeks to recognize a regular structure to its social narratives (i.e., Boyd et al., 2020). Yet, a significant amount of repetition does not make a narrative repetitious in a negative way nor do departures make them any less engaging. There is evidence, in fact, that from a Hawaiian perspective repetition in a story is desired and perceived in a positive light. The linguist Samuel Elbert wrote about Hawaiian storytelling that "repetition of key words in successive verses is much admired" and generally serves as "proof that intellectual virtuosity was much esteemed in the culture" (Elbert, 1951: 64). More recent writers have supported this sentiment in their analyses of Hawaiian storytelling. Kimura (2002) and Perreira (2013) make use of the Hawaiian term *pīnaʻi* ("repetition") to include repetition as a foundational feature of Hawaiian oratory and to suggest that it can provide a sense of *mana* ("power") to speech (see Saft, 2019: 62–73 for further discussion).

To be sure, SI is speaking in Pidgin and not Hawaiian, but here we need to recall from Chapter 2 a historical connection between the two languages that derives from the fact that pre-creolized forms of pidgin were based largely on Hawaiian and also from the fact that, as Kimura (1983) notes, speakers of Hawaiian turned to Pidgin to preserve their Native Hawaiian identity after Hawaiian was banned. When we also consider that the speaker SI is Native Hawaiian and speaks both Pidgin and Hawaiian, then it is possible to make the suggestion that there is a strategic reason for his frequent repetitions, that he is employing repetition as a resource for adding *mana* to his testimony.

Furthermore, there is another reason for believing that his repetitions are strategic resources. This reason is connected to the fact that narrative departures add a more interactional tone to the testimony that is reminiscent of a style of speech used frequently by Pidgin speakers known as "talk story." Talk story, which has been called a "major speech event in Hawaiian culture" (Au, 1980: 91), refers to a lively interaction among people in Hawai'i marked by the telling of stories, discussions, and different types of verbal play that includes joking. SI's remark in lines 1–2 of Excerpt (1) to Collette about the differences between their hair is the type of joking that might occur as a part of a talk story. Of course, SI's departures do not take on the full character of talk story, but they do, as departures, have an interactional effect of redirecting the attention of the audience for a quick moment.

And, because of this "talk story" aspect of the departures that redirect attention, the departures allow the speaker to shift back to his testimony and thereby highlight key points by repeating them. This narrative departures, therefore, allow the speaker to repeat his main points without necessarily repeating the points directly one after another. This is specifically what he does in lines 6–7 when returns from his departure of "Hi auntie" to repeat that getting nothing for 200 years *nevah just occur*. He does it again in line 24 after addressing *how you Bob*? He subsequently returns to the testimony to restate and thus emphasize his question in line 25 *why is nothing so prevalent?* In this light, these so-called departures may be understood as an effective narrative strategy for making a powerful and effective testimony. Indeed, one final excerpt below shows that SI continues using this strategy. This excerpt, Excerpt (4), occurs a few lines after the conclusion of Excerpt (3). Six lines of his testimony from 26–31 have been omitted. It begins as SI urges the committee again in lines 32–33 to *figure out who da corrupt kanakas in power*.

Excerpt (9): Skippy Ioane testimony

32	SI:	*whatever it takes for get one somebody for figure out who da*
33		*corrupt kanakas in power (.) how come Hawaiian Homes jus so dumb (.) dey*
34		*born dumb, or dey got creat- or somebody paid em to be dumb (.) you know*
35		*what I mean Collette? (.) How come we get alas for so long (.) alas is such*
36		*a prevalent things in our communities*

In this excerpt, it can be seen that SI poses another "question" in line 33, *how come Hawaiian Homes jus so dumb*. And, like his earlier questions, this serves as a rhetorical strategy as he offers nothing more than a short micropause at the end of line 33. Instead of waiting for an answer, he continues in line 34 to pose the issue in terms of either-or, either *dey born dumb* or *dey got creat-or somebody paid em to be dumb*. Then, after another short pause near the end of line 34, SI engages in an action that is similar to a narrative departure in line 35 when he addresses Collette in 35 with the question *you know what I mean Collette*? It is similar to a narrative departure because he moves temporarily away from addressing the collectivity of people there to address one individual. It is also different, though, from the previous narrative departures because he is not asking her a question that temporarily moves away from the main topic of the testimony. There is a micropause after this question to Collette in line 35, but it is impossible to tell if the addressee provides any type of response, verbal or non-verbal. Still, though, this departure accomplishes an important function as it enables SI, on the one hand, to emphasize his point about Hawaiian Homes being dumb through his address of this question directly to Collette and, on the other hand, to then return from this departure to emphasize another related point. Indeed, the excerpt shows that SI continues his testimony with another rhetorical question in line 35 that repeats one of the main points of his testimony thus far. Using the term *alas* again, he asks *how come we get alas for so long*. Without waiting for a response, he then performs another repetition at the end of line 35 through line 36, this time using a statement structure, to restate that *alas is such a prevalent thing in our community*.

SI thus has employed interactional strategies that include repetition, rhetorical questions, and narrative departures in these 36 lines of testimony to make, first of all, the central point that the Native Hawaiian community has received nothing as it remains on the waiting list for land and, second of all, to request that a separate committee be established to investigate Native Hawaiians who may have been paid off to keep the general community of Native Hawaiians on the waiting list. These interactional strategies are all accomplished primarily through a Pidgin grammar and lexicon but also feature creative components from the speaker that come from outside of Pidgin itself. While it is perhaps not a good idea to accord significant validity to the comments made on Youtube in response to this videoclip, it is nonetheless striking that SI's testimony was overwhelmingly praised. Comments included statements such as, "I KEEP GOING BACK TO THIS VID ... NAILED IT" (original all in caps), "It doesn't get more straight up then that," "BRILLANT! NOTHING BUT CORRUPTION! THIS MAN IS MAN! (original all in capital letters)," "At least this guy knows some truth.......The Hawaiians on the top are intent on keeping the Hawaiians on the bottom DOWN!" "BRAVO!! This is truth! amerika is well known for this behavior," and "I love this! I am so proud of this speech. Truth hurts sometimes." As these comments attest to, the repetitions, rhetorical questions, and narrative departures should be appreciated as strategies that greatly contributed to the effectiveness of this testimony. Moreover, the testimony on the overall, together with Tonouchi's story, speaks to the potential of Pidgin as a voice for the expression of resistance in public domains of Hawaiian society. The speaker SI does suggest that some Native Hawaiians may be implicated in wrongdoing, but his testimony is largely a critique of the fact that Native Hawaiians are not being given the land promised to them by the Hawaiian Homeland Commission. Pidgin in this sense serves as a resource for demanding answers and actions concerning the land that was taken from the Native Hawaiians as a part of American Colonialism.

4.3 Talking About Pidgin in Hawaiian

The first two analyses of this chapter have served to emphasize the utility of Pidgin in the public domain as a resource for expressing resistance. Both the writer Tonouchi in the first analysis and the speaker SI in the second use Pidgin to accomplish complex linguistic processes that include switches in person perspectives, indirect quotation, repetitions, and narrative departures as a part of formulating important sociopolitical criticisms. For the last analysis of this chapter, I change the focus and explore the relationship between Pidgin and Hawaiian through interviews with two Hawaiian speakers who are known to be speakers and supporters of Pidgin. As the excerpts presented in the analysis will show, both interviewees grew up speaking Pidgin and both also learned Hawaiian later in life as a second language. One of the interviewees, JA, serves as a teacher at the Nāwahī Hawaiian medium school, and the other, CL, works as a lecturer in the Ka Haka ʻUla Hawaiian Language College at the University of Hawaiʻi at Hilo. CL teaches courses in Ethnobotany and Ethnozoology and teaches primarily through the medium of English. CL is also a well-known entertainer in Hawaiʻi who has produced at least one album. The analysis begins with JA describing in Excerpt (10) the basic organization of the two languages in her life.

Excerpt (10): Interview with JA

1 SS: *Mau nō kou hoʻohana ʻana i ka ʻŌlelo Paʻiʻai ma kou- kou ola*
Still EP your use NOM O the Pidgin in your your life
"Do you still use Pidgin in your life?"

2 JA: *ʻAe kēlā lā kēia lā ma- keu hoʻi ma ka hale ʻoiai ke hele au i*
Yes that day this day especially EP in the house because when go I D
3 *ke ke kula ʻo ka ʻŌlelo Hawaiʻi wale nō akā ke pau hoʻi ka hale*
The the school S the Hawaiian only EP but when done return the house
4 *ʻŌlelo Paʻiʻai piha ka ʻohana no laila [ʻae*
Pidgin full the family so yes

"Yes, this and every day, especially at home because when I go to school It is only Hawaiian but when finished and I go home, the family speaks fully in Pidgin and so yes

5 SS: *[maikaʻi aa kou mau mākua kekahi =*
Good aa your PL parents also
"Good, your parents too?
6 JA: = *ʻae*
Yes
"Yes."
7 SS: *mai kou wā liʻiliʻi*
From your time small
"from when you were small?"

8 JA: *'ae mai ko'u wā li'ili a laila wala'au pū au me kekahi o ko'u mau 'ānake*
Yes from my time small and talk also I with some of my PL aunts

9 *no O'ahu mai*
From O'ahu D

"Yes, from when I was small, and I also speak (in Pidgin) with some of my aunts "from O'ahu."

Employing the term *'Ōlelo Pa'i'ai*, the Hawaiian term for Pidgin that was discussed in Chapter 2, the interviewer asks JA in line 1 if she still uses Pidgin in her life. In response, JA answers in line 2 that she does every day, and then she next adds through line 3 that she especially uses it at home since she only speaks Hawaiian at school. She then continues in line 4 to note that when she returns home, her family speaks *'Ōlelo Pa'i'ai* fully (*piha*). When the interviewer asks confirmation questions in lines 5 and 7 about whether this was true of her parents and whether this started from the time she was young, JA responds affirmatively in line 8 that this had been the case since she was a child.

As noted at the outset of this chapter, Pidgin is typically juxtaposed with English, with Pidgin considered a private language in contrast to the belief that Pidgin speakers employ English in public. JA, however, offers a different take on this division. Instead of Pidgin versus English, it is Hawaiian that stands in a specific arrangement in her life; she is expected to leave Pidgin at home and speak only Hawaiian at school. Pidgin still remains valued as she appears to be proud that she speaks it every day, but she needs to maintain a division between the two. This type of division is also apparent later in the interview with JA as discussion focuses on her sister, who did not follow her in pursuing the study of Hawaiian.

Excerpt (11): Interview with JA

1 JA: *i ko'u mana'o 'ano like kona pae 'Ōlelo Pa'i'ai me ka'u akā i kona mana'o*
In my idea kind like her level Pidgin with my but in her idea

2 *ʻoi aku ʻoi iki aku kaʻu ma luna ona akā ke walaʻau me kekahi ke launa*
More little D mine above her but when talk with some when meet

3 *me kekahi o kona mau hoa*
With some of her PL friends

"In my mind, her level of Pidgin is like mine but in her mind my level of Pidgin is a little bit above hers, when talking with when meeting with some of her friends

4 SS *ʻae*
Yes
"yes"

5 JA *ʻo ka mea mua hō um like ʻoe me kou kaikaina ke lohe aku a laila pane*
S the thing first wow like you with your sister when listen D and answer

6 *ʻau aʻale like ʻo ia me aʻu*
I no like she with me

"the first thing is wow um you sound like your sister and I answer, no, she is like me."

7 SS *o:[:*
Oh
"oh"

8 JA *[ʻo au ma mua ona like ʻo ia me aʻu*
S I before her like she with me
"I came before her, she is like me"

9 SS *ʻae kākoʻo kākoʻo akā ʻaʻole ʻo ia hāhai iā ʻoe ma ka ʻōlelo Hawaiʻi ea*
Yes agree agree but not she follow O you with the Hawaiian right

10 *ʻa ʻole ʻo ia i komo i ka papa*
Not she PST enter O the class

"yes, I agree, I agree but she did not follow you with the Hawaiian, right? She did not take a course."

11 JA *ʻae ʻaʻole ʻo ia a ua komo iki liʻiliʻi wale nō*
Yes not she and PST enter bit little only EP
"yes she did not and she took just a little bit (of Hawaiian)"

12 SS *aa =*
Ah
"aa"
13 JA *=aloha mahalo a laila ke hana nei ʻo ia i kekahi um ʻoihana hou no laila*
Aloha mahalo and working she at certain company new so
14 *makemake ʻo ia i kuʻu ʻōlelo o ka lā a laila kaʻana au i kekahi hua ʻōlelo*
Want she O my word of the day and share I O some words
15 *Hawaiʻi me ia no laila ke hoʻāʻo nei e hoʻohana ʻo ia ma kekahi ʻano*
Hawaiian with her so trying to use she in some way

" 'Aloha' and 'mahalo' and she is working at a new company and so she wants my word of the day and I share some Hawaiian words with her and so she is trying to use Hawaiian to some degree."

After first expressing in line 1 her belief that she and her sister speak Pidgin at the same level, JA notes through line 2 that her sister believes that JA's Pidgin is stronger. JA then describes in line 5 how her sister's friends think JA speaks Pidgin at the same level as her sister, which prompts JA to suggest proudly through line 8 that it is her sister who followed her in her speaking of Pidgin.

These first 8 lines thus indicate, at least as described by JA, that there may be something special in the level of Pidgin spoken by both her and her sister that makes it noticeable by her sister's friends. This suggests that there are different "levels" of Pidgin, with JA and her sister speaking what is sometimes called "thick Pidgin," that is, the basilect variety. It is also probably what Dr. Llewellyn Young, who was quoted at the outset of the chapter, meant when he used the superlative "harshest" to describe the Pidgin spoken in Kekaha. JA, though, seems to express pride in this excerpt in the fact that she speaks such a level of Pidgin.

These first 8 lines indicate that there may be some choice about the degree to which a Pidgin speaker employs a thick Pidgin, but at the same time, the rest of this excerpt focuses on the fact that JA's sister decided not to follow her in studying Hawaiian. In response to the interviewer's question about this in lines 9–10, JA replies in line 11 that her sister studied a little bit and provides examples of *aloha* and *mahalo* in lines 13 to show the degree of the sister's knowledge. At the same time, JA notes in lines 13–14 that that her sister is currently attempting to employ

Hawaiian in her new business and she has asked JA to share Hawaiian knowledge with her on a daily basis. JA sums this up in line 15 as her sister is trying to use Hawaiian "in some way" (*ma kekahi ʻano*).

The latter part of this excerpt thus suggests that JA's sister, despite choosing not to study Hawaiian, is finding that Hawaiian is useful in business in society. This reflects, on the one hand, the idea that the value of Hawaiian in society has risen to the degree that it can be advantageous in business, but also, on the other hand, that studying Hawaiian is still very much a choice within society. Speaking Pidgin in society may also be a choice—JA suggests that she and her sister speak a thicker form of Pidgin than some of those around her—but at the same, there is no indication that either JA or her sister is finding Pidgin as valuable a resource at work. In fact, as JA already made clear, she is expected to speak only Hawaiian at her place of work, in school.

A similar type of division between Pidgin and Hawaiian was apparent in the interview with CL. This excerpt occurs very early in the interview just after the interviewer had asked CL about his usage of Pidgin. In response, CL had mentioned a new CD he was working on with songs in Pidgin and how he had been talking with his producer, Charles, about the categories of awards given at the Grammy Music Awards.

Excerpt (12): Interview with CL

1 CL: *Loaʻa nō kekahi māhele no ka ʻōlelo Hawaiʻi no ka mele akā aia ia*
Has EP some part for the Hawaiian for the song but exist that
2 *ʻāpana ma loko o ka māhele regional roots category*
Part inside of the part

"There is a category for Hawaiian language songs but it is in the grouping within the category regional roots category."

3 SS: *o::*
Oh
"oh"
4 CL: *a no laila ʻano ʻē pehea e hoʻohālike ai kekahi mele ʻōiwi o Hawaiʻi*
And so strange how compare some song native of Hawaiʻi
5 *me ka mele ʻōiwi o Louisiana nō hoʻi a i ʻole Zydeco a ia ʻano mele*
With the song native of EP EP or and that kind song

6 *aia ka nui o ia ʻano mele i loko o hoʻokahi māhele ʻo regional roots*
Exist the big of that kind song within o one category
7 *category a so ʻano ʻē*
And strange

"and so it strange, how can you compare some song native to Hawaiʻi with the song native to Louisiana or Zydeco and that type of song, most of those songs are within the category Regional Roots and so it is strange."

8 SS: *ʻae*
Yes
9 CL: *ʻo Kalani Peʻa ka mea nāna i lanakila no ʻelua makahiki no ia māhele*
TM Kalani Peʻa the one who PST win for two years for that category
10 *so nīnau au iā ia ʻo Charles ʻē inā ua haku au i kekahi inā hoʻopuka*
Ask I O him TM Charles hey if Pst wrote I O some if put out
11 *au i kekahi CD hou me ka ʻōlelo Paʻiʻai ka hapalua a me ka ʻōlelo*
I o some new with the Pidgin the half and with the Hawaiian
12 *Hawaiʻi kekahi hapalua pehea ka ʻoiaʻiʻo ʻana o ka o ka māhele*
Also half how the truth NOM of the of the category
13 *hiki ke hoʻokomo ma Regional Roots a i ʻole ʻaʻole hiki*
Can put in or not can

"Kalani Peʻa is the one who won for two years for that category so I asked him, Charles, hey if I wrote a song, if I put out a new CD half in Pidgin and half in Hawaiian, how will that work in the category of Regional Roots, or is that not Possible? What does that say about the truth of the category."

14 SS *a:*
Ah
"ah"
15 CL: *a wahi āna no ka ʻōlelo Paʻiʻai ʻaʻole ʻo ia ʻike*
And according to him for the Pidgin not he know
"And according to him, he did not know about Pidgin."

CL notes in line 1 that there is a Grammy award category for the Hawaiian language but also notes in line 2 that it falls under the category of "Regional Roots." Following a short response from the interviewer in line 3, CL describes in lines 4–7 the problem of such a category, namely, that it covers a lot of different types of music, from Hawaiian music to indigenous music of Louisiana and that of Zydeco. In doing this, he employs the Hawaiian term *'ōiwi*, which means "native" or "indigenous," noting in line 4 that Hawaiian music is indigenous music and noting in line 5 that Louisiana has indigenous music. He remarks in lines 6–7 that putting all of these types of music together in one category of "Regional Roots" is "strange" (*'ano 'ē*). He then offers the information in line 9 that a musician from Hawai'i, Kalani Pe'a, won the award in this category for two years. Kalani Pe'a is known in Hawai'i for singing in Hawaiian, and probably for that reason, CL remarks that he asked his producer Charles in line 10 about the category for a song by CL that was half in Pidgin and half in Hawaiian. As he states in line 13, he asked Charles directly if it would fall under the category of Regional Roots. As CL reports in line 15, Charles did not know.

CL has relayed this story that includes interaction with his producer to demonstrate the contrast between Hawaiian and Pidgin. Hawaiian has received recognition through the world through a Grammy award bestowed upon a Hawaiian singer, but it is not clear whether Pidgin would even be recognized in the same category. This contrast is a potential problem for CL because he has chosen to record music that is half in Pidgin and half in Hawaiian, and he is concerned that it might not make him eligible for consideration in the same category as Hawaiian. While CL is speaking specifically about the music industry and not Hawaiian society per se, his concern about the lack of recognition of Pidgin in the industry is reflective of the differing statuses of Hawaiian and Pidgin in Hawai'i. Bolstered by the Hawaiian language revitalization movement and the creation of Hawaiian-specific educational structures, Hawaiian's value has increased significantly while Pidgin still faces stigma that lead many to try to keep it out of educational institutions altogether.

As the next excerpt shows, even though CL struggles to find a place for Pidgin in the music industry, Pidgin stills remains the main language spoken with his family.

Excerpt (13): Interview with CL

1 SS: *me kou 'ohana kekahi wala- me kāu mau keiki 'ōlelo Pa'i'ai 'oe*
With your family also speak- with your PL child Pidgin you
2 *me [lākou*
With them

"Also with your family, with your children, do you speak Pidgin with them."

3 CL: *['ae 'ae akā 'o wau wale nō he 'ōlelo Hawai'i*
Yes yes but TM I only EP Hawaiian
"yes, yes, but I am the only one that speaks Hawaiian
4 SS: *'ae ['ae*
Yes yes
"yes, yes"
5 CL: *[inā makemake au e ukiuki lākou me ka 'ōlelo Hawai'i i nā manawa a*
If want I annoy them with the Hawaiian on Pl time
6 *pau a i 'ole 'o he aha ia mea a i 'ole 'o ha'akoi iā lākou e 'ōlelo Hawai'i*
All or what that thing or push O them to Hawaiian
7 *akā me ka ma'alahi akā ke komo nei ka'u keiki waena i ka 'ōlelo Hawai'i*
But with the easy but enter my child middle O the Hawaiian
8 *ua puka ka'u ko'u ka'u hiapo ma ma ke kula 'o Kamehameha akā 'a'ole*
PST graduate my my my oldest in in the school Kamehameha but not
9 *'o ia kāna mea ikaikai ka 'ōlelo Hawai'i*
He his thing strong the Hawaiian

"If I want them to be annoyed, (I can do it) with Hawaiian all the time or, what is that thing? or push them to speak Hawaiian, but I can do that easily but my middle child is taking Hawaiian, my oldest graduated from Kamehameha Schools but Hawaiian was not his strong point."

10 SS: *a: a:*
Ah, ah
"ah, ah"
11 CL: *akā ma ka 'ōlelo Pa'i'ai o- ma'a ma'amau he mea ma'amau*
But in the Pidgin use to regular thing regular
"But in Pidgin, oh, it is a regular thing, it is regular"

In response to the interviewer's question in lines 1–2 if he uses Pidgin with his family, CL responds in line 3 with two *'ae* ("yes") but then quickly moves to emphasize that he is the only one who speaks Hawaiian. He next expands on this information in lines 5–6 and a part of line 7 by saying that he can sometimes frustrate his family members by speaking to them in Hawaiian and by forcing them to use Hawaiian. He then adds in line 7 that one of his children is studying Hawaiian in a class and, in line 8, that his oldest child graduated high school from Kamehameha, which is the largest private school system in the state specifically for children of Hawaiian blood. They do have requirements for studying some Hawaiian language at Kamehameha, but as CL notes in line 9, Hawaiian language is not one of his strong suits. Following a brief acknowledgment from the interviewer in line 10, CL offers in line 11 that Pidgin is the "regular" (*ma'amau*) language. Here, he does not specify that Pidgin is the regular language of the home, but his choice of the descriptor *ma'amau* ("regular") seems to attribute to Pidgin the status of "regular" language for him and his family.

It is interesting in this excerpt that CL, like JA, recognizes that even though Hawaiian is gaining in value within society, speaking Hawaiian is still very much a choice in society that some people, such as CL choose, and others, like members of his family, do not. And while Hawaiian may still be a choice, speaking Pidgin in CL's family is not described as a choice; instead, it is treated as the regular and accepted thing to do.

Yet, even though the employment of Pidgin may be regular and accepted in CL's family, he reveals in the interview a belief in the inappropriateness of Pidgin, at least in comparison with English. Excerpt (14) shows such an orientation.

Excerpt (14) Interview with CL

1 CL: *'A'ole 'o ia hoihoi i ka 'ōlelo Hawai'i akā 'o ka 'o ka 'o ia ka mea ua*
Not he interested in the Hawaiian but TM the TM the it the thing PST

2 *ʻōlelo nui ka ʻōlelo Haole makemake ʻo ia e ʻōlelo Haole ma waho o ma*
Say big the English want he to English outside of the
3 *kahi o ka ʻōlelo Paʻiʻai*
Instead of the Pidgin

"He is not interested in Hawaiian but the thing is that he speaks a lot of English, he wants to speak English outside instead of Pidgin."

4 SS: *o: hoihoi m- ma Kamehameha ea ʻōlelo Hao[le koi ʻia*
Oh interesting at Kamehameha right English required PAS
"that's interesting, at Kamehameha, right, English is required."
5 CL *[yeah no ka mea*
because
6 *ʻano koi ʻia (.) e ʻōlelo kūpono ma laila*
Kind of require PAS to speak properly at there

"yeah because they are kind of required to speak properly there."

CL reports in line 1 that his oldest is not interested in Hawaiian and continues in line 2 to note that he/she speaks mostly in English. Next, he remarks in lines 2–3 that he/she likes speaking English outside instead of Pidgin (*ma kahi o ka ʻōlelo Paʻiʻai*), thus indicating that his oldest child's decision to speak English goes against the typical practice in his family, namely, the use of Pidgin. The interviewer next in line 4 connects the fact that his oldest child attended Kamehameha with his/her desire to speak in English. As the interviewer employs the term *koi ʻia* ("require") to suggest that students are required to use English at the school, CL begins in overlap in line 5 and then continues on to repeat the term *koi ʻia* in line 6 to note that the *ʻōlelo kūpono* ("appropriate language") is what is required at the school. His choice of the modifier *kūpono* indicates an evaluation as well as a hierarchy, specifically, that English is the appropriate language, which stands in contrast to Pidgin and also possibly to Hawaiian. His usage of this evaluation does not necessarily indicate that it is his own outright belief, but it does suggest that even a staunch supporter of Pidgin and Hawaiian such as himself may reveal an orientation to the public ideology that English is in fact recognized as the most appropriate language in Hawaiʻi.

JA did not go as far as to reveal a similar orientation in her interview, but did she relate a story from her experience as a student in the public school system that can help explain the development of such an orientation to ideological beliefs about linguistic appropriateness within people in Hawai'i. She explains this in Excerpt (15), the last excerpt of this chapter.

Excerpt (15): Interview with JA

1 JA: *no laila ma ko'u wā li'ili'i mai ka pae papa malo'ō a i ka puka kula 'ana*
So in my time small from the level kindergarten to graduating NOM
2 *mai ke kula ki'eki'e a ua kūpa'a au ma ka 'ōlelo Pa'i'ai ua loa'a nā*
From the high school and PST steadfast I in the Pidgin PST have PL
3 *kumu i um 'ano pāpā i ka 'ōlelo ma kekahi 'ano akā 'a'ole i koi 'ia*
Teacher PST kind ban O the language in some way but not PST require PAS
4 *au e 'ōlelo Pelekānia*
I to speak English

"So when I was small from kindergarten level to graduating from high school, I was steadfast in my Pidgin, there were some teachers who kind of banned the
language but I was not required to speak English."

5 SS: *hmm*
6 JA: *ua loa'a kekahi papahana kek- 'a'ole papahana he mau ha'awina kekahi*
PST have some program not program PL lesson some
7 *mau hō'ike'ike i pono ai ia'u e 'ōlelo ma'ema'e 'a'ole na'e ka 'ōlelo*
PL presentation PST have to I to speak clean not though the language
8 *Pelekānia piha akā ma'ema'e a ma kēia 'oiai kēlā he pāhana papa*
English full but clean and at this since that program class
9 *'umikumalua a laila ka'u kumuhana nui ua pili i ka hoewa'a 'ana*
Twelve and my topic big PST related O the paddle NOM

"There was a program, not program, some lessons, some presentations that I had to speak cleanly at, not fully in English though but cleanly and in this (presentation), since it was the program for senior students and my big topic was paddling."

10 SS *o:*
Oh
"oh"
11 JA *a laila ma ka'u hō'ike'ike 'ana 'oiai aia au e ha'i'ōlelo ana ua poina au i*
And in my present NOM since there I speaking PST forget I O
12 *kahi hua'ōlelo a laila ua ho'opuka au i ka hua'ōlelo 'o dakine*
Little word and PST blurt out I O the word dakine
"and in presenting since I was up there speaking I forgot one little word and I blurted out the word 'dakine.'"
13 SS *a:*
Ah
"ah"
14 JA *no laila ma muli o kēlā ua 'ano: ua hā'awi 'ia ho'okahi 'ai ma lalo*
So due to that PST kind of PST give PAS one point down
"So because of that, it was kind, I had one point taken off."

Through lines 1–2, JA expresses her commitment to Pidgin throughout her school experience from kindergarten through high school, but she then notes in line 3 that there was a type of ban on Pidgin (*'ano pāpā 'ia*) even though it was not strong enough to require her to speak English. After a short response from the interviewer in line 5, JA continues in line 6 with an example. She states in lines 6–7 that she was expected to "speak cleanly" (*'ōlelo ma'ema'e*) when it was time for a school presentation. The term *'ōlelo ma'ema'e* is potentially an ideologically laden expression, but she attempts to clarify this in line 8 by saying that the expected way of speaking was not English but was still *ma'ema'e* ("clean"). She does not attempt to explain this further but adds that it was her senior project on the "big" (*nui*) topic of canoe paddling. After another short response from the interviewer in line 10, JA tells the story in lines 11–12 that as she was making her presentation, she forgot a word and in its place produced the word *dakine*, which is a Pidgin term that probably derives from the English words "the kind" and has many uses in Pidgin. After another short response from the interviewer in line 13, JA reports that her grade was dropped by one point due to her inclusion of the word *dakine.*

JA is thus careful not to equate speaking cleanly with speaking English as opposed to Pidgin, but it is clear from her explanation that her speech was not "clean" due to one Pidgin term and that this one Pidgin term was the reason she did not receive the highest possible grade. In short, then, if students are penalized for including Pidgin in a formal speech, this sends the message that they are not to use Pidgin in their speeches. Moreover, the fact that JA lost points for the inclusion of one Pidgin term in an otherwise "clean" speech reveals the persistence of ideological beliefs that have left Pidgin as a stigmatized language since it developed over one hundred years ago. Even for those who speak and support Pidgin throughout different domains of society, it is English and not Pidgin that represents the appropriate or clean way of speaking in society. This ideological belief, then, may also be responsible for the division expressed by both interviewees between Pidgin and Hawaiian, namely, that Hawaiian has gained recognition in public areas such as the workplace and also music awards while Pidgin still struggles for acceptance.

4.4 Concluding Remarks

The last analysis of this chapter suggests that the stigma attached to Pidgin as inferior, at least compared to English, is still apparent in Hawaiʻi. Even for the interviewees, who are supporters and proud speakers of Pidgin, it was difficult for them to manage this stigma in their interviews as they both used terms such as "appropriate" (*kūpono*) and "clean" (*maʻemaʻe*) when referring to formal English speech.

This stigma exists even though there is growing evidence from research demonstrating that the notion of Pidgin as inferior has no basis in the reality of actual language usage. The first two analyses provide further proof of this as both the written story by Tonouchi and the spoken testimony by SI employed a wide range of discursive strategies to produce texts that stood as well-stated criticisms of aspects of society resulting from American settler colonialism. And while we may also point out that the very choice of Pidgin, as a much maligned language, serves a show of resistance to the hierarchical structure that puts English first, this by no means detracts from the fact that Pidgin is and can be used a regular medium of communication in society. As shown especially by Tonouchi, who used Pidgin to explain aspects of recent history as part of his story,

Pidgin can be used to tell stories from first- and third-person perspectives.

The analyses in this chapter, then, contribute to a growing Pidgin advocacy that has been attempting to raise critical language awareness about the situation of Pidgin in Hawai‘i. These efforts at advocacy, which include university coursework, a video project that engaged high school students, a position paper by a group known as Da Pidgin Coup, and Pidgin summits (Higgins, 2021a, 2021b), have certainly been a factor in the recognition in 2015 of Pidgin as an official language of Hawai‘i on the census and have served as inspiration for continued research, such as this chapter, on the use of Pidgin at the discourse level. Through a combination of research showing Pidgin used in society for different purposes and further advocacy efforts, the hope is that society at large, especially educators and other gatekeepers, will realize the value of Pidgin in society. Pidgin is one of the first languages of many people in Hawai‘i, and it is thus very important to their identity as individuals born and raised in the islands. A greater understanding and appreciation of Pidgin, among both people from the outside and speakers themselves, will be empowering as it will help break down the hierarchy between Pidgin and English and provide speakers with a stronger belief in their own creative abilities.

Finally, it is worth noting that the interviews are suggestive of an interesting dynamic developing between Pidgin and Hawaiian that may be unfavorable to Pidgin. As noted by the interviewee JA, she is required to leave her Pidgin at the door and speak Hawaiian in her role as a teacher at a Hawaiian medium school. This experience is probably similar to many of the students in the Hawaiian medium pathway; they are encouraged to speak Hawaiian and discouraged from using Pidgin at school. However, as I discuss further in Chapter 7, students in some Hawaiian medium schools are offered opportunities, through a heritage language program, to study foreign languages such as Latin, Japanese, and Chinese through the medium of Hawaiian. This program is intended to take advantage of the developing multilingual abilities of the students to facilitate further cognitive development and enhance the metalinguistic ability of students to understand and analyze language. Additionally, English is introduced into the curriculum in the 5th grade, a result of a compromise with state government officials who were fearful of having Hawaiian medium education without any English at all. To be sure, there are Hawaiian language educators (Cabral, 2018; Wilson, 2017) who note that the similarity between the structure of *ʻŌlelo Paʻiʻai* and Hawaiian aids speakers of Pidgin in learning Hawaiian and in the process helps them appreciate their Pidgin knowledge. Still, it is not readily apparent what role, if any, Pidgin may have in the Hawaiian language educational pathway that continues to gain momentum in Hawaiian society. Granted, it is difficult to ascertain a clear picture of the intersection of Hawaiian and Pidgin through the two interviews in the chapter, but if Pidgin speakers such as JA are expected to check their Pidgin at the door in Hawaiian medium schools, it is worth considering whether a new hierarchy may be in the making, one which puts Hawaiian (and English) above Pidgin. Keeping an eye on the Hawaiian-Pidgin connection in future may make it possible to find ways to use the growing Hawaiian revitalization movement to garner support for Pidgin as well.

References

Au, K. H. (1980). Participation structures in a reading lesson with Hawaiian children: Analysis of a culturally appropriate instructional event. *Anthropology & Education Quarterly, 11*, 91–115.

Bahktin, M. (1981). *The dialogic imagination*. Texas University Press.

Bahktin, M. (1986). *Speech genres and other late essays*. University of Texas Press.

Balaz, J. (2019). *Pidgin eye*. Ala Press.

Boyd, R. L., Blackburn, K. G., & Pennebaker, J. W. (2020). The narrative arc: Revealing core narrative structures through text analysis. *Science Advances, 6* (32). https://doi.org/10.1126/sciadv.aba2196

Cabral, J. (2018). *E Ola ka ʻŌlelo Paʻiʻai. Keynote speech at the Hawaii-Pidgin summit*. University of Hawaiʻi at Mānoa. Retrieved from https://www.hawaii.edu/satocenter/?p=1713

Chock, E. (Ed.). (1978). *Talk story: An anthology of Hawaii's local writers*. Petronium.

Chock, E. (1990). *Last days here*. Bamboo Ridge.

Cooren, F. (2012). Communication theory at the center: Ventriloquism and the communicative constitution of reality. *Journal of Communication, 62*(1), 1–20.

Drager, K. (2012). Pidgin and Hawai'i English: An overview. *IJLTIC, 1*(1), 61–73.

Elbert, S. (1951). Hawaiian literary style and culture. *American Anthropologist, 53*(3), 345–354.

Ellis, J. (2020). Da decolonizing real: Liberating humour in Joe Balaz's Pidgin eye. *The Journal of Commonwealth Literature, 1*, 1–14.

Han, C. H. (2002). Interpreting interrogatives as rhetorical questions. *Lingua, 112*(3), 201–229.

Higgins, C. (2015). Earning capital in Hawai'i's linguistic landscape. In R. Tupas (Ed.), *Unequal Englishes across multilingual spaces* (pp. 145–162). Palgrave Macmillan.

Higgins, C. (2021a). Promoting Pidgin at the University of Hawai'i at Mānoa. In G. Clements & M. J. Petray (Eds.), *Linguistic discrimination in U.S. higher education: Power, prejudice, impacts, and remedies* (pp. 174–188). Routledge.

Higgins, C. (2021b). Engaging the public in sociolinguistics for social justice: Advocating for Pidgin speakers in Hawai'i. In D. S. Warriner & E. R. Miller (Eds.), *Extending applied linguistics for social impact* (pp. 13–34). Bloomsbury Academic.

Kimura, L. (1983). The Hawaiian language. In *Native Hawaiians study commission: Report on the culture, needs, and concerns of native Hawaiians* (pp. 173–224). Department of Interior.

Kimura, L. (2002). *Nā mele kau o ka māhele mua o ka mo'olelo 'o Hi'akaikapoliopele na Joseph M. Poepoe: He kālailaina me ke kālele ma luna i nā ku'inaiwi kaulua*. M.A. Thesis, University of Hawai'i at Hilo.

Lum, D. (1986). Local literature and lunch. In E. Chock & D. Lum (Eds.), *The best of bamboo ridge* (pp. 3–5). Bamboo Ridge Press.

Lum, D. (1990). *Pass on, no pass back*! Bamboo Ridge.

MacKenzie, I., Francis, F., & Rutter Giappone, K. B. (2018). *Comedy and critical thought: Laughter as resistance.* Washington, D.C.: Rowan and Littlefield.

Mossman, B. (2021). Keeping the faith. *Midweek.* Retrieved from https://www.midweek.com/dr-llewellyn-young/

Odo, C. (1975). *Phonological processes in the English dialect of Hawaii* (Ph.D. Dissertation). University of Hawai'i at Mānoa.

Odo, C. (1977). Phonological representations in Hawaiian English. *University of Hawaii Working Papers in Linguistics, 9*(3), 77–85.

Perreira, H. (2013). He ki'ina ho'okuana'ike mauli ma ke kālailai mo'okalaleo. *Hūlili: Multidisciplinary Research on Hawaiian Well-being, 9*, 53–114.

Reinecke, J. (1969). *Language and dialect in Hawai'i: A sociolinguistic history to 1935*. University of Hawai'i Press.

Romaine, S. (1994). Hawai'i Creole English as a literary language. *Language in Society, 23*(4), 527–554.

Romaine, S. (1995). Birds of a different feather: Tok Pisin and Hawai'i Creole English as literary languages. *The Contemporary Pacific, 7*(1), 81–123.

Romaine, S. (1996). Pidgins and Creoles as literary languages: *Ausbau* and *Abstand*. In M. Hellinger & U. Ammon (Eds.), *Contrastive sociolinguistics* (pp. 271–289). Mouton de Gruyter.

Romaine, S. (2005). Orthographic practices in the standardization of Pidgins and Creoles: Pidgin in Hawai'i as anti-language and anti-standard. *Journal of Pidgin and Creole Languages, 20*(1), 101–140.

Saft, S. (2019). *Exploring multilingual Hawai'i: Language use and language ideologies in a diverse society*. Lexington Books.

Saft, S., Tebow, G., & Santos, R. (2018). Hawai'i Creole in the public domain: Humor, emphasis, and heteroglossic language practice in university commencement speeches. *Pragmatics, 28*(3), 417–438.

Sakoda, K., & Siegel, J. (2003). *Pidgin grammar: An introduction to the Creole language of Hawai'i*. Bess Press.

Schegloff, E. (1984). On some questions and ambiguities in conversation. In J. M. Atkinson & J. Heritage (Eds.), *Structures of social action: Studies in conversation analysis* (pp. 71–93). Cambridge University Press.

Siegel, J. (2008). Pidgin in the classroom. *Educational Perspectives, 41*(1–2), 55–65.

Sorensen, M. J. (2008). Humor as a serious strategy of nonviolent resistance to oppression. *Peace & Change: A Journal of Peace Research, 33*(2), 167–190.

Tamura, E. (1994). *Americanization, acculturation, and ethnic identity: The Nisei generation in Hawai'i*. University of Illinois Press.

Tannen, D. (1995). Waiting for the mouse: Constructed dialogue in conversation. In D. Tedlock & B. Mannheim (Eds.), *The dialogic emergence of culture* (pp. 198–217). University of Illinois Press.

Tonouchi, L. (2001). *Da Word*. Bamboo Ridge Press.

Tonouchi, L. (2009). *Living Pidgin: Contemplations on Pidgin culture*. Tinfish Press.

Weaver, S. (2010). The 'other' laughts back: Humour and resistance in anti-racist comedy. *Sociology, 44*(1), 31–48.

Wilson, W. H. (2017). Hawaiian language revitalization. In H. Sato & J. Bradshaw (Eds.), *Languages of the Pacific Islands: Introductory readings* (pp. 220–237). CreateSpace Independent Publishing Platform.

Wong, L. (1999). Language varieties and language policy: The appreciation of Pidgin. In T. Huebner & K. Davis (Eds.), *Sociopolitical perspectives on language policy and planning in the USA* (pp. 221–237). Benjamins.

Yamanaka, L. A. (2000). *Heads by Harry*. Harper.

Yamanaka, L. A. (2006). *Wild meat and the bully burgers: A novel.* Picador.

Yokota, T. (2008). The 'Hawai'i Creole problem': Attitudes about Hawai'i Creole. *Educational Perspectives, 41*(1–2), 22–29.

5

"Filipino" and "Micronesian" as Categories of Immigrant Languages in Hawai'i

Having focused the previous two chapters on Hawaiian and Pidgin, respectively, I concentrate this chapter on immigrant languages, the category I use to describe languages that are not indigenous to Hawai'i but instead arrived with people who came and stayed in Hawai'i. This includes the plantation laborers who began coming in the mid-late 1800s with languages such as Cantonese, Mandarin, Japanese, Portuguese, Korean, Spanish, Tagalog, and Ilokano, and it also includes more recent arrivals who speak Marshallese, Kosraean, Palauan, Pohnpeian, Chuukese, and Yapese, languages that have frequently been grouped together in the category of "Micronesian."

As discussed in Chapter 2, consideration of the role of immigrant languages in Hawai'i's language ecology should be undertaken with awareness that the infusion of immigrants and their languages in Hawai'i coincided with the decimation of the native Hawaiian population and the near extinction of the Hawaiian language. Unlike languages like Japanese, Portuguese, Ilokano, and the "Micronesian" languages, Hawaiian is, except for a few pockets of diaspora on the mainland United States, spoken only in Hawai'i. The same also should be said about

S. Saft, *Language and Social Justice in Context*,
https://doi.org/10.1007/978-3-030-91251-2_5

Pidgin. Despite the complex relationship between Hawaiian and Pidgin, Pidgin is a language unique to Hawai'i. Although both Hawaiian language revitalization and Pidgin advocacy continue to expand, any attempts to promote immigrant languages without consideration of these two languages is to risk further endangerment of Hawaiian and increased stigmatization of Pidgin.

That having been said, this chapter emphasizes a need to advocate for social justice for immigrant languages in Hawai'i given that many immigrants to Hawai'i suffer from linguistic injustices that can prevent them from gaining access to crucial information and services and can also result in the placement of their children in "special" programs for "English learners," which in turn may hinder their access to "mainstream" educational pathways as well as their ability to make advances in society. The Hawai'i Department of Education (DOE) reports that "in any given year Hawai'i's Els [English Learners] represent about 70 different languages,"[1] a statistic that emphasizes the tremendous linguistic diversity in Hawai'i but also raises questions about the degree to which the needs of these students and their families are being met.

This chapter explores these questions by focusing on two groups of people in Hawai'i, those typically covered by the categories "Filipino" and "Micronesian." These are two very diverse groups in and of themselves that actually represent multiple languages. Nonetheless, I choose them here for two major reasons: (1) the categories "Filipino" and "Micronesian" are commonly employed in Hawai'i in everyday discourse and also in the media (see Saft, 2019 for discussion and analysis); and (2) included within these categories is some of the most recent and active immigration to Hawai'i. Although the year 1906 is used as the official starting point of Filipino immigration, people from the Philippines, many of whom are extended family members of the plantation laborers, continue to immigrate to Hawai'i. 1986 is usually given as the beginning of the arrival of people in the "Micronesian" category because that is the date of the Compact of Free Association (COFA), an agreement the United States has with the Republic of the Marshall Islands, the Republic of

[1] http://hawaiidxp.org/quick_data/datastory/el.

Palau, and the Federated States of Micronesia that allows people from those three places to move to the United States without a visa (Talmy, 2006). As a group, "Micronesians" have been referred to as the most recent immigrants. Although the two groups are different from each other in many ways, this chapter will show that both have faced hardships that stem from the linguistic hierarchy that has developed in Hawai'i.

This chapter is divided into four larger sections, starting with a basic overview of the status of immigrant languages in the current educational system in Hawai'i. This section will set the stage for the next two sections, which focus specifically on the categories of "Filipino" and "Micronesian" and their experiences in attempting to achieve upward mobility in a social system dominated by English. The original plan for these sections was to engage in interviews with speakers of "Filipino" and "Micronesian" languages in Hawai'i about their experiences, but my research revealed the existence in the literature of numerous voices from within the "Filipino" and "Micronesian" communities, some of which appear in academic publications but also others in alternative sources such as poetry, interviews, reports, videos, and blogs. These two sections accordingly center on these voices because they provide critical perspectives on the linguistic and other injustices that some people face in Hawaiian society. Finally, the fourth and final section presents a critical analysis of newspaper discourse in Hawai'i in order to shed light on how newspapers reinforce a public discourse that disadvantages speakers of immigrant languages through the promotion of a public monolingualism.

5.1 Immigrant Languages and Hawai'i's Schools

As described in Chapter 2, there was a time in Hawai'i when some groups of immigrants readily pursued the teaching of their first languages to children. This includes the creation of language schools that functioned separately from the regular public schools to teach German, Chinese, Korean, and Japanese. In particular, Japanese schools were the most prominent with 37,762 students at its peak in 1941 (Shimada,

1998). According to Shimada (1998), this number represented 84.3 of the second generation Japanese schoolchildren.

However, as already noted, the American territorial government went to a lot of trouble to control and ultimately close the language schools. The German language schools were forced to close at the beginning of World War I (Wagner-Seavey, 1980) and the onset of World War II resulted in the end of the Japanese and Chinese languages schools. As Shimada (1998) reports, the Japanese schools were forced to liquidate their assets as many of the school leaders were placed in internment camps at the beginning of the US involvement in World War II. By forcing the closure of these schools, Hawai‘i followed the campaign in the United States to promote English as the key to demonstrating allegiance to America by making it difficult for immigrant parents to transmit ancestral languages to their children.

Despite continued opposition to the language schools following the war (Shimada, 1998), they began again in the late 1940s with the Japanese and Chinese communities leading the way. The number of students in the Japanese language schools increased from 67 schools with 11,631 students in 1948 (Niyekawa-Howard, 1974) to a peak of 87 schools with 13,054 students in 1965 (Shimada, 1998). Still, enrollment did not approach the peak it had reached prior to the war with Niyekawa-Howard (1974: 13) observing that, “compared with the decade immediately preceding World War II when a fairly steady enrollment of 38,000 to 40,000 was maintained, it is obvious that the war had drastically reduced the role the Japanese language schools played in the community.” Niyekawa-Howard (1974) also reports that the number had decreased to about 7,000 prior to the publication of her article in 1974, and it is likely that the number has continued to decline. The largest school that offers Japanese language education, Rainbow Gakuen School in Honolulu, lists its student population at 623 as of 2016.[2] Yet, while enrollment may not be as high as it once was, it is important to note that language schools and programs do still exist in Hawai‘i, including those that focus on teaching Japanese, Chinese, Korean,

[2]https://en.hjschl.org/SchoolLife/Enrollment.aspx.

Samoan, and Tokelauan. It is also important to recognize that these schools exist outside of the public school system that developed in Hawai'i.

In fact, Niyekawa-Howard (1974) suggests that one of the reasons for the decline of students in language schools is the increase in availability of public schools offering Japanese. Shimada (1998) gives 1958 as the year that public high schools began to offer Japanese classes as a secondary language. This trend continues to the current time as the Hawai'i Department of Education (DOE) offers options for learning not only Japanese but also other immigrant languages under a program that is called "World Languages." Although just how many languages a school offers will depend on that particular school's resources and interest in the community, the DOE Web site states that "The World Languages Program consists of instruction in 11 languages including American Sign Language, French, German, Hawaiian, Ilokano, Japanese, Korean, Mandarin Chinese, Russian, Sāmoan, or Spanish, at the elementary and secondary school levels."[3] The website also notes that the program's vision is "that all students will communicate and demonstrate cultural competence in at least two languages."

Moreover, the Hawai'i DOE has taken two steps in order to bolster the World Languages programs in their schools. First, it instituted in 2016 a "Multilingualism for Equitable Education Policy" which states that "all Hawai'i State Department of Education (HIDOE) schools embrace, promote, and perpetuate multilingualism to support and advance learners, families, and communities."[4] Through this policy, the DOE promises that it will, among other goals, "provide a range of language programs for multilingual students," "provide effective educators with the appropriate knowledge, skills, and materials," and "provide outreach supports to families" (Multilingualism). As stated on the website, such goals "were written to be inclusive of all major language groups in Hawai'i: Hawaiian, English, World/Heritage Languages, and

[3]https://www.hawaiipublicschools.org/TeachingAndLearning/StudentLearning/Multilingualism/Pages/WL.aspx.

[4]https://www.hawaiipublicschools.org/TeachingAndLearning/StudentLearning/Multilingualism/Pages/default.aspx.

American Sign Language" (Multilingualism). Toward achieving these goals, the website notes that the DOE has, among other activities, been hosting a Multilingualism and Arts Symposium since 2019 and also worked on making information available in various languages on the Internet.

The second step has been the creation of a "Seal of Biliteracy" to award to students who graduate from high school with a high proficiency in the two languages of the state, Hawaiian and English, or in one of the two languages of the state and at least one additional language that includes American Sign Language (Seal of Biliteracy). The Seal of Biliteracy has been used to recognize students in the Hawaiian medium education pathway who have achieved strong levels of literacy in both Hawaiian and English. In fact, the DOE website lists separately that one of the purposes of the seal is "to support opportunities for the study of and increase proficiency in 'Ōlelo Hawai'i" (Seal of Biliteracy). Since the program began, the number of recipients of the seal has increased from 37 in 2017 to 361 in 2020 (Seal of Biliteracy).

Both of these programs, "Multilingualism for Equitable Education Policy" and the "Seal of Biliteracy," signify that the Hawaiian state government does not just passively pay lipservice to multilingualism as a positive aspect of society. It has also taken action by putting these two initiatives into place to allow students to be recognized for their multilingual skills.

At the same time, however, it still needs to be recognized that, in terms of language, there remains a very lopsided emphasis in public education system on English. In order to graduate from high school, for instance, students are required to pass two courses in English Language Arts, a course in expository writing, as well as other language arts electives that are aligned with the so-called Common Core of courses (Graduation Requirements). Yet, despite offering incentives for achieving proficiency in multiple languages, the reality is that students are not in fact required to study any world languages to gain their diploma. Students are given a choice among two courses in World Languages, two courses in Fine Arts, and two courses in another category entitled "Career and Technical Education/JROTC." In other words, languages are available if students should choose to study them (although availability will differ depending on staffing and resources at each school), but students may complete their graduation requirements without ever studying any language other than English, which is of course required. This reality is supported by statistics from the 2017 report entitled "The National K-12 Foreign Language Enrollment Survey" which showed that only 18.61% of students in K-12 schools in Hawai'i enrolled in foreign language study.[5] This number is slightly below the national average for all states, 20%, and significantly below that of states such as New Jersey, Maryland, and Vermont which had over 35% enrollment in foreign languages. This information suggests that the two initiatives "Multilingualism for Equitable Education Policy" and the "Seal of Biliteracy" are not necessarily viewed as programs for the general population of public students but rather as elective programs that may function as incentives for students who already have a background in languages other than English.

With world languages optional, it is possible to see the real pressure in the school system in terms of language is to make sure students can fulfill the English language requirements so they can earn their high school degrees. This pressure has led the Hawai'i DOE to label a significant number of its students as either EL (English Learners) or LEP (Limited English Proficiency) and to pull them out of regular courses to receive special English instruction. The DOE notes that EL status is determined via an English proficiency test given to students whose families indicate that they "use a language other than English," and it also reports that every year 17% of students in the K-12 system "are, or have been, Els" (Hawai'i's English Learners). Although Ilokano, Chuukese, Marshallese, Tagalog, and Spanish are listed as the five most common first languages, these special English courses are usually populated by speakers of various different languages, which means that the students do not typically receive instruction in their first language. All instruction, regardless of first language, is tailored to meet the English requirement and there is no evidence that these programs pay much, if any, attention to the first languages of the students. To be sure, the statistic offered previously in

[5]https://www.americancouncils.org/sites/default/files/FLE-report-June17.pdf.

this chapter, namely, that EL programs are populated by speakers of 70 different first languages, seems to suggest how impossible it would be to expect teachers and staff to administer programs that developed English and the first languages of the students.

Yet, even though 70 may be impossible, the success of Hawaiian medium education provides evidence that it is possible to produce bilingual students with strong English skills even if the focus is not solely on English. Although Hawaiian medium education began in the 1980s outside of the DOE through the non-profit ʻAha Pūnana Leo, it is now supported within the DOE through what is called *ka papahana kaiapuni* that "delivers instruction exclusively through the medium of Hawaiian language until grade 5, whereupon English is formally introduced" ("Hawaiian language immersion program").[6]

Yet, even though English takes a backseat to Hawaiian in the classroom, reports from educators working in Hawaiian medium suggest that students perform well with academic English. Wilson and Kamanā (2011: 51) relate findings in Hawaiʻi with that of other indigenous language programs to emphasize that "programs that use the indigenous language and its heritage to an exceptional level, including full immersion through Grade 12, produce the same (or better) results in the nationally dominant language (e.g. English in the United States) and academics as standard English-medium programs … for indigenous students." They furthermore report that as of 2009, "the Nāwahī school has had a 100% high-school graduate rate and 80% college attendance rate" (Wilson and Kamanā, 2011: 46). It is not surprising then to read a recent newspaper article stating that popularity of Hawaiian language immersion has grown by 40% in the last five years (Lee, 2020), a statistic suggesting that many parents in the community are excited by this educational option. The Hawaiian medium school pathway may still be viewed as special because it focuses on the indigenous language of the islands and not on an immigrant language, but the success and popularity of the program should prompt leaders to wonder about the possible effectiveness of bilingual immersion programs for other languages in Hawaiʻi as well.

[6]https://www.hawaiipublicschools.org/TeachingAndLearning/StudentLearning/HawaiianEducation/Pages/translation.aspx.

Indeed, there is evidence in the private school sector in Hawai'i that bilingual educational techniques can be implemented. Maryknoll School launched a 50/50 Mandarin-English bilingual immersion program in 2017 that begins from kindergarten and currently goes through grade 4. The program has been featured in the local news and has been called "groundbreaking."[7]

Furthermore, the suggestion has been made to the DOE to consider similar types of bilingual programs available for other languages in Hawai'i. For instance, when the DOE solicited letters from the community as part of testimony in support of the "Multilingualism for Equitable Education Policy" in 2016, an instructor of Ilokano at the University of Hawai'i at Mānoa added the following suggestions to her statement:

> While I support the intent and purpose of the proposed BOE [Board of Education] policy 105.14, I believe that it can be made stronger. There is nothing in the policy that binds the BOE to implement the policy and it reads more like a series of recommendations. I urge the BOE to implement a bilingual education program that would allow the students to use their native languages while they are learning the English language. I would also urge the BOE to allocate money to this program to train teachers in each school in bilingual education and other languages. (Ortega, 2016)

This "urging" stems from the fact that, outside of the Hawaiian medium pathway, there is little emphasis on developing the students' first languages in the public education system.

5.2 Concerns About the EL Category

Although EL programs in Hawai'i do not emphasize teaching approaches that encourage students to develop their first languages, there is evidence that they do promote academic success, at least for some categories of

[7]https://www.kitv.com/story/39935283/a-groundbreaking-chinese-immersion-program-on-oahu-is-expanding.

learners. According to the website that shows the most recent data as the school year 2018–2019, one statistic indicates that students who were EL but exited the program prior to high school graduated at a rate of 90%, which was higher than the 86% graduation rate for students who were never in an EL program.[8] In short, students in EL but exiting before high school were more likely to graduate high school on time than "regular" students who were never EL. Moreover, the same holds for college enrollment; students who were in EL programs but exited them before high school were "more likely to enroll in college immediately in the first fall after high school than students who were Never EL," and are they are also more likely to complete college within six years of high school (Hawai'i's English Learners).

However, these positive outcomes unfortunately do not hold for students unable to make it out of the EL program before high school. Students who were in the category "active EL" in high school fall significantly below the "Never EL" students who follow the mainstream pathway. The 90% on-time graduation rate of the students who exited EL prior to high school falls to 70% for students still categorized as "active EL" in high school. This 70% rate also falls significantly below the 86% rate of graduation for "regular" non-EL students.

Further alarming is the fact that graduation rates vary significantly according to the first language of the student. For students who exited EL prior to high school and who spoke Ilokano, Tagalog, Japanese, and Spanish as a first language, the graduation rate is higher than students who were "never EL." In particular the rates for Ilokano (96%), Tagalog (93%), and Japanese (93%) are very high. But for speakers of Marshallese and Chuukese, the rates were significantly lower, 70% and 52%, respectively, for students who exited EL before high school. Furthermore, for Marshallese and Chuukese students who remained "active EL" in high school, the numbers are even lower, 51% for Marshallese speakers and 29% for Chuukese speakers. These low numbers contrast sharply with Ilokano and Tagalog speaking students, but even in those latter two groups, the graduate rate for "active EL" in high

[8]The data from this section is taken from: http://hawaiidxp.org/quick_data/datastory/el.

school falls to a number lower than "regular" students who were "never EL." The graduate rate for Ilokano "active EL" students in high school is 82% and for Tagalog speaking students it is 81%, both slightly lower than the 86% rate of "Never EL."

Statistics, of course, do not tell the entire story, but the numbers do suggest a couple of tendencies that are troubling. First, they underscore the degree to which English is valued over the first languages of the students. The students' ability to demonstrate the desired proficiency in English prior to high school can, according to the numbers, make or break their ability to graduate. If they do not exit the EL track before high school, their chances of graduating decrease significantly. Note here that the first languages of the students are basically inconsequential as they do not seem to figure into the assessment of the students' abilities in terms of oral and written communication. It is English or bust, which is to say then, that the approach to EL in Hawai'i public schools essentially falls into a subtractive category in which first languages are, more or less, disregarded. This therefore flies directly in the face of a growing literature suggesting that the development of literacy in an L1 can transfer over to success in English literacy, which also seems to be the case in the Hawaiian medium pathway with its achievement of a 100% graduation rate while not officially introducing English as an academic subject until the 5th grade.

The second troubling tendency is that the graduation percentages for speakers of some languages falls considerably for students unable to exit EL programs prior to high school. Specifically, there should be concern for students who speak Marshallese and Chuukese as a first language, but this concern should also extend to speakers of Tagalog and Ilokano as the on-time graduation rates for speakers of both fell significantly when they were unable to exit EL programs prior to high school. This result for speakers of all four languages begs the question not just of why this was the case but also, more importantly, of how can such a result be avoided in the future. The next section seeks to shed light on these questions through further consideration of the experiences of speakers of these languages in Hawai'i.

5.3 "Filipino" and "Micronesian" Languages

The basic point to be made in this section is that a social system that places pressure on teachers and students to achieve standards for the dominant language without giving systematic consideration to the diverse languages spoken by the students results in severe injustices for those who struggle with the dominant language. These injustices, in turn, create critical disadvantages for speakers who cannot demonstrate proficiency in the dominant language in school. Although "Filipino" and "Micronesian" are very different categories, they both share a history of struggles in Hawai'i that make them relevant in this chapter and in this section. I first consider the "Filipino" situation and then turn to the "Micronesian" category.

5.3.1 Stigmatizing and then Recapturing Filipino Languages as Heritage Languages

Researchers have recognized three waves of immigration of people to Hawai'i from the Philippines (Teodoro, 1981). The first wave began in 1906 when the first immigrants arrived to work on the plantations but ended in 1934 when the number of Filipino arrivals was limited to an annual quota of fifty after the Tydings-McDuffie Act granted commonwealth status and eventual independence to the Philippines. This quota, however, was lifted temporarily in 1946 due to a shortage of plantation workers, thus leading to the second wave of Filipino immigration. The third wave began in 1965 with the Immigration Act that abolished the quota system and allowed for existing Filipino families to petition "for the entry of extended-family kin" (Teodoro, 1981: 30), which led to the admittance of 26,626 family members between 1970 and 1976 (Teodoro, 1981). This type of immigration from the Philippines still continues today with Agbayani stating in 2011 that "we're number one in the number of immigrants coming in every year, and we have been since 1965" (quoted in Gutierrez, 2011).

The first wave of immigrants faced extreme racial and linguistic discrimination as they arrived at a time when English had already been declared the language of education, when Pidgin was emerging as a creole language, and when Japanese language schools were increasing. Unable to speak any of those languages, the first immigrants were at the will of their employers, who exploited them by making them work long hours for little wages. Yet, both Teodoro (1981) and Ramos (1996) note that despite continued hardships, language was one of the main reasons that this first wave of immigrants was able to create and maintain a strong Filipino community. Teodoro (1981: 43) asserts first that, "the use of Philippine languages and the retention of certain aspects of Filipino culture, undeniably part of that heritage, enabled the Filipinos to cope with the hostile conditions of the plantation era," and he later emphasizes that "given the circumstances Filipinos were thrown into, ... this retention essentially served as a basic source of group cohesiveness and strength." Although the Philippines is known to be very diverse with over 170 languages that are not necessarily mutually intelligible, this bonding was made possible due to the prominence of speakers of Ilokano. Both Teodoro (1981) and Ramos (1996) refer to early sociolinguistic work in Hawai'i by John Reinecke to make this point. This next passage from Ramos (1996: 163) refers specifically to the first wave of Filipino immigrants:

> According to Reinecke (1969), the Filipino immigrant group's large size, its short term of Residency in Hawaii, the attitude of transiency held by many of its members, and isolation from the rest of the population made it possible for them to maintain the use of the Philippine languages, especially Ilokano.

In addition, the Filipino community also took the initiative to promote its own language in the media. Reinecke (1969) reports the existence of eight Filipino newspapers, mostly in Ilokano, in 1935. Additionally, Teodoro (1981: 46) finds that "several radio stations have had broadcasts in Philippine languages since 1933." And even though Tedoro bemoans the fact that, unlike Japanese, Chinese, and Korean, "the Filipinos have not operated private schools where the mother tongue could be taught to their children" (Teodoro 1981: 46), it is important to note the strength of the linguistic heritage of the Filipino community in Hawai'i for two reasons. The first is because it contrasts with the belief that Filipino immigrants are unconcerned with the education of their children. Although the early immigrants may have been uneducated in terms of a schooling background (Teodoro 1981), they did construct a community with a Filipino language background for later waves of immigrants to build on. Due to the usage of Tagalog and English as languages of education in the Philippines, later Filipino immigrants, especially those from the third wave, sometimes arrived in Hawai‘i speaking three languages, including a regional language such as Ilokano. Ramos (1996) makes note of findings by Lasman et al. (1971: 92) "that out of 503 immigrants to Hawaii interviewed in 1971, 96% spoke Ilokano, but that 67.4% could speak Tagalog. In addition, 78.4% reported the ability to speak English, although this varied in degree." If we consider that the arriving immigrants, particularly children in Hawai‘i's schools, probably picked up Pidgin in school and on the playgrounds, this means that some in the Filipino community may be highly multilingual with a command of at least four languages.

In fact, writers of Filipino background have specifically attempted to debunk the so-called uneducated Filipino as a "myth," "misconception," and/or a "stereotype" (Teodoro 1981). Teodoro (1981: 26) emphasizes that the Filipinos viewed "education as a primary means through which one may not only enhance the quality of one's life, but acquire status and prestige as well" as a part of insisting that "the contention that Filipinos do not value education simply will not stand scrutiny." As he further notes, the first wave of immigrants "were compelled to concern themselves with economic survival" and therefore they did "not attend schools, but instead worked to help out their families" (Teodoro 1981: 24). Yet, it was this hard work in the face of racial and linguistic discrimination that enabled the first wave of immigrants to lay the groundwork of a community that enabled subsequent generations and subsequent Filipino immigrants to achieve social mobility in Hawai‘i. Indeed, the high graduation rates noted earlier of 96% and 93% for EL speakers of Ilokano and Tagalog, respectively (for students exiting EL programs before high school), are strongly suggestive of the degree to which education is emphasized within the family and the community.

The second reason it is important to stress the establishment of a linguistic heritage by the first wave of Filipino immigrants is because, as Labrador (2015) points out, continued immigration from the Philippines prompted many children of Filipino immigrants to attempt to distance themselves from their heritage because of the association with immigrants who spoke English with a "Filipino accent" and thus were marked as FOB (fresh-off-the boat). In particular, the use of a Filipino accent has been employed by local comedians as a part of what has been called "mock Fillipino" (Furukawa, 2007; Hiramoto, 2011) to poke fun at the Filipino community and help stereotype them as, among other things, "dog eaters" and "the perpetual immigrant or JOJ (Just-off-the-jet)" (Labrador, 2015: 7). Despite suggestions that the usage of Mock Filipino is all done in fun in a society where ethnic comedy is very common, Labrador insists that Mock Filipino not only "implies stupidity or lack of intelligence" (Labrador, 2015: 7), but it also "produces stigmatizing discourses of immigrant Filipinos, which in turn work to stigmatize Locals as immigrants" (Labrador, 2015: 51). Such stigmatizing discourse has resulted in young Filipinos born in Hawai'i attempting to distance themselves from these stereotypes by "disregarding or denying their cultural roots and not self-identifying as Filipino" (Labrador, 2015: 5).

Interestingly, instead of identifying as Filipino, these young people have chosen the identity of "Local" and have decided to speak Pidgin, which helps separate them from the category of "non-Local." (Labrador, 2015). As Labrador (2015: 9–10) notes, non-Local can refer to many other categories of people in Hawai'i that includes "haole," but he also asserts that "for Filipino identity making, 'immigrant', referring to those born in the Philippines, is the most salient non-Local category, although with the increased movement of Filipinos from the continental United States to Hawai'i, a Local Filipino/mainland Filipino polarity has also emerged." Pidgin works well then as an identifier of localness since it separates Filipino youth from both the stereotyped accents of immigrants and also from people from the mainland who speak English in a way associated with standard English that comes off as "uppity," "pushy," "know-it'all," and "materialistic" (Labrador, 2015: 11). Teodoro (1981: 58) sums this up by writing that, "for many local Filipinos speaking English that is not pidgin is interpreted as wanting to be considered better than the locals; speaking with a non-pidgin Filipino accent means that a person is a 'noninsider Filipino."

Indeed, the repercussions of sounding like a "noninsider Filipino" in Hawai'i can be severe. In an article in National Geographic (from Imani Altemus-Williams & Marie Eriel Hobro, 2021) that reconsiders the tendency to view Hawai'i as a multicultural paradise, Nadine Ortega says the following about her experience in Hawai'i's schools:

> "They would make fun of my accent" she says. "I stopped speaking for most of that school year. I was scared to speak because if I spoke, they would make fun of me." Fellow students even pushed her down the stairs. "It caused me to internalize shame," she says. "The summer after sixth grade, I watched a lot of TV and tried really hard to change that accent. I was like, 'How do I speak in a way that they would accept me? Why can't they accept me as I am?' I used to cry to my mom: I want to go back to the Philippines."

For Ortega, the "they" in the first sentence refers mostly to fellow students, particularly others of a Filipino heritage. As Labrador (2015) notes, young Filipinos were often the most disparaging of a Filipino accent in an attempt to show that they themselves were different.

In the passage from Ortega, the ridicule came from within school, but there is evidence that the stigma attached to a Filipino accent has even wider ramifications within society. Matsuda (1991) reports the story of a Filipino man in Hawai'i named Manuel Fragante who, despite being a combat veteran of two wars on the side of the United States and despite receiving the highest score on a civil service examination, was turned down for a job at the Division of Motor Vehicles. According to Matsuda (1991: 1334), "when he asked why, he learned that he was rejected because of his Filipino accent." At the urging of a Filipino member of the state senate, Fragante hired a lawyer and took the case to court, where interviewer notes revealed that Fragante was judged as having a "difficult manner of pronunciation" and a "heavy Filipino accent." Matsuda (1991: 1337) also notes that "the administrator in charge of hiring recommendations stated, 'because of his accent, I would not recommend him for this position.'" After four days, the judge, who Matsuda notes "was on assignment from Arizona" (Matsuda, 1991: 1337) sided with the original interviewers and concluded that "Manuel Fragante was denied the job *not* because of national origin, but because of legitimate difficulties with his accent." The Judge admitted that Fragante "has extensive verbal communication skill in English," but also added that "he has a difficult manner of pronunciation and that some listeners would 'stop listening' when they hear a Filipino accent" (Matsuda, 1991: 1339).

A more recent case that makes a similar point is Aris vs. Hawai'i (Aris v. Hawaii, 2013), in which the plaintiff, described as a full-time special education teacher and as a Filipino who "speaks English with a Filipino accent," filed a complaint after observing another teacher "mocking people of Filipino ancestry by mockingly using Filipino accents in the classroom 3–4 times per week, which resulted in the non-Filipino students laughing" (Aris v. Hawaii, 2013: 1). Although the plaintiff directly asked the teacher to stop this practice, the teacher continued to do so, which prompted the plaintiff to lodge complaints with her superiors. Eventually, the plaintiff was "terminated for false allegations of alleged performance issues" (Aris v. Hawaii, 2013: 2), which prompted the plaintiff to file a lawsuit. The lawsuit was ultimately dismissed after the court determined that "the Plaintiff failed to file the Complaint in the instant case within ninety days after receipt of the right to sue letter" (Aris v. Hawaii, 2013: 7).

The content of these two lawsuits together with the ridicule suffered by Nadine Ortega for a Filipino accent suggest a twofold stigma attached to a Filipino accent. It is ridiculed, first of all, because it does not sound local, thus making it a problem for children who are bullied by other Filipino youth wishing to make it clear that they are not FOB. Second of all, a Filipino accent is discriminated against in society because it is perceived as not conforming to a perceived standard English, which means that it may be difficult to understand for speakers of standard English.

At the same time that a Filipino accent remains a source of discrimination, Labrador (2015) interestingly notes that there has been a push by younger Filipinos in Hawai'i to reconnect with Filipino culture and identities through a process that Labrador (2015), following Strobel

(1996), refers to as indigenization and multiculturality.[9] As Labrador (2015: 14) explains, "for Strobel, indigenization is the process of rediscovering 'native' Philippine oral traditions, folklore, beliefs, and values as well as returning to a Filipino language as a medium of communication." It is by rediscovering oral traditions, folklore, beliefs, and languages that Filipinos in Hawai'i can assert and also transmit their culture and heritage to future generations. In the words of Labrador (2015: 14), "indigenization and multiculturality are seen as strategies to reclaim a cultural identity thought to be lost in the process of immigration and assimilation or repressed by United States colonialism and contemporary American racism."

This push to reconnect has occurred at a level of intersection between the community and the university, with the university responding to increased calls to serve the growing Filipino community and the growing number of Filipino students in University of Hawai'i system. In particular, the Pamantasan Council, established in 1987 and open to all students, administrators, faculty and staff from the various UH campuses, has been active in forging connections in actively promoting events at the university level (see Labrador, 2015 and also University of Hawai'i System Testimony on SB 1418 SD1).[10]

Activities described by Labrador on the campus of the University of Hawa'i at Mānoa include a student conference called "Rediscovering Filipino Identity" in 2002 and a song festival entitled Pag-ibig Sa Tinubuang Lupa ("Love for the Native Land"). Both of these activities were sponsored by the Katipunan Club which Labrador (2015: 75–76) describes as "Filipino/Tagalog language-based student organization that is a major component of the Filipino and Philippine Literature program at UH-Mānoa." Additionally, Labrador (2015: 76) notes that "the University of Hawai'i at Mānoa is the only institution in the world to offer a bachelor of arts degree with a specialization in Ilokano" and that

[9]Despite listing Strobel (1996) in the text, Labrador does not include such a reference in the bibiliography. There is, though, a reference to Strobel (1996), and hence, that is the source listed at the end of this book.

[10]https://www.capitol.hawaii.gov/session2019/testimony/SB1418_SD1_TESTIMONY_LHE-LAB_03-15-19_.PDF.

“students are also able to earn a minor and a certificate in Ilokano in addition to the bachelor’s.” The Ilokano program began, he notes, in 1972 but only became a BA granting track in 2013, which is consistent with a more recent emphasis on Filipino cultures and languages.

The Hilo campus of the University of Hawai‘i system also established a Filipino Studies Program in 2012 that includes language courses taught under the name of “Filipino.” The Filipino Studies Program offers a certificate and it also co-sponsored recent conferences such as the International Conference on Multidisciplinary Filipino Studies and the Pamantasan Conference that focuses on sustainability and is held in conjunction with the College of Agriculture. That the two largest 4-year campuses of the University of Hawai‘i system have recently increased their degree and certificate granting capabilities for programs in Filipino studies provides both a response and a reinforcement to the attempts to rediscover a Filipino identity within Hawaiian communities. The Filipino Studies website at UH-Hilo posts testimonials from some of its students that are indicative of the effects of recent efforts to help students reconnect with their Filipino heritage[11]:

> The Filipino Studies Program at UH Hilo has taught me so much about who I am as a Filipino. Throughout my elementary to high school years, I never got to be around anyone who lived the same life as me. My classmates had Filipino blood in them but were only 10%-30% Filipino, and none of them had a parent or family member who was born and raised in the Philippines. I also got teased on my middle name when asked by my classmates, and my Filipino food home lunches would be made fun of as well. For example, in 6th grade, I brought eggplant and pork with black bean sauce for lunch one day. And, when everyone in my class looked at my lunch, it seemed like everyone wanted to get away from me and not eat lunch with me. I only had about one or two friends in intermediate and high school who were more than 50% Filipino and could relate to my life.
>
> The biggest accomplishment that I took from the Filipino Studies Program was learning the basics of the Philippine national

[11]https://hilo.hawaii.edu/academics/filipinostudies/testimonials.php.

language: Tagalog. Growing up, I only knew how to speak and understand the Ilocano dialect because my family comes from the Ilocos Sur region of the Philippines.

Being a part of the Filipino-Studies program helped me realize the importance and impact that Filipinos have made in our Hawai'i society. As a Filipino-American living in Hawai'i, it gives me a sense of ownership and duty to keep the culture and traditions alive wherever I go. Being surrounded by individuals who come from the same culture as I do and who are proud to be Filipino is such a beautiful and empowering feeling.

Overall, Filipino Studies was an unforgettable experience that was a big part of my college career. The program gave me knowledge not just about Filipino culture and language, but it also helped me to grow personally and appreciate my Filipino identity more.

As a Filipino myself and being a part of an Ilocano family, the courses showed me a different side of the Filipinos. From my first few classes I learned about the language, grammar, how to construct sentences, and how to speak them. One of the assignments was to create a film in Filipino. The making of the film was very enjoyable as we got to bond with our classmates and practice the language. The other courses focused more on the cultural aspects such as the practices of the Filipinos, their history and beliefs, and much more. Learning about what the Filipinos have been through and accomplished has inspired me to keep working hard and continue to pursue my dreams.

While we may expect that the organizer of the website housing these testimonials would choose those that best promote the program, the comments nonetheless strongly suggest the importance of (re)connecting with their cultural heritage. It can be, as one of them states, "a beautiful and empowering feeling."

The very first testimonial above, in which a student describes being teased for a Filipino middle name and feeling isolated due to her Filipino heritage, brings the discussion back to education at the secondary school level. Despite the existence of a World Languages program in the public schools and also the implementation of two programs to support the multilingual talents of their students, there are no real educational procedures that enable students to maintain languages such as Ilokano and Tagalog at the elementary, junior, and high school levels. The lack of these programs helps reinforce a system that centers on English—and specifically a way of speaking English that may stigmatize a Filipino accent and result in bullying. Some educators, in fact, insist that lack of pathways for Filipino students hinders their development. Working with HIDOE (Hawai'i Department of Education) data from 2015, Halagao (2016) notes not just that Filipino students on the overall score lower than Asian peers in Language Arts and Math but also that there is a great disparity between performance of non-EL students to current active EL students. In her words, "the disparity was significant, with current/active EL students underperforming in English language arts and math," an observation which led to the conclusion that, "these findings from the K-12 state assessments also quantitatively validate what we have known about our students in the K-12 public school system based on traditional forms of assessment: Filipino youth are not academically performing up to their potential and abilities" (Halagao, 2016: 15).

Halagao relates the underperformance of Filipino youth to findings from the U.S. Census Bureau for the years 2006–2010 showing that "among family households with school-aged children, Filipinos have the second lowest mean income among the state's major ethnic groups" (Halagao, 2016: 16), and she also makes a clear call for the development and application of "culturally appropriate methods" that include the use of Filipino languages spoken by the students:

> We need to instead build on their strengths. One area of strength for our Filipino youth is our multilingual abilities. Many Filipino youth come to school knowing languages such as Filipino, Ilokano, and English. Instead of labeling our Filipino students as English Learner (EL), their multilingual abilities should be viewed as rich assets that should be nurtured, valued, and used as resources for learning. A suite of linguistic and cultural Hawai'i Board of Education (BOE) policies like the Seal of Biliteracy and Multilingualism for Equitable Education reinforces the value of Filipino immigrant student languages and supports evidence-based interventions like dual language and bilingual education for our Filipino EL students. (Halagao, 2016: 16)

Halagao does mention the two programs Seal of Biliteracy and Multilingualism for Equitable Education in this passage but she mentions them as evidence for the need of further interventions within the school system such as dual language and bilingual education that, outside of the Hawaiian language pathway, have not yet been fully explored. Halagao also bemoans the fact that the standardized testing procedures in language arts and math do not give an accurate depiction of the abilities of the students. As she writes, "if success had been assessed on different indicators such as the number of languages that students know, then Filipinos would be ranked higher. I also acknowledge that standardized tests are often culturally-biased and not a complete indication of what a child knows—especially children whose first language is not English" (Halagao, 2016: 16). This critique of both teaching and testing methods serves as a rather straightforward statement of the need to make languages other than English, Ilokano and Tagalog in this case, more at the forefront of education in Hawai'i for students of Filipino heritage. Evidence suggests that students are becoming increasingly able to explore their heritage cultures and languages at the university level, but the ability to do so earlier in the educational process may represent another major step in making education more equitable for students of immigrant backgrounds. To be sure, it is difficult to predict the degree that bilingual and dual language programs will reduce social stigma against Filipino accents, but they would hold much potential in encouraging speakers of Filipino languages to take more pride in their linguistic abilities and also in encouraging schools to recognize the true academic and linguistic abilities of their students. Moreover, bilingual education involving Filipino languages would make it possible to build on the linguistic skills already possessed by the students to further enhance their overall cognitive development.

5.3.2 "Micronesian"

Although the "Micronesian" experience in Hawai'i is typically traced back to 1986, which gives this group a much shorter history in Hawai'i than people in the category of "Filipino," it is clear that the

"Micronesian" experience in Hawai'i has been replete with hardships and discrimination.

One of the sources of discrimination is that the category of "Micronesian" has become a convenient scapegoat for a number of social problems that existed prior to 1986; these problems include homelessness, budget crises, lack of health care options, and crime. To put this in perspective, it should be understood that even though a primary motivation for the COFA agreement was to enable COFA citizens to migrate to the United States in order to seek health care and places to live because of the radioactive damage inflicted by the United States to the COFA islands, "Micronesians" have been scapegoated for doing what they were expected to do, seek affordable housing and health care. The following quotation in an article by Blair (2011) is from William Hoshijo, the executive director of the Hawai'i Civil Rights Commission, and begins to speak to the type of public backlash that has developed:

> I have no doubt that there is discrimination against migrants from the Compact States in Hawai'i. You can see it in some of the insider-outsider rhetoric used to describe them as a drain on resources, particularly in health and human services. While much of that is focused on the responsibility of the federal government and whether Hawai'i is getting its fair share of funding to offset the impact of migration, there is also some pretty vitriolic rhetoric in the mix. (quoted in Blair, 2011)

The same article by Blair (2011) also provides the voice of another advocate, Deja Ostrowski, who describes her concern about "an underlying assumption of "Micronesians" as a leech on social services."

In an effort to explore in more depth the usage of the category of "Micronesian" in public discourse, I undertook in previous research a search of local newspapers and found an overwhelming tendency to reinforce the idea that "Micronesians" are responsible for a "strain" on local resources (Saft, 2019). One example is presented below from the Honolulu Star-Advertiser, recognized as the largest newspaper in Hawai'i. It begins by discussing the work of Josie Howard at a non-profit organization titled "We are Oceania" that provides services and assistance to people in the "Micronesian" category.

From the Honolulu Star-Advertiser, July 24, 2017

> We are Oceania aims to help Micronesians retain communal values and succeed in a modernized world. Being successful, she said, means "to be able to navigate both worlds … find that safe place that works for you." Howard, who moved here from Chuuk to study in 1989, said Micronesians in Hawaii often face discrimination. "We feel very unwelcome," she said. Her three Hawaii-born children are "bullied at school because they're Micronesian," she said. Many newcomers are homeless, without job skills and in dire need of health care—which places a major strain on social services and has led to some resentment.

This article contains quotations from Howard that speak directly to discrimination in Hawai'i. She states that "we feel very unwelcome" and that her children are "bullied at school." Yet, while the bullying is itself a concern, it is also problematic that the writer of this article adds commentary at the end with a final sentence that reinforces the public sentiment that "many newcomers are homeless, without job skills and in dire of need of health care—which places a major strain on social services and has led to resentment." Far from being neutral, this type of discourse encourages media consumers to view people in the category of "Micronesian" in terms of their negative effects on society. With this type of sentiment reinforced in the media, it is not surprising that there have been suggestions made from within the Hawaiian state government to curb COFA migration completely (Blair, 2011) and also that the government made it more difficult for COFA participants to get access to health insurance by moving adults aged 18–64 off of state-funded Medicaid in 2015 (Hofschneider, 2020).[12]

[12]The U.S. federal government "cut COFA citizens off federal safety net programs like Medicaid, forcing states to figure out whether and how to provide health care to the poorest members of this immigrant community" (Hofschneider, 2020). It should also be noted that after 25 years without access Medicaid, the federal government restored COFA citizens' eligibility at the beginning of 2021.

As would be expected, those falling within the category of "Micronesian" feel the heavy burden of this type of public discourse that makes them the target for resentment from the rest of society. For example, the Marshallese poet and activist Kathy Jetnit-Kijiner shows her understanding of the so-called "Micronesian Problem" when she writes the following:

> We seem to be the problem that needs fixing. Within all of these discussions that centered around "The Micronesian Problem," our voices were generally absent, deemed unnecessary. And so our history was also ignored. A history that explained our need for migration and survival, a history of colonization, dispossession, and war—which left our countries crippled. This racism is also portrayed in how we've been revoked rights to healthcare benefits that we need to simply live. (Jetnit-Kijiner, 2013)

Another poet, Emelihter Kihleng, from the island of Pohnpei, shows a similar orientation in her poem titled "The Micronesian Question" (Kihleng, 2019), part of which is shown below.

> We are a "BURDENSOME" group
> of more than 10,000
> 50% living below
> federal poverty level,
> relying "not on educational services but on social-welfare services, health care and
> safey-net programs"

Jetnit-Kijiner (2013) also describes how this racism led her to adopt a negative self-view.

> When I first came to Hawai'i, I didn't know I was inferior- but I soon learned to adopt that mindset. I was told to speak more English. I was made fun of for my accent. I was always left out, for reasons I couldn't fully grasp. Teachers were constantly surprised at my ability to succeed. I was told I wasn't Marshallese—that Micronesian was easier to understand.

Another example of how this type of public discourse pushes people in this group toward self-hate is taken from an interview with Leroy Ittu in the article by Altemus-Williams and Hobro (2021) that questions the view of Hawai'i as a harmonious melting pot. In the interview, Ittu describes how people placed in the category "Micronesian" feel compelled to lie about and deny their background.

> All I see here is discrimination [and] faded dreams … People in Hawai'i call us cockroaches and say horrible things about us. They blame us for everything… when you go to a job interview, you have to hide the fact that you're Micronesian. 'Tell them you're something else. Say you're from an island by Guam.' But why should I lie about who I am? … I hope I will find peace here … We are humans too.

This idea that people placed in the "Micronesian" category feel a need to hide their ethnic heritages is used by Jetnit-Kijiner (2013) to describe how her poetry, as well as that of Emelihter Kihleng, which can be "angry, visceral, and in-your-face," is intended to serve as a response to the tendency among Micronesians to engage in self-hatred.

> This was—is—my story. And I wanted more people to talk about this issue—because it was the elephant in the room. And I didn't want that kind of hatred to live in other Micronesian kids raised in Hawai'i—the way it lived inside of me for so long. I didn't want them to hate their own culture or lose their language and connection to their homeland, because of this hatred.

In this passage, Jetnit-Kijiner (2013) expresses her fear that this self-hatred may lead other children raised in Hawai'i to move away from their cultural and linguistic heritages, in a similar way that Filipino youth eschewed a Filipino identity for a local one (Labrador, 2015). In fact, there is evidence that this is already happening. Vidalino Raatior states that "the young people growing up are beginning to disclaim their roots and heritage. If they were proud Micronesians, they are hiding it now because of possible negative impact. They start hearing negative jokes and begin doubting the label 'Micronesian' and begin to disclaim that" (quoted in Blair, 2015). Talmy (2006) notes a similar occurrence based on his critical ethnography of an ESL program in a Hawaiian high school. He reports that a 15-year-old girl born in Chuuk "admitted that she did not miss Chuuk much, since she had not lived there for a long time, and claimed with a halting laugh that she had 'no idea' when asked where she felt 'home' was" (Talmy, 2006: 28).

In terms of this connection between self-hatred and loss of cultural identity, significant scrutiny should be given to education. Discrimination against COFA citizens reverberates through many public and private domains of society, but the school system in Hawai'i certainly occupies a central role in promoting beliefs about the category of "Micronesians" and for allowing students themselves to be negatively impacted by these beliefs. Jetnit-Kijiner (2013) provides an example that probably represents the experience of many Micronesian children in school:

> My cousins in public schools had it way worse. They were spit on in hallways, jumped in the corners, pulled into fights, bullied and harassed. My cousin was placed in English
>
> As a Second Language class for an entire year, without any questions asked, before her teacher finally realized she could actually speak fluent English.

These experiences of Jetnit-Kijiner and her cousin were supported by the observations of Talmy (2006: 37) in his critical ethnography:

> There were also more overt expressions of non-Micronesian students' racism, mostly manifest in comments about Micronesians' appearance, intelligence, hygiene, classroom behavior, and motivations for being in the U.S. As one 9th grader from Hong Kong noted about his Micronesian classmates: "They disgust me. They spit, they dig their nose in the middle of the class, they talk so ((loud screeching voice)) wa ya wa wa ya! They don't do their work. They're thieves. I can't work with people like that.`` Said another, "They talk too much. They so loud. They don't even work. They lazy.`` A Taiwanese boy said he was "embarrassed`` being in the same class as Micronesians, while a Korean refused to touch them because

> he believed they had *uku*, or lice. These comments are similar to those made by a number of teachers as well. (37)

Especially notable in this passage from Talmy (2006) is that the quotations come from other students who have been marked by the school as deficient in English and placed together with "Micronesian" students in special classes for English learners. These EL students, who have already been "othered" by the school, are they themselves creating a "we" versus "other" distinction with the Micronesians as the "other," thus leading Talmy (2006) to describe the "Micronesian" students as the "other-other."

Also especially disheartening is the last sentence of this passage that includes teachers as contributors to this process of othering. Talmy (2006: 35), in fact, explicates this idea by writing the following about his observations at the school:

> What was most striking about teachers' interaction with Micronesian students at Tradewinds was how little they knew about Micronesia, and by extension, about their students from Micronesia. Even in the ESL classes, where Micronesians often comprised upwards of one third of the students, teachers clearly lacked understanding not only of the different cultures, customs, languages, and educational systems of Micronesia, but even of the countries that make up the geographical area. Teachers routinely confused Marshallese with Chuukese, Palauans with Pohnpeans, and appeared not to realize that students from these countries spoke different first languages. (LIs)

This lack of knowledge is a problem if we note that students from parts of the Pacific labeled as "Micronesian" increased from 1,100 in the late 1990s to more than 8,100 in 2014 (Lee, 2018). Lee (2018) reports in an article in 2018 that "today, a handful of DOE schools are more than 25% Micronesian."

Moreover, it is apparent that a high percentage of "Micronesian" students are placed in EL programs. Talmy (2006: 23) notes that in one district in Hawai'i in 2001, 30% of "Micronesian" students were considered "non-English proficient," 65% "limited English proficient," and 5% “fully-English proficient.“ While those figures are for one district over 20 years ago, more recent statistics indicate that the overall percentage of “Micronesian” students in EL programs is higher than ever. Heine (2002) notes that in 2002, 13% of the EL population in Hawai‘i came from “Micronesia,” but according to statistics from 2018 to 2019, speakers of Chuukese, Marshallese, Pohnpeian, and Kosraean accounted for a combined 32% of the EL designees.[13]

Often overlooked in these statistics are the concerned voices of parents as they watch their children placed in EL programs until they are “stopped out” for not being able to graduate by the required age of 18. Although “drop out” is the term for a student “who has been guided toward alternative education because she won’t have the right credits to not drop out” (Matsuda, 2016), COFA parents believe their children are “pushed out” and not “dropping out” (Matsuda, 2016). As Matsuda (2016) states in a report partly based on interviews with COFA parents, “parents say that their children are labeled as incompetent and trapped by the English Language Learner (ELL) designation… many parents blame the schools for cultural and linguistic discrimination that prevents their children from benefiting fully from Honolulu schools. Parents believe these and other factors cause Micronesian students to be ‘pushed out’ from the public school system.” Talmy (2006), in fact, reports the case of two EL students in his critical ethnography. The name “Tradewinds” refers to the pseudonym given to the school at which he conducted his observations.

> Mona and Nell were two 17 year-old 9th graders who came from different outer islands of Chuuk. Both were at very early stages of L2 English proficiency, were unable to read or write much in their L1s, and had sporadically attended public school in Chuuk. Their circumstances were similar to a number of other Micronesian students at Tradewinds, both Chuukese and non-Chuukese, whose formal educations were interrupted and/or who had dropped out of school in Micronesia: they had come to Hawai’i because there were few educational and employment prospects for them in Micronesia. Both girls struggled mightily in all of their

[13]http://hawaiidxp.org/quick_data/datastory/el.

> Tradewinds classes. Unfortunately, any aspirations they may have held of graduating from a U.S. high school ended when they were both pre-emptively "released" from Tradewinds because they would not have the necessary credits to graduate by age 18. Many ESL students, particularly Micronesians, were similarly released at Tradewinds, and directed to "alternative education" programs where they could get job training and a chance at a GED. (Talmy, 2006: 29)

The "releasing" or "pushing out" of "Micronesian" students prior to graduation was common in 2006 when Talmy published this article and it continues to be a concern (Matsuda, 2016).

In fact, the voices of parents are especially clear in a report from several educators in Hawai'i who were asked to research viable educational options available to meet the needs of the children of COFA communities (Kala'i et al., 2015). In order to complete their report, the authors conducted interviews with parents across the Hawaiian Islands and found that the "participants discussed several areas of policy needs, including those related bilingual/multilingual students, changes in the system to better understand "Micronesian" students and culture, and the most mentioned area of policy need: student grade placement should be based on readiness not in age" (Kala'i et al., 2015: 18). In particular, they found great concern about two "institutional problems," the fact that "students are often placed into ELL programs regardless of their academic ability to succeed in regular classes," and the fact that they are "getting 'aged out' of high schools before they can graduate because they cannot attend after the age of 18" (Kala'i et al., 2015: 54). The three passages below from the report demonstrate the concerns of the parents and how these concerns were sometimes linked to still another concern of the parents, the maintenance of the children's first languages and cultures.

> Several parents discussed how their child's school automatically placed their child in ELL classes because of their ethnicity; in one case, a mixed-race family labeled one of their children as Samoan and one as Micronesian and the school did not place the Samoan child in ELL but did place the Micronesian child in ELL. (p. 19)

> A majority of the comments concerned the loss of language and culture as a result of moving to Hawai'i and the dissatisfaction with the placement of students in the English Language Learner program based on ethnicity and/or assumptions that the students are incapable of speaking English and are illiterate. (p. 21)

> Both men and women, mostly from O'ahu, made 11 statements about home language. The concern is the loss of their home, heritage language because Hawai'i is now their new home and the influx of English is so strong. There is desire to teach languages such as Chuukese and Marshallese to students so the younger generations can communicate with the older generation. (p. 22)

The initial passage suggests a concern about racial inequality in the placement of children in EL programs, and the second and third passages show a linkage between EL placement and another concern of the parents, the maintenance of the children's first languages and cultures. Toward this point, the report offers a direct quotation from one of the parents:

> "Not to undermine or belittle the importance of the English language, but that it just helps the children empower their sense of who they are, that their language and culture is important". (p. 22)

Without dismissing the importance of English, this quotation shows an understanding of the connection among language, culture, and identity, namely, that the learning of one's language and culture can be empowering in terms of developing one's own sense of self. This empowerment through education would be diametrically opposed to the learning of self-hatred that some COFA residents have made reference to.

As a part of their report, Kala'i et al. (2015) discuss options of educational programs that can be created to aid the parents and students. They provide six options: (1) enrichment programs that provide services on non-instructional days; (2) Saturday school programs that allow students to focus on their cultures and languages; (3) afterschool programs; (4) family-based preschools that could function like 'Aha Pūnana Leo Hawaiian language preschools and also encourage parent participation; (5) a satellite campus of existing charter school that would make implementation easier because it would be administered by already established school; and (6) a charter school that would allow for an innovative approach to education which could be based on culture and language development. For option (5), the report uses the Hawaiian medium school Ke Kula ʻO Nāwahīokalaniʻōpuʻu as an example because it now has satellite campuses in Waimea on the Big Island and Waiʻanae on Oʻahu, both of which are also Hawaiian medium. The report does not suggest to which charter schools a campus based on "Micronesian" cultures and languages may be attached. Interestingly, for option (6), the report does not offer one of the Hawaiian medium schools as a model, even though a school such as Ke Kula ʻO Nāwahīokalaniʻōpuʻu is classified as a charter school. Instead, it lists three examples of schools established after 2010 that appear to be more focused on culture than language.

Ultimately, Kalaʻi et al. (2015) conclude "that while opening a Micronesian culture based charter school is not feasible at this time there are promising signs of the progress toward that goal" (Kalaʻi et al., 2015: 52). In the short run, they suggest that enrichment programs, better outreach to parents, and working more closely with DOE teachers to "address misunderstandings and misinterpretations between families and schools" (Kalaʻi et al., 2015: 53). One of the complicating factors noted toward the creation of a charter school is the diversity of the "Micronesian" community with "different cultural practices, history, and languages." They note that "while the participants and our clients articulated similar values, the language barrier among these politically different groups was still a limiting factors" (Kalaʻi et al., 2015: 52). They do, however, emphasize the need to take some form of action and they do include language as major reason for this need:

> Opening a charter school may not be possible in the near future, but the evidence shows that Micronesian parents and other stakeholders do want a different approach to the education of their children. They are fearful of the complete loss of Micronesian culture and language among the new generation of Micronesians growing up in the less-than-perfect public school environments. (Kalaʻi et al., 2015: 52)

Kala'i et al. (2015) do not argue for a form of bilingual education at the particular moment that the report was completed, but it is interesting to note that Heine (2002) had suggested nearly twenty years ago that the Micronesian community could potentially benefit from an educational approach that focused on the development of the children's first languages. She noted that many students come from educational systems in their home islands that focused on English but ignored "the development of cognitive academic language proficiency in the mother tongues" (Heine, 2002: 6), thus leaving them with limited academic proficiency in both. Moreover, she cites research by Cummins (1984) and Hakuta (1987) that "home language proficiency is a strong predictor of second language development" (Heine, 2002: 6).

Nonetheless, even though the reports by Kala'i et al. (2015) and Matsuda (2016) indicate that educators are taking notice of the situation of students in the "Micronesian" category, it has yet to have significant effects on the current secondary educational practices in Hawai'i. Students labeled as "Micronesian" are still frequently placed in EL programs that pay little or no attention to their first languages and, as a result, they still are at high risk of being "pushed out" of high school due to an inability to complete all of the requirements by the age of 18.

5.4 An Analysis of Media Discourse

The reports by Kala'i et al. (2015) and Matsuda (2016) are based on interviews with parents in the COFA community in Hawai'i and therefore help insert important voices into the discourse about language and education in Hawaiian society. Likewise, academic work such as Labrador (2015), which also features interviews with people in the community and affected by public policies, is also critical in terms of ensuring that a variety of voices are "heard." Moreover, alternative media outlets, including social media, provide avenues for the dissemination of opinions that may not make it into more mainstream forms of media. For example, the Civil Beat is an online platform in Hawai'i that has offered a variety of perspectives on the Micronesian and Filipino communities in Hawai'i. Similarly, it is via personal websites and blogs that

I was able to learn of the important work of the poets Kathy Jetnit-Kijiner and Emelihter Kihleng. In this sense, we are lucky that recent technologies offer the opportunity to learn about and pursue such diverse perspectives in the media.

At the same time, however, it is still true that a lot of public discourse still is controlled by mainstream media that includes newspaper and television news discourse. The mainstream media may influence public opinion so that people are unable to see the full range of options that are actually available. Specifically in terms of education, a public discussion that considers the importance of learning English in one of the states of the United States but does not describe the existence of various types of bilingual education can help convince the public of the necessity of EL programs that focus, naturally enough, only on English and not the development of the students' first languages. A public not aware of possible educational pathways is one that will not be able to push for such pathways. In this last main section of this paper, I explore public discourse on language and language education in Hawai'i through a critical analysis of discourse in newspapers in Hawai'i.

In order to do so, I make use of a database available through the University of Hawai'i at Hilo library called "Access World News" that makes it possible to do a keyword search of 30 local newspapers in Hawai'i, including the most circulated newspapers such as the Midweek Oahu and the Honolulu Star-Advertiser and also lesser circulated ones that include university and community college publications.[14]

In an attempt to gain a sense of recent public discourse related to English language education as well as education of world languages in Hawai'i, I conducted a search of the following keywords and phrases on May 26th, 2021: (1) "English language learners;" (2) "Limited English proficiency;" (3) "world languages;" (4) "bilingual education;" (5) "dual language;" (6) "bilingual;" (7) "Iloc/kano;" (8) "Tagalog;" (9) "Marshallese;" and (10) "Chuukese." I then chose the first ten mentions of these keywords and phrases in the database and engaged in a

[14]According to the Honolulu Star-Advertiser website, the two most circulated newspapers, the Midweek and the Honolulu Star-Advertiser are both owned by the same publisher, Oahu Publications, Inc. https://www.staradvertiser.com/about/star-advertiser-contact-information/.

discourse analysis of the content of the articles. The discourse analysis follows below, but it should be noted that some of the terms, such as "English language learner," "limited English proficiency," "Ilokano," "Tagalog," "Marshallese," and "Chuukese" appeared very frequently in the data. In comparison, the terms "world languages," "bilingual education," and "dual language," appeared less frequently, and it sometimes required a longer span of time to find ten mentions in the database.

The analysis shows that there are certain ways that some of these categories are discussed in the newspaper discourse. The first way is that English language learners are viewed as an underprivileged group that is need of special attention. Excerpts (1)–(4) provide examples:

Excerpt (1): Honolulu Star-Advertiser, December 13, 2020
This past week, media outlets were reporting discouraging news about the state of education in America: Our K-12 students are falling behind and failing at a drastically higher rate than in previous, non-COVID-19 years. Worse yet, the data seems to show that at-risk students — a demographic that lumps together low-income, minority, **English language** and special education learners — are being disproportionately affected.

Excerpt (2): Honolulu Star-Advertiser, March 28, 2021
The directive for remedial education by the U.S. DOE "validates the direction the department has already been heading with designating previous relief funds for this effort," said Nanea Kalani, state DOE communications specialist. There is some work being done along those lines, she said. A range of summer school models would include remediation, extended learning opportunities for **English language learners** and special education.

Excerpt (3): Honolulu Star-Advertiser, May 18, 2021
All distance-learning classes would be led by a certified teacher in that particular subject. The distance-learning platform must have accommodations for 504 Plan and special education students and **English Learners**.

Excerpt (4): Honolulu Star-Advertiser, September 20, 2020
The school's math and English proficiency rates were more than 17 percentage points above state averages. About a quarter of Liholiho's students are **English language learners** and more than 30% are economically disadvantaged, Small said.

Excerpt (1) focuses more generally on the state of education in the United States, but it sets the tone by defining the category "at-risk students" as a broad category that "lumps together" other specific categories of "low-income, minority, English language and special education learners." These categories of students are put together because they "are being disproportionately affected" during the COVID-19 period. Excerpts (2)–(4) support this approach to the categorization of English language learners. Taken from an article discussing how summer school could be used to help students, Excerpt (2) groups English language learners and special education with each other under the category of "remedial education." Excerpt (3) comes from an article discussing the composition of appropriate distance-learning platforms and also places English learners with "special educations students" and "504 Plan" students, which is a plan for students with disabilities. Excerpt (4) describes the positive trend of math and English proficiency rates in one particular school in Hawai'i, and in doing so it groups the categories of English language learners with "economically disadvantaged."

These articles may certainly be well-meaning in terms of their attempts to look after particular sets of students, but they create a discourse that reinforces to the public not only that English language learners is a "real" category but also that it is a category akin to special education and populated by people who are economically disadvantaged. Put bluntly, this discourse helps to stigmatize English learners as a kind of "helpless" group in need of special assistance from the greater educational system. This construction of English learners as helpless, thus, puts the well-meaning school system in charge of their well-being, which serves as the motivation for EL programs to fulfill this need. This discourse is further reinforced by another category frequently found in the newspaper database, namely "limited English proficiency." Excerpts (5)–(7) speak to this point.

Excerpt (5): Honolulu Star Advertiser, April 18 2021
Increasing the number of schools serving free meals to all students is important because there are many students from low-income households who don't qualify for SNAP. They could be from households with **limited English proficiency**, making it difficult for them to navigate the eligibility system.

Excerpt (6): Honolulu Star Advertiser, December 4, 2020
Tai Jung, who was also at the rally, has been helping her parents, Korean American immigrants who speak **limited English**, file their unemployment claims. "It's been very difficult and very straining," said Jung. "It is very difficult to navigate."

Excerpt (7): Honolulu Star Advertiser, April 8, 2021
We urge health care providers and public health stakeholders to conduct outreach to vaccinate vulnerable Asian American populations, such as those who are low-income and who have **limited English proficiency**.

Excerpt (5) begins by mentioning students from low-income households who may not qualify for a program that provides them with free meals. The article then connects these households to the category of "limited English proficiency" by suggesting that such students from low-income households may be "limited English proficiency." Excerpts (6) and (7) are slightly different as they do not focus on an educational context, but they nonetheless represent the fact that a connection is frequently drawn in the newspaper discourse between "limited English proficiency" and low-income status. In Excerpt (6) this is done through a link between limited English and unemployment, and in Excerpt (7), which is an article that was reprinted in the Honolulu Star Advertiser from a national newspaper, the connector "and" is used to put "low-income" together with "limited English proficiency." Once again, it is noteworthy that the intent is probably to attempt to provide assistance and guidance, but the pervasiveness of these categories and the connections drawn in this discourse undoubtedly aid in reinforcing stereotypes that people perceived to belong to the categories of "English language learner" and "limited English proficiency" are somehow deficient in terms of their ability to navigate basic social services, especially education, and thus in need of special care.

The public discourse that reinforces stereotypes about "English language learners" and "Limited English proficiency" contrasts sharply with the mentions of "world languages" in the newspapers. Unlike the two categories mentioning "English," "world languages" appears much less frequently; my search of the database yielded only two mentions of world languages in 2020 and I had to go back to the year 2014 to get the tenth mention of this category. Also, instead of the urgent tone found in calls to protect "English learners," there was no such urgency in discussion of the students taking courses in "world languages," even during the COVID-19 pandemic and even though world languages is a described as an important program by the Department of Education on its website. Excerpts (8) and (9) show the two most recent occurrences of "world languages" in 2020.

Excerpt (8): West Hawai'i Today, August 20, 2020
Designed for DOE employees who serve as emergency hires, substitute teachers or educational assistants, the initiative directly addresses teacher shortage areas in Hawaiian language, **world languages**, English, mathematics and science.

Excerpt (9): Ke Alaka'i, (Laie, HI), April 2, 2020
In a school where the general student body represents the United States, Asia and the Pacific Islands, Rahel Meyer, studying communication and media studies, and triple minoring in political science, peacebuilding and **world languages**, is one of few European students and was born and raised in Germany. She said she loves having the opportunity to be creative and establish herself in a career, and she loves the multicultural family she has made on campus.

Excerpt (8) focuses on an initiative to offer scholarships to people already working in education so that they may go back to the university for a Master of Education in Teaching. As the article notes, the category of "world languages" is listed together with other areas that are facing a teacher shortage. Excerpt (9) comes from the school newspaper of Brigham Young University-Hawai'i and it reports on a particular student whose triple minor includes "world languages." Excerpt (9) is interesting because "world languages" is used in a positive way to describe the accomplishments of a particular person. Such a positive usage contrasts with descriptions of English learners that depict them more negatively as deficient and in need of help.

Similar to the category of "world languages," references to "bilingual education" and "dual language education" were comparatively rare in the database. Of the two categories, "dual language" was more common; Excerpt (10) provides an example as part of a report about the Chinese program at the private school Maryknoll in Honolulu.

Excerpt (10): Honolulu Star-Advertiser, February 1, 2021
Maryknoll students currently may attend classes in person on campus, via distance learning, or through a hybrid approach that combines both options. The school offers a **Dual Language Chinese immersion program**, a strong project-based science and technology curriculum, and a Scholar Pathway program with options in aerospace, medical innovations, business and diplomacy, and creative arts and expression.

This excerpt does not begin with a focus on the Chinese dual language program; the first sentence describes more generally the current state of education at Maryknoll during the pandemic. The writer though makes explicit mention of the "Dual Language Chinese immersion program" in the second sentence and also mentions other notable aspects of the curriculum at Maryknoll. While the Maryknoll dual program did not appear again in the ten mentions, dual language was mentioned in a positive way in reference to programs focusing on Hawaiian. It was also mentioned in a positive way when reference to the language skills of people. Excerpts (11) and (12), both taken from articles published in 2017, show examples of both.

Excerpt (11): Honolulu Star-Advertiser, March 27, 2017
A class for youngsters 3 to 6 years old conducted in both Hawaiian and English was cited as a "uniquely innovative" option for keiki and helped to earn Kawaiaha'o Church School its gold star accreditation earlier this month. The report said the **dual-language class** was "uniquely

innovative," an option that parents may enroll their keiki in for no additional cost. The class has been led by Kala'iku Kaowili since its inception five years ago; it currently consists of 24 multiethnic students age 3 to 6, assisted by Nani Nagao and Birgitta Grace.

Excerpt (12): The Garden Island (Lihue, HI), August 20, 2017
"Charlie" Rice — who was **bilingual** in English and Hawaiian, while many of his fellow legislators were not — also informed Krauss that early on in his legislative career all speeches on the floor of both houses were required to be given both in English and Hawaiian. Rice said he occasionally utilized his **dual language** skills to gain favor with the opposition Home Rule party, whose members were predominately of Hawaiian descent and spoke only Hawaiian.

Excerpt (11) focuses on a dual language class for children aged 3 to 6 and is described as "uniquely innovative." Excerpt (12) offers a report of person named "Charlie Rice" who is described as "bilingual in English and Hawaiian" and also using "his dual language skills" for political advantage. These two articles point to a basic contradiction; even though dual language programs and dual language skills are discussed in very positive terms in the newspapers, there is no discussion, at least in the articles found in this study, about the application of dual language programs or bilingual language programs to languages other than Hawaiian (and the one mention of Chinese). It is as if the dual language approach is just accepted for Hawaiian and English but does not factor into the realm of possibilities for the teaching of other languages in the public school system.

This contradiction is further apparent when we observe that the category of "bilingual"—without education following it—is frequently used when the discussing of language services that are necessary in the community. Excerpts (13)–(16) all come from articles mentioning bilingual as a part of some service or work in society.

Excerpt (13): The Garden Island (Lihue, HI), November 23, 2020
This includes people with disabilities and senior citizens. Many sites are also able to assist individuals for whom English is a second language.

During the 2019 filing season, volunteers helped prepare over 3.5 million returns at thousands of tax sites nationwide. Volunteering can be exciting, educational and enjoyable, Tucker said. **Bilingual volunteers** are particularly needed.

Excerpt (14): Honolulu Star Advertiser, November 11, 2020
Roberson said her agency has a number of **bilingual speakers on staff**, but would like to hire more to reach out to Pacific Islanders of various backgrounds who may not speak English as a first language.

Excerpt (15): Honolulu Star-Advertiser, June 30, 2020
DOH funds at KKV pay for an easy- access Walk-In Family Planning Clinic, where **bilingual counselors** provide pregnancy tests, birth control and early prenatal care. Ninety-five percent of these patients live on incomes at or below federal poverty level.

Excerpt (16): The Garden Island (Lihue, HI), January 27, 2021
Recognizing the language barriers within the agriculture-laboring community, the department mobilized outreach utilizing **bilingual health workers** and public-health nurses on Kaua'i.

Excerpt (13) reports that "bilingual volunteers" are needed to help people file their income taxes, Excerpt (14) is from an article in which one of the leaders involved in contact tracing of COVID-19 cases notes that her agency in the Department of Health (DOH) "has a number of bilingual speakers on staff," Excerpt (15) features another service of the DOH, family planning, and notes there are "bilingual counselors" providing services, and Excerpt (16) is also health related in that it mentions how "bilingual health workers" are needed to deal with language barriers in the "agriculture-laboring community." As these excerpts indicate, there is a need for workers who speak languages other than English. In fact, there are some excerpts in which references to the categories "English language learner" and "limited English proficiency" are mentioned in articles that also put out a call for bilingual services. Two examples appear below in excerpts (17) and (18).

Excerpt (17): Honolulu Star-Advertiser, April 8, 2020
For students with disabilities, schools should have close contact with families to determine appropriate technology, aids, at-home support services, and accommodations. Schools should establish communication plans for **English language learners**, and ensure all updates and support materials for parents have **multilingual translations**. Community organizations and volunteers have a powerful role to play as these materials are created.

Excerpt (18): Honolulu Star Advertiser, September 4, 2020
The letter, penned by attorney Lance Collins, says "the state has a legal obligation to provide contact tracing and relevant health information in minority languages to **limited English proficient** individuals at the levels established by statute. From the available information information to Kokua Council, the state has failed to act contrary to its legal obligation to do so."

Excerpt (17) is telling because at the same time that the article calls for schools to "establish communication plans for English language learners," it also calls for "multilingual translations" of materials and updates concerning the communication plan. The article then suggests these multilingual translations will not come from the schools themselves but instead from "community organizations and volunteers." Excerpt (18) does not focus on the schools, but it features a letter claiming that the state of Hawaiʻi has failed to do an adequate job of providing "contact tracing and relevant health information in minority languages to limited English proficient individuals." The article does not state whether this failure stems from the lack of qualified multilingual people to perform this service or if it due to some other cause, but both this excerpt and Excerpt (17) point out a significant contradiction in the system. Even though public discourse frequently speaks of a necessity for bilingual workers, the educational system is not designed, with the exception of the Hawaiian medium pathway, to meet this need. Given that the school system has numerous students with multilingual abilities, one very obvious way of satisfying the multilingual needs of society would be to assist bilingual and multilingual youth in developing their language skills.

In fact, it is further revealing that many of the references in the articles to specific languages such as Chuukese, Ilokano, Marshallese, and Tagalog concern some service in the community through those languages. Excerpts (19)–(22) provide examples.

Excerpt (19): Honolulu Star-Advertiser, May 3, 2021
The clinic was organized by a Kalihi coalition of agencies and partners, including the Hawaii Public Housing Authority and the nonprofit Parents and Children Together. Kaiser Permanente administered about 500 first doses of the Pfizer vaccine on a walk-up basis, with no appointments necessary. Language interpreters were on hand, with the ability to translate in **Chuukese, Marshallese, Korean, Samoan** and **Ilocano**.

Excerpt (20): Honolulu Star-Advertiser, August 11, 2020
The desk will troubleshoot for students connecting to DOE systems, including connectivity, access and security concerns as well as support with devices. "While other school districts provide tech support to families, HIDOE's help desk is statewide and was designed with a higher level of support, with phone support in multiple languages, chat support and an online portal," the department said in a news release. "The help desk will be able to provide phone support in languages most commonly spoken in Hawaii households – **English, Hawaiian, Ilokano, Tagalog, Chuukese** and **Marshallese**."

Excerpt (21): Associated Press State Wire: Hawaii, September 4, 2020
Derauf stressed the need for the state to talk to Pacific Islander community leaders, determine what services are most needed and then quickly create and publicize those services. Derauf also warned against stigmatizing the Pacific Islander community in communication campaigns and said information should be presented in the languages of the Pacific Islands, including **Marshallese** and **Chuukese**.

Excerpt (22): Honolulu Star-Advertiser, August 5, 2020
Three nonprofits are calling on the state attorney general and election officials to provide translated ballots and voting materials to **non-English** and **Hawaiian language** speakers. In this year's election, the translated language materials for Honolulu voters are only made available in **Ilokano** and **Chinese** upon request at the Honolulu City Clerk's office, according to Collins. "All other voting materials in the ballot package, including ballots, instructions, and information, are exclusively in English and no notation is made on neighbor island ballot packages," Collins said in his letter to state Attorney General Clare Connors.

Excerpts (19) and (20) refer to services that have already been or are in the process of being implemented. Excerpt (19) focuses on a health clinic that provides vaccines and had interpreters on hand for five languages, Chuukese, Marshallese, Korean, Samoan, and Ilokano, and Excerpt (20) describes the construction of a help desk by the DOE (Department of Education) that can provide support in five languages, Hawaiian, Ilokano, Tagalog, Chuukese, and Marshallese, in addition to English. Excerpt (21) is part of an article concentrating on medical services and works as a reminder or request not to stigmatize the Pacific Islander community and to make sure information is presented Marshallese and Chuukese. Excerpt (22) is interesting in that it first describes a call to election officials to provide translated ballots to two categories of speakers, "non-English" and "Hawaiian language," which is quite rare in recognizing "Hawaiian language speaker" as a separate category for social services. It then notes that translations are "only" made available in Ilokano and Chinese "upon request." Thus, even though translations are available in two languages besides English, the voice in this article suggests that this is not enough and calls for the inclusion of more languages.

All four of these articles appeared in Hawai'i's newspapers in less than a year's time, thus suggesting the relative frequency with which these languages are mentioned in terms of services in society. Moreover, it is noticeable that these mentions stand in contrast to the lack of mentions in the newspapers of these languages in an educational context. Instead, in terms of language, the emphasis in the public discourse on education is on serving the aggregate group of "English learners" without concern about their first languages. It seems to send a mixed message to the multilingual students themselves; services in languages such as Ilokano, Tagalog, Chuukese, and Marshallese are necessary for society but the languages themselves are not important enough to be emphasized in schools. Not only does this teach the young students to devalue their home languages in favor of English but it also, due to the subtractive nature of the EL programs, potentially deprives those students of future jobs that they may have filled had they been in programs that helped them develop bilingual skills.

This contradiction is further seen in a newspaper discourse that often praises people for their multilingual abilities. Excerpts (23)–(25) contain examples.

Excerpt (23): Honolulu Star Advertiser, September 29, 2020
Coldwell Banker Realty has announced the designation of Leian Harosky (R) as a Luxury Property Specialist to the firm's Kapolei office. Harosky has more than 16 years of varied experience that ranges from residential sales to corporate and government housing. She currently leads the Harosky Homes Team, a diverse group of multilingual individuals whose mission is to provide the best guidance and service possible to help their clients achieve their real estate goals. Harosky is fluent in **Tagalog, Indonesian** and **Mandarin**.

Excerpt (24): Garden Island, May 23, 2021
Fulgencio, a Leo Club member, has been serving in many aspects of the community, school and the underprivileged. Fluent in **Tagalog** and **Spanish**, Fulgencio is looking forward to completing her Hawai'i Pacific Health internship and is planning to study nursing.

Excerpt (25): West Hawaiʻi Today, May 25, 2021
As the first Hilo High School student to graduate from high school and community college simultaneously, a young **Chuukese** student aspires to set a positive example for all Micronesian students.

Excerpt (23) describes the promotion of an employee to a new position, and in the process notes the employee "is fluent in Tagalog, Indonesian, and Mandarin." Her language abilities are relevant because the articles notes that the employee leads "a diverse group of multilingual individuals," but it also has a laudatory sense to it in that it serves to praise the employee for her abilities. Excerpts (24) and (25) praise recent high school graduates, with Excerpt (24) adding that the student is fluent in Tagalog and Spanish. Excerpt (25) does not mention the language ability of the graduate but it does use the descriptor "Chuukese" to make his ethnicity relevant as part of praising him for his potential as "a positive example for all Micronesian students."

Once again, here, the praise given to people for possessing multiple languages and cultures leads to questions as to why different approaches cannot be employed in schools to enable more young people opportunities to develop their linguistic talents. It seems more than a bit of an irony that members of society are praised for their cultural backgrounds and multilingual abilities within a larger social system that labels many of them as "English language learners" and "limited English proficiency" and thereby provides very little, if any, support in preserving their cultures and languages.

5.5 Conclusions

With a focus on the situation of people labeled as "Filipino" and "Micronesian" and with consideration also given to the secondary schooling system, this chapter has attempted to explore the place of immigrant languages with Hawaiian society. Although immigrant languages have played an important role in a Hawaiian history that once had a flourishing set of language schools devoted to some languages and particularly Japanese, the discussion in this chapter leads to the conclusion that modern Hawai'i is not currently, on the overall, very conducive to the maintenance and development of immigrant languages. Moreover, we may conclude that this general lack of attention to immigrant language in the domain of education disadvantages recent immigrants such as those in the categories of "Filipino" and "Micronesian," and we may therefore suggest that their struggles in school may be alleviated if schools offered opportunities for them to maintain their first languages.

Additionally, the analyses in this chapter lead to the suggestion that the priority placed in schools on English (to the detriment of other languages) may help facilitate discriminatory views toward immigrant groups who are stigmatized for speaking English differently (with an accent) and who see their children also stigmatized through placement in EL programs that, for some of them, are difficult to test out of.

While these are criticisms that need to be addressed, discussion should also end with recognition of the resilience that continues to be shown by immigrants in Hawai'i. Even in the face of an educational system that provides relatively little support for their languages, there continue to be community spurred programs such as those that were started to teach Samoan and Tokelauan to children. While there currently are not, to my knowledge, any similar programs for languages such as Marshallese and Chuukese, there are non-profit organizations in place such as "We are Oceania" and "Micronesians United-Big Island" that help sponsor annual events for the youth such as the "Micronesian Youth Summit" and the "Pacific Youth Empowerment for Success" conference and that also play a role in pushing society to consider educational alternatives. Kala'i et al. (2015) relied heavily on the these non-profit organizations to conduct the interviews for their report on educational alternatives and it is worth noting that they conclude their report by making note of the resilience of the larger Micronesian community:

> Finally, if we have learned anything from our research it would be this fact: the Micronesian community is filled with optimism amidst very difficult and often hostile and discriminatory environments for their children. Resiliency and perseverance define this community and enables them to overcome the challenges and barriers that are both seen and unseen; both heard and unheard. (Kala'i et al., 2015: 55)

Indeed, we have seen that this type of perseverance has started to pay off in the Filipino community as there are now Filipino Studies programs at both the University of Hawai'i at Mānoa and also the University of Hawai'i at Hilo that have been aided by advocacy groups such as the Pamantasan Council. As noted in this chapter, these university programs are allowing younger Filipino students to reconnect with their heritage languages and cultures. And even though the DOE does not currently offer programs to facilitate the maintenance of languages such as Ilokano, Tagalog, Marshallese, and Chuukese, there can be optimism that continued resilience and activism from these immigrant groups may lead to improvements in school programs that address inequalities built into the educational system and that enable speakers of these languages to develop their linguistic skills.

References

Altemus-Williams, I., & Hobro, M. E. (2021). Hawai'i is not the multicultural paradise some say it is. *National Geographic.* https://www.nationalgeographic.com/culture/article/hawaii-not-multicultural-paradise-some-say-it-is

Aris v. Hawai'i. (2013). Document retrieved from https://casetext.com/case/aris-v-hawaii

Blair, C. (2011). *No Aloha for micronesians in Hawaii.* Honolulu Civil Beat. https://www.civilbeat.org/2011/06/no-aloha-for-micronesians-in-hawaii/

Blair, C. (2015). *An untold story of American immigration.* Honolulu Civil Beat. http://www.civilbeat.org/2015/10/an-untold-story-of-american-immigration/

Cummins, J. (1981). The role of primary language development in promoting educational success for language minority students. In California State Department of Education (Ed.), *Schooling and language minority students: A theoretical framework* (pp. 3–49). California State University, Evaluation, Dissemination and Assessment Center.

Cummins, J. (1984). *Bilingualism and special education.* College Hill Press.

Furukawa, T. (2007). No flips in the pool: Discursive practice in Hawai'i Creole. *Pragmatics, 17*(3), 371–386.

Hakuta, K. (1987). Degree of bilingualism and cognitive ability in mainland Puerto Rican children. *Child Development, 58*(5), 1372–1388.

Halagao, P. E. (2016). Exposing K-12 Filipino achievement gaps and opportunities in Hawai'i public schools. *Educational Perspectives, 48*(1 & 2), 6–19.

Heine, H. C. (2002). Culturally responsive schools for micronesian students. *Pacific resources for education and learning: Prel briefing paper* (pp. 1–17).

Hiramoto, M. (2011). Is dat dog you're eating? Mock Filipino, Hawai'i Creole, and local elitism. *Pragmatics, 21*(3), 341–371.

Hofschneider, A. (2020). *Congress poised to restore medicaid for micronesians*. Honolulu Civil Beat. https://www.civilbeat.org/beat/congress-poised-to-restore-medicaid-for-micronesians/

Jetnit-Kijiner, K. (2013). The micronesian question. *Kathy Jetnil-Kijiner*. https://www.kathyjetnilkijiner.com/the-micronesian-question/

Kala'i, K., Nimmer, N., Noh, E., Raatior, V., & Watanabe, J. (2015). *Feasibility study for a micronesian culture based school and other educational programs*. University of Hawa'i at Mānoa College of Education. http://www.weareoceania.org/wp-content/uploads/2016/01/Final-Report-Feasibility-Study-for-a-Micronesian-Culture-Based-Charter-School.pdf

Kihleng, E. (2019). The micronesian question. In E. Flores, E. Kihleng, & C. Santos Perez (Eds.), *Indigenous literatures from micronesia* (pp. 183–187). University of Hawai'i Press.

Labrador, R. (2015). *Building Filipino Hawai'i*. University of Illinois Press.

Lasman, I. (1971). *A study of the attitudes of Filipino immigrants about Hawai'i* (Unpublished M.A. Thesis). University of Hawai'i.

Lee, S. (2020). *Building a Hawaiian language curriculum classroom by classroom*. Honolulu Civil Beat. https://www.civilbeat.org/2020/02/building-a-hawaiian-language-curriculum-classroom-by-classroom/

Lee, S. (2018). *How Hawaii schools are building bridges to micronesian students*. Honolulu Civil Beat. https://www.civilbeat.org/2018/05/how-hawaii-schools-are-building-bridges-to-micronesian-students/

Matsuda, M. (1991). Voices of America: Accent, anti-discrimination law, and a jurisprudence for the last reconstruction. *The Yale Law Journal, 100*(5), 1329–1407.

Matsuda, S. (2016). Drop-out or push-out? micronesian students in Honolulu. *Pass*. https://www.pass-usa.net/micronesian-students-honolulu

Niyekawa-Howard, A. (1974). History of the Japanese language school. *Educational Perspectives, 13*, 6–14.

Ortega, N. (2016). *Testimony to BOE student achievement committee meeting*. https://boe.hawaii.gov/Meetings/Notices/Documents/2016-02-02%20SAC/2016-02-02%20SAC%20Testimony.pdf

Ramos, T. (1996). Philippine languages in Hawai'i: Vehicles of cultural survival. *Social Processes in Hawai'i, 37*, 161–170.

Reinecke, J. (1969). *Language and dialect in Hawai'i: A sociolinguistic history to 1935*. University of Hawai'i Press.

Saft, S. (2019). *Exploring multilingual Hawai'i: Language use and language ideologies in a diverse society.* Lexington Books.

Shimada, N. (1998). Wartime dissolution and revival of the Japanese language schools in Hawai'i: Persistence of ethnic culture. *Journal of Asian American Studies, 1*(2), 121–151.

Strobel, L. M. (1996). "Born-again Filipino": Filipino identity and Asian panethnicity. *Amerasia Journal, 22*(2), 31–53.

Talmy, S. (2006). The other *other*: Micronesians in a Hawai'i high school. In C. Park, R. Endo, & A. L. Goodwin (Eds.), *Asian and Pacific American education: Learning, socialization, and Identity* (pp. 19–49). Information Age Publishing.

Teodoro, L. (Ed.). (1981). *Out of this struggle: The Filipinos in Hawaii.* University Press of Hawaii.

Wagner-Seavey, S. (1980). The effect of world war i on the German community in Hawaii. *Hawaiian Journal of History, 14,* 109–140.

Wilson, W. H., & Kamanā, K. (2011). Insights from indigenous language immersion in Hawai'i. In D. J. Tedick, D. Christian, & T. W. Fortune (Eds.), *Immersion education: Practices, policies, possibilities* (pp. 36–57). Multilingual Matters.

6

Recognizing and Appreciating Translanguaging

The previous chapter, Chapter 5, suggested that the emphasis in the public school system on English deprives students who enter school as speakers of immigrant languages of a great opportunity to develop their first languages and, in the process, expand their linguistic and cognitive abilities. In this chapter, I focus on the phenomenon of language mixing and show how it presents another mismatch between language practices in society and the educational emphasis on English. Supporting previous research that has shown language mixing to be prevalent in public domains of society in Hawai'i (Saft, 2019; Saft et al., 2018), I use the analyses in this chapter to underscore the creative linguistic abilities that many people from the Hawaiian Islands develop as they grow up in a multilingual society.

In the literature on sociolinguistics and discourse analysis, researchers have employed various terms, including code-switching, code-meshing, heteroglossia (Bailey, 2012; Ivanov, 2001), polylanguaging (Jorgensen, 2008; Jorgensen et al., 2011), metrolingualism (Otsuji & Pennycook, 2010; Pennycook & Otsuji, 2015), plurilingualism (Garcia & Otheguy, 2019), and translanguaging, to name just a few, to describe language

S. Saft, *Language and Social Justice in Context*,
https://doi.org/10.1007/978-3-030-91251-2_6

mixing. In past publications (Saft, 2019; Saft et al., 2018), I have employed the term heteroglossia in an attempt to underscore the fact that the mixing of languages entails the combining of not only referential meanings but also non-referential indexical meanings that are attached to certain ways of speaking and even to whole languages. Focusing one analysis on the website of a private school system in Hawai'i, I described how headlines such as "*i mua* newsroom" and "*na'au* or never" bring together Hawaiian and English, two languages with very different historical trajectories in Hawai'i, and place them on equal footing in a publicly available space (Saft, 2019).

In this chapter, I frame the analysis of language mixing in terms of translanguaging. This decision is not due to any lack of satisfaction with the concept of heteroglossia; the analysis will still include discussion of the indexical meanings attached to languages in Hawai'i. Instead, I choose translanguaging because translanguaging has been called a "transformative" approach that promotes social justice. As Garcia and Leiva (2014: 200) state, "what makes translanguaging different from these other fluid languaging practices is that it is transformative, attempting to wipe out the hierarchy of languaging practices that deem some more valuable than others." Translanguaging wipes out language hierarchies because speakers do not limit themselves in their speech to individual named languages such as "English," "Japanese," or "Hawaiian," and in the process do not show an orientation to the fact that one language may be considered more desirable than another. In short, bilingual and multilingual speakers who translanguage do not conform to the boundaries of named languages and do not follow recognized hierarchical social norms (such as "speak in proper English") but rather use the languages together on purpose to achieve creative and strategic goals. Translanguaging is therefore not the result of some kind of "bilingual interference" but is instead more representative of the full linguistic competence of speakers than are assessments intended to measure narrowly English skills. If educators and other gatekeepers in society can appreciate translanguaging as an indication of linguistic competence, then translanguaging can help transform the lives of people previously discriminated against for not speaking an idealized form of a dominant language like English.

This understanding is present in Otheguy et al.'s (2015: 283) definition of translanguaging as the "deployment of a speaker's full linguistic repertoire without regard for watchful adherence to the socially and politically defined boundaries of named (and usually national and state) languages," and its relationship to the idea of transformation is apparent in Garcia and Otheguy's (2019: 16) statement that "the purpose of translanguaging could be transformative of socio-political and socio-education structures that legitimize the language hierarchies that exclude minoritized bilingual students and the epistemological understandings that render them invisible." The ultimate hope, then, is that translanguaging, by recognizing the linguistic skills of people who are frequently criticized for not properly speaking a dominant language such as English, can "transform society to be more inclusive of difference" (Garcia & Otheguy, 2019: 8 referring to the work of Mignolo, 2000).

In order to demonstrate how understanding of translanguaging may be transformative in Hawaiian society, this chapter considers language mixing in several different speech situations, including public testimony from a meeting with members of the Hawaiian Homelands Commission, a public theater performance by students from the Hawaiian medium high school Ke Kula o Nāwahīokalaniʻopuʻu, a televised debated between mayoral candidates, and a speech by a Hawaiian Congress member on the floor of the Congress in Washington D.C. These analyses are meant, first and foremost, to highlight that the actual linguistic abilities of people in Hawaiʻi do not start and end with named languages. At the same time, the analyses also relate translanguaging to processes such as translation and identity construction, which in turn leads to a discussion of the relationship between translanguaging and power that is applicable to a multilingual society such as Hawaiʻi.

6.1 Translanguaging and Public Testimonies

The first analysis is from a public meeting with members of the same Hawaiian Homelands Commission to which SI made a testimony in Pidgin that was described in Chapter 4. This analysis is based on a different meeting, but like the one in Chapter 4, it took place on the Big

Island of Hawai'i and was posted on YouTube.[1] The analysis in this section shows how two speakers engaged in translanguaging as a part of their testimonies. Excerpt (1) represents the beginning of a testimony by LT. Following the practice employed in Chapters 2–4, I print Hawaiian and Pidgin portions of the data in italics. This is done to assist readers in following the discussion presented after the data, but it should be noted that, as emphasized in this chapter, the boundaries among languages used in the data are not necessarily fixed.

Excerpt (1): LT, October 21, 2019

1	LT:	*Mahalo nui* um to Halealoha for showing a clear example for the
2		commission for the Chair himself of what proper leadership looks like, *you*
3		*not doing the job, you not doing the job* step aside and let one *kanaka* who can,
4		*no keep taking orders* from the state *no keep taking orders* from the henchmen ya
5		step aside And let *kanaka* (*) that's why we're here because *kanaka* need, *kanaka*
6		needs *'āina* yah we all know that 44,000 applications 33 on the list 33,000 on the
7		list hundreds of thousands who have died waiting for justice

LT begins this with two terms *mahalo nui* that are recognizable as Hawaiian meaning "thank you a lot," but LK then uses language that can be labeled as English through line 2 to express his thanks to the speaker who spoke just prior to him. That speaker, named Halealoha, had just stated that he was resigning from his position with the Department of Hawaiian Homelands because he no longer could believe in the work of the department in light of the recent controversy over Mauna Kea and specifically over the Mauna Kea Access Road.[2] He then employs grammatical forms in lines 3–4 that are recognizably Pidgin. Specifically, his usage of *not* in line 3 without an auxiliary verb is a Pidgin negation form

[1]https://www.youtube.com/watch?v=eY17To_p0pA&t=1035s.

[2]Reported at https://www.bigislandvideonews.com/2019/10/22/video-halealoha-ayau-testifies-resigns-dhhl-position/.

(Sakoda & Siegel, 2003). He uses another Pidgin negation form, the negative command form beginning with *no* in line 4 to tell the commission first not to take orders from the state government and then again not to "take orders from the henchmen." As he does this, he uses the category term *kanaka* in line 3 to refer to Native Hawaiians. As discussed in Chapter 3, this terms originates in the Hawaiian language. And even though he employs an English grammar in lines 5–7, he uses the term *kanaka* three additional times, combining it in line 6 with another term of Hawaiian origin, *'āina* ("land"), to express that Native Hawaiian people need land and that is the reason they are there, to fight for land for the Native Hawaiians. The excerpt ends as he cites statistics about how many Native Hawaiians are on the list and have applied for land and as he notes through line 7 that there are "hundreds of thousands who have died waiting for justice."

The majority of this introduction would probably be characterized as English, but it is noticeable that the speaker LT has also mixed in forms and lexical items recognizable as Hawaiian and Pidgin. Given that LT seems to have knowledge of English, Pidgin, and Hawaiian, these first seven lines may raise the question as to why the speaker would choose to mix languages and not just deliver the content in one language such as English that is comprehensible by everyone present. Yet, the very premise of such a question reveals an orientation to a monolingual mindset that would expect speakers to "stick to" the dominant language. Given that LT has access to linguistic resources that include but are not limited to English, we could just as well deem it natural for him to employ the resources at his disposal, in this case English, Pidgin, and Hawaiian. A phenomenon such as translanguaging that appears to be extraordinary when viewed from the dominant monolingual perspective may be a regular practice for people such as LT accustomed to language mixing in Hawai'i.

Moreover, through a closer look at Excerpt (1), we can see that LT is not just randomly mixing languages. His decision to employ words derived such as *kanaka* and *'āina* is a strategic choice since these are words that will be meaningful to an audience in Hawai'i who are aware of the struggles by Native Hawaiian people (*kanaka*) for their native lands (*'āina*). This is to say, then, that his usage of these terms goes beyond the level of referential meaning to the indexical level since these terms from the Hawaiian language carry with them a deeper meaning related to being Native Hawaiian in a place where the land is of utmost importance to a Native Hawaiian identity but is mostly controlled by the United States. Furthermore, it is surely not a coincidence that LT employs Pidgin negative markers in line 4 to direct the members of the commission *no keep taking orders from the state no keep taking orders from the henchmen*. As a language that conflicted with English from the time it developed into a creole, Pidgin carries with it, as discussed in earlier chapters, an indexical meaning that is steeped in resistance to English dominance. LT's decision to provide directives in Pidgin thus carries with it this indexical meaning of resistance as a part of his urging the members to take a stance and resist authority. LT's knowledge of the indexical meanings attached to Hawaiian and Pidgin is part of his linguistic competence, as is his ability to mix languages to construct his argument in a creative, strategic, and effective manner. Excerpt (2) shows how he continued to do so in his speech.

Excerpt (2): LT, October 21, 2019

8 sounds like spinning my tires yah sounds like spinning the tires so no no matter
9 how much gas *you give em the ting keep digging into the ground.* That's what I
10 see with the Department of Hawaiian Homelands. It's not your guys' fault it's the
11 state of Hawai'i, they control this whole operation here yah so I I urge the
12 commissioners to exercise your guys' authority. You guys have the power to *huli*
13 *da ship to bail em out little bit,* take some of the water out kick out the *buggahs*
14 *that stay dragging us back,* you guys have that authority don't wait for the chair to
15 do it

LT employs the phrase "spinning tires" twice in line 8 and although this phrase is not Pidgin per se, it does consist of an act of "stylizing" since it is a metaphorical expression that varies slightly from English. He adds to the stylization of this phrase by adding Pidgin pronunciations such as *em* ("them") and *ting* ("thing") in line 9 as a part of making further criticism of the work of commission for just spinning its wheels and thus not getting much work done. He then employs English sentence structure with English pronunciations through the end of line 12 to add more criticism and to urge the commissioners "to exercise your guys' authority" in line 12. Then, at the end of line 12, he employs the phrase *huli da ship* with the term *huli*, a Hawaiian term meaning "turn over," that is also used frequently by Pidgin speakers. He continues with another Pidgin expression, *buggahs*, in line 13 when he says kick out the *buggahs that stay dragging us back*. Moreover, as a part of expressing *buggahs that stay dragging us back*, the speaker makes use of the Pidgin grammatical construction *stay* that, according to Sakoda and Siegel (2003), has its origins in the Portuguese verb "estar." Finally, we see that LT in line 14 employs another command form, "don't wait for the chair to do it," but unlike the two *no* led negative commands in line 4 of Excerpt (1), this form is expressed through an English grammar, not a Pidgin one.

An interesting aspect of the translanguaging practices of LT is that many of the terms he employs are "bivalent" (Woolard, 1998), which is to say that they are used across languages. *Huli* is one example as are both *kanaka* and *'āina*. They have their origin in Hawaiian but are used in Pidgin and probably, at least in the case of *kanaka and 'āina*, also by speakers of Hawaiian English. Due to this bivalency, they can be employed by speakers such as LT in "mixed company," that is with people who are not Hawaiian or even Pidgin speakers (but presumably are familiar enough with Hawai'i to know the terms), and still transmit the indexical meanings of these terms to the audience. This therefore means that linguistic competence involved in this translanguaging includes not just referential and indexical meanings but also an awareness of terminology that is bivalent and thus usable with various types of audiences.

Another aspect of the construction of meaning in this excerpt lies in the very act of switching languages itself. In my prior work on heteroglossia (Saft, 2019; Saft et al., 2018), I argued that the act of switching from one language to another can have the effect of highlighting the utterance marked by the switch. Here, I suggest the possibility that LT’s usage of English in the last statement in lines 14–15 “you guys have that authority don’t wait for the chair to do it” is emphasized because of its juxtaposition with the previous lines in 12–14 that contain Pidgin expressions *huli da ship* and *buggahs that stay dragging us back.* The creation of emphasis may explain why LT employs the negative command English construction in lines 14–15 that leads with “don’t” even though he had constructed the two negative commands in Excerpt (1) using the Pidgin structure that begins with *no.* LT is able to choose from either the English or Pidgin negative constructions according to which one best fits the immediate communicative context. This then suggests that part of the linguistic competence of multilingual speakers exhibited through translanguaging is the ability to know how to mix languages so as to emphasize certain points in the discourse. One further excerpt from LT’s testimony, Excerpt (3), underscores his translanguaging skills. It continues from Excerpt (2) as LT is criticizing the Chair of the commission.

Excerpt (3): LT, October 21, 2019

15 LT: he was appointed by the governor, recycled, thrown back into the mix, right
16 DLNR, deputy, now you got a promotion and what does he do with that
17 promotion, evict Hawaiians on Hawaiian homelands, himself, he was there,
18 helping take apart the *hale, Hale o Kūhiō,* yah, on the solstice, that’s how you
19 celebrate solstice, that’s how you honor Kānehoalani, *’Ai lā nō ho‘i* ya that’s what
20 we have been seeing and witnessing and so *mahalo nui* to Mauna Kea for
21 bringing all of these issues from the department from the fixed state of Hawai‘i to
22 the head for the whole world to see how corrupt how *buss up dis is*

The speaker LT continues in line 15 to note, in a critical tone, that the appointment of the Chair of the commission by the governor was the result of him being recycled from another commission, the DLNR (Department of Land and Natural Resources). LK then notes in line 17 that this "promotion" led him to "evict Hawaiians on Hawaiian homelands," and he proceeds to describe a particular action in which the Chair oversaw the dismantling of a structure called *Hale o Kūhiō* that had been erected on the base of the mountain Mauna Kea. He also notes in lines 18–19 that this occurred on the solstice and in doing so invokes the name of Kānehoalani, a Hawaiian god of the solstice. These Hawaiian names are important as they index and hence invoke an official Hawaiian voice. Except for the Hawaiian names of *Hale o Kūhiō* and *Kānehoalani*, LT has mostly employed in lines from 15 to 19 an English grammar. However, in line 19, he switches to Hawaiian and utters the phrase *'Ai lā nō ho'i*, which plays on the last name of the Chair to whom he has been referring. The last name of the Chair is Ailā, a Hawaiian name, but the first part of the Hawaiian phrase, *'Ai lā,* consists of two words that mean "eat sun" and is translated into English as "scorched" or "sunburned."[3] To indicate that this is meant to be Hawaiian, and not just the name of the Chair as one part of an otherwise English structure, LK, he adds the two Hawaiian emphatic particles *nō ho'i*, which are commonly used by Hawaiian speakers and thus makes this recognizable as Hawaiian (as opposed to just using the Chair's name as part of an utterance in English). LK then switches back in lines 19–21 to English before uttering the Hawaiian thank you *mahalo nui* to credit the Mauna Kea telescope issue for creating awareness of issues with Hawaiian homelands throughout the world. At the very end of the clip, though, there is one more switch as he moves from stating in line 22 "how corrupt" to *how buss up dis is*. *Buss up* is a phrase used frequently in Pidgin to mean "broken" or "damaged." Like his switch to English at the end of Excerpt (2), it is possible that this switch here at the end of Excerpt (3) from English to Pidgin has the effect of underscoring his point that it is *buss up*. This especially seems likely since his expression *buss up* is basically a reformulation of "how corrupt" the situation is, with repetition of the same idea but through a different language working to emphasize the speaker's point.

[3]This translation can be found at Wehewehe Wikiwiki https://hilo.hawaii.edu/wehe/?q=ai+la.

Excerpt (3) is mostly characterized by English, but LK's switch to Hawaiian to play on the name of the Commission's chair is a strikingly creative play on words that crosses languages. LT's translanguaging shows off his creative skills, skills that represent the linguistic competence that he undoubtedly developed from growing up in a multilingual society with access to languages such as Hawaiian, Pidgin, and English.

LT's translanguaging in excerpts (1)–(3) consisted of a mixing of Hawaiian, Pidgin, and English, which, given the increasing number of Hawaiian speakers, is a common combination in Hawaiian. Yet, it is by far not the only combination of languages found in examples of translanguaging in Hawai'i. Excerpt (4), taken from the same public meeting but focusing on a different speaker, provides an example.

Excerpt (4): NE, October 21, 2019

1 *Aloha kākou. Taeao manuia i le alofa ma le agalelei o Tagaloalagi.* I want to
2 address Chairman Aila and the members of the Board the members of the
3 commission, yesterday, Sunday, October 20th marked the 100th day of the *lāhui*'s
4 time on the *mauna*, there was a birthday, there was music, there was ceremony
5 and good food, within the length of those 100 days 36 arrests have been made
6 the majority which are DHHL beneficiaries by definition, all faces that carry
7 themselves with *kapu aloha* everyday I see them up at camp, we're the *kūpuna*
8 we're the *mākua*, this is a disturbing development given the fact that the state has
9 no real jurisdiction on DHHL *'āina* bearing in mind that the access road
10 stands on DHHL *'āina* illegally so as to serve the private interests of private
11 corporations and external entities, by definition, everybody but the beneficiaries
12 my time up on this podium will function as a prayer of reminders (.) growing up
13 in Sāmoa, I am no stranger to corruption

After leading with the Hawaiian greeting *aloha kākou*, NE offers a prayer in line 1 in the Samoan language. It is unlikely that many in the audience will understand his prayer, but it does position him as someone with a specific identity, something he confirms later in this excerpt in lines 12–13 by stating in English "growing up in Sāmoa, I am no stranger to corruption." Following his Samoan prayer, NE begins a speech that consists of mostly English except for key words in Hawaiian. He employs the terms *lāhui* ("tribe" or "nation of people" line 3), *mauna* ("mountain" line 4), *kapu aloha* (" line 7), kūpuna ("elders" line 7), *mākua* ("parents" line 8), and *'āina* ("land" lines 9 and 10). These are key words because they are categories that refer to the Native Hawaiian people (*lāhui, kūpuna, mākua*), their land (*'āina*), and also their philosophy (*kapu aloha*), and they allow NE, even though he might not be Native Hawaiian, to refer to and access the important indexical meanings attached to these Hawaiian terms at the beginning of a speech that is going to be critical of the way the Commission has handled Hawaiian lands.

It is unknown the degree to which NE engaged in translanguaging while he was growing up in Sāmoa, but, as Excerpt (4) indicates, he has embraced translanguaging as a strategy to initiate a speech on behalf of the Native Hawaiian. In addition to offering multilingual speakers an opportunity to explore and employ their full linguistic competence, translanguaging also allows people to express and utilize their identities in creative ways. In just the first thirteen lines of this speech, NE has not only invoked his Samoan identity as something that makes him "no stranger to corruption" but he also positioned himself through his usage of key Hawaiian terms as a supporter of the Native Hawaiians resistance to corruption against their people and land.

6.2 Public Translanguaging by Hawaiian Medium School Students

To build on the last point that translanguaging is empowering because it allows speakers to explore their developing identities as well as their linguistic competence, this section offers an analysis of a public theater performance called *Ho'oulu* ("Grow") by a group of students at the high school level from the Hawaiian medium school Nāwahiokalaniʻōpuʻu on the Big Island of Hawaiʻi.[4] It is transformative and an act of empowerment in that it was written and performed by the students in order to consider issues that young people frequently face in the modern world. It is also empowering in that it allowed the students to choose the language for the script, and although the analysis will show that the language mostly consisted of Hawaiian, the script is also marked by translanguaging. The play was performed in 2019 and it was video-recorded by ʻŌiwi TV and posted on its website. It is posted with a description that is in and of itself a form of translanguaging as it has a Hawaiian description first followed by an English translation (I discuss translation more in the third analysis of this chapter). The analysis is concerned with the language used in the play itself, but since the description of the play fits the focus in this chapter on translanguaging, I have reproduced the description below.[5]

> *He haʻawina ko nā hana a pau. Ua like nō ma kēia mau hana keaka a nā haumāna o ka papahana ʻo Hoʻoulu Pāhiahia i kahu ai. Hōʻike ʻia kekahi ʻano pilikia, alaina a hana kolohe nō paha. ʻO ka mea nui o nā hana kolohe, ʻo ia ka paʻa o ka haʻawina nui a me ke ala e hoʻoponopono a holomua ai ma hope mai. E ulu like kākou a pau mai kā lākou mau moʻolelo haku o kēia au kanaka.*
>
> Hoʻoulu Pāhiahia students from Ke Kula ʻO Nāwahīokalaniʻōpuʻu explore the choices they face as young people in today's complex world. Via original scripts written and performed by the students, a glimpse into decisions to bully, lie, steal, and disrespect elders is looked at from different angles, dealt with, and resolved, leading to deep learning for all involved.

As shown below, the fact that the play focuses on issues possibly relating to students' current lives factors into their usage of translanguaging.

[4]Available on Youtube at https://www.youtube.com/watch?v=ruEOGIIY_9Y&t=414s and also on ʻŌiwi TV at https://oiwi.tv/oiwitv/hooulu/.

[5]This description comes from https://oiwi.tv/oiwitv/hooulu/.

The analysis focuses on a scene in the play as three young women gather at one of their homes to watch the Super Bowl. Excerpt (5) shows how the characters interact with one another.

Excerpt (5): Hoʻoulu

1 Wah1: *e piholo ana kāu kime =*
lose your team
"your team is going to lose"
2 Wah2: *= piholo wale ana kāu kime*
lose just your team
"your team is just going to lose"
3 Wah1: *bet au iā ʻoe*
I O you
"I bet you"
4 Wah2: *Inā lanakila kāu kime, e hāʻawi au iā ʻoe he kaʻa*
If win your team give I O you car
"If your team wins, I will give you a car"
5 Wah1: *well inā lanakila kāu kime, e holoi au i kāu mau pā no ʻekolu makahiki*
If win your team wash I O your PL dish for three years
"If your team wins, I will wash dishes for you for three years."
6 Wah2: *well inā lanakila kāu kime, kuke au he ʻaina ahiahi ʻulu nāu*
If win your team cook I dinner bread fruit for you
"If your team wins, I will cook a breadfruit dinner for you"

This excerpt begins as Wah1 and Wah2 begin arguing in lines 1 and 2 about whose team is going to win the game. In these two lines, the language used is recognizable as Hawaiian. It can be noted that both Wah1 and Wah2 employ the *a*-class of the *ko* possessive that was discussed in Chapter 3 in telling each other that "your team" (*kāu kime*) is going to lose. Line 3 is where the translanguaging begins as Wah1 uses a recognizable English term "bet" to state that they bet on the game. This is an interesting place to translanguage and is salient as translanguaging not only because of the English term "bet" but also because there is a Hawaiian term, *piliwaiwai*, that could have been used to have the same referential meaning. Wah2 indicates in line 4 that she is willing to engage in the bet as she offers to give Wah1 a car should Wah1's team wins.

In doing so, she does not engage in translanguaging. In response, Wah1 in line 5 does translanguage as she begins with "well" before moving back to Hawaiian to state that she will wash dishes for Wah2 for three years if Wah1's team wins. In line 6, Wah2 provides a very parallel response as she also leads with English "well" before continuing in Hawaiian to state that she will cook a breadfruit dinner for Wah1 if Wah1's team wins. Wah1 has thus offered to wager a car and a breadfruit dinner while Wah2 has wagered three years of dish washing.

This short excerpt thus contains translanguaging between English and Hawaiian, although the English is quite minimal. Moreover, in contrast to "bet" in line 3, the two "well" tokens in lines 5 and 6, respectively, while certainly not devoid of meaning, do not consist of significant referential meaning. I will return to this usage of "bet" later in the analysis, but it is interesting to note that a pattern develops in the dialogue such that much of the referential content is communicated through Hawaiian with other non-referential meanings expressed at times through English. Excerpt (6) shows how the amount of English in the dialogue increases as the participants begin watching the game that is the source of the bet between Wah1 and Wah2. This excerpt follows directly after Excerpt (5) and begins with a knock at the door.

Excerpt (6): Ho'oulu

7	Mom:	*'O wai kēlā* Who that "Who is that?"
8	Wah3:	*'O coach kēnā ua kono mākou iā ia e nānā i k a super bowl me* S that PST invite we O him watch O the with
9		*mākou* We "That's Coach. We invited him to watch the Super Bowl with us"
10	Mom:	*Hiki ia'u ke ki'i* Can I get "I can get it"

11	Wah1:	*[No*
12	Wah2:	*[No*
13	Wah3:	*[No*
14	Wah3:	*E ki'i au i ka puka, hiki iā 'oe ke noho i lalo Mā* Get I O the door can you sit down Mom "I will get the door, you can sit down Mom"
15	??	((low voice)) eew
16	Wah3:	*Oh aloha coach* Hello "Oh, hello Coach"
17	Coach:	*Aloha mai kākou mahalo i ke kono 'ana mai, e Leahi he* Hello D we thanks the invitation NOM D Leahi
18		*Seahawks fan 'oe kekahi* You also "Hello to us all, thank you for inviting me, hey Leahi are you Also a Seahawks fan?"
19	Wah3:	*'Ae, māua 'o Hau'oli (wahine 1)* Yes we S "yes, Hau'oli and I"
20	Mom:	*hey coach*
21	Wah1:	*[eww*
22	Wah2:	*[eww*
23	Wah3:	*[eww*
24	Coach:	*yeesh*
25	Wah1:	*oh*
26	Wah2:	*ooh*
27	Coach:	*look at that [pa*
28		*[look at that*
29	Coach:	*[ya*
30	Wah3:	*[ya*

In response to mom's question in Hawaiian in line 7, Wah3 responds in lines 8–9 that it is Coach, who has come to watch the Super Bowl with them. This explanation is accomplished primarily through Hawaiian, but she does employ the term "coach" even though there is a Hawaiian equivalent for coach, namely *ka'i.* Here, though, it is notable that coach is used as more than just a title (as in "he is the coach"); "Coach" serves as this character's name in this part of the play. Moreover, it is notable that the term Super Bowl in line 8 is also expressed through its English name. This might be considered inevitable as it would seem easier just to "borrow" this term from English when speaking Hawaiian, but it is interesting that the writers and performers have chosen a very American event, as opposed to some cultural event that might be more linked specifically to Hawai'i and Hawaiian culture.

Although not shown in the transcript, the "mom" becomes recognizably excited when she hears that it is coach and offers in line 10 to answer the door. In overlap, all three of the young female characters respond with the English "no" before Wah3 states in Hawaiian in line 14 that she will get it. After she tells "mom" to sit down, an "eew" is audible from one of the three young women in line 15 as a seeming reaction to mom's excited state. After Wah3 answers the door and greets Coach in line 16 with "Oh aloha coach" that seems to be a mix of English and Hawaiian, Coach expresses his gratitude for being invited in line 17 and then, with the phrase "Seahawks fan," mixes in some English in order to ask Wah3 in line 18 if she is also a fan of the Seahawks. Wah3 responds using Hawaiian in line 19 that "yes she and Hau'oli are both Seahawks fans," but then the dialogue is cut short as "mom" stands up, begins moving toward Coach, and states in English "hey Coach." This draws laughter from the crowd as one of the young women steps in front and cuts mom off as all three of the women utter "eew" in overlap in lines 21–23, which seems to be a reaction borrowed from English. Even Coach utters "yeesh" in line 24 as a reaction to mom's action. This "yeesh" also seems to be a reaction derived from English. Finally, at the end of this excerpt, the coach and the three young female characters sit down and act as they are watching and reacting to a game. This is expressed in lines 25–30 through a series of yells and calls that sound as if they are English in nature.

Excerpt (6) thus features dialogue that consists of considerable translanguaging between English and Hawaiian. Nonetheless, there is an observable pattern which features Hawaiian grammatical structures with reactions sounding much more similar to English. These reaction sounds, though, are not devoid of meaning. They are expressions of emotions, particularly disgust at the mom's infatuation with Coach and also excitement in lines 25–30 as Coach and the women watch the game. Excerpt (7) below shows more translanguaging that displays emotions as this particular scene of the play reaches a teachable moment.

Excerpt (7): Ho‘oulu

31 Wah1: *yessah lanakila ka‘u kime e ‘Iwalani, na‘u kēlā ka‘a*
Win my team for me that car
"Yessah, my team won, that is car belongs to me"
32 Wahi2: *Pani kou mau maka*
Close your PL eye
"Close your eyes"
((Wah2 walks away and fiddles with something in her hands))
33 Wah3: *‘o ia nō ke kī*
That EP the key
"that is the key"
34 Wah1: *‘ae, ‘o ia paha ke kī o ke ka‘a*
Yes, that maybe the key of the car
"yes, maybe that is the key for the car"
35 Wah2: *melemele nā kī*
Yellow PL key
"the keys are yellow"
36 Wah3: *ke ho‘oma‘ema‘e nei paha ‘o ia*
Cleaning maybe she
"maybe she is cleaning it"
((Wah2 places a small play car in Wah1's hand))
37 Wah1: *[aw:: junk*
38 Wah3: *[aw:: junk*
39 Coach: *[aw:: junk*
40 Wah1: [*aw brah mana‘o au he ka‘a maoli*
Think I car real
"Aw brah, I thought it was going to be a real car"
41 Wah2: *‘A‘ole au i ‘ōlelo he ka‘a e kau ai ‘oe*
Not I PST say car ride you
"I never said it was a car you could ride"
42 Coach: *‘a‘ole maika‘i iki nā 49ers*
Not good little PL 49ers
"The 49ers are not good at all"
43 Wah2: *whatever ua laki wale kāu kime i kēia lā*
PST lucky only your team this day
"Whatever, your team was just lucky today"
44 Wah3: *hamau ‘o kā mākou kime ka heke o nā heke*
Shut up S PS we team the best of PL best
"Shut up, our team is the best of the best"
45 Wah1: *mai ho‘ohalahala i ka‘u kime*
Do not criticize O my team
"don't criticize my team"

46 Wah2: *hey you guys e mālie mai ua kuke ʻo ʻAnake i kēia mau meaʻai a pau*
Relax D PST cook S aunt O this PL food all
47 *no kākou a ua hele pū coach no ka launa pū me kākou ʻaʻole*
For we and PST come also for the meeting also with we not
48 *maikaʻi ka hoʻohalahala*
Good the criticizing

"hey you guys, relax, Auntie cooked all of this food for us and Coach
also came to be with us, it is not good for us to just criticize"

49 Mom: *e mālie ʻoukou ʻaʻohe kumu e hoʻopaʻa ai, he pāʻani leʻaleʻa*
Relax you PL not reason argue a game for fun
50 *wale kēia*
Only this

"relax all of you, there is no reason to argue, it is supposed to just be a game for fun"

51 Coach: *ʻAe pololei. Mahalo no ke kono ʻana mai. ʻO ka piholo kekahi*
Yes correct thanks for the invitation NOM D S losing also
52 *māhele o ka pāʻani. Pono kekahi kime e lanakila a pono kekahi kime e*
Part of the game Need one team win and need one team
53 *pīholo maikaʻi kākou*
Lose good we

"Yes correct. Thank you for the invitation. Losing is a part of the game One team has to win and one team has to lose. We are all fine."

((the groups starts to get ready to eat))

At the beginning of this excerpt in line 31, Wah1 exclaims "yessah" and then states that her team won and also announces in Hawaiian that the car now belongs to her, which serves as a reminder of the bet made between her and Wah2. This prompts Wah2 to tell them in line 32 in Hawaiian to close their eyes and then stand up and start fidgeting with something with her back turned to the others. This then leads the other participants to speculate through line 36 that she is getting prepared to hand over the key to the car. Wah2 produces, however, a small yellow toy car that she places in the hand of Wah1, which in turn leads the other two young women and Coach to utter the English exclamation of disappointment "aw junk" in unison (lines 37–39). The receiver of the toy car, Wah1, next utters in line 40 "aw brah" which consists of the Pidgin address term "brah" before exclaiming in Hawaiian that she thought it was a real car. This then escalates into an argument as Wah2 states in Hawaiian in line 41 that she never said it was a real car and as Wah1, Wah3, and Coach make critical statements through line 46. The argument is primarily through Hawaiian, but it does feature a response from Wah2 in line that begins with the English "whatever." Then, in line 46, instead of further escalating the argument, Wah2 leads with English "hey you guys" and attempts to ameliorate the controversy by pointing out through line 48 in Hawaiian with the Hawaiian term *'Anake* that the "Auntie" has cooked all of this food and that Coach has come to visit and so it is therefore not good to criticize and argue. This then prompts "mom" to express in Hawaiian in lines 49–50 that everyone should relax and not worry about just a game for fun. Coach next agrees in line 51 and further explains that losing is just part of the game before finally stating with the first-person plural inclusive pronoun *kākou* ("we") that "we" are all fine (*maika'i kākou*). The group then sit down in preparation to eat as mom begins to distribute food.

We thus get a teachable moment that demonstrates that games are just games and that betting can be divisive and lead to arguments. Losing is part of the nature of games, and it is, as the characters show us, better to get along than to argue over just a game. In presenting this lesson, an organization has emerged in terms of language; quick expressions of emotion are accomplished through English, but the majority of the ideas are expressed through Hawaiian. The Hawaiian includes fairly complex structures, including the possessives, pronouns, and regular grammatical constructions that enable the participants to criticize, argue, complain, and also make peace.

Although Hawaiian is much more prominent than English in this play, this still stands as an example of translanguaging given that the characters have purposely mixed in English expressions. It is important to note that these English expressions are not due to some problem or something lacking with the Hawaiian language. Hawaiian does have words such as "bet" and "coach" that are not included in the play. Hawaiian also has exclamations that could have been used instead of terms such as "junk," "whatever," "Aw brah," and "yessah." A good example occurs near the end of Excerpt (10) when Wah2 states in line 46 *hey you guys e mālie mai* and then when mom follows in line 49 in full Hawaiian *e mālie mai 'oukou* that employs the pronoun '*oukou*' ("you guys") instead of "hey you guys." It may be argued that there are different nuances between the Hawaiian and the English, but in terms of referential expressions, they more or less work the same. It may also be argued that the student writers and creators may not be aware of the Hawaiian equivalents of these English expressions and thus left them in English. This, however, is very unlikely; given their Hawaiian medium education and given that it is a scripted performance, it is probable that they would have been able to create the entire dialogue in Hawaiian.

Instead of looking for possible "deficiencies" in the languages or the speakers to explain the usage of one language instead of the other, it makes more sense to consider that the translanguaging in the play is a purposeful action by a group of young Hawaiian speakers who are in the process of making sense of their social worlds and their identities as bilingual Hawaiian and English speakers (and possibly trilingual if we include Pidgin). Much of their schoolwork in Hawaiian medium pushes them to learn the ways of their ancestors, but they also live in a modern world that consists of super bowls, gambling, arguing, bullying, etc. The translanguaging in the play enables the participants to demonstrate their fluency in Hawaiian but also at the same time their identities as young people who are reacting to and living in modern society. Thus, it is certainly not a coincidence that English appears in the constructed interactions as lexical chunks and exclamations of emotions and that the grammar is almost primarily Hawaiian. This procedure allows the young speakers to demonstrate their command of Hawaiian, thus leaving no doubt about their identities as Hawaiian speakers, even though some purists may be troubled by the inclusion of English. I say more about the relationship between translanguaging and Hawaiian language revitalization in the conclusion, but it is clear that the students have used this play to create for themselves a "translanguaging space" to express their linguistic competence and emerging identities (Li, 2011). In developing the concept of "translanguaging space," (Li, 2011: 1223) writes the following:

> The act of translanguaging then is transformative in nature; it creates a social space for the multilingual language user by bringing together different dimensions of their personal history, experience and environment, their attitude, belief and ideology, their cognitive and physical capacity into one coordinated and meaningful performance, and making it into a lived experience. I call this space "translanguaging space", a space for the act of translanguaging as well as a space created through translanguaging. (Li, 2011: 1223)

This quotation assists in seeing the transformative nature of the students' performance as they made an explicit decision to take control of this particular space in society to express themselves as emerging Hawaiian-English speakers in their modern world.

6.3 Translanguaging and Translating

To contribute to our understanding of translanguaging in Hawai'i as it pertains to the linguistic competence and identity construction of some people in Hawai'i, I consider as the last analysis of this section the act of translation. I do this here partly because some proponents of translanguaging have emphasized that translanguaging and translation represent different actions. Garcia et al. (2020: 81), for instance, recognize that translation "has always been a bridge between two cultures," but they also take the position that "for language minoritized students, translation has never been an accepted strategy to make meaning, either in monolingual or bilingual or multilingual programmes of all types." In terms of educational programs, they surely have a point given that translation as a learning technique may restrict the ability of the young people to create their own meanings through language. At the same time, though, as a general practice used in discourse, translation can allow for creativity and has, in fact, been noted for its emancipatory effect in relation to political activism (Carcelen-Estrada, 2018; Strani, 2020; Tymoczko, 2010; Wroblewska, 2020). In the words of Carcelen-Estrada (2018: 255), "translation redresses power asymmetries and smuggles alternative meanings to incorporate different worldviews and concepts into an imperial grammar putting an end to monolingualism." Indeed, in my own examination of potential sources of data in doing research for this book, I was surprised not only at the number of times I came across translation, particularly involving the Hawaiian language, but also at the relationship between power and translation that emerged from the data. At times, the translation seemed a mere necessity, given that not everybody involved was a speaker of Hawaiian. Further consideration, however, makes it more obvious that power was involved, that is to say that the very act of translating from Hawaiian to English or English to Hawaiian often carries with it, in some form or another, a challenge to long accepted hierarchies. I begin with an analysis of an excerpt that appears at first to be quite straightforward. It came at the very beginning of a debate between candidates for the position of mayor in Hawai'i that was broadcasted on 'Ōiwi TV. Occurring during the COVID-19 pandemic in 2020, the debate occurred through technology with the candidates as well as the moderator and the moderator's assistant in different locations. Excerpt (8) shows how the moderator HM begins the debate with a greeting in Hawaiian and then offers basically the same greeting in English.

Excerpt (8): From the 2020 mayoral debate on Hawaiian Issues

1 HM: *A 'o ia (.) aloha nui nō ho'i iā kākou a pau loa e ko Hawai'i pae 'āina*
And it aloha much EP EP O us all to PS Hawai'i island chain
2 *ke aloha 'āina iā kākou a pau, mahalo a nui i ko kākou hui 'ana i ke*
the aloha land O us all thank and much o PS us meet NOM at the
3 *ahiahi nei, mahalo a nui no ko 'oukou kipa 'ana mai i kēia, ka*
Evening here thank and much for PS you PL visit NOM D in this the

4	*ho'opa'apa'a 'ana ma waena o nā moho e holo ana no ke kūlana o* Debate NOM between PS PL candidate running for the position of
5	*meia no kēia no ke kūlana kauhale 'o Honolulu nei* Mayor for this for the city Honolulu here

And here we go (.) much aloha to each and every one of us of the Hawaiian Island Chain. Much "aloha 'āina" to all of us, thank you very much for our meeting this evening, thank you very much for your visiting this, the debate between the candidates running for the position of mayor of the city of Honolulu.

6	Welcome ah to all of you, welcome everyone for attending the Honolulu mayoral
7	debate on kanaka maoli issues. I am your hostess Hinalei Moana Wong Callu and
8	I'd like to acknowledge each and every one of you for tuning in. I'd also like to
9	acknowledge our two candidates ah to Rick Blangiardi and Keith Amemiya
10	mahalo to both of you for joining us and also I'd like to recognize our two sign
11	language interpreters.

This excerpt is at first glance fairly neatly divided into five lines of Hawaiian and then the next six lines in English. Also at first glance, this seems to be a basic greeting in Hawaiian followed, loosely speaking, by a translation of that greeting into English. There is slight overlap in the usage of the two languages as HM employs the city name Honolulu in line 5. Also, after switching to English in line 6, HM does utilize the Hawaiian term *kanaka maoli* in line 7 as a modifier that specifies the type of issues to be focused on. As noted previously in Chapter 3, *kanaka maoli* literally means "real people but is used specifically to refer to Native Hawaiians." Also, the moderator HM uses the bivalent thank you term *mahalo* in line 10 to directly express gratitude to the two mayoral candidates.

However, a more careful examination of the two greetings reveals some important differences. In particular, the moderator HM employs the first-person plural inclusive pronoun *kākou* three times in the first two lines of the Hawaiian greeting. She uses it first in her initial expression of greeting expression *aloha nui nō ho'i iā kākou a pau loa e ko Hawai'i pae 'āina* ("warm greeting to all of us in the Hawaiian Island Chain") to emphasize that the greetings go to all of "us" in Hawai'i. She then employs *kākou* again twice in line 2 first to greet everyone with the expression *aloha 'āina* (literally "love of the land") and then to give thanks to everyone for coming together this evening with the phrase *mahalo a nui i ko kākou hui 'ana i ke ahiahi nei* ("thank you to all of us for gathering this evening"). Not only are the inclusive *kākou* pronouns not represented in the English greeting, the English uses a version of the pronoun "you" on several occasions, but her usage of *aloha 'āina* ("love of the land") is also not found in the English. *Aloha 'āina* has an important historical meaning as a type of catch phrase for Hawaiian speakers (and later included those who did not speak Hawaiian) desiring to preserve their land and it thus foreshadows that many of the issues discussed during the debate will focus on preservation of the land for Native Hawaiians.

These differences may raise questions about whether the English greeting is actually a translation of the Hawaiian, but if we see that both the English and Hawaiian basically accomplish the same action, greeting the audience and explaining that the purpose of the program is the debate, then we may see this as a form of translation that functions to invest the Hawaiian version with power not found in the English version. It is, first of all, empowering that the moderator, as a Hawaiian speaker taking the leading role of the debate, can choose to put Hawaiian first, thus making a statement about the hierarchy between the two languages. In other words, she is using her power as moderator to display to the audience that the Hawaiian language needs to be included and that it should come first. Second of all, her inclusion in the Hawaiian version of linguistic resources such as the pronoun *kākou* is powerful in that it moves to establish a sense of community among Hawaiian-speaking participants. Moreover, the fact that she creates this inclusive community through the phrase *aloha 'āina* sends a message to her fellow Native Hawaiians that one of the purposes of this debate about Hawaiian issues is to preserve their lands. This is not to say that the English greeting is devoid of power; the usage of the term *kanaka maoli* in the English version is a strong statement to all of the English speakers that they will be focusing on Native Hawaiian issues. Nonetheless, the ultimate power lies in the hands of the moderator to determine who in the audience is to get what message, the message of an inclusive community effort to preserve the native lands or the English version that seems to provide more of standard greeting that uses the pronouns "you" and "your" to greet everyone and explain the basic agenda for the evening.

This connection between translation and power is also readily apparent in some of the excerpts presented in Chapter 3 in the discussion of the media representation of the usage of the Hawaiian language in public domains such as courtrooms and floor meetings of the House of Representatives. Two of these excerpts are reproduced below: Excerpt (9) shows the interaction between the judge and Samuel Kaʻeo and Excerpt (10) shows the discourse that occurred on the floor of the House of Representatives.

Excerpt (9): Language Battle

1	Judge:	You know I'm going to give you another opportunity, Mr. Kaʻeo to just
2		identify yourself just so the record is clear, I'm going to ask you (.) one
3		last time (.) is your name Samuel Kaʻeo
4	SK:	*Eia au ke kū nei i mua ou, ʻo ia ke kanaka āu i kāhea mai nei. Ke kū nei*
5		*i mua ou e ka lunakānāwai (.) aloha*
6	Judge:	Okay, the court is unable to get a definitive determination for the record
7		that the defendant (seated here is Samuel Kaʻeo)

Excerpt (10): The Controversial Hanohano

16	AP:	But when embattled representative of Puna spoke in her native language
17	JM:	Representative Hanohano
18	FH:	*Mahalo hoʻomalu ʻōlelo. Kākoʻo loa. Makemake au i ka haʻiʻōlelo o*
19		*ka luna makaʻāinana mai Kapolei mai e komo i loko o ka puke hale*
20		*no nā makaʻāinana [mahalo*
21	AP:	[it touched off a mini firestorm as vice speaker John
22		Mizuno presided over the chamber
23	JM:	Representative Hanohano could you please translate for the members

24		(1)
25	FH:	*'A'ole au e makemake e unuhi mai* I don't wanna translate mahalo
26	AP:	That exchange prompted a clearly frustrated Mizuno to bang the gavel
27	JM:	Recess, subject to the ca- call of the chair recess ((bangs gavel once))
28	AP:	After a short interval, Mizuno came back with this
29	JM:	Rule 60.1 provides members should conduct themselves in a respectful
30		manner

In Excerpt (9), it is Ka'eo's (SK) decision not to switch languages that, even though it led to a warrant for his arrest, functioned as a very powerful action that was reported in the news and discussed significantly in the social media. As the news report stated, Ka'eo can speak English but his decision not to translate from Hawaiian served as a political statement about discrimination against Hawaiian speakers despite the declaration of Hawaiian as an official language of the state.

The move by FH in Excerpt (10) makes a similar political statement. Although the discussion had been in English, FH employs Hawaiian in lines 18–20, a move which elicits a request from JM in English in line 23 to translate for the other members. FH, however, refuses to translate in line 25 as she stays in Hawaiian with *'a'ole au e makemake e unuhi mai* ("I do not want to translate") before, ironically, engaging in an act of translanguaging at the end of line 25 by translating her last statement into English with "I don't wanna translate." She has engaged in translanguaging here but she has done so in order to refuse the request to translate her Hawaiian.

The participants in both of these excerpts thus demonstrate the power involved in translation by refusing to translate. Moreover, in their decisions not to translate, the participants demonstrate an understanding of the relationship among translation, translanguaging, and identity. Both Ka'eo and FH are most certainly aware, as speakers of Hawaiian and English, that they have the ability to translanguage and thus also have the ability to translate between the two languages if necessary. Whether they grew up speaking Hawaiian or learned it later in life, their emergent identities as Hawaiian and English speakers made them aware of the power attached to the usage of Hawaiian and to the act of translation. It also made them aware that their refusal to translate in situations such as court and official governmental meetings would be problematic, thus making this refusal a political statement about the asymmetries between the two languages in society. The uproar from their refusal reinforces their identities as Hawaiian speakers and also leads to labels such as political activist and/or problem-maker depending on the perspective of the recipient of the information.

This relationship among translanguaging, translation, and identity leads to two final excerpts that show translanguaging done in a formal political context. It is from a speech made by Kaialiʻi Kahele, one of the representatives from Hawaiʻi in Congress in Washington, D.C. This speech was made on the floor of the U.S. Congress in February of 2021 in Washington, D.C., and while the speech did not occur in Hawaiʻi, it nonetheless serves as a display of the power of translation and translanguaging involving an indigenous language such as Hawaiian. Excerpt (11) shows the beginning of the speech.[6]

Excerpt (11): Kaialiʻi Kahele: February 26, 2021

1 KK: I rise this morning to honor *mahina ʻōlelo Hawaiʻi* or Hawaiian language month
2 colleagues I have the wonderful privilege of being Native Hawaiian. My culture
3 has served as a guiding light throughout my entire life, a light that has survived
4 because of the many *kūpuna*, our elders, who protected this light and who
5 protected our native indigenous language. For Native Hawaiians and for so many
6 indigenous peoples, our languages is essential for our people to live and thrive
7 In fact, we have an *ʻōlelo noʻeau*, a proverb that says *i ka ʻōlelo no ke ola, i ka*
8 *ʻōlelo no ka make*, in the language rests life and in the language rests death

---

[6]https://www.youtube.com/watch?v=X9D1XDHXM_0.

KK employs Hawaiian four times in opening his speech: first in line 1 with *mahina ʻōlelo Hawaiʻi*, next in line 4 with the word *kūpuna*, then in line 7 *ʻōlelo noʻeau,* and finally in line 7–8 with the proverb *i ka ʻōlelo no ke ola, i ka ʻōlelo no ka make*. And each time he does this, he follows immediately with a translation of the Hawaiian expression into English, letting his audience know that *mahina ʻōlelo Hawaiʻi* means "Hawaiian language month," *kūpuna* is "our elders," *ʻōlelo noʻeau* translates as "proverb," and *i ka ʻōlelo no ke ola, i ka ʻōlelo no ka make* means "in the language rests life and in the language rests death." KK continues this practice of employing Hawaiian and then providing immediate English translations, but as he gets to the end of his five-minute speech, he alters this practice in some instances. Excerpt (12) shows the end of his speech.

Excerpt (12): Kai Kahele: February 26, 2021

1	KK:	it is no longer novel to hear Hawaiian spoken in our local coffee shops
2		and our grocery stores and my family proudly joins alongside fellow firekeepers
3		to stoke the *ʻōlelo Hawaiʻi* flame as my daughters attend Hawaiian language
4		schools *Pūnana Leo o Hilo and Ke Kula ʻo Nāwahīkalaniʻōpuʻu.* While I am
5		filled with pride, Mr. Speaker, it comes with a mix of other emotions
6		Disappointment underfunding, frustration at the lack of equity in government use
7		of Hawaiian as an official language, and trepidation knowing how close we came
8		to having our language snuffed out. While I am encouraged by our progress, I
9		know there is more work ahead. We must to continue to raise up the languages of
10		all of America's First Peoples. UNESCO states that a third of the world's
11		languages have fewer than one thousand speakers left. Language is essential to
12		cultural diversity and diversity is essential to our shared humanity. While *mahina*

13 *'ōlelo Hawai'i* or our month of celebrating Hawaiian language is coming to a
14 close, we will continue to stoke the flames of *'ōlelo Hawai'i*, month-by-month,
15 year-by-year, generation to generation because, Mr. Speaker, *i ka 'ōlelo no ke ola,*
16 *i ka 'ōlelo no ka make*, in language rests life, in the language rests death, and our
17 resolve is greater than ever to ensure that our languages will live on. *E ola mau*
18 *ka 'ōlelo Hawai'i a me nā 'ōlelo 'ōiwi a pau loa. Mahalo* and I yield.

As KK moves through a forceful statement about the importance of the Hawaiian language, he uses the term *'ōlelo Hawai'i* ("Hawaiian language") in line 3 without translation, which is probably due to the fact that he had used the term several times earlier in his speech and had earlier translated it as "the Hawaiian language." He then names two schools in line 4 that have Hawaiian names, the *Pūnana Leo o Hilo* and *Ke Kula 'o Nāwahīkalani'ōpu'u.* He had previously employed the two names in his speech and made it clear that they were Hawaiian medium schools. Later, in lines 12–13, he utters the phrase *mahina 'ōlelo Hawai'i,* for which he provided a translation in Excerpt (11) as "Hawaiian language month." Here again, he chooses to provide a translation in line 13 with "or our month of celebrating Hawaiian language." He repeats *'ōlelo Hawai'i* in line 14 without a translation and then he also repeats in lines 15–16 the proverb from Excerpt (11) *i ka 'ōlelo no ke ola, i ka 'ōlelo no ka make* with basically the same translation "in language rests life, in the language rests death." Finally, he ends his speech in lines 17–18 with a statement in Hawaiian that did not appear before and is not translated into English here, *e ola mau ka 'ōlelo Hawai'i a me nā 'ōlelo 'ōiwi a pau loa. Mahalo* ("let the Hawaiian languages and all Indigenous languages live. Thank you").

As noted, the decision not to translate some of the Hawaiian terms in Excerpt (12) probably derives from the fact they have been used previously in the speech, which would not make translation necessary. KK's decision to translate the repetition of the longer proverb in lines 15–16 may be due to the length and difficulty of the proverb, thus necessitating a second translation. Yet, neither of these reasons can explain why KK ends his speech with a comparatively long expression in Hawaiian without any translation. Here again, though, the explanation undoubtedly lies in the connection between translation and power. By ending his speech with Hawaiian without the English translation, he is demonstrating his power to employ language, particularly the language of the cultural and ethnic group with which he identifies, in a way that leaves the listeners unable to comprehend. Doing so puts the power in the speaker's hands as he becomes the one who decides whether they understand or not and, in doing so, creates, at least for the moment, a power asymmetry between those able to speak Hawaiian and those who cannot with meaning only available to those who can. At the same time, by not translating this final Hawaiian statement into English, he allows the last words of his speech to be Hawaiian, another act of power that undoubtedly leaves an impression upon the audience even though there is no translation on which they can rely.

KK has thus accomplished a series of interrelated actions in his decision to engage in translanguaging in his speech. He first puts his linguistic competence to use to produce a speech that mixes English and Hawaiian. Second, by doing so, he makes a display of a particular identity, namely that he is a Native Hawaiian who has linguistic competence and who is passionate about the revitalization of the Hawaiian language and culture. Third, he turns this particular context, the floor of the Congress, into his own "translanguaging space" by deciding to employ Hawaiian words with English translations. This is a powerful move because from the perspective of communication, there is no necessity for him to employ Hawaiian given that the other Congress members are able to understand a speech all in English. The fact he does so, as just noted above, serves as a display that the power lies in his hands to allow (or not to allow) them to understand. Finally, his ultimate act of power is his decision not to translate his very last statement, thus exerting his control over the audience by denying listeners without Hawaiian language knowledge access to the ending of his passionate speech.

While translation and translanguaging may still be considered separate activities, the data in this section suggest that the act of translating can be a critical component of translanguaging. This is true not only because translation often requires a mixing of languages but also because translation can be an act of power that is transformative because it enables speakers with multilingual abilities to overcome and transform power asymmetries through language.

This chapter has predominantly focused on translanguaging among three languages, Hawaiian, Pidgin, and English. A full consideration of translanguaging in Hawaiian society should consider in the future translanguaging that occurs with other languages, for example, in spaces of tourism where visitors, residents, and local business owners surely negotiate decisions about which language(s) to use. Moreover, future research must also examine the degree to which translanguaging occurs in schools. Based on earlier chapters, the basic presumption is that the public school system in Hawaiʻi, outside of Hawaiian medium schooling, places a strong emphasis on the usage of English. Part of this presumption is that, at least in the classroom, translanguaging is not a desirable practice due to the ideological belief that formal communication should be in English. However, more detailed examination will surely uncover interesting ways that students attempt to use language, possibly translanguaging, to rebel against the expectation of English dominance in school as well as to negotiate their emerging identities.

6.4 Conclusions: Translanguaging and the Revitalization of Hawaiian

This chapter has suggested that translanguaging is a skill that many people in Hawaiʻi develop and readily use in various social situations, including public discourse such as public testimonies, theater performances, and government speeches. Translanguaging enables people to go beyond the boundaries of named languages and employ their entire linguistic competence which not only empowers them to display and reinforce emerging identities but also allows for tremendous creativity in using a diverse set of linguistic resources. Translanguaging is not, I maintained, a skill nurtured formally in school but instead picked up by people in Hawaiʻi based on their lived experiences in a multilingual society. The fact that translanguaging matches life experiences outside of school suggests that educators may wish to recognize the translanguaging skills of students rather than focusing solely in class on their English skills. For instance, if not already doing so, teachers of English learners may want to explore ways of using translanguaging in classes in order to encourage emerging bilinguals to appreciate their developing overall linguistic competence.

This does not mean, however, that people in Hawai'i are not aware of named languages or of their importance to society. As I showed in previous work (Saft, 2019), named languages such as Hawaiian, Pidgin, and English are psychologically very real within individuals and also throughout Hawai'i in general. One example is Pidgin; even though in actuality there are different types of Pidgin, including "thick" and "weak" forms that overlap considerably with English, the category of Pidgin is very real and, for many people in Hawai'i, the categorization of their speech as Pidgin is crucial to their identity as "local." Another example is Hawaiian. The existence of the language category "Hawaiian" is central to the revitalization movement, and revitalization of the category of "Hawaiian" is of utmost importance to the identity of many Native Hawaiians. In fact, Hawaiian medium teachers are well-known for insisting that students in the schools speak only Hawaiian. This is probably a main reason that the students in the *Ho'oulu* performance in the second analysis made sure to demonstrate their proficiency in Hawaiian even as they engaged in some translanguaging; they may have been aware of the critical eyes their teachers and other members of the Hawaiian-speaking community had they used a lot of English and/or Pidgin. From the perspective of many involved in Hawaiian revitalization, a fuller mixture of English and Hawaiian would no longer be "Hawaiian" and would not demonstrate the "success" of the Hawaiian movement. Instead, it may suggest that Hawaiian speakers cannot exist without the crutch of English.

Indeed, this is where translanguaging and language revitalization seem to be in conflict. Proponents of translanguaging typically follow language critics such as Reagan (2004) and Makoni and Pennycook (2005, 2006) in insisting that named languages are historical constructions that in reality do not exist. Otherguy et al. (2015: 294) explain this viewpoint in their research promoting translanguaging:

> It follows from our discussion that from the standpoint of lexicon and structure, the only thing anyone actually speaks is his or her own idiolect, something that no one else speaks...and given that the idiolects that comprise a named language are all ultimately different, it follows that no one really speaks a named language.

They also underscore why this critique of named languages is necessary:

> The named language adopts the view from outside the speaker, a perspective from which the speaker has to fit as a member of a set group; it offers a description based on external categories that emanate from, and in turn reaffirm, sociocultural or national (and often also political) structures. (Otherguy et al., 2015: 294)

Thus, emerging bilinguals, despite being able to display a deep linguistic competence through translanguaging, are often forced through education to fit into an already designated category, proficient English speaker. Translanguaging is transformative because it helps reveal those named categories of languages as illusions, which in turn can be liberating for emergent bilinguals who can appreciate their own creative language skills and also have them appreciated by others.

This, however, seemingly creates a conundrum if we simultaneously want to revitalize an indigenous language such as Hawaiian and also allow young bilinguals to feel empowered through translanguaging. Yet, there is no reason why we cannot achieve the two separate goals, learning Hawaiian and appreciating translanguaging, in a society such as Hawaiʻi. The recognition of translanguaging, in theory, does not have to conflict with the learning of named languages. Speakers of Hawaiian can proudly (and surely do) speak Hawaiian in some contexts and then also proudly engage in translanguaging. In fact, the ability to distinguish between contexts of adherence to the boundaries of named languages and contexts of translanguaging surely constitutes part of a speaker's full linguistic competence. As this chapter has shown, speakers such as the students who created and performed *Hoʻoulu* are capable of using the named language of Hawaiian (for instance, in school) and can also engage in translanguaging for different creative effects.

The crucial key, however, in making it possible to recognize both translanguaging and the pursuit of a named indigenous language such as Hawaiian is overcoming the monolingual mindset. It is the monolingual mindset in the United States that pushes people to expect English to be the language of education and therefore to judge the mixing of languages in a negative manner. As discussed earlier, it is what makes it difficult for people in power in Hawai'i to accept that there could be two equally official languages of the state and it is also what stops educators from allowing and even encouraging students to take advantage of their full linguistic competence. Until we figure out not only that the human linguistic faculty is capable of both translanguaging and speaking named languages but also that engaging in both may be good for the development of the human brain, it will prove difficult to appreciate translanguaging and to understand how it can serve as an empowering practice in society.

References

Bailey, B. (2012). Heteroglossia. In A. Martin-Jones, A. Blackledge, & A. Creese (Eds.), *The Routledge handbook of multilingualism* (pp. 499–507). Routledge.

Carcelen-Estrada, A. (2018). Translation and activism. In J. Evans & F. Fernandez (Eds.), *The Routledge handbook of translation and politics* (pp. 254–269). Routledge.

Garcia, O., Aponte, G. Y., & Le, K. (2020). Primary bilingual classrooms: Translations and translanguaging. In S. Laviosa & M. Gonzalez-Davies (Eds.), *The Routledge handbook of translation and education* (pp. 81–94). Routledge.

Garcia, O., & Leiva, C. (2014). Theorizing and enacting translanguaging for social justice. In A. Blackledge & A. Creese (Eds.), *Heteroglossia as practice and pedagogy* (pp. 199–216).

Garcia, O., & Otheguy, R. (2019). Plurilingualism and translanguaging: Commonalities and divergences. *International Journal of Bilingual Education and Bilingualism*. https://doi.org/10.1080/13670050.2019.1598932

Ivanov, V. (2001). Heteroglossia. In A. Duranti (Ed.), *Key terms in language and culture* (pp. 95–97). Blackwell.

Jorgensen, J. N. (2008). Polylingual languaging around and among children and adolescents. *International Journal of Multilingualism, 5*, 161–176.
Jorgensen, J. N., Karrebæk, M. S., Madsen, L. M., & Moller, J. S. (2011). Polylanguaging in superdiversity. *Diversities, 13*, 24–37.
Li, W. (2011). Moment analysis and translanguaging space: Discursive construction of identities by multilingual Chinese youth in Britain. *Journal of Pragmatics, 43*, 1222–1235.
Makoni, S., & Pennycook, A. (2005). Disinventing and (re)constituting languages. *Critical Inquiry in Language Studies: An International Journal, 2*(3), 137–156.
Makoni, S., & Pennycook, A. (Eds.). (2006). *Disinventing and reconstituting languages*. Multilingual Matters.
Mignolo, W. (2000). *Local histories/global designs. Coloniality, subaltern knowledges, and border thinking*. Princeton University Press.
Otheguy, R., Garcia, O., & Reid, W. (2015). Clarifying translanguaging and deconstructing named languages: A perspective from linguistics. *Applied Linguistics Review, 6*, 281–307.
Otsuji, E., & Pennycook, A. (2010). Metrolingualism: Fixity, fluidity and language in flux. *International Journal of Multilingualism, 7*, 240–254.
Pennycook, A., & Otsuji, E. (2015). *Metrolingualism: Language in the city*. Routledge.
Reagan, T. (2004). Objectification, positivism and language studies: A reconsideration. *Critical Inquiry in Language Studies: An International Journal, 1*(1), 41–60.
Saft, S. (2019). *Exploring multilingual Hawai'i: Language use and language ideologies in a diverse society*. Lexington Books.
Saft, S., Tebow, G., & Santos, R. (2018). Hawai'i Creole in the public domain: Humor, emphasis, and heteroglossic language practice in university commencement speeches. *Pragmatics, 28*(3), 417–438.
Sakoda, K., & Siegel, J. (2003). *Pidgin grammar: An introduction to the Creole language of Hawai'i*. Bess Press.
Strani, K. (2020). Multilingualism and politics revisited: The state of the art. In K. Strani (Ed.), *Multilingual and politics: Revisiting multilingual citizenship* (pp. 17–45). Palgrave Macmillan.
Tymoczko, M. (2010). Translation, resistance, activism: An overview. In M. Tymoczko (Ed.), *Translation, resistance, activism* (pp. 1–22). University of Massachusetts Press.

Woolard, K. (1998). Simultaneity and bivalency as strategies in bilingualism. *Journal of Linguistic Anthropology, 8*(1), 3–29.
Wroblewska, M. N. (2020). Theory, practice, activism: Gramsci as a translation theorist. In R. R. Gould & K. Tahmasebia (Eds.), *The Routledge handbook of translation and activism*. Routledge.

7

Linguistics as a Resource for Social Justice

7.1 Introduction

The preceding four chapters have, on the one hand, emphasized through analyses and discussion the importance of Hawaiian, Pidgin, immigrant languages, and translanguaging to Hawaiian society, and, on the other hand, been critical of society, especially education, for not encouraging residents to freely employ languages other than English and to explore and develop a multilingual linguistic competence. In light of these criticisms, the purpose of this chapter is to provide an example of how an academic program in linguistics is attempting to work for linguistic justice in Hawai'i. In order to pursue this goal, I focus specifically on the Linguistics program at the University of Hawai'i at Hilo, the program for which I currently work as program coordinator. The decision to concentrate on this program is due largely to my familiarity as program coordinator but it also stems from a belief that there are unique aspects of the program that contribute to linguistic justice in Hawai'i. As this chapter hopes to demonstrate, the program is designed with three specific goals: (1) support the movement to revitalize the Hawaiian language; (2) promote multilingualism in Hawai'i; and (3) facilitate a general

S. Saft, *Language and Social Justice in Context*,
https://doi.org/10.1007/978-3-030-91251-2_7

critical awareness of how language can serve as a resource for combatting social discrimination.

With its focus on linguistic justice, the discussion in this chapter is meant to contribute to what is actually a long list of language specialists who use their role as academics in institutions of higher learning to promote critical reflection on language-based social inequalities. This includes linguists such as William labov, Geneva Smitherman, John Rickford, and John Baugh who have spoken out in public forums on behalf of African American Vernacular English (see Baugh, 2018; Rickford & King, 2016; Rickford & Rickford, 2000), the growing research focusing on language endangerment and language revitalization (i.e., Hinton et al., 2018; Olko & Sallabank, 2021), as well as linguistic research in areas of critical language awareness and critical discourse analysis that attempt to raise the collective consciousness about language-based inequalities. As Wolfram and Dunstan (2021: 157) recently emphasize, "socially responsible linguists and sociolinguists are called on to challenge extant ideologies about language, and to implement strategies that promote the practice of sociolinguistic equality."

This chapter also hopes to build on social justice activism in Hawai'i that centers on language. The focus of this chapter, UH-Hilo, is located in the city of Hilo on the Big Island of Hawai'i, but there is a growing amount of work through our sister school in Honolulu on the island of O'ahu, the University of Hawai'i at Mānoa. This includes especially the work at the Hawai'inuiākea School of Hawaiian Knowledge with its mission "to pursue, perpetuate, research, and revitalize all areas and forms of Hawaiian knowledge."[1] Work in the school features Hawaiian language teaching, but it also extends well beyond language in the research, outreach, and education provided throughout society.[2] Also from UH-Mānoa have been significant efforts to promote Pidgin, both at the university and in the community. Higgins (2021a) notes a few of these efforts at the university such as the creation of a working group entitled

[1]https://manoa.hawaii.edu/hshk/.

[2]An example is that the current Dean of the School, Jonathan Osorio, has written one of the most prominent books on Hawaiian history that adopts a critical perspective on American colonialism in Hawai'i (Osorio, 2002).

Da Pidgin Coup, the establishment of the Charlene Sato Center for Pidgin and Creole in 2002, the approval of an undergraduate certificate in Pidgin and Creole studies, and the implementation of courses focusing on "Pidgin and Creole in Hawai'i." In terms of the community, Higgins describes in another publication (Higgins, 2021b) how teams consisting of faculty members, students, and people from the community have engaged in projects, for example, a student documentary film, an installation on Pidgin at the Hawai'i Plantation Village Museum, and a summit focusing on the role on Pidgin in education. UH-Hilo is much smaller in size than its sister school UH Mānoa, with significantly fewer faculty in linguistics and also in Hawaiian Studies, but this chapter hopes to show that it is no less focused on linguistic activism.

With its emphasis on linguistic activism, this chapter hopes to continue to dispel perceptions that have lingered about linguists as academics tending to use research for their own gains, especially when dealing with indigenous minority languages. In particular, these concerns deal with situations in which linguists enter communities as "lone wolves" (Bowern & Warner, 2015; Crippen & Robinson, 2013) and, after working directly with speakers of indigenous languages, employ their findings to further their own careers through academic publications. The penchant for doing so has resulted in a situation in which "language communities often perceive fieldworkers as seeking 'one-way' relationships meant only to fulfill their own academic goals" (Guerin & Lacrampe, 2010: 23). Crystal Richardson, a graduate student in linguistics from the Karuk tribe of California, notes that her tribal elders refer to such linguists as "brain pickers" and explains that "the reality of broken relationships held between 'informants' and 'researchers' has left a bitter taste in the mouths of many Karuk people." She extends her criticism to say that "the job of collecting information to be disseminated to the outside world is considered one of the foulest forms of exploitation known to Karuk traditionalists" (Richardson, 2017: 5–6, quoted in Hinton et al., 2018: xxv).

Part of the problem is, as underscored by Leonard (2017, 2018), that traditional linguistics encourages students to consider language in separation from the people who speak languages. As Leonard (2018: 58) writes:

> Contemporary linguistic science privileges certain ways of defining language, particularly by structural units that can and often are described and analyzed not only separately from each other, but that are also disembodied from the people who use them, thus contradicting Indigenous values of interrelatedness as a framework for describing and interacting with the world. This trend of conceiving of languages as structurally-defined objects emerges in linguists' analyses.

This conception of languages as "structurally-defined objects," in turn, makes it much easier for linguistics to believe that it is acceptable to impose their own wills on these detached objects. In the words of Dobrin and Berson (2011: 202, also quoted in Leonard, 2018: 56), "linguists' scientific authority … takes for granted one group's power derived from its association with the high-status western institution of the academy, to cast its gaze upon cultural others through the research process, and to represent them according to its own, externally imposed analytic categories in the resulting scholarly products."

In the place of a hierarchical relationship that enables linguists to employ fieldwork results for their own gain in the name of "science," many have endeavored to reexamine the "ethics" involved in linguistic fieldwork (Grinevald, 2006; Rice, 2010, 2011; Warner et al., 2007) and to reinvision the relationship of the linguist to the community in terms of a collaboration that puts community interests ahead of academic ones (Amery, 2014; Grenoble, 2009; Leonard, 2018). As Grenoble (2009: 63) asserts, "ethical linguistic research starts with community involvement." McCarty (2018) notes, for example, how collaboration involving Miami tribal elders such as Julie Olds and Daryl Baldwin and the linguistic work of David Costa (1994) led to a community-based Miami language learning program in 1996 (Baldwin et al., 2013). Baldwin, in fact, describes how his initial reading of Costa's (1994) thesis prompted him to begin graduate study in linguistics (Gerdts, 2017). Native educators' engagement with linguistics suggests a changing view that sees the potential to employ linguistics as a resource for programs designed to promote indigenous languages.

Indeed, this potential of linguistics for collaboration and community has been behind academic-led endeavors to achieving larger goals such as language revitalization. This includes the Master-Apprentice Language Learning Program developed by Leanne Hinton and her colleagues (Hinton et al., 2018), the Northwest Indian Language Institute at the University of Oregon, and also the various programs in indigenous language revitalization offered at the University of Victoria in British Columbia, which Wilson (2018: 83) notes as offering "a certificate, diploma, B.Ed. and M.A./M.Ed." Such programs provide language courses and also linguistic-related coursework for students wishing to gain not just speaking proficiency but also the knowledge that will enable them to contribute to the perpetuation of their languages. As I begin to show in the next section, the Linguistics program at UH-Hilo has been (re)designed to make such contributions.

7.2 Linguistics at UH-Hilo: A Resource for Hawaiian Revitalization

Gerdts (2017: 612) notes that "around the middle of the twentieth century, most top-tier universities created stand-alone linguistics departments," and she likewise notes this was done "to distinguish themselves from the anthropology and foreign language departments out of which they were born." At UH-Hilo, a basically opposite process occurred; the Linguistics program existed as an interdisciplinary program within the College of Arts and Sciences but was moved into the already existing Ka Haka ʻUla o Keʻelikōlani College of Hawaiian Language (henceforth Ka Haka ʻUla or the College) in 2008 to provide support for the expanding movement to revitalize the Hawaiian language. The move of Linguistics into Ka Haka ʻUla brought with it two faculty, myself (SS) and Yumiko Ohara (YO), who had been doing the majority of the teaching in the program. The program still offers a stand-alone undergraduate major in Linguistics, but in terms of administration, Linguistics is a program that now falls under the Hawaiian Studies Department. Accordingly, in terms of hierarchical structure, as the coordinator of the program, I answer directly to the Chair of the Hawaiian Studies Department, a position which falls directly beneath the Director of the

Hawaiian Language College. It is important to note, then, that the structure in Ka Haka ʻUla contrasts with traditional hierarchies that place indigenous languages and their speakers in linguistics departments and thus require adherence to the greater policies and frameworks created by linguists. In Ka Haka ʻUla, the Linguistics program is required to follow the policies put in place by Hawaiian language activists whose foremost goal is promotion of the Hawaiian language and culture. In fact, one of the first policies that I and YO had to follow is the strict language policy of the College, Hawaiian only as the medium of communication among faculty and staff. In order to so, we developed a proficiency in Hawaiian by attending the language courses with the regular Hawaiian language students (more on the College language policy later in this chapter).

Another order of business was collaborating with faculty in Ka Haka ʻUla to revise the Linguistics curriculum to further meet the needs of the Hawaiian language revitalization movement. After the curricular revisions, Linguistics was redesigned to consist of three areas of specialization, with students required to take courses from all three areas and specialize in one by taking at least three courses from that area. Box 7.1 below shows the major with the areas of specialization, Structure/Grammar, Applied/Sociolinguistics, and Language Maintenance, Revitalization, and Policy.

Box 7.1: The Linguistics Major

The Linguistics Major and Assigned Credits (46 credits)

Core Courses

LING 102 Introduction to Linguistics (3)
LING 311 Phonetics and Phonology (3)
LING 321 Morphology And Syntax (3)
LING 490 Research and Methods in Linguistics (3)

Areas of Specialization

Select one of the 3 areas below as an area of concentration and take at least 3 courses in that area. From the other 2 areas, take at least 1 course. (15 credits)

Structure/Grammar

LING 345 Historical & Comparative Linguistics (3)
ENG 324 Modern English Grammar & Usage (3)
LING 410 Semantics & Pragmatics (3)
JPNS 451 Structure Of Japanese I (3)
JPNS 452 Structure Of Japanese II (3)
KHAW 453 Hawaiian Phonetics & Phonology (3)
KHAW 454 Hawaiian Morphology & Syntax (3)

Applied/Sociolinguistics

LING 347 Pidgins And Creoles (3)
LING 356 Language and Gender (3)
LING 412 Discourse Analysis (3)
LING 432 Critical Applied Linguistics (3)**
LING 442 Languages in Hawaiʻi (3)**
ANTH 331 Language in Culture & Society (3)
ENG 350 s Language Acquisition Theory (3)
JPNS 345 Methods for Teaching Japanese (3)

Language Maintenance, Revitalization, and Policy

KIND 240 Culture Revitalization Movements (3)
LING 432 Critical Applied Linguistics (3)**
LING 442 Languages in Hawaiʻi (3)**
LING 434 Indigenous Languages of the US (3)
LING 445 Explorations in Bilingual & Immersion Education (3)
KHAW 455 Hawaiian: Polynesian Languages (3)
KHWS 496 Hawaiian Studies Seminar (3)

Three additional semester hours in Linguistics (or other related and approved field) at the 300- or 400-level (3).

16 university credits in second/auxiliary language study, 4 credits of which must be in a different language from the other credits. In certain circumstances, students may substitute demonstrated fluency in a second/auxiliary language in lieu of up to 8 credits. (16)

**Courses are listed in two areas but count toward only one.

As observed in Box 7.1, there is some crossover between the two specializations Applied/Sociolinguistics and Language Maintenance, Revitalization, and Policy as two courses, Critical Applied Linguistics and Languages in Hawaiʻi, can count in the two areas (although they cannot count toward both), but this division between sociolinguistics and language revitalization gives majors the option of specializing in the specific area of revitalization. It should be emphasized that most of the courses are delivered through the medium of English and that there is no requirement that the majors study the Hawaiian language, but since the revision of the major, we have seen a large increase in the number of students who decide to pursue a double major in both Hawaiian Studies and Linguistics. Helping facilitate the ease with which a double major may be pursued is the fact that some of the courses listed in Box 7.1, the ones beginning with the alphas KHAW and KHWS, are administered through Hawaiian and already count toward a major Hawaiian Studies. Accordingly, these courses count toward the two majors, thus encouraging students to do both. Students who choose to major in both are typically those who recognize a reciprocal relationship between Linguistics and Hawaiian Studies. The study of linguistics facilitates their understanding of the structure and sociopolitical situation of the Hawaiian language, and, likewise, the study of Hawaiian enhances the students' understanding of both language structure and sociolinguistic aspects surrounding languages, especially minority and endangered languages.

I will refer again to Box 7.1 later in this chapter, but I want to note that the placement of the Linguistics program in Ka Haka ʻUla makes even more sense if we consider that a considerable amount of the work in the Hawaiian language revitalization movement and in the development of the Hawaiian Studies major has been based on linguistics. In Wilson's (Wilson, 2018: 87) account of the establishment of the major in the late 1970s, he writes that "from the beginning of its B.A. program, Ka Haka ʻUla has extensively incorporated insights from linguistics into its courses." Moreover, Wilson also emphasizes that linguistics has exerted significant influence on the teaching of Hawaiian in the undergraduate Hawaiian language courses. He writes (Wilson, 2018: 88), "Ka Haka ʻUla language courses also focus heavily on teaching linguistically informed lexicon, grammar, and diagramming of sentences. The grammatical diagrams are based in Hawaiian, facilitating teaching through Hawaiian." In fact, Kamanā and Wilson (2012) apply the idea of lexical categories, i.e., nouns, verbs, adjectives, etc., to Hawaiian, but they do so by creating categories such as *hamani, hehele, ʻaʻano, kikino, and papani* that better reflect meaningful lexical distinctions in the language. In addition, Kamanā and Wilson (2012) employ the image of a squid to describe the way that these categories are placed together to create syntactical patterns that are used systematically by speakers of Hawaiian. Given the importance of the ocean to traditional Hawaiian ways of survival, the squid provides a more culturally centered way of conceptualizing grammar. Wilson (2018) emphasizes that "this grammatical focus allows students to rapidly access the full language beyond memorized phrases." To be sure, there may be other available ways of teaching Hawaiian that do not adopt such a linguistic focus, but it is difficult to deny that this method has been largely successful in increasing the number of adult Hawaiian speakers of the language through the B.A. program in Hawaiian Studies in Ka Haka 'Ula. Here again, it is evident that insights from linguistics have been used as resources for language revitalization.

Insights from linguistics have also been instrumental to efforts of Hawaiian language revitalization at lower levels of education. As noted earlier in this book, early work in the movement started with the creation of Hawaiian language preschools under the non-profit organization the 'Aha Pūnana Leo in 1984. A few years later, Hawaiian medium education was extended to the elementary school level, and then to the junior high and high school levels, with several schools designated now as Ka Haka 'Ula laboratory schools. Educators at these schools are employing knowledge from the area of first language acquisition to develop a literacy program starting with kids at a young age. Wilson and Kamanā (2017) describe the development of a syllabic reading program that begins in the 'Aha Pūnana Leo preschools. Known as "Hakalama," the reading program takes advantage of the syllable structure of Hawaiian and English to employ the roman alphabet to prompt preschool students to make connections between syllables and written symbols, such as "ha, ka, la, ma, pa, wa, 'a …" As they explain (Wilson & Kamanā, 2017: 134), "The Polynesian Hawaiian language is especially well-suited for learning to read by syllables, a method unavailable for English." The preschoolers then develop the ability to recognize these syllables as part of words, leading to the ability to read words as well as sentences at a time that is "approximately 2 years before their peers in English medium reading English" (Wilson & Kamanā, 2017). Additionally, when the children move into elementary school and are ready to read by phonemes, they will be able to transfer skills in reading Hawaiian to other languages, most notably English, which students start studying officially in Hawaiian medium education in the 5th grade (Wilson & Kamanā, 2017). There is recent research on the Hakalama reading program, most notably the Wilson and Kamanā paper mentioned here, but this method has been employed since the mid-1980s in the Hawaiian medium preschools to promote literacy, not just in Hawaiian but in English as well. Here again, the focus was not on doing research in linguists; instead, an aspect of linguistics was culled for the practical application it could lend to the Hawaiian revitalization movement.

Faculty at Ka Haka 'Ula, including the Linguistics faculty, has also facilitated the development at one of the laboratory schools, Ke Kula 'o Nāwahīokalani'ōpu'u, of a heritage language program to provide instruction to the students, starting from early in elementary school, in languages such as Japanese, Chinese, and Latin (Wilson & Kamanā, 2011). This is the same program that was described briefly in Chapter 5 as a means of enabling the young students not only to gain exposure to languages that may be part of their ethnic heritage but also to take advantage of and further develop their metalinguistic skills in comparing and analyzing languages. Focusing specifically on Latin instruction, Wilson and Kamanā (2011: 50) write the following:

> Latin instruction is from a perspective based in Hawaiian language, culture and history with a contrastive analysis, grammar-translation approach. This instruction also includes comparison with English language, culture and history from the time of the early Anglo-Saxon tribes. Metalinguistic skills developed from contrastive analysis with Latin provide Nāwahī students with tools to consciously improve overall vocabulary development and language performance, be it in Hawaiian, English or other languages.

Although not mentioned overtly here, instruction in Latin and in Japanese and Chinese as well occurs through the medium of Hawaiian, hence further strengthening their Hawaiian skills at the same as their metalinguistic abilities. This heritage language program is partly based on the research of Bialystok and others on bilingualism and multilingualism showing the cognitive benefits of learning multiple languages at a young age (Bialystok, 2018; Bialystok et al., 2012).

Since moving to Ka Haka ʻUla, the two Linguistics faculty have played a prominent role in the implementation of the heritage language programs. Both myself and YO have a background in Japanese and have spent time in the classroom at Nāwahī teaching Japanese. In addition, we have sent double majors in Linguistics and Hawaiian Studies who speak Japanese to Nāwahī to serve as teachers and assistants. In fact, throughout the COVID-19 pandemic as Nāwahī moved to online instruction, YO supervised a team of Japanese and Hawaiian speakers that was delivering Japanese instruction to students starting in the first grade of elementary school. I have also used my background studying Latin in college to assist in the Latin instruction, which has been handled mostly by Pila Wilson (PW), one of the early pioneers in Hawaiian revitalization who has his doctorate in linguistics and teaches courses in Hawaiian linguistics through the medium of Hawaiian at Ka Haka ʻUla. Linguistics therefore has been central in developing this heritage language program that, instead of engaging in "typical" academic work in linguistics, is focusing on aiding Hawaiian revitalization and also in the development of the metalinguistic abilities of Hawaiian-speaking children.

Additionally, linguistics has also been part of a program at the university to provide Nāwahī students at the high school level with a head start in earning university credits. This program enables the students to take some of the Hawaiian language courses at the university level that have an emphasis on grammatical structures, and it also enables them to enroll in other courses especially created to fit their needs and abilities. Examples here are a course taught through Hawaiian by PW focusing on the Hawaiian language revitalization movement, a course on English composition taught by a UH-Hilo professor from the English department, and another course on dual literacy that was taught by me as part of my course load as a UH-Hilo faculty member. For the dual literacy course, students were to read articles in both Hawaiian and English and also to write various types of essays in both Hawaiian and English. The course, which was taught through Hawaiian, adopted a comparative perspective that attempted to increase the students' ability to compare and analyze formal writing styles across Hawaiian and English. All of these courses are taught as regular university courses and thus open to all students at the university, but the content has been tailored to foster the abilities of the Hawaiian medium high school students in the two official languages of the state. This type of program has been implemented with the hope of grooming the high school students from Nāwahī to become not only leaders of the Hawaiian revitalization movement in the future but also leaders within a Hawaiian society that recognizes, at least, the importance of the Hawaiian language. To be sure, not all graduates from Nāwahī pursue career paths that focus on the Hawaiian language, but the belief is that this type of early college credit program that focuses on linguistic abilities across languages will provide them with metalinguistic knowledge and skills that will serve them in any field they choose. Once again, the goal is not linguistics per se; linguistic knowledge and the Linguistics faculty themselves are viewed as resources for the attainment of various life goals.

7.3 The Contributions of Linguistics to Multilingualism and Other Minority Languages

The above section explained some of the ways that the Linguistics program, from its position in Ka Haka ʻUla, functions as resource for the Hawaiian Language revitalization movement. This section describes how the Linguistics program also plays a role as a resource in providing assistance to other minority languages and in promoting multilingualism. To do so, I first refer back to Box 7.1 and note that in addition to courses on Hawaiian, the Linguistics program also features courses that concentrate directly on Japanese, as indicated by the JPNS alpha that precedes the course names. Unlike the courses with Hawaiian alphas that are taught through Hawaiian, these courses on Japanese are taught through English and not Japanese, but they are nonetheless designed for students with at least a beginner's background in the Japanese language. As Box 7.1 shows, there are two courses focusing on Japanese structure and a third on Japanese language pedagogy.

Japanese is also featured in the course entitled "Languages in Hawai'i," which counts in either the Applied/Sociolinguistic or Language Maintenance, Revitalization, and Policy specialization. This is a survey course that spends significant time on Hawaiian and Pidgin but also covers immigrant languages such as Japanese, Chinese, Portuguese, various Filipino languages, Ryukyuan languages, Korean, Samoan, and the languages of so-called Micronesia. Adopting a comparative perspective, this course attempts to underscore the diverse linguistic structures within these languages and it also attempts to consider sociopolitical aspects of the co-existence of these languages in the Hawaiian Islands. Pidgin is also featured in "Pidgins and Creoles" as a part of a consideration of pidgin and creole languages throughout the world.[3] Moreover, language diversity is also emphasized in the course "Indigenous Languages of the U.S." which provides students with a general survey of indigenous languages in North America and explicates some of the sounds and structures of those language that differ from English and European languages.

In addition to developing survey courses that cover indigenous and minority languages, Linguistics at UH-Hilo has also sought ways to work specifically with speakers of indigenous and minority languages so as to facilitate their ability to promote their own languages. To do so, we have, since moving into Ka Haka 'Ula, created an academic certificate within the Linguistics program entitled "Contemporary Indigenous Multilingualism." Academic certificates require fewer credit hours than majors and allow students to pursue specific academic topics without necessarily pursuing majors, although students frequently pursue certificates related to their majors. The intention of the certificate in "Contemporary Indigenous Multilingualism" is to enable speakers of indigenous languages to explore their own languages so that they may deepen their knowledge and proficiency and also prepare themselves to teach their languages to others. Among the languages focused on by

[3]Prior to the COVID-19 pandemic, plans were being made to offer a Linguistics course focusing specifically on Pidgin in Hawai'i, but this class was to be instructed by a part-time lecturer and was unable to be offered due to budget cuts due to the pandemic. We are hoping to offer the course in the near future.

students who have completed the certificate or are currently in the process of completing it are Ojibwe, Samoan, Tahitian, Marquesan, Nahuatl, Uchinaaguchi (Ryukyuan), and Sonsorolese, a language of the Pacific Islands. Box 7.2 shows the requirements to complete the certificate.

Box 7.2: Certificate in Contemporary Indigenous Multilingualism

Certificate in Contemporary Indigenous Multilingualism

Requirements (21–25 credits):

Required Courses (6)

LING 102 Introduction to Linguistics (3)
KIND 240 Culture Revitalization Movements (3)

Core Electives (6–8), Taken from:

LING 133 Elementary Indigenous Languages (3)
LING 233 Intermediate Indigenous Languages (3)
KHAW 103 First Level Transitional Hawaiian Immersion (4)
KHAW 104 First Level Partial Hawaiian Immersion (4)
KHAW 133 First Level Hawaiian for Speakers (4)
KHAW 233s Level Hawaiian for Speakers (4)

Transfer semester hours in an indigenous language other than Hawaiian (i.e., Lakota, Samoan) from a tribal college or other college

Related Electives (9–11), Taken from:

LING 442 Languages in Hawaiʻi (3)
LING 347 Pidgins And Creoles (3)
LING 331 Language in Culture & Society (3)

Courses in indigenous languages other than Hawaiian

Courses pertaining to indigenous multilingualism with prior permission from the Hawaiian Studies department chair

Hawaiian language courses; however, no more than a total of 8 credits may be applied to this certificate

Note: This certificate may be taken by linguistics majors or any other major.

As Box 7.2 indicates, courses in Hawaiian language count and so the certificate is open to Hawaiian-speaking students. However, the Hawaiian language students tend not to pursue this certificate, which is probably due to the fact that a major in Hawaiian Studies will provide them with a much more detailed study of their language.

For students focusing on indigenous languages besides Hawaiian, the courses LING 133 and LING 233 are key to the certificate as it is in these courses that they work closely with the Linguistics faculty to explore the structure and sociolinguistic situation of their languages of focus. These courses are taught by myself and YO, and, while we are almost never proficient in the languages focused on by students, we are able to direct them in terms of analysis and description. For instance, we are able to push students to examine structural facets of their language such as pluralization, tense and aspect, and transitivity, and we can likewise direct them to examine language policies and other events that may have led to language shift. Students then present different aspects of their languages in class in front of each other and the instructor, which allows students to view their languages through a comparative lens and also develop a capacity to explain their languages to others. These courses do, then, encourage students to engage in work typically associated with linguistics, namely the examination of structural features such as phonemes, morphemes, and grammatical categories. However, it does not treat them merely "as objects to be described in scientific materials" (Leonard, 2018: 56) but instead does so as part of an attempt to seek the means to support, maintain, and revitalize languages that may have a minority or even endangered status. The certificate in "Contemporary Indigenous Multilingualism" is thus an example of the approach adopted toward Ka Haka 'Ula toward linguistics, namely, that linguistics not only be viewed as a separate discipline in and of itself but, more importantly, also be conceived of as a resource for the greater goal of preserving languages.

In addition to this certificate program, the Linguistics program provides assistance in other ways to minority languages. For instance, YO works closely with a community-based group in Hawai'i that is endeavoring to reconnect with Ryukyuan languages and cultures. The Ryukyuan languages, which include the language Uchinaaguchi mentioned above, are the indigenous languages of the Ryukyuan Islands, a set of islands off the coast of Japan that, prior to be forcibly annexed by Japan in 1879, functioned as an independent kingdom. Since annexation, the six recognized languages of the islands have become endangered as the Japanese embarked on the process of colonization, which included forcing people of the islands to be educated in Japanese. There is a close connection between the Ryukyuan Islands and Hawai'i due to arrival of Ryukyuans beginning in 1900 to work as plantation laborers. Accordingly, there are many descendants of these laborers still living and working in Hawai'i, which means that these languages should be recognized as heritage languages. A group of these descendants have been holding monthly workshops that feature Ryukyuan language and culture classes, and YO has been involved for several years in a leadership role. We have also encouraged many of the linguistics majors to participate, and some have come to play active role and to participate in larger conferences devoted to Ryukyuan languages and cultures. In fact, one of the original conveners of the meetings has recently returned to school at UH-Hilo to complete a B.A. as a major in Linguistics at UH-Hilo with a specialization in "Language Maintenance, Revitalization, and Policy."

Involvement with the Ryukyuan languages has also led the Linguistics program to forge ties between the Hawaiian language revitalization movement and the growing interesting in preserving the Ryukyuan languages. This includes several trips by faculty from Ka Haka 'Ula of Ryukyuan ancestry to deliver workshops and attend symposiums and conferences in the Ryukyuan islands. Likewise, Ka Haka 'Ula has hosted academics from universities in the Ryukyuan islands who wanted to observe the revitalization activities in Hawai'i with the hope of developing programs for their languages in the Ryukyus. Indeed, a recent book published in Japanese on the future of the Ryukyuan languages contains articles written by YO and one other Ka Haka 'Ula faculty member, Kanani Maka'imoku, and it also contains the Japanese translation of a speech delivered by the Director of Ka Haka 'Ula, Keiki Kawai'ae'a (Hateruma et al., 2021).

The Linguistics program has also been involved in a similar relationship with another indigenous language group in Japan, the Ainu. Ainu is indigenous to the island of Hokkaido, which is now a part of Japan. Ainu educators at Sapporo University in Hokkaido have brought members of its Urespa club, which was established in order to provide students with a safe place to study Ainu language and culture, to Hawai'i to participate in a cultural and linguistic exchange with Hawaiian language students at UH-Hilo. This cultural exchange also included short homestays with Hawaiian families. YO also traveled with several Ka Haka 'Ula Hawaiian language students to visit Hokkaido for further linguistic and cultural exchange, and she also accompanied faculty and students of the Urespa club to New Zealand to visit several sites of Māori revitalization. The relationship between the UH-Hilo Linguistics program and the Urespa club progressed to a point where Ka Haka 'Ula and Sapporo University signed an agreement to support each other's efforts. Through this agreement, YO and I had begun plans to host a summer institute offering courses in Hawaiian, English, and language revitalization, but such plans were interrupted by the COVID-19 pandemic. We are hopeful that such an institute may be possible in the future.

Finally, it is noteworthy in this section that the Linguistics program is working with a local high school on the Big Island of Hawai'i to offer training in translation to students who speak minority languages in the community that surrounds the school. This project, termed "student translators," was initiated by a teacher at the school to make sure that important information from the school was being delivered equally to parents that may not be proficient in English. The project is being piloted starting in September of 2021, and I have agreed to provide the initial training class on a volunteer basis to the high school or to the students. The school will give the students high school credit for the class training, and the school also has secured a small grant to hire the students, upon completion of the training, to translate official school letters of communication into their languages. This project will not only provide the students with basic skills in translation but it will show the students, many of whom were originally designated as English language learners and put into special programs, that their languages are valued in the school and in the community. It is hoped that this pilot attempt will lead to a partnership between the UH-Hilo Linguistics program and the high school that can be continued and possibly expanded to other high schools across the island as a part of appreciating and developing the multilingualism that already exists in Hawai'i.

7.4 Linguistics at the Graduate Level

Discussion in this chapter has thus far focused on linguistic work primarily at the undergraduate level and below, but it should be noted that linguistics contributes at the graduate level to both the Hawaiian language revitalization movement and the preservation of minority and/or indigenous languages. Prior to the movement of Linguistics into Ka Haka ʻUla, Ka Haka ʻUla had already implemented four graduate programs, one graduate certificate program, two M.A. programs, and one doctoral program. The graduate certificate program, called the Kahuawaiola Indigenous Teacher Education Program, prepares teachers to work primarily in the Hawaiian medium schools. The two M.A. programs, one in Hawaiian Language and Literature and one in Indigenous Language and Culture Education, have also, to date, focused primarily on the Hawaiian language and providing students with skills to engage in research on the Hawaiian and/or to further their understanding of a Hawaiian-based educational philosophies and practices. The Ph.D. program, titled Hawaiian and Indigenous Language and Culture and Revitalization, has, since its start in 2005, simultaneously worked with groups of students focusing specifically on Hawaiian as well as those focusing on other indigenous languages. Since its inception in 2005, the program has had students from a variety of language communities that include Māori, Tlingit, Chamoro, Mohawk, Lakota, Arapaho, Dakota, Ojibwe, and Ryukyuan. All of these graduate level programs center on indigenous languages, but are not programs in linguistics, although they all in one way or another rely on insights from linguistics.

Of the graduate programs, linguistics has arguably had the most influence on the Ph.D. program. Box 7.3 shows the basic curriculum for the Ph.D. program and the utilization of linguistic terminology for some of the course names.

Box 7.3: Ph.D. in Hawaiian and Indigenous Language and Culture Revitalization

Graduation Requirements

1. KIND 730 Research Methods in Hawaiian and Indigenous Languages and Cultures (3)
2. Eight Credits in Advanced Study of Language of Focus:

   KLAN 701 Semantics/Pragmatics of Indigenous Languages (1)
   KLAN 702 Stylistics/Domains of Indigenous Languages (1)
   KLAN 703 Semantics/Pragmatics of an Indigenous Language (3)
   KLAN 704 Stylistics/Domain of an Indigenous Language (3)

   These credits are directed toward improved analytical and fluency skills in the student's language of focus and its culture. KLAN 701–702 are seminars taken by all students to develop common understandings and form the basis for KLAN 703–704, which focus specifically on Hawaiian or other indigenous languages depending on student interests.
3. Additional Language Requirement:
   For students whose language of focus is Hawaiian, the additional language requirement will be met by demonstrated fluency and academic knowledge of any approved second language equivalent to the 102 level as taught at UH Hilo. For students whose language of focus is other than Hawaiian, the additional language requirement will be met by demonstrated fluency and academic knowledge of Hawaiian equivalent to the 102 level as taught at UH Hilo.
4. Two Areas of Specialization:
   Students will focus on two of the four areas of specialization provided in the program: (a) Indigenous Language and Culture Education, (b) Indigenous Language and Culture In Society, (c) Language Planning, and (d) Hawaiian Language and Culture.

   KED 794 Indigenous Language and Culture Education (3) (Pre: KED 660 Indigenous Culture-based Education (3), KED 662 Indigenous Well-being Through Education (3) or equivalent)

KIND 794 Indigenous Language and Culture in Society (3) (Pre: KIND 601 Language Maintenance and Shift (3), KIND 602 Methods/Resolutions in Indigenous Language Community Building (3) or equivalent)
KLIN 794 Language Planning (3) (Pre: KIND 601 Language Maintenance and Shift (3), KIND 602 Methods/Resolutions in Indigenous Language Community Building (3) or equivalent)
HWST 794 Hawaiian Language and Culture (3) (Pre: HAW 631 History of Hawaiian Language & Literature (3), HAW 654 Advanced Hawaiian Grammar (3), HWST 663 Traditional Hawaiian Literature (3), HWST 665 Ethnological & Historical Narratives (3) or consent of instructor)

5. Students may take up to six semester credits (or equivalent) at another accredited university in courses pre-approved by the program chair and transfer the credits to the University of Hawaii at Hilo in place of any of the listed program courses.
6. Completion of all graduate courses with a grade no lower than "B."
7. Successful completion of a comprehensive examination consisting of oral and/or written questions, after the student's Graduate Committee determines the student has had sufficient preparation in the field of study to begin work on the dissertation.
8. Submission and approval of a portfolio which documents the student's work to improve public opinion and/or government policy concerning the revitalization of the student's language and culture of focus. The portfolio may include newspaper or periodical articles or oral presentations aimed at the student's indigenous community or the larger public; it may include written material or oral testimony given at government forums concerned with indigenous language and culture revitalization.
9. Successful completion of a dissertation, with enrollment in a minimum of six credits of KIND 800 Doctoral Dissertation Research (1–6) (V) during the writing of the dissertation. A final oral examination in defense of the dissertation is then required upon completion of the dissertation.

To explain these curricular requirements, it is important to realize that for some of the courses, both the Hawaiian language students and other students focusing on other Indigenous languages are expected to enroll together. For such courses, instruction occurs primarily in English. But for other courses, the groups are kept separate, an arrangement that stems largely from the desire to provide the Hawaiian language students with instruction solely in Hawaiian. One example is the courses listed in requirement #2. For the first two courses in the list, KLAN 701 and KLAN 702, all students are together in an attempt to discuss the application of ideas of pragmatics, semantics, and stylistics and domains, all concepts used in Linguistics, to indigenous languages at a general level. For the courses KLAN 703 and KLAN 704, they are each divided into two sections, one for Hawaiian and the other for non-Hawaiian indigenous students, in order to begin applying in more specific detail the topics to their own languages and cultures.

Although linguistic terminology is employed, the purpose of these courses and of the Ph.D. program is not to engage in the work of linguistics. It is to use linguistics to provide graduate students with the knowledge, skills, and training to progress with their own language revitalization that will strengthen indigenous languages across the globe. Indeed, of the nine graduates from the program to date, six of whom have focused on Hawaiian and three on other indigenous languages (one each on Māori, Tlingit, and Mohawk), there have been some that have concentrated on linguistic topics. One graduate focused on relative clause constructions in the Hawaiian language and their usage in Hawaiian literature (Cabral, 2016) and another graduate on a comparison of Hawaiian speakers from two different generations at the discourse level (Kimura, 2012). There have been dissertations written on topics that, if forced to categorize, may fall under the umbrella of "applied linguistics," such as the language testing and assessment in Māori (Edmonds, 2008), language pedagogy in Mohawk (Green, 2020), and immersion education and school construction in Tlingit (Twitchell, 2018). At the same time, there have been topics that seem removed from linguistics, for instance a focus on conflict resolution in Hawaiian medium schools (Kamanā, 2010), Hawaiian literature (Perreira, 2011; Warfield, 2020), and Hawaiian performing arts (Harman, 2020). While these topics range quite widely, the one constant is that all topics are meant to apply to and contribute to the promotion and revitalization of indigenous languages. For example, the dissertation that explicated and analyzed relative clauses in Hawaiian featured a discussion of how to teach these complex structures to learners, and those that focused on Hawaiian literature aimed to uncover and unpack cultural knowledge that could be used to teach students and deepen their cultural knowledge. Thus, despite a linguistic focus in some of the courses and in some of the dissertation topics, linguistics is approached as just one resource for the larger purpose of the program, language, and cultural revitalization.

Moreover, the Linguistics program is heavily involved in the work at the M.A. level, particularly on the side of Indigenous Language Culture Education. Until recently, students in this M.A. program have focused on Hawaiian as all of the courses were conducted through the medium of Hawaiian except for portions of some of the courses in which the students would interact via technology with indigenous students from other parts of the world. The program, though, has recently begun to link with the Linguistics program and faculty to offer courses in English in order to begin accepting students focusing on other indigenous languages. These students still take some courses with the Hawaiian-speaking students through the medium of Hawaiian, which would require them to study Hawaiian and work with the faculty and classmates to receive translation, but they would also enroll in courses offered by the Linguistics faculty in English. This revision has been piloted since August 2020 with one student working on a Ryukyuan language and hoping to make progress in transmitting the language to younger generations in the Ryukyuan Islands. There are plans for another student from the island of Palau from a small community of Sonsorolese speakers to join the program in 2021 as an undeclared graduate student. Among other areas of focus, this student hopes to develop an orthography in order to promote the teaching and transmission of her language. Both of these students have a background in linguistics as they earned B.A. degrees in our Linguistics program, but for them, linguistics will continue to serve as a resource for their larger goals.

7.5 Navigating Standard Language Ideologies at UH-Hilo

The linguistic-related activities described above have been undertaken within Ka Haka ʻUla, which, as one of several colleges at UH-Hilo, adheres to the general policies through which the university is administered. It is, therefore, possible to say that there is administrative support for activities to promote the revitalization of indigenous languages and work with minority languages. The university, in short, has not done anything to limit these activities and has allowed Ka Haka ʻUla, more or less, to create and revise its curricula as it so desires.

At the same time, though, one of the general policies of the university is to support English as the unwritten official language of the university. This is the case because even though both Hawaiian and English stand as official languages of the state, only English is required as a part of the general education curriculum established by the university. All students at the university must pass an English composition class in order to graduate. Even students choosing to major in Hawaiian Studies must pass the English composition course. In contrast, students are not required to take any Hawaiian language courses before graduation. This means that all students must take at least one English course, but they can graduate without taking any courses in Hawaiian. There is a general education requirement that students take one course in a category designated as "Hawai'i Pan-Pacific," and there are Hawaiian languages that count toward the satisfaction of this requirement. However, the majority of courses in this category are taught through English (see discussion in Lockwood & Saft, 2016).

Not only does the university place English above Hawaiian in this way, but it also leaves the other language unique to Hawaiʻi, Pidgin, completely out of the picture. The latest statistics shows that 74 percent of the student body comes from Hawaiʻi, all of whom have certainly been exposed to Pidgin and many undoubtedly have grown up speaking the language.[4] Yet, Pidgin receives no mention in the educational

[4]Statistics taken from http://www.hawaii.edu/campuses/hilo/.

curriculum and is, according to interview research conducted by Lockwood and Saft (2016), considered by some to be a controversial topic at the university. Lockwood and Saft (2016) conducted interviews with 18 faculty members representing 10 different majors and found that 8 of the interviewees asked to remain anonymous because of "the sensitive nature of the topic in Hawai'i" and because of "concerns that positive views toward HC [Hawai'i Creole] might be seen as going against university policy" (Lockwood & Saft, 2016: 5–6).

In their interviews, Lockwood and Saft did find support among the faculty for Pidgin with some faculty stating that they accept papers written in Pidgin. As stated by one of the interviewees:

> Papers and presentations can be submitted in the official languages of Hawai'i which Should include Pidgin. Historically, the languages and cultural aspects of these islands have been crushed numerous times. We are instructing the generation that can change this. If we allow them to be themselves and support the revitalization of the Hawaiian culture and languages, then we are helping to right the wrongs done in the past.

Nonetheless, they also found several opinions that reinforce a standard language ideology:

> English is the language of science. Speaking Pidgin in a scientific setting does nothing but confuse others and disorganize data recording. (Lockwood & Saft, 2016: 7)

> Our students must pass a national board exam in order to become high school and elementary teachers. The test is done in English and if they can't pass it, they don't get to be teachers. Plain and simple, they need English more than they need Pidgin when it comes to that sort of thing. (Lockwood & Saft, 2016: 7)

The interviews also showed that some faculty expressed support for Pidgin but did so in a way that also revealed adherence to ideologies that promote English.

> It [HC] should be used but only in the right context. Not because it is improper or dysfunctional, but because it is inappropriate for certain settings just as any other language. If a Japanese student tried writing an English paper in my freshman comp class using Japanese, I would ask them to change it to English. (Lockwood & Saft, 2016: 7)

> Pidgin is a creative and sometimes comical language. It doesn't always seem to fit in school. I have nothing against it, I allow and encourage its use, but I have a hard time taking it seriously in some of the more academic uses such as writing. (Lockwood & Saft, 2016: 7)

Both of these interviewees attempt to compliment Pidgin, but by treating it as a language not appropriate for more serious uses such as academic writing, they are following and simultaneously reinforcing the standard language ideology that English is the more appropriate language for those "formal" contexts.

It is not just Pidgin, though, that takes a backseat to English. The university has a general education curriculum that makes the study of other languages, including Hawaiian, optional. In order to graduate, students are required to fulfill six credits (usually fulfilled by taking two three-credit courses) of a general education requirement with the label "diversification requirement." In addition to Hawaiian, the university does offer students the option to study a range of languages that includes Japanese, Chinese, Filipino, and Spanish that count toward the "diversification requirement," but students can also fulfill this requirement by taking a long list of courses that include art and dance.[5] Interestingly, the introductory linguistics course taught through the Linguistics program (Linguistics 102) also counts toward this requirement. Thus, students can engage in the general study of linguistics without studying a specific language. To be sure, even though UH-Hilo is a comparatively small university that carries slightly less than 3,000 undergraduate students, it does offer language instruction in languages like Hawaiian, Japanese, Chinese, and Filipino that are part of the heritage of many of its local students. Nonetheless, by making English the only mandatory language,

[5]The list of courses that satisfy this requirement can be viewed at: https://hilo.hawaii.edu/academics/gened/ArtsHumanitiesLiterature.php.

and by enabling English to serve as the de facto language of the university, it falls in line with and continues to reinforce the general belief that English is "the" language that really matters.

In order to navigate the university's lack of emphasis on languages other than English, the Linguistics program has implemented its own language requirement for students who major in Linguistics. As shown in Box 7.1, majors are required to engage in 16 credits of what it called "second/auxiliary language study" that must come from at least two different languages. Since language courses are typically four credits per course, this means that majors are generally expected to take four semesters of language study, with many students opting to take three courses of one language and one of another or to take two semesters each of two languages. Students may also take more than two languages; they may, for instance, take one semester each of four different languages.

While the program is strict about enforcing the language requirement, it does offer flexibility for students who enter the program with proficiency in languages other than English. For instance, we regularly have students who are first language speakers of languages in the Pacific (i.e., Samoan, Tongan, Marshallese, Palauan, Chuukese) and Asia (i.e., Japanese, Korean, Chinese), and in those cases, we give them eight credits of language study, four for their first language and four for English since they have already demonstrated proficiency in English by passing the university's mandatory English course. Such students, thus, are required to engage in two semesters worth of a study of a third language. As a program, the goal is to make sure that all students have exposure to at least three languages to satisfy the Linguistics major. For students whose first language is English, the language requirement leads them to study two additional languages, thus giving them exposure to three languages.

Students may also demonstrate proficiency in a language that may not be their first language and receive credit toward the language requirement. Here, we sometimes have students who have learned American Sign Language, and in such cases, we ask them to meet with someone at UH-Hilo to confirm their proficiency. Likewise, we count language courses at the community college or higher that have been taken at other institutions. This includes tribal colleges as the program looks to promote Native American and other indigenous languages.

This means that students are not limited to the language courses offered here at UH-Hilo and fits with our desire to encourage student exposure to a diverse array of languages.

The Linguistics program also participates with colleagues in the Hawaiian Language College to counter the de facto English language policy of the university by creating what might be called a meso-level language policy focusing on Hawaiian. A meso-level language policy was first discussed by Kaplan and Baldauf (1997) as a level that, since it may be created within institutions, falls between the micro- and macro-levels. In fact, when Ka Haka ʻUla was established in 1997 as a separate college at the university, one of the stipulations was that interaction in the administration of the college would be through Hawaiian. All communication among faculty and staff, whether it be face-to-face or electronic (such as e-mail), occurs through Hawaiian. Additionally, there are some beginning level Hawaiian courses and courses in Linguistics that employ English, but all interaction among faculty and students of Hawaiian, inside and outside of the classroom, is through Hawaiian. This meso-level language policy has encouraged faculty and students to develop the routine of speaking to each other solely in Hawaiian, which has carried over to interaction outside of Ka Haka ʻUla. For example, faculty and staff in the college employ Hawaiian with one another regardless of whether they meet on or off of campus. Students also develop such a routine as they advance through the Hawaiian Studies program. As noted in Chapter 3, Ka Haka ʻUla has designed their undergraduate and graduate programs to include a focus on instilling the "crucial disposition" (Wilson & Kawaiʻaeʻa, 2007) to lead students to employ Hawaiian among themselves.

This meso-level language policy was aided greatly when Haleʻōlelo, the name given to the Hawaiian Studies building, was completed in 2014. All communication within the building, unless otherwise directed, occurs through the medium of Hawaiian. The building name Haleʻōlelo literally means "house of language" and is derived from the College's namesake, Princess Ruth Keʻelikōlani, who was a staunch supporter of the Hawaiian language and who referred to her own dwelling as "Haleʻōlelo." This building provides faculty, staff, and students with a *honua* (environment) for speaking Hawaiian on a campus that otherwise expects English to be the official language of communication.

In addition to the meso-level language policy developed by Ka Haka ʻUla, the university has made attempts to appreciate minority and indigenous languages. It is relevant here to note that UH-Hilo is typically recognized as one of the most, if not the most, diverse universities in the United States. The UH-Hilo website notes that "U.S. News & World Report has ranked the University of Hawaiʻi at Hilo as the most ethnically diverse campus among national universities."[6] The website also reports that "The Chronicle of Higher Education's 2018 Almanac named UH-Hilo the most diverse four-year public university in the nation."[7] Part of the reason for this diversity is that many of the local students, who as noted before comprise 74% of the student population, are themselves multiethnic and thus count toward this high rate of diversity. At the same time, the UH-Hilo website also notes that as many as 42 countries are represented in the student population.[8]

While the university is unable to offer language courses for all of the languages represented by this diversity, the university employs a student club model to facilitate the students' abilities to organize their own student clubs based on a language and/or culture. For instance, the UH-Hilo website has a list of clubs that includes the Pohnpei Kaselehlie Club, the Japanese Student Association, the Kosrae Hilo Organization, the Tupulaga O Sāmoa Mo A Taeao (Samoan), the Filipino Studies Group, the Ngelekel Belau Club (Palau), the Waab Student Organization (Yap), and the Marshallese Iakwe Club.[9] These organizations do not just focus on language, but many of them consist of first language speakers who support each other's usage of their languages. Many of these languages and cultures are on display at the annual International Nights performances that are open to the public.

As noted earlier in this chapter, Linguistics at UH-Hilo has attempted to create a curriculum that supports the efforts of the students to

[6] https://hilo.hawaii.edu/chancellor/stories/2019/09/09/uh-hilo-ranked-most-ethnically-diverse/.
[7] https://hilo.hawaii.edu/chancellor/stories/2019/09/09/uh-hilo-ranked-most-ethnically-diverse/.
[8] https://hilo.hawaii.edu/international/IN.php.
[9] https://hilo.hawaii.edu/international/IN.php.

appreciate and promote their own languages. Even speakers of languages with few speakers are encouraged to develop ways of studying and teaching their languages via the Linguistics major and the certificate program in Contemporary Indigenous Multilingualism. In addition, Linguistics has tried to foster linguistic tolerance through courses that focus on languages such as Hawaiian and Pidgin and by providing chances to consider indigenous languages of the world. Yet, despite these efforts, critical reflection may suggest that even more effort is still necessary to challenge standard language ideologies that foster linguistic inequality. To make this point, I point to research that has emphasized the need for linguistic intervention on university campuses. In a dissertation focusing on university students from Appalachia, Dunstan (2013) found that perceptions about their own way of speaking, so-called Appalachian English, affected their participation in their courses. As described recently by Wolfram and Dunstan (2021: 157):

> The study showed, for example, that course participation was affected by the perception that the students' dialect did not align with the normative standards expected in an academic setting such as the classroom. As a result, some students were hesitant and defensive because of their dialect and did not feel comfortable speaking in class. Furthermore, students felt that their dialect was an academic barrier, and that they needed to 'prove their intelligence' and overcome stereotypes associated with their academic background.

The results of this study led Wolfram and Dunstan (2021: 157) to note that even with an emphasis on diversity training in American universities, "language is one of those overlooked issues that goes unrecognized in the diversity canon as it actively and insidiously promotes and enhances inequality on campus." They likewise describe how they created an "intervention program" called "Educating the Educated" that led the university of focus, a large Southern university, to incorporate more emphasis on language in their diversity initiatives (Dunstan et al. 2015; Dunstan et al. 2018). The Linguistics program at UH-Hilo has geared itself to support indigenous and minority languages in Hawai'i and across the globe, but, to end this section with a brief statement of critical reflection, it will be beneficial for the program to consider more ways to promote linguistic awareness among the entire set of students, faculty, and staff on campus.

7.6 Conclusion

Referring to work such as Dunstan (2013), Andrews (2018), and Myrick (2019), Wolfram and Dunstan (2021: 156) note that "substantive empirical evidence reveals that institutions of higher learning are conducive sites for the practice of linguistic inequality and, in fact, may serve as active agents in its reproduction." Wolfram and Dunstan (2021: 171) also assert that "Linguists and sociolinguists can play a prominent role in confronting linguistic inequality in higher education. But they cannot do it simply by espousing their ideas in the limited linguistic courses they teach or in conversations that they have with other professionals." As discussed in this chapter, the Linguistics program at UH-Hilo does use its courses to promote critical language awareness of languages that include Hawaiian, Pidgin, and other minority and indigenous languages. But more than that, from its place as a smaller program within the larger Hawaiian Studies Department, Linguistics focuses its efforts inside and outside of its classrooms on providing direct support to indigenous and other minority languages and to the work of language revitalization. It is hoped that this work, which sometimes includes engaging one-on-one with speakers of lesser spoken languages, helps make contributions toward linguistic justice at the local level in Hawai'i as well as at a more global level. The next chapter, the Conclusion, puts the ideas of this chapter together with those of the other chapters to further consider the possibility of linguistic justice in Hawai'i.

References

Amery, R. (2014). Reclaiming the Kaurna language: A long and lasting collaboration in an urban setting. *Language Documentation & Conversation, 8*, 409–429.

Andrews, P. (2018). *Comfortably White or uncomfortably Black: The racialization of Black students in undergraduate classrooms* (Unpublished Paper). North Carolina State University.

Baldwin, D., Baldwin, K., Baldwin, J., & Baldwin, J. (2013). Kyaamiaataweenki Oowaaha: Miami spoken here. In L. Hinton (Ed.), *Bringing our languages home: Language revitalization for families* (pp. 3–18). Heyday Books.

Baugh, J. (2018). *Linguistics in pursuit of justice.* Cambridge University Press.

Bialystok, E. (2018). Bilingual education for young children: Review of the effects and consequences. *International Journal of Bilingual Education and Bilingualism, 21*(6), 666–679. https://doi.org/10.1080/13670050.2016.1203859

Bialystok, E., Craik, F. I. M., & Luk, G. (2012). Bilingualism: Consequences for mind and brain. *Trends in Cognitive Science, 16*(4), 240–250.

Bowern, C., & Warner, N. (2015). 'Lone wolves' and collaboration: A reply to Crippen & Robinson (2013). *Language Documentation & Conservation, 9*, 59–85.

Cabral, J. (2016). *He Kālailaina i nā Kāhulu Pepeke Poke Ki'a a Waila ho'i o ka 'Ōlelo Hawai'i a me ka Ili 'ana o ia mau Kāhulu Pepeke i Loko o ka Mo'olelo 'o Kalapana* (Unpublished Ph.D. Dissertation). University of Hawai'i at Hilo.

Costa, D. (1994). *The Miami-Illinois language* (Unpublished Ph.D. Dissertation). University of California.

Crippen, J., & Robinson, L. (2013). In defense of the lone wolf: Collaboration in language documentation. *Language Documentation & Conservation, 7*, 123–135.

Dobrin, L. M., & Berson, J. (2011). Speakers and language documentation. In P. K. Austin & J. Sallabank (Eds.), *The Cambridge handbook of endangered languages* (pp. 187–211). Cambridge University Press.

Dunstan, S. B. (2013). *The influence of speaking a dialect of appalachian English on the college experience* (Unpublished Ph.D. Dissertation). North Carolina State University.

Edmonds, C. A. (2008). *The reliability and validity of the Māori language proficiency in writing test: Kaiaka Reo year eight* (Unpublished Ph.D. Dissertation). University of Hawai'i at Hilo.

Gerdts, D. (2017). Indigenous linguists: Bringing research into language revitalization. *IJAL, 83*(4), 607–617.

Green, J. (2020). *The oral literacy approach* (Unpublished Ph.D. Dissertation). University of Hawai'i at Hilo.

Grenoble, L. (2009). Linguistic cages and the limits of linguists. In J. Reyhner & L. Lockard (Eds.), *Indigenous language revitalization: Encouragement, guidance & lessons learned* (pp. 61–69). Northern Arizona University.

Grinevald, C. (2006). Worrying about ethics and wondering about "Informed consent": Fieldwork from an americanist perspective. In A. Saxena & L. Borin (Eds.), *Lesser-known languages of South Asia: Status and policies, case studies and applications of information technology* (pp. 339–370). Mouton de Gruyter.

Guerin, V., & Lacrampe, S. (2010). Trust me, I am a linguist: Building partnership in the field. *Language Documentation & Conversation, 4*, 22–33.

Harman, K. L. (2020). *I Lālā Mau Nā Hula Ilalaole He Kālailaina i Nā Kuhi Lima o Nā Hula A Joseph Kealiikuikamoku Ilalaole-O-Kamehameha* (Unpublished Ph.D. Dissertation). University of Hawai'i at Hilo.

Hateruma, E., Kojima, Y., & Teruya, O. (Eds.). (2021). *Ryuukyuu Shogo to Bunka no Mirai*. Iwanami Shoten.

Higgins, C. (2021a). Promoting Pidgin at the University of Hawai'i at Mānoa. In G. Clements & M. J. Petray (Eds.), *Linguistic discrimination in U.S. higher education: Power, prejudice, impacts, and remedies* (pp. 174–188). Routledge.

Higgins, C. (2021b). Engaging the public in sociolinguistics for social justice: Advocating for Pidgin speakers in Hawai'i. In D. S. Warriner & E. R. Miller (Eds.), *Extending applied linguistics for social impact* (pp. 13–34). Bloomsbury Academic.

Hinton, L., Huss, L., & Roche, G., (Eds.). (2018). *The Routledge handbook of language revitalization*. Routledge.

Kamanā, K. (2010). *Mo'oki'ina Ho'oponopono: Ke Ō o ka 'Ike Ku'una Hawai'i ma ke Kula 'o Nāwahīoklani'ōpu'u* (Unpublished Ph.D. Dissertation). University of Hawai'i at Hilo.

Kamanā, K., & Wilson, W. H. (2012). *Nā Kai 'Ewalu: Beginning Hawaiian lessons*. Hale Kuamo'o.

Kaplan, R. B., & Baldauf, R. B. (1997). *Language planning: From practice to theory*. Multilingual Matters.

Kimura, L. (2012). *He Kālailaina i ka Panina 'Ōlelo a ka Mānaleo Hawai'i: Ka Ho'ohālikelike 'ana i ka 'Ōlelo Mānaleo a nā Hanauna 'Elua, 'o ka 'Ōlelo Kūmau a ka Makua a me ka 'Ōlelo Kūpaka a ke Keiki* (Unpublished Ph.D. Dissertation). University of Hawai'i at Hilo.

Leonard, W. Y. (2017). Producing language reclamation by decolonising 'language'. In W. Y. Leonard & H. de Korne (Eds.), *Language documentation and description* (Vol. 14, pp. 15–36). EL Publishing.

Leonard, W. Y. (2018). Reflections on (de)colonialism in language documentation. In D. McDonnell, A. L. Berez-Kroeker, & G. Holton (Eds.), *Reflections on language documentation 20 yeas after Himmeleman 1998* (pp. 55–65). NFLRC.

Lockwood, H., & Saft, S. (2016). Shifting language ideologies and the perceptions of Hawai'i Creole among educators at the university level in Hawai'i. *Linguistics and Education, 33*, 1–13.

McCarty, T. L. (2018). Community-based language planning: Perspectives from indigenous language revitalization. In L. Hinton, L. Huss, & G. Roche (Eds.), *The Routledge handbook of language revitalization* (pp. 22–35). Routledge.

Myrick, C. (2019). *Language and gender ideologies in higher education: An examination of faculty discourses* (Unpublished Ph.D. Dissertation). North Carolina State University.

Olko, J., & Sallabank, J. (2021). *Revitalizing endangered languages: A practical guide*. Cambridge University Press.

Osorio, J. (2002). *Dismembering lāhui: A history of the Hawaiian nation to 1887*. University of Hawai'i Press.

Osorio, J. (2006). On being Hawaiian. *Hūlili: Multidisciplinary research on Hawaiian well-being, 3*, 19–26.

Perreira, H. K. (2011). *He Ha'i'ōlelo Ku'una: Nā Hi'ohi'ona me nā Ki'ina Ho'āla hou i ke Kākā'ōlelo* (Unpublished Ph.D. Dissertation). University of Hawai'i at Hilo. .

Rice, K. (2010). The linguist's responsibilities to the community of speakers: Community-based research. In L. A. Grenoble & N. Louanna Furbee (Eds.), *Language documentation: Practice and values* (pp. 25–36). John Benjamins.

Rice, K. (2011). Ethics in fieldwork. In N. Thieberger (Ed.), *The Oxford handbook of linguistic fieldwork* (pp. 407–429). Oxford University Press.

Rickford, J. R., & King, S. (2016). Language and linguistics on trial: Hearing Rachel Jeantel (and other vernacular speakers) in the courtroom and beyond. *Language, 92*(4), 948–988.

Rickford, J. R., & Rickford, R. J. (2000). *Spoken soul: The story of Black English*. Wiley.

Twitchell, X. L. (2018). HAA DACHX̱ÁNX'I SÁANI KAGÉIYI YÍS: HAA YOO X̱'ATÁNGI KEI NALTSEEN. *For our little grandchildren:*

Language revitalization among the Tlingit (Unpublished Ph.D. Dissertation). University of Hawai'i at Hilo.

Warfield, S. K. (2020). *Ka Na'i Aupuni: The emergence and development of a true Hawaiian leader* (Unpublished Ph.D. Dissertation). University of Hawai'i at Hilo.

Warner, N., Luna, Q., & Butler, L. (2007). Ethics and revitalization of dormant languages: The Mutsun language. *Language Documentation & Conservation, 1*, 58–76.

Wilson, W. H. (2018). Higher education in indigenous language revitalization. In L. Hinton, L. Huss, & G. Roche (Eds.), *The Routledge handbook of language revitalization* (pp. 83–93). Routledge.

Wilson, W. H., & Kamanā, K. (2011). Insights from indigenous language immersion in Hawai'i. In D. J. Tedick, D. Christian, & T. W. Fortune (Eds.), *Immersion education: Practices, policies, possibilities* (pp. 36–57). Multilingual Matters.

Wilson, W. H., & Kamanā, K. (2017). The Hakalama: The 'Aha Pūnana Leo's syllabic Hawaiian reading program. In C. J. McLachlan & A. W. Arrow (Eds.), *Literacy in the early years: Reflections on international research and practice* (pp. 133–150). Springer.

Wilson, W. H., & Kawae'ae'a, K. (2007). I Kumu Lālā: Let there be sources; let there be branches: Teacher education in the college of Hawaiian language. *Journal of American Indian Education, 46*(3), 37–53.

Wolfram, W., & Dunstan, S. (2021). Linguistic inequality and sociolinguistic justice in campus life: The need for programmatic intervention. In G. Clements & M. J. Petray (Eds.), *Linguistic discrimination in U.S. higher education* (pp. 156–173). Routledge.

8

Conclusion: Toward a Public Multilingualism

Through analyses focusing on Hawaiian, Pidgin, immigrant languages, and translanguaging, the chapters in this book have suggested that Hawaiian society, despite a multilingual history and despite existing pockets of multilingualism, fails to do as much as it could to facilitate social justice for non-English languages and their speakers. Chapters 3 and 4 added to prior research by demonstrating that Hawaiian and Pidgin are critical components of the local linguistic landscape. With rich sets of category terms and possessive forms, Hawaiian is a valuable resource for (re)anchoring a Native Hawaiian identity to the land. Pidgin, the analysis demonstrated, is highly effective in both written and spoken form in expressing critique and resistance in public discourse. At the same time, though, both chapters gave an indication of the obstacles that prevent speakers from using Hawaiian and Pidgin freely in society. Despite being an official language of the state, Hawaiian still struggles to gain acceptance in public, with even the local mainstream media sometimes unwilling to engage in a discussion that may promote increased usage in critical domains like the legal system and formal

S. Saft, *Language and Social Justice in Context*,
https://doi.org/10.1007/978-3-030-91251-2_8

government. For Pidgin, a stigma derived from over one hundred years of comparisons with English makes it difficult for even speakers themselves to move beyond the ideological belief that Pidgin is somehow not "appropriate" or "clean."

Chapter 5 described the emphasis in the public school system on learning English and how this emphasis makes it difficult for speakers of immigrant languages to leave EL programs and also, in many cases, to graduate from high school. Discussion in this chapter focused specifically on the groups "Filipino" and "Micronesian," and it featured increased calls from parents and other social critics for alternative forms of education, including bilingual education, that would be socially just for these groups. Chapter 6 showed that the educational focus on English stands in contrast with the regularity in which speakers engage in translanguaging in actual contexts of language usage. This chapter suggested that a deeper understanding of translanguaging, including the power associated with the act of translation, has the potential to be transformative in an educational context because it can help speakers of languages other than English appreciate their full linguistic competence.

Chapter 7 described a program in Linguistics that was designed to contribute to social justice through its support, specifically, of the work of Hawaiian language revitalization and, generally, of endangered and minority languages throughout the world, including Pidgin and immigrant languages in Hawai'i. As noted in that chapter, the program in Linguistics is only one of several efforts in Hawai'i to maintain, revitalize, and promote languages such as Hawaiian and Pidgin. Yet, as the book makes clear, while advocacy is definitely making a difference—there has, for example, been a steady increase in the number of Hawaiian speakers since the 1980s and there has also been a reestablishment of intergenerational transmission, much more needs to be done to dismantle the effects of the monolingual mindset that has been entrenched in Hawaiian society as a result of American colonialism. The rest of this chapter continues to reflect on the chapters as a part of offering further consideration of the relationship between language and social justice in Hawai'i.

8.1 Group-Differentiated Language Rights

In a published report of the hearing before the Select Committee on Indian Affairs in the U.S. Senate in Washington D.C. in 1987, a member of the committee asked the following question when the issue of Hawaiian medium education was raised (Culturally Relevant Early Education Programs, 1987: 87):

> A second objection to establishing Hawaiian language medium schools comes from Hawaii's multi-ethnic culture. If bilingual education is good for Hawaiians, why not Japanese language medium schools and Ilocano language medium schools and Portuguese medium schools and Portuguese language medium schools and on and on?

Below is the response provided by the Hawaiian language educator and activist Larry Kimura:

> I'm not against that. But all the other languages here—Japanese, Korean, Chinese, Portuguese and so on—are thriving some place in the world. This is the only place Hawaiian is spoken. If Hawaiian is going to survive, we have to do something about it here. Chinese is not going to die if Hawaii doesn't establish schools. (Culturally Relevant Early Education Programs, 1987: 87)

Kimura's response serves as an appropriate way to segue into a final point about the organization of languages in Hawaiʻi. As part of a linguistic human rights, all people deserve the right to speak their own languages (Skuttnab-Kangas, 2018). There is no reason that Hawaiʻi cannot be a place with multiple pathways to learn, transmit, and employ a variety of languages. But, as alluded to by Kimura, linguistic justice in Hawaiʻi must start with Hawaiian. Hawaiʻi cannot be a linguistically or socially just place until people of Native Hawaiian ancestry are allowed to use their language, the indigenous language of the Hawaiian Islands, in all public domains. There cannot, to reiterate, be social justice until we have a thriving Hawaiian language that stands in true equality with English as the two official languages of the state.

To maintain that Hawaiian be given preference because of its status as the indigenous language of the land is to make a case for what May (2011, 2014), building on the ideas of the political theorist Will Kymlicka (1995, 2001, 2007), has called "group-based language rights" or "group-differentiated language rights." Some may argue that Hawaiian is already given preferential treatment as an official language that has its own educational pathway, but as the analysis of media discourse in Chapter 3 showed, this so-called preferential treatment does not ensure access in most public domains. Through a group-differentiated language rights approach, Hawai'i would be pushed to grant Hawaiian speakers the right to employ Hawaiian in all public interaction, something which would require governmental agencies to hire Hawaiian speakers and which, in theory, would lead more Native Hawaiians to study and speak their language.

In outlining the notion of group-differentiated language rights, May suggests that the differentiation in language rights would be based on a distinction between two groups, "national minorities" and "ethnic minorities." National minorities are those people who have always lived in a particular territory but have become a minority due to colonization and/or conquest. In addition to Native Hawaiians in Hawai'i, these groups include the Welsh in Britain, Catalans and Basques in Spain, Bretons in France, Quebecois in Canada, and they also include indigenous people such as Native Americans in the United States (May, 2011, 2014). Ethnic minorities are groups who have migrated from another place, including refugees who may have been either removed by force or had to flee from their homelands. Many of the groups and languages discussed in this book, including the immigrants that came from Japan, China, Portugal, and the Philippines to work the plantations and also more recent immigrants from the islands in the Pacific such as Sāmoa and also Micronesia, would be considered ethnic minorities. The basic idea is that the languages of national minorities would be entitled to more rights in society than the languages of ethnic minorities. Accordingly, in Hawai'i then, this means that Hawaiian speakers would be granted more language rights than speakers of other languages.

Concerning the types of rights that would be offered to the two minority groups, May (2011, 2014) refers to a distinction made by Kloss (1977) between "tolerance-oriented" and "promotion-oriented" rights.

According to Kloss, ethnic minorities would be granted "tolerance-oriented" language rights, described as rights that "ensure the right to preserve one's language in the private, nongovernmental sphere of national life" (May, 2011: 266). May further notes that tolerance-oriented rights "include the right of individuals to use their first language at home and in public, freedom of assembly and organization" (May, 2011: 266). In contrast, "national minorities" would be given "promotion-oriented" rights which, according to Kloss (1977: 2, quoted by May, 2011: 266), "involve public authorities [in] trying to promote a minority [language] by having it used in public institutions-legislative, administrative, and educational, including the public schools." May makes a note to point out that both tolerance-oriented and promotion-oriented rights can be applied narrowly or widely, depending on the situations.

In terms specific to Hawai'i, this approach to group-based language is attractive because of the preference it accords to the Hawaiian language. To illustrate briefly, we may imagine a Hawaiian speaker walking into a governmental office and making written and/or spoken requests in Hawaiian, which would be responded to by a Hawaiian speaking or by written correspondence in Hawaiian. The same would be true in court; the court system would, in theory, have Hawaiian-speaking staff, Hawaiian-speaking lawyers, and even Hawaiian-speaking judges. If they did not, then there would be, at least, Hawaiian interpreters readily available. This approach is also attractive because it recognizes a place for immigrant languages in society, even though languages of immigrants may not enjoy quite the same rights as national minorities. Hence, unlike speakers of Hawaiian, speakers of immigrant languages may not be able to walk into a government office and utilize their languages. At the same time, though, tolerance-oriented means that they would still be able to pursue the usage of their languages outside of public offices. For example, after school programs or weekend programs run by the community of speakers would allow immigrant groups not only to use their languages but also transmit them to future generations. In fact, as noted in this book, this does in fact occur in Hawai'i with examples being language schools focusing on Japanese, Chinese, Samoan, and Tokelauan.

However, despite the attractive quality of a group-based rights approach with a distinction between tolerance and promotion-oriented rights, there is a sense that it does not go far enough in terms of facilitating a public multilingualism, at least in the case of Hawai'i. For instance, as the analysis in Chapter 6 made apparent, newspaper discourse refers to a need in Hawai'i to offer public services in immigrant languages, particularly for "Micronesian" and "Filipino" languages. In fact, as discussed in the Introduction, Hawai'i has begun offering services in various immigrant languages, including court interpretation and driver license tests. This does not mean that the courts and the Department of Motor Vehicles always have speakers of "Micronesian" and "Filipino" languages on hand, but the attempts to make these services available suggest the possibility that Hawai'i go beyond tolerance-oriented rights and consider further the implementation of regular services in immigrant languages in the public domain. As long as such services do not replace or detract from the ability to increase the presence of Hawaiian, then the availability of services in immigrant languages would only enhance the lives of speakers of those languages.

Also, crucially, the division between national minorities and ethnic minorities makes it difficult to find a place for Pidgin. Although born out of communication involving immigrants, Pidgin does not fit the category of an ethnic minority language given that it is spoken both by the offspring of immigrants and by Native Hawaiians. Nor, though, does it fit into the category of national minority, even though it has been, as discussed in Chapter 2, sometimes viewed in terms of indigeneity as an indigenous resource. Pidgin is a language spoken by a large number of the current population of Hawai'i, and it still, despite evidence that it is widely used in public domains for various purposes, suffers from a stigma that results in discrimination and also leads to a situation in which speakers growing up with Pidgin learn to be critical of their own language when it is used in public domains. Even the two Pidgin advocates interviewed in Chapter 4 showed this type of view when they described English as the "clean" (*ma'ema'e*) or "appropriate" (*kūpono*) way of speaking.

Even though Pidgin does not fit easily into the group-differentiated rights framework of May (2011, 2014), it is apparent that an approach to language rights and social justice needs to ensure Pidgin a primary role in society. Given evidence showing that Pidgin is used in public interactions more than previously thought (Higgins, 2015; Saft, 2019), it makes sense that efforts at advocacy continue to educate the public about Pidgin and also to encourage educators to adopt a more accepting approach to Pidgin in the classroom. Why, for instance, would a student in Hawai‘i be denied the opportunity to display his/her linguistic competence by translanguaging between Pidgin and English (and possibly other languages) in a formal presentation? As indicated in the interview with JA in Chapter 4, the educational norm is still to penalize students for using Pidgin. If Pidgin speakers are going to be further empowered in society, the belief in the subordination of Pidgin to English must change, and we can start to make that change by teaching and showing children in Hawai‘i that Pidgin is an acceptable form of communication.

Finally, one further criticism of the idea of promotion-oriented rights is that it seems weak when referring to Hawaiian, the language that stands with English as the official language of Hawai‘i. Given Hawaiian's status as an endangered language, it makes sense that there is a need to promote the language, and in a sense, the government is already promoting Hawaiian by granting educational pathways, but the goal should not stop at mere promotion. The goal needs to be a full-fledged commitment, as a part of the current revitalization movement that builds out from educational structures toward the renormalization of Hawaiian in society. This includes ensuring that the Hawaiian educational pathways are equipped with the funding necessary to train teachers and that Hawaiian medium schools have the positions they need to deliver quality education in Hawaiian. As noted in the Introduction in Chapter 1, Hawaiian medium education currently struggles to meet the demands from the community and teachers struggle to find the time both to create curriculum and to teach in Hawaiian. Moreover, as noted above, this commitment would mean equipping government services with Hawaiian speakers, which would encourage more younger people to study Hawaiian as it would represent a path leading to a choice of stable jobs related to the state government. Hawaiian has made significant gains due to the educational structures that have been put into place, but it still suffers from the belief that the main career path for a Hawaiian speaker to go back into one of the educational structures as an educator.

To be sure, genuine attempts to develop group-differentiated rights for Hawaiian would require creativity at the political level in terms of state budgeting and job allocation, but such a commitment to the Hawaiian language would, arguably, create more opportunities in the long run to develop educational and social pathways for immigrant languages as well. As noted in Chapter 5, a desire to see improvement in the educational situation for "Micronesian" students led to the establishment of a task group that included leaders from Hawaiian medium education and that considered how insights from Hawaiian medium and other culture-based approaches might be applied to the "Micronesian" groups (Kala'i et al., 2015). As the status of Hawaiian continues to grow throughout different public domains of society, we may anticipate an increase in bilingual and multilingual leaders in society who develop the knowhow, the flexibility, and the willingness to aid immigrant groups in the promotion of their languages.

8.2 The Monolingual Mindset

A group-differentiated rights approach that gives priority to Hawaiian but also actively works to create educational pathways for immigrant languages would certainly face challenges, but perhaps the biggest challenge is that Hawai'i, despite being a multilingual society since the 1800s, is pervaded by an English monolingual mindset due to the U.S. backed government's efforts to install English as the dominant language. It is this monolingual mindset that makes it difficult for the Hawaiian language to make gains in public domains of society beyond education. It is the monolingual mindset that leads to discrimination against Pidgin and prompts speakers to demean their own language. It is the same monolingual mindset that serves as the impetus for placing minority language students in subtractive EL programs that prevent immigrants and their children from enjoying the transmission of their ancestral languages and from reaping the cognitive benefits of bilingualism. And, it is the monolingual mindset that prevents academic school programs from taking advantage of the emerging translanguaging skills of the students that serve as a better measure of their linguistic abilities. Instead of using the monolingual mindset to compel speakers of other languages to feel insecure and anxious for not concentrating their efforts on English, we need to convince speakers of the dominant language that a public monolingualism is not a healthy strategy for them either.

Here, it is imperative that the general population be better informed about the research findings described in the Introduction, namely, the potential cognitive benefits of bilingualism, the positive results of initiatives to teach indigenous languages in terms of healing, health, and general well-being, and also the availability of various approaches to bilingual education throughout the U.S. As noted in the Introduction, bilingual programs are trending upward in the U.S., but in Hawai'i, outside of Hawaiian medium education, there are not many such programs available. Sometimes the dominant English group may express understanding that it is important for speakers of Hawaiian and other languages to learn their own languages, but rarely do they turn the focus on themselves. In other words, they may recognize the benefits of public multilingualism for speakers of other languages who need to get easier access to important social services, but they tend not to appreciate how living in an environment filled with languages offers them and their children invaluable opportunities to: (1) expand their cognitive capabilities by learning and speaking languages; (2) gain exposure to various cultures; and (3) live among and learn from alternate worldviews.

Unfortunately, as detailed in Chapter 2, in the long history of American colonialism, the Americans in power have often pitted English against other languages as a part of making English dominant and pushing all other to the periphery and sometimes to the brink of elimination. The remnants of this linguistic struggle, I would argue, leave many first language speakers of English fearful about according other languages, Hawaiian included, a central place in public domains, including education. If we are to achieve linguistic justice in Hawai'i, then we must find a way to persuade more people to adopt the type of multilingual mindset that enables them to embrace a society that has two equally strong official languages in English and Hawaiian, a beautiful creole language called Pidgin, and also a place, including more bilingual programs, for immigrant languages.

8.3 Resistance Continues

Luckily, though, until speakers of English can be fully convinced of the advantages of a public multilingualism, it is readily apparent that speakers of other languages in Hawai'i will remain committed to the tradition of resistance that began in the 1800s. In fact, most of the analyses presented in this book can be viewed from the vantage point of resistance. This includes the Hawaiian language newspapers in Chapter 2 that spoke out on behalf of the Native Hawaiians and the Hawaiian language, and it also includes Hawaiian voices in Chapter 3 from the 1972 radio program Ka Leo Hawai'i and the speech contests held in 2018 and 2019. Both the elder speakers on the radio program and the youth in the speech contests demonstrated a dedication to their ancestral tongue by going against the monolingual mindset and speaking in Hawaiian in broadcasted events. Resistance was also readily apparent in the decisions by Samuel Ka'eo in the court and Faye Hanohano on the floor of the House of Representatives to speak in Hawaiian. It is brave decisions such as these to speak Hawaiian, at the risk of consequences such as arrest, that will, together with the educational structures put into place by leaders of the Hawaiian language revitalization, continue to pave a way for justice for Hawaiian language speakers.

Resistance was also obvious in the usage of Pidgin in public in Chapter 4. The written fiction by Tonouchi and the spoken testimony by SI display the vitality and utility of Pidgin in the public domain. To be sure, the inclusion of Tonouchi's fiction in a local "English" magazine required magazine staff members willing to go against the grain and print a piece in Pidgin, but it is Tonouchi's creative and strategic usage of Pidgin that makes a statement about Pidgin as a language that can be put to work in writing. Much the same is true of SI's spoken testimony in front of the Hawaiian Homelands Commission; his usage of Pidgin, complete with the narrative departures, repetitions, and rhetorical questions, demonstrates Pidgin's potential in society as an expression of resistance. Even the willingness of the two interviewees in Chapter 4 to express their support for Pidgin through the medium of Hawaiian has connections to resistance as it shows that it is possible in a multilingual society such as

Hawai'i to engage in interviews and have discussions about serious content in a language other than English.

Chapter 5 did not feature voices in immigrant languages, but it presented the opinions of community members and other advocates of "Filipino" and "Micronesian" languages who were willing to be critical of the discrimination faced by speakers of these languages. These critical views came from parents who watched their children struggle in an educational system that label them as "English learners" and "limited English proficiency" and willingly expel them from school once they are too old, and they also came from people who themselves experienced discrimination in the public school system. Chapter 6 focused on translanguaging in order to demonstrate that languages can be mixed (and sometimes purposely not mixed) in ways that are transformative and empowering. Translanguaging allows speakers to control the flow of information and it also enables them to take charge of their own identity construction. The content in Chapter 7 was also related to resistance as it described a linguistics program that was redesigned to support Hawaiian and other minority languages despite an institutional structure that stresses English as the default language policy. The linguistics program, it should be emphasized, is not looking to replace English as a language of focus but rather working to demonstrate that an educational institution such as a university can actively promote the type of multilingualism that includes justice for endangered and minority languages. This, in fact, reflects the larger position of this book; despite the fears of those in power, a public multilingualism in Hawai'i does not mean sacrificing English proficiency. Instead, by allowing English speakers to be surrounded by and learn from multiple languages, a public multilingualism will enhance the linguistic and overall cognitive abilities of all Hawaiian residents. As long as some people in Hawai'i continue to show resistance by speaking and promoting a variety of languages, hope remains for enlightened linguistic perspectives that can improve the lives of speakers of Hawaiian, Pidgin, and immigrant languages.

8.4 Final Comments

On occasion, Hawaiian society has been regarded as a multicultural, multiracial, and/or multilingual paradise. Dekneef (2016), for example, notes that Martin Luther King visited several times and spoke of Hawai'i as "a place where we see the glowing daybreak of freedom and dignity and racial justice." This book, however, has adopted the viewpoint that, at least from a linguistic perspective, Hawai'i has much to work on before it can be considered "just." Still, though, despite the critical tone of many of the points made within, there are plenty of reasons to hold onto optimism for the future. Hawai'i already has one alternative educational pathway (Hawaiian medium), it has a growing number of Pidgin advocates, and it is seeing the emergence of a critical consciousness toward immigrant languages such as those in the "Filipino" and "Micronesian" categories. With continued resistance by speakers of Hawaiian, Pidgin, immigrant languages, and those who translanguage, together with further efforts to raise critical awareness about the cognitive benefits of speaking multiple languages and about the positive results of bilingual approaches to education, Hawai'i, perhaps more than any other place in the United States due to its multilingual history and present has the potential to make great advances toward linguistic justice. This book has attempted to offer insight into how the usage of language in Hawai'i, on the one hand, can serve as a resource for social justice and, on the other hand, how it sometimes works as a hindrance. The basic hope is that this insight will be of use in the future as we continue to fight for and make progress toward linguistic justice for people in Hawai'i and throughout the world.

References

Culturally Relevant Early Education Programs. (1987). *Hearing before the Select Committee on Indian Affairs, United States Senate One Hundredth Congress*. U.S. Government Printing Office.

Dekneef, M. (2016, January 18). Why Martin Luther King Jr. wore a Hawaiian lei on Selma march. *Hawaiian Magazine*. http://www.hawaiimagazine.com/content/why-martin-luther-king-jr-wore-hawaiian-lei-selma-march

Higgins, C. (2015). Earning capital in Hawai'i's linguistic landscape. In R. Tupas (Ed.), *Unequal Englishes across multilingual spaces* (pp. 145–162). Palgrave Macmillan.

Kala'i, K., Nimmer, N., Noh, E., Raatior, V., & Watanabe, J. (2015). *Feasibility study for a micronesian culture based school and other educational programs*. University of Hawa'i at Mānoa College of Education. http://www.weareoceania.org/wp-content/uploads/2016/01/Final-Report-Feasibility-Study-for-a-Micronesian-Culture-Based-Charter-School.pdf

Kloss, H. (1977). *The American bilingual tradition*. Newbury House.

Kymlicka, W. (1995). *Multicultural citizenship: A liberal theory of minority rights*. Clarendon Press.

Kymlicka, W. (2001). *Politics in the vernacular: Nationalism, multiculturalism, and citizenship*. Oxford University Press.

Kymlicka, W. (2007). *Multicultural Odysseys: Navigating the new international politics of diversity*. Oxford University Press.

May, S. (2011). Language rights: The "Cinderella" human right. *Journal of Human Rights, 10*, 265–289.

May, S. (2014). Contesting public monolingualism and diglossia: Rethinking political theory and language policy for a multilingual world. *Language Policy, 13*, 371–393.

Saft, S. (2019). *Exploring multilingual Hawai'i: Language use and language ideologies in a diverse society*. Lexington Books.

Skutnabb-Kangas, T. (2018). Language rights and revitalization. In L. Hinton, L. Huss, & G. Roche (Eds.), *The Routledge handbook of language revitalization* (pp. 13–21). Routledge.

References

Agbo, S. A. (2001). Enhancing success in American Indian students: Participatory research at Akwesasne as part of the development of a culturally relevant curriculum. *Journal of American Indian Education, 40*(1), 31–56.

Altemus-Williams, I., & Hobro, M. E. (2021). Hawai'i is not the multicultural paradise some say it is. *National Geographic.* Retrieved from https://www.nationalgeographic.com/culture/article/hawaii-not-multicultural-paradise-some-say-it-is

Amery, R. (2014). Reclaiming the Kaurna language: A long and lasting collaboration in an urban setting. *Language Documentation & Conversation, 8*, 409–429.

Andrews, P. (2018). *Comfortably White or uncomfortably Black: The racialization of Black students in undergraduate classrooms* (Unpublished Paper). North Carolina State University.

Antoniou, M., & Wright, S. (2017). Uncovering the mechanisms responsible for why language learning may promote healthy cognitive aging. *Frontiers in Psychology, 8.* Retrieved from https://www.ncbi.nlm.nih.gov/pmc/articles/PMC5736569/

Aris v. Hawai'i. (2013). Document retrieved from https://casetext.com/case/aris-v-hawaii

Asato, N. (2006). *Teaching Mikadoism: The attack on Japanese language schools in Hawaii, California, and Washington.* University of Hawai'i Press.

Asensio, R. (2010). Language policy in the Kingdom of Hawai'i: A worldly English approach. *Second Language Studies, 28*(2), 1–48.

Aspinwall, D. B. (1960). Languages in Hawaii. *PMLA, 75*(4), 7–13.

Au, K. H. (1980). Participation structures in a reading lesson with Hawaiian children: Analysis of a culturally appropriate instructional event. *Anthropology & Education Quarterly, 11*, 91–115.

S. Saft, *Language and Social Justice in Context*, https://doi.org/10.1007/978-3-030-91251-2

Avineri, N., Graham, L. R., Johnson, E. J., Conley Riner, R., & Rosa, J. (Eds.). (2019a). *Language and social justice in practice.* Routledge.

Avineri, N., Graham, L. R., Johnson, E. J., Conley Riner, R., & Rosa, J. (2019b). Introduction: Reimagining language and social justice. In N. Avineri, L. R. Graham, E. J. Johnson, R. Conley Riner, & J. Rosa (Eds.), *Language and social justice in practice* (pp. 1–16). Routledge.

Bahktin, M. (1981). *The dialogic imagination.* University of Texas Press.

Bahktin, M. (1986). *Speech genres and other late essays.* University of Texas Press.

Bailey, B. (2012). Heteroglossia. In A. Martin-Jones, A. Blackledge, & A. Creese (Eds.), *The Routledge handbook of multilingualism* (pp. 499–507). Routledge.

Bak, T. H., Nissan, J. J., Allerhand, M. M., & Deary, I. J. (2014). Does bilingualism influence cognitive aging? *Annals of Neurology, 75*, 959–963.

Baker, C. (2001). *Foundations of bilingual education and bilingualism.* Multilingual Matters.

Baker, C., & Jones, S. P. (1998). *Encyclopedia of bilingualism and bilingual education.* Multilingual Matters.

Balaz, J. (2019). *Pidgin eye.* Ala Press.

Baldwin, D., Baldwin, K., Baldwin, J., & Baldwin, J. (2013). Kyaamiaataweenki Oowaaha: Miami spoken here. In L. Hinton (Ed.), *Bringing our languages home: Language revitalization for families* (pp. 3–18). Heyday Books.

Ball, J., & Moselle, K. (2013). *Contributions of culture and language in Aboriginal head start in urban and northern communities to children's health outcomes: A review of theory and research.* Prepared for Division of Children, Seniors & Healthy Development, Health Promotion and Chronic Disease Prevention Branch.

Barakos, E. (2020). Linguistic and social justice: Toward a debate of intersections and disjuncture. *Journal of Sociolinguistics, 24*, 265–277.

Bastos, C. (2018). Portuguese in the cane: The racialization of labour in Hawaiian plantations. In S. Aboim, P. Granjo, & A. Ramos (Eds.), *Changing societies: Legacies and challenges* (pp. 65–96). Imprensa de Ciências Sociais.

Baugh, J. (2018). *Linguistics in pursuit of justice.* Cambridge University Press.

Beamer, K. (2014). *No Mākou Ka Mana: Liberating the nation.* Kamehameha Schools Press.

Beechart, E. (1985). *Working in Hawai'i: A labor history.* University of Hawai'i Press.

Benham, M. K. P. (1998). The voice "less" Hawaiian: An analysis of educational policymaking, 1820–1960. *The Hawaiian Journal of History, 32*, 121–140.

Benton, R. (1981). *The flight of the Amokura: Oceanic languages and formal education in the South Pacific. New Zealand Council for Educational Research.*

Bialystok, E., Craik, F. I. M., & Freedman, M. (2007). Bilingualism as a protection against the onset of symptoms of dementia. *Neuropsychologia, 45*, 459–464.

Bickerton, D. (1998). Language and language contact. In M. Haas (Ed.), *Multicultural Hawai'i: The fabric of a multiethnic society* (pp. 53–64). Garland Publishing.

Bickerton, D., & Wilson, W. H. (1987). Pidgin Hawaiian. In G. Gilbert (Ed.), *Pidgin and Creole languages: Essays in memory of John E. Reinecke* (pp. 61–76). University of Hawai'i Press.

Biddle, N., & Swee, H. (2012). The relationship between wellbeing and indigenous land, language and culture in Australia. *Australian Geography, 43*, 215–232.

Billig, M. (2008). The language of critical discourse analysis: The case of nominalization. *Discourse & Society, 19*(6), 783–800.

Blair, C. (2011). *No Aloha for micronesians in Hawaii.* Honolulu Civil Beat. Retrieved from https://www.civilbeat.org/2011/06/no-aloha-for-micronesians-in-hawaii/

Blair, C. (2015). *An untold story of American immigration.* Honolulu Civil Beat. Retrieved from http://www.civilbeat.org/2015/10/an-untold-story-of-american-immigration/

Boas, F. (1911). *The mind of primitive man.* The Macmillan Company.

Bougie, E., Wright, S. C., & Taylor, D. M. (2003). Early heritage-language education and the abrupt shift to a dominant-language classroom: Impact on the personal and collective esteem of inuit children in Arctic Québec. *International Journal of Bilingual Education and Bilingualism, 6*(5), 349–373.

Bowern, C., & Warner, N. (2015). 'Lone wolves' and collaboration: A reply to Crippen & Robinson (2013). *Language Documentation & Conservation, 9,* 59–85.

Boyden, J. (2016). The true tragedy of Attawapiskat. *Maclean's.* Retrieved from https://www.macleans.ca/news/canada/attawapiskat-and-the-fallout-of-intergenerational-trauma/

Brenzinger, M., & Heinrich, P. (2013). The return of Hawaiian: Language networks of the revival movement. *Current Issues in Language Planning, 14*(2), 300–316.

Bucholtz, M., Castillas, D. I., & Lee, J. S. (2015). Team collaboration and educational partnership in sociocultural linguistics. *American Speech, 90*(2), 230–245.

Bucholtz, M., Castillas, D. I., & Lee, J. S. (2016). Beyond empowerment: Accompaniment and sociolinguistic justice in a youth research program. In R. Lawson & D. Sayers (Eds.), *Sociolinguistic research: Application and impact* (pp. 25–44). Routledge.

Bucholtz, M., Castillas, D. I., & Lee, J. S. (2017). Language and culture as sustenance. In D. Paris & H. S. Alim (Eds.), *Culturally sustaining pedagogies: Teaching and learning for justice in a changing world* (pp. 43–59). Teachers College Press.

Bucholtz, M., Castillas, D. I., & Lee, J. S. (2018). *Feeling it: Language, race, and affect in Latinx youth learning.* Routledge.

Bucholtz, M., Lopez, A., Mojarro, A., Skapoulli, E., Van der Stouwe, C., & Werner-Garcia, S. (2014). Sociolinguistic justice in schools: Student researchers as linguistic experts. *Language and Linguistics Compass, 8*(4), 144–157.

Cabral, J. (2016). *He kālailaina i nā kāhulu pepeke poke ki'a a waila ho'i o ka 'Ōlelo Hawai'i a me ka ili 'ana o ia mau kāhulu pepeke i loko o ka Mo'olelo 'o Kalapana* (Unpublished Ph.D. Dissertation). University of Hawai'i at Hilo.

Cabral, J. (2018). *E ola ka 'Ōlelo Pa'i'ai. Keynote speech at the Hawaii-Pidgin Summit. University of Hawai'i at Mānoa.* Retrieved from https://www.hawaii.edu/satocenter/?p=1713

Carcelen-Estrada, A. (2018). Translation and activism. In J. Evans & F. Fernandez (Eds.), *The Routledge handbook of translation and politics* (pp. 254–269). Routledge.

Casumbal-Salazar, I. (2017). A fictive kinship: Making "modernity", "ancient Hawaiians", and the telescopes on Mauna Kea. *Native American and Indigenous Studies, 4*(2), 1–30.

Cervantes-Soon, C. G., Dorner, L., & Palmer, D. (2017). Combating inequalities in two-way language immersion programs: Toward critical consciousness in bilingual education spaces. *Review of Research in Education, 41*(1), 403–427.

Chandler, M., & Lalonde, C. (1998). Cultural continuity as a Hedge against suicide in Canada's first nations. *Transcultural Psychiatry, 35*(2), 191–219.
Chapin, H. G. (1984). Newspapers of Hawai'i 1834 to 1903: From "He Liona" to the Pacific cable. *The Hawaiian Journal of History, 18*, 47–86.
Charlot, J. (2005). *Classical Hawaiian education: Generations of culture*. The Pacific Institute.
Chock, E. (Ed.). (1978). *Talk story: An anthology of Hawaii's local writers*. Petronium.
Chock, E. (1990). *Last days here*. Bamboo Ridge.
Chrisjohn, R., Young, S., & Maraun, M. (2006). *The circle game: Shadows and substance in the Indian residential school experience in Canada*. Theytus Books.
Clare, L., Whitaker, C. J., Mrtyr, A., Martin-Forbes, P. A., Bastable, A. J. M., Pye, K. L., Quinn, C., Thomas, E. M., Mueller Gathercole, V. C., & Hindle, J. V. (2016). Executive control in older welsh monolinguals and bilinguals. *Journal of Cognitive Psychology, 28*(4), 412–426.
Clyne, M. (2005). *Australia's language potential*. University of New South Wales Press.
Clyne, M. (2008). The monolingual mindset as an impediment to the development of plurlingual potential in Australia. *Sociolinguistic Studies, 2*(3), 347–366.
Collier, V. P., & Thomas, W. P. (2009). *Educating English learners for a transformed world*. Dual Language Education of New Mexico-Fuente Press.
Cooren, F. (2012). Communication theory at the center: Ventriloquism and the communicative constitution of reality. *Journal of Communication, 62*(1), 1–20.
Costa, D. (1994). *The Miami-Illinois language* (Unpublished Ph.D. Dissertation). University of California.
Coup, D. P. (2008). Pidgin and education: A position paper. *Educational Perspectives, 40*, 30–39.
Cowell, A. (2012). The Hawaiian model of language revitalization: Problems of extension to mainland native America. *International Journal of the Sociology of Language, 218*, 167–193.
Craik, F. I. M., Bialystok, E., & Freedman, M. (2010). Delaying the onset of Alzheimer disease. *Neurology, 75*, 1726–1729.
Crippen, J., & Robinson, L. (2013). In defense of the lone wolf: Collaboration in language documentation. *Language Documentation & Conservation, 7*, 123–135.
Cummins, J. (1978). Bilingualism and the development of metalinguistic awareness. *Journal of Cross Cultural Psychology, 9*, 131–149.
Cummins, J. (1981). The role of primary language development in promoting educational success for language minority students. In California State Department of Education (Ed.), *Schooling and language minority students: A theoretical framework* (pp. 3–49). California State University, Evaluation, Dissemination and Assessment Center.
Cummins, J. (1984). *Bilingualism and special education*. College Hill Press.
Cummins, J. (2007). Rethinking monolingual instructional strategies in multilingual classrooms. *Canadian Journal of Applied Linguistics, 10*(2), 221–240.
Cummins, J. (2009). Fundamental psycholinguistic and sociological principles underlying educational success for linguistic minority students. In T. Skutnabb-Kangas, R. Phillipson, A. K. Mohanty, & M. Panda (Eds.), *Social justice through multilingual education* (pp. 19–35). Multilingual Matters.

Cushman, E. (2011). "We're taking the genius of Sequoyah into this century": The Cherokee syllabary, peoplehood, and perseverance. *Wicazo Sa Review, 26*(1), 67–83.

Davis, J. (2017). Resisting rhetoric of language endangerment: Reclamation through indigenous language survivance. *Language Documentation and Description, 14*, 37–58.

de Jong, E., & Bearse, C. I. (2012). Dual language programs as a strand within a secondary school: Dilemmas of school organization and the TWI mission. *International Journal of Bilingual Education and Bilingualism, 17*(1), 15–31.

Dekneef, M. (2016, January 18). Why Martin Luther King Jr. wore a Hawaiian lei on Selma march. *Hawaiian Magazine*. Retrieved from http://www.hawaiimagazine.com/content/why-martin-luther-king-jr-wore-hawaiian-lei-selma-march

Demmert, W. G. (2001). *Improving academic performance among native American students: A review of the research literature* (ERIC Number: ED463917). Retrieved from https://eric.ed.gov/?id=ED463917

Diez, B. (2019). 'English only': The movement to limit Spanish speaking in US. *BBC*. Retrieved from https://www.bbc.com/news/world-us-canada-50550742

Dobrin, L. M., & Berson, J. (2011). Speakers and language documentation. In P. K. Austin & J. Sallabank (Eds.), *The Cambridge handbook of endangered languages* (pp. 187–211). Cambridge University Press.

Dolson, D. (1985). Bilingualism and scholastic performance: The literature revisited. *NABE Journal, 10*(1), 1–35 (ERIC Document Reproduction Service No. EJ 367 966 and ED 291 257).

Drager, K. (2012). Pidgin and Hawai'i English: An overview. *IJLTIC, 1*(1), 61–73.

Dunstan, S. B. (2013). *The influence of speaking a dialect of appalachian English on the college experience (Unpublished Ph.D. Dissertation). North Carolina State University.*

Dunstan, S. B., Eads, A., Jaeger, A. J., & Wolfram, W. (2018). The importance of graduate student engagement in a campus language diversity initiative. *Journal of English Linguistics, 46*(3), 215–228.

Dunstan, S. B., Wolfram, W., Jaeger, A. J., & Crandall, R. E. (2015). Educating the educated: Language diversity in the university backyard. *American Speech, 90*, 266–280.

Duranti, A. (1994). *From grammar to politics: Linguistic anthropology in a Western samoan village*. University of Berkeley Press.

Eades, D., Jacobs, S., Hargrove, E., & Menacker, T. (2006). Pidgin, local identity, and schooling in Hawaii. In S. J. Nero (Ed.), *Dialects, Englishes, Creoles and education* (pp. 139–163). Lawrence Erlbaum Associates.

Edmonds, C. A. (2008). *The reliability and validity of the Māori language proficiency in writing test: Kaiaka Reo year eight* (Unpublished Ph.D. Dissertation). University of Hawai'i at Hilo.

Elbert, S. (1951). Hawaiian literary style and culture. *American Anthropologist, 53*(3), 345–354.

Ellis, J. (2020). Da decolonizing real: Liberating humour in Joe Balaz's Pidgin eye. *The Journal of Commonwealth Literature, 1*, 1–14.

Fairclough, N. (1995). *Critical discourse analysis: The critical study of language*. Routledge.

Fishman, J. (1967). Bilingualism with and without Diglossia. *Journal of Social Issues, 23*(2), 29–38.

Fishman, J. (1991). *Reversing language shift*. Multilingual Matters.
Fleming, J., & Ledogar, R. J. (2008). Resilience, an evolving concept: A review of the literature relevant to aboriginal research. *Pimatisiwin: A Journal of Aboriginal and Indigenous Community Health, 6*, 7–23.
Flores, N., & Garcia, O. (2017). A critical review of bilingual education in the United States: From basements and pride to boutiques and profit. *Annual Review of Applied Linguistics, 37*, 14–29.
Fortune, T. W., & Tedick, D. J. (2008). *Pathways to multilingualism: Evolving perspectives on immersion education*. Multilingual Matters.
Friedman, A. (2015). America's lacking language skills. *The Atlantic*. Retrieved from https://www.theatlantic.com/education/archive/2015/05/filling-americas-language-education-potholes/392876/
Fuchs, L. (1961). *Hawaii Pono*. Harcourt, Brace, and World.
Fujikane, C. (2008). Introduction: Asian settler colonialism in the U.S. colony of Hawai'i. In C. Fujikane & J. Okamura (Eds.), *Asian settler colonialism: From local governance to the habits of everyday life in Hawai'i* (pp. 1–42). University of Hawai'i Press.
Fuller-Thomson, E. (2015). Emerging evidence contradicts the hypothesis that bilingualism delays dementia onset. A commentary on "age of dementia diagnosis in community dwelling bilingual and monolingual Hispanic Americans" by Lawton et al. *Cortex, 66*, 170–172.
Furukawa, G. (2018). Stylization and language ideologies in Pidgin comedic skits. *Discourse, Context and Media, 23*, 41–52.
Furukawa, T. (2007). No flips in the pool: Discursive practice in Hawai'i Creole. *Pragmatics, 17*(3), 371–386.
Galla, C. K., & Wilson, W. H. (2019). Early and emergent literacy practices as a foundation for Hawaiian language medium education. In A. Sherris & J. K. Peyton (Eds.), *Teaching writing to children in indigenous languages* (pp. 25–43). Routledge.
Garcia, O., Aponte, G. Y., & Le, K. (2020). Primary bilingual classrooms: Translations and translanguaging. In S. Laviosa & M. Gonzalez-Davies (Eds.), *The Routledge handbook of translation and education* (pp. 81–94). Routledge.
Garcia, O., & Leiva, C. (2014). Theorizing and enacting translanguaging for social justice. In A. Blackledge & A. Creese (Eds.), *Heteroglossia as practice and pedagogy* (pp. 199–216).
Garcia, O., & Otheguy, R. (2019). Plurilingualism and translanguaging: Commonalities and divergences. *International Journal of Bilingual Education and Bilingualism*. Retrieved from https://doi.org/10.1080/13670050.2019.1598932
Genesee, F., Geva, E., Dressler, C., & Kamil, M. (2006). Synthesis: Cross-linguistic relationships. In D. August & D. Shanahan (Eds.), *Developing literacy in second-language learners* (pp. 153–174). Center for Applied Linguistics.
Genesee, F., & Lindholm-Leary, K. (2013). Two case studies of content-based language education. *Journal of Immersion and Content-Based Language Education, 1*(1), 3–33.
Gerdts, D. (2017). Indigenous linguists: Bringing research into language revitalization. *IJAL, 83*(4), 607–617.

Gifford, S. (2020). Navajo nation coronavirus rates higher than 48 states: Records. *New York Daily News*. Retrieved from https://www.nydailynews.com/coronavirus/ny-coronavirus-navajo-nation-20200414-yy53wpkbcjb55psckvbosgbma4-story.html

Goldmacher, S. (2016). Trump's English-only campaign. *Politico*. Retrieved from https://www.politico.com/story/2016/09/donald-trumps-english-only-campaign-228559

Gonschor, L. (2020). *A power in the world: The Hawaiian Kingdom in Oceania*. University of Hawai'i Press.

Goodenough, F. (1926). Racial differences in the intelligence of school children. *Journal of Experimental Psychology, 9*, 388–397.

Goodhue, K. P. (1998). We are who we were: From resistance to affirmation. *'Ōiwi: A native Hawaiian Journal, 1*, 36–39.

Goodwin, C. (2000). Action and embodiment within situated human interaction. *Journal of Pragmatics, 32*(10), 1489–1522.

Goodyear-Ka'ōpua, N. (2017). Protectors of the future, not protestors of the past: Indigenous Pacific activism and Mauna a Wākea. *The South Atlantic Quarterly, 116*(1), 184–194.

Goodyear-Ka'ōpua, N., Hussey, I., & Wright, E. K. (Eds.). (2014). *A nation rising: Hawaiian movements for life, land, and sovereignty*. Duke University Press.

Graduation Requirements. *Hawaii State Department of Education Website*. https://www.hawaiipublicschools.org/TeachingAndLearning/StudentLearning/GraduationRequirements/Pages/Requirements.aspx

Green, J. (2020). *The oral literacy approach* (Unpublished Ph.D. Dissertation). University of Hawai'i at Hilo.

Greene, J. (1998). *A meta-analysis of the effectiveness of bilingual education*. University of Texas-Austin.

Grenoble, L. (2009). Linguistic cages and the limits of linguists. In J. Reyhner & L. Lockard (Eds.), *Indigenous language revitalization: Encouragement, guidance & lessons learned* (pp. 61–69). Northern Arizona University.

Grenoble, L. (2021). Why revitalize? In J. Olko & J. Sallabank (Eds.), *Revitalizing endangered languages: A practical guide* (pp. 9–22). Cambridge University Press.

Grenoble, L., & Whaley, L. (2006). *Saving languages: An introduction to language revitalization*. Cambridge University Press.

Greymorning, S. (1997). Going beyond words: The Arapaho immersion program. In J. Reyhner (Ed.), *Teaching indigenous languages* (pp. 22–30). Northern Arizona University.

Grinevald, C. (2006). Worrying about ethics and wondering about "Informed consent": Fieldwork from an americanist perspective. In A. Saxena & L. Borin (Eds.), *Lesser-known languages of South Asia: Status and policies, case studies and Applications of information technology* (pp. 339–370). Mouton de Gruyter.

Grosjean, F. (2010). *"Bilingual" life and reality*. Harvard University Press.

Guerin, V., & Lacrampe, S. (2010). Trust me, I am a linguist: Building partnership in the field. *Language Documentation & Conversation, 4*, 22–33.

Gumperz, J. (1982). *Discourse strategies*. Cambridge University Press.

Guschov, S. (2018). *Puerto Rico: An update on new statehood bill and official English status*. The nation's leading English language advocates. Retrieved from https://proenglish.org/2018/10/30/puerto-rico-an-update-on-new-statehood-bill-and-official-english-status/

Hagiwara, M. K. I., Miyamura, J., Yamada, S., & Sentell, T. (2016). Younger and sicker: Comparing micronesians to other ethnicities in Hawaii. *American Journal of Public Health, 106*(3), 485–491.

Hajet, J., & Slaughter, Y., (Eds.). (2015). *Challenging the monolingual mindset*. Multilingual Matters.

Hakuta, K. (1987). Degree of bilingualism and cognitive ability in mainland Puerto Rican children. *Child Development, 58*(5), 1372–1388.

Hakuta, K. (1989). *Bilingualism and intelligence testing: An annotated bibliography*. Bilingual Research Group.

Halagao, P. E. (2016). Exposing K-12 Filipino achievement gaps and opportunities in Hawai'i public schools. *Educational Perspectives, 48*(1 & 2), 6–19.

Halet, D., Chandler, M. J., & Lalonde, C. E. (2007). Aboriginal language knowledge and youth suicide. *Cognitive Development, 22*, 392–399.

Han, C. H. (2002). Interpreting interrogatives as rhetorical questions. *Lingua, 112*(3), 201–229.

Hanks, W. (1996). *Language and communicative practices*. Westview Press.

Hanneman, M. (2015). Harvard Lauds Samoan language center. *Midweek*. Retrieved from https://www.midweek.com/harvard-lauds-samoan-language-center/

Harman, K. L. (2020). *I Lālā Mau Nā Hula Ilalaole He Kālailaina i Nā Kuhi Lima o Nā Hula A Joseph Kealiikuikamoku Ilalaole-O-Kamehameha* (Unpublished Ph.D. Dissertation). University of Hawai'i at Hilo.

Hateruma, E., Kojima, Y., & Teruya, O. (Eds.). (2021). *Ryuukyuu Shogo to Bunka no Mirai*. Iwanami Shoten.

Hawaiian Language Immersion Program. *Hawaii State Department of Education*. https://www.hawaiipublicschools.org/TeachingAndLearning/StudentLearning/HawaiianEducation/Pages/translation.aspx

Hawai'i Leads Country. (2016). Hawai'i leads country in non-English speakers. *Star Advertiser*. Retrieved from https://www.staradvertiser.com/2016/05/23/breaking-news/hawaii-leads-country-in-non-english-speakers/

Heath, S. B. (1983). *Ways with words: Language, life, and work in communities and classrooms*. Cambridge University Press.

Heine, H. C. (2002). Culturally responsive schools for micronesian students. *Pacific resources for education and learning: Prel briefing paper*, 1–17.

Higashionna, R., Ikehara, G., & Matsukawa, L. (2011). The Okinawans. In J. McDermott & N. N. Andrade (Eds.), *People and cultures of Hawai'i: The evolution of culture and ethnicity* (pp. 131–151). University of Hawai'i Press.

Higgins, C. (2010). Raising critical language awareness in Hawai'i at Da Pidgin coup. In B. Migge, I. Leglise, & A. Bartens (Eds.), *Creoles in education: An appraisal of current programs and projects* (pp. 31–54). John Benjamins.

Higgins, C. (2015). Earning capital in Hawai'i's linguistic landscape. In R. Tupas (Ed.), *Unequal Englishes across multilingual spaces* (pp. 145–162). Palgrave Macmillan.

Higgins, C. (2019). The dynamics of Hawaiian speakerhood in the family. *International Journal of the Sociology of Language, 255*, 45–72.

Higgins, C. (2021a). Promoting Pidgin at the University of Hawai'i at Mānoa. In G. Clements & M. J. Petray (Eds.), *Linguistic discrimination in U.S. higher education: Power, prejudice, impacts, and remedies* (pp. 174–188). Routledge.

Higgins, C. (2021b). Engaging the public in sociolinguistics for social justice: Advocating for Pidgin speakers in Hawai'i. In D. S. Warriner & E. R. Miller (Eds.), *Extending applied linguistics for social impact* (pp. 13–34). Bloomsbury Academic.

Higgins, C., Nettell, R., Furukawa, G., & Sakoda, K. (2012). Beyond contrastive analysis and codeswitching: Student documentary filmmaking as a challenge to linguicism in Hawai'i. *Linguistics and Education, 23*, 49–61.

Him, M. L. (2000). Transmitting the Chinese heritage: Chinese schools in the United States mainland and Hawaii. In T. Ang See (Ed.), *Intercultural relations, cultural transformation, and idenity: The ethnic Chinese* (pp. 124–158). Kaisa Para Sa Kaunlaran, Inc.

Him, M. L. (2010). The Chinese community press in Hawai'i, Chinese America: History & perspectives. *The Journal of the Chinese Historical Society of America*, 95–103.

Hinton, L. (2013). *Bringing our languages home: Language revitalization for families*. Heyday.

Hinton, L., Florey, M., Gessner, S., & Manatowa-Bailey, J. (2018). The master apprentice language learning program. In L. Hinton, L. Huss, & G. Roche (Eds.), *The Routledge handbook of language revitalization*. Routledge.

Hinton, L., Huss, L., & Roche, G., (Eds.). (2018). *The Routledge handbook of language revitalization*. Routledge.

Hiramoto, M. (2011). Is dat dog you're eating? Mock Filipino, Hawai'i Creole, and local elitism. *Pragmatics, 21*(3), 341–371.

Hisatake, K. (2018). Hawaiian hospitality and hostility: Camp in Rap Reiplinger's Pidgin comedy. *Amerasia Journal, 44*(3), 27–48.

Hofschneider, A. (2020). *Congress poised to restore medicaid for micronesians*. Honolulu Civil Beat. Retrieved from https://www.civilbeat.org/beat/congress-poised-to-restore-medicaid-for-micronesians/

Holm, A., & Holm, W. (1995). Navajo language education: Retrospect and prospects. *Bilingual Research Journal, 19*(1), 141–167.

Hovey, R., Delormier, T., & McComber, A. (2014). Social-relational understandings of health and well-being from an indigenous perspective. *International Journal of Indigenous Health, 10*(1), 35–54.

Hughes, J. (1993). The demise of the English standard school system in Hawai'i. *The Hawaiian Journal of History, 27*, 65–89.

Hymes, D. (1962). The ethnography of speaking. In T. Gladwin & W. C. Sturtevant (Eds.), *Anthropology and human behavior* (pp. 13–53). Anthropology Society of Washington.

Hymes, D. (1996). *Ethnography, linguistics, narrative inequality: Toward an understanding of voice*. Routledge.

Ing, T. L. (2019). *Reclaiming Kalākaua: Nineteenth-century perspectives on a Hawaiian sovereign*. University of Hawai'i Press.

Ivanov, V. (2001). Heteroglossia. In A. Duranti (Ed.), *Key terms in language and culture* (pp. 95–97). Blackwell.

Jacob, M. (2013). *Yakama rising: Indigenous cultural revitalization, activism, and healing.* University of Arizona Press.

Jespersen, O. (1922). *Language: It's nature, origin, and development.* Henry Holt & Company.

Jetnit-Kijiner, K. (2013). The micronesian question. *Kathy Jetnil-Kijiner.* Retrieved from https://www.kathyjetnilkijiner.com/the-micronesian-question/

Jorgensen, J. N. (2008). Polylingual languaging around and among children and adolescents. *International Journal of Multilingualism, 5,* 161–176.

Jorgensen, J. N., Karrebæk, M. S., Madsen, L. M., & Moller, J. S. (2011). Polylanguaging in superdiversity. *Diversities, 13,* 24–37.

Jung, M.-K. (2006). *Reworking race: The making of Hawaii's interracial labor movement.* Columbia University Press.

Kachru, B. B. (1977). Linguistic schizophrenia and language census: A note on the Indian situation. *Linguistics, 15*(186), 17–32.

Kala'i, K., Nimmer, N., Noh, E., Raatior, V., & Watanabe, J. (2015). *Feasibility study for a micronesian culture based school and other educational programs.* University of Hawa'i at Mānoa College of Education. Retrieved from http://www.weareoceania.org/wp-content/uploads/2016/01/Final-Report-Feasibility-Study-for-a-Micronesian-Culture-Based-Charter-School.pdf

Kam, R. T. (2006). Language and loyalty: Americanism and the regulation of foreign language. *The Hawaiian Journal of History, 40,* 131–147.

Kamanā, K. (2010). *Mo'oki'ina ho'oponopono: Ke ō o ka 'ike ku'una Hawai'i ma ke Kula 'o Nāwahīokalani'ōpu'u* (Unpublished Ph.D. Dissertation). University of Hawai'i at Hilo.

Kamanā, K., & Wilson, W. H. (2012). *Nā Kai 'Ewalu: Beginning Hawaiian lessons.* Hale Kuamo'o.

Kame'eleihiwa, L. (1992). *Native land and foreign desires: Pehea lā e Pono ai.* Bishop Museum Press.

Kanahele, G. (1982). *Hawaiian renaissance.* Project WAIAHA.

Kana'iaupuni, S. M., Malone, N., & Ishibashi, K. (2005). *Ka Huaka'i: 2005 Native Hawaiian educational assessment.* Kamehameha Schools Pauahi Publications.

Ka'opua, L. S., Braun, K. L., Browne, C., Mokuau, N., & Park, C. B. (2011). Why are native Hawaiians underrepresented in Hawai'i's older adult population? Exploring social and behavioral factors of longevity. *Journal of Aging Research.* Retrieved from https://www.hindawi.com/journals/jar/2011/701232/

Kaplan, R. B., & Baldauf, R. B. (1997). *Language planning: From practice to theory.* Multilingual Matters.

Kauhi, E. K. (2000). *He mo'olelo no Kapa'ahu: The story of Kapa'ahu.* Pili Productions.

Kavé, G., Eyal, N., Shorek, A., & Cohen-Mansfield, J. (2008). Multilingualism and cognitive state in the oldest old. *Psychology of Aging, 23,* 70–78.

Kawai'ae'a, K., Housman, A., & Alencastre, M. (2007). Pū'ā i ka 'ōlelo, ola ka 'ohana: Three generations of Hawaiian language revitalization. *Multidisciplinary Research on Hawaiian Well-Being, 4,* 183–237.

Kawakami, A. J. (2004). Issues central to the inclusion of Hawaiian culture in k-12 education. *Hūlili: Multidisciplinary Research on Hawaiian Well-Being, 1*(1), 111–130.

Kecskes, I., & Papp, T. (2000). *Foreign language and Mother Tongue.* Lawrence Erlbaum Associates Publishers.

Kihleng, E. (2019). The micronesian question. In E. Flores, E. Kihleng, & C. Santos Perez (Eds.), *Indigenous literatures from micronesia* (pp. 183–187). University of Hawai'i Press.

Kim, S., Jeon, S. G., Nam, Y., Kim, H. S., Yoo, D., & Moon, M. (2019). Bilingualism for dementia: Neurological mechanisms associated with functional and structural changes in the brain. *Frontiers in Neuroscience, 13*. Retrieved from https://www.ncbi.nlm.nih.gov/pmc/articles/PMC6868000/pdf/fnins-13-01224.pdf

Kimura, L. (1983). The Hawaiian language. In *Native Hawaiians study commission: Report on the culture, needs, and concerns of native Hawaiians* (pp. 173–224). Department of Interior.

Kimura, L. (2012). *He kālailaina i ka panina 'ōlelo a ka mānaleo Hawai'i: Ka ho'ohālikelike 'ana i ka 'ōlelo mānaleo a nā hanauna'elua, 'o ka 'ōlelo kūmau a ka makua a me ka 'ōlelo kūpaka a ke keiki* (Unpublished Ph.D. Dissertation). University of Hawai'i at Hilo.

Kimura, L., Kamanā, K., & Wilson, W. H. (2003, April 23). *Hawaiian: Back from the brink.* Honolulu Advertiser. Retrieved from http://the.honoluluadvertiser.com/article/2003/Apr/24/op/op04a.html

King, M., Smith, A., & Gracey, M. (2009). Indigenous health part 2: The underlying causes of the health gap. *The Lancet, 374*, 76–85.

Kipp, D. R. (2000). *Encouragement, guidance, insights, and lessons learned for native language activists developing their own tribal language program.* Grotto Foundation.

Kloss, H. (1977). *The American bilingual tradition*. Newbury House.

Krashen, S., & Biber, D. (1988). *On course: Bilingual education's success in California.* California Association for Bilingual Education.

Krauss, M. (1992). The world's languages in crisis. *Language, 68*, 4–10.

Kymlicka, W. (1995). *Multicultural citizenship: A liberal theory of minority rights.* Clarendon Press.

Kymlicka, W. (2001). *Politics in the vernacular: Nationalism, multiculturalism, and citizenship.* Oxford University Press.

Kymlicka, W. (2007). *Multicultural Odysseys: Navigating the new international politics of diversity.* Oxford University Press.

Labor Strikes. *Hawai'i Digital newspaper project.* Retrieved from https://sites.google.com/a/hawaii.edu/ndnp-hawaii/Home/subject-and-topic-guides/labor-strikes

Labov, W. (1966). *The social stratification of English in New York City.* Center for Applied Linguistics.

Labrador, R. (2004). "We can laugh at ourselves": Hawai'i ethnic humor, local identity and the myth of multiculturalism. *Pragmatics, 14*(2/3), 291–316.

Labrador, R. (2015). *Building Filipino Hawai'i.* University of Illinois Press.

Laddaran, K. C. (2015). Pidgin English now an official language of Hawaii. *CNN.* Retrieved from https://www.cnn.com/2015/11/12/living/pidgin-english-hawaii/index.html

Lasman, I. (1971). *A study of the attitudes of Filipino immigrants about Hawai'i* (Unpublished M.A. Thesis). University of Hawai'i.

Lee, S. (2018). *How Hawaii schools are building bridges to micronesian students.* Honolulu Civil Beat. Retrieved from https://www.civilbeat.org/2018/05/how-hawaii-schools-are-building-bridges-to-micronesian-students/

Lee, S. (2020). *Building a Hawaiian language curriculum classroom by classroom.* Honolulu Civil Beat. Retrieved from https://www.civilbeat.org/2020/02/building-a-hawaiian-language-curriculum-classroom-by-classroom/

Leonard, W. Y. (2017). Producing language reclamation by decolonising 'language'. In W. Y. Leonard & H. de Korne (Eds.), *Language documentation and description* (Vol. 14, pp. 15–36). EL Publishing.

Leonard, W. Y. (2018). Reflections on (de)colonialism in language documentation. In D. McDonnell, A. L. Berez-Kroeker, & G. Holton (Eds.), *Reflections on language documentation 20 yeas after Himmeleman 1998 (pp. 55–65). NFLRC.*

Lewis, P., & Simons, G. (2010). Assessing endangerment: Expanding Fishman's GIDS. *Revue Romaine De Linguistique, 55*(2), 103–120.

Li, W. (2011). Moment analysis and translanguaging space: Discursive construction of identities by multilingual Chinese youth in Britain. *Journal of Pragmatics, 43*, 1222–1235.

Liebenberg, L., Ikeda, J., & Wood, M. (2015). "It's just part of my culture": Understanding language and land in the resilience process of aboriginal youth. In L. C. Theron, L. Liebenberg, & M. Ungar (Eds.), *Youth resilience and culture.* Springer.

Lili'uokalani. (1990). *Hawai'i's Story: By Hawai'i's Queen.* Mutual Publishing.

Lindholm-Leary, K. (2001). *Dual language education.* Multilingual Matters.

Lindholm-Leary, K., & Borsato, G. (2006). Academic achievement. In F. Genesee, K. Lindholm-Leary, W. Saunders, & D. Christian (Eds.), *Educating English language learners* (pp. 157–179). Cambridge University Press.

Lindholm-Leary, K., & Genesee, F. (2010). Alternative educational programs for English learners. In *Improving education for English learners: Research-based approaches* (pp. 323–382). California Department of Education.

Lindholm-Leary, K., & Howard, E. (2008). Language and academic achievement in two-way immersion programs. In T. W. Fortune & D. J. Tedick (Eds.), *Pathways to bilingualism: Evolving perspectives on immersion education.* Multilingual Matters.

Lippi-Green, R. (1994). Accent, standard language ideology, and discriminatory pretext in the courts. *Language in Society, 23*(2), 163–198.

Liu, J. C., & Var, T. (1986). Resident attitudes toward tourism impacts in Hawaii. *Annals of Tourism Research, 13*, 193–214.

Lockwood, H., & Saft, S. (2016). Shifting language ideologies and the perceptions of Hawai'i Creole among educators at the university level in Hawai'i. *Linguistics and Education, 33*, 1–13.

Look, M. A., Trask-Batti, M. K., Agres, R., Mau, M. L., & Kaholokula, J. K. (2013). *Assessment and priorities for health & well-being in native Hawaiians & other Pacific peoples.* Center for Native Health.

Louis, W., & Taylor, D. M. (2001). When the survival of a language is at stake: The future of Inuttitut in Arctic Quebec. *Journal of Language and Social Psychology, 20*(1–2), 111–143.

Lucas, P. N. (2000). E Ola Mau Kākou i ka 'Ōlelo Makuahine: Hawaiian language policy and the courts. *The Hawaiian Journal of History, 34*, 1–28.

Lum, D. (1986). Local literature and lunch. In E. Chock & D. Lum (Eds.), *The best of bamboo ridge* (pp. 3–5). Bamboo Ridge Press.

Lum, D. (1990). *Pass on, no pass back*! Bamboo Ridge.

Mac Ionnrachtaigh, F. (2013). *Language, resistance and revival: Republican prisoners and the Irish language in the North of Ireland.* Pluto Press.

Makoni, S., & Pennycook, A. (2005). Disinventing and (re)constituting languages. *Critical Inquiry in Language Studies: An International Journal, 2*(3), 137–156.

Makoni, S., & Pennycook, A. (Eds.). (2006). *Disinventing and reconstituting languages.* Multilingual Matters.

Matsu, C., Takeshita, J., Izutsu, S., & Hishinuma, E. (2011). The Japanese. In J. McDermott & N. N. Andrade (Eds.), *People and cultures of Hawai'i: The evolution of culture and ethnicity* (pp. 107–130). University of Hawai'i Press.

Matsuda, M. (1991). Voices of America: Accent, anti-discrimination law, and a jurisprudence for the last reconstruction. *The Yale Law Journal, 100*(5), 1329–1407.

Matsuda, S. (2016). Drop-out or push-out? micronesian students in Honolulu. *Pass.* Retrieved from https://www.pass-usa.net/micronesian-students-honolulu

Mauer, M., & King, R. (2007). *Uneven justice: State rates of incarceration by race and ethnicity.* The sentencing project. Retrieved from https://www.sentencingproject.org/publications/uneven-justice-state-rates-of-incarceration-by-race-and-ethnicity/

May, S. (2011). Language rights: The "Cinderella" human right. *Journal of Human Rights, 10,* 265–289.

May, S. (2013). Indigenous immersion education: International developments. *Journal of Immersion and Content-Based Language Education, 1*(1), 34–69.

May, S. (2014). Contesting public monolingualism and diglossia: Rethinking political theory and language policy for a multilingual world. *Language Policy, 13,* 371–393.

McCarty, T. L. (2008). Schools as strategic tools for indigenous language revitalization: Lessons from native America. In N. Hornberger (Ed.), *Can schools save indigenous languages? Policy and practice on four continents* (pp. 161–179). Palgrave Macmillan.

McCarty, T. L. (2009). Empowering indigenous languages—What can be learned from native American experiences? In T. Skutnabb-Kangas, R. Phillipson, A. K. Mohanty, & M. Panda (Eds.), *Social justice through multilingual education* (pp. 125–139). Multilingual Matters.

McCarty, T. L. (2011a). *The role of native languages and cultures in American Indian, Alaska native, and native Hawaiian student achievement.* Brief prepared for the promising practices and partnerships in Indian education (P3IE) program evaluation group, under a contract from the U.S. Department of Education Office of Indian education programs to Kauffman & Associates Inc. of Spokane.

McCarty, T. L. (2011b). *Ethnography and language policy.* Routledge.

McCarty, T. L. (2018). Community-based language planning: Perspectives from indigenous language revitalization. In L. Hinton, L. Huss, & G. Roche (Eds.), *The Routledge handbook of language revitalization* (pp. 22–35). Routledge.

McGregor-Alegado, D. (1979). *Hawaiian resistance, 1887–1889* (Unpublished Thesis for Master of Arts in Pacific Island Studies). University of Hawai'i.

McGuire, P. D. (2010). Exploring resilience and indigenous ways of knowing. *Pimatisiwin: A Journal of Aboriginal and Indigenous Community Health, 8,* 117–131.

McIvor, O. (2013). *Protective effects of language learning, use and culture on the health and well-being of indigenous people in Canada.* Retrieved from https://www.semanticscholar.org/paper/Protective-Effects-of-Language-Learning%2C-Use-and-on-McIvor/66b23f335bc571f735ce62124a5883da93994089

Mignolo, W. (2000). *Local histories/global designs. Coloniality, subaltern knowledges, and border thinking.* Princeton University Press.

Mindness, H. (2006). Humor in Hawai'i: Past and present. *The Hawaiian Journal of History, 40,* 177–199.

Morcom, L. A. (2017). Self-esteem and cultural identity in Aboriginal language immersion Kindergarteners. *Journal of Language, Identity & Education, 16*(6), 365–380.

Morcom, L. A., & Roy, S. (2017a). Learning through language: Academic success in an indigenous language immersion kindergarten. *Journal of American Indian Education, 56* (2), 57–80.

Morcom, L. A., & Roy, S. (2017b). Is early immersion effective for aboriginal language acquisition? A case study from an Anishinaabemowin Kindergarten. *International Journal of Bilingual Education and Bilingualism, 22*(5), 551–563.

Morisako, A. K., & Tauali'I, M., Ambrose, A. J. H., & Withy, K. (2017). Beyond the ability to pay: The health status of native Hawaiians and other Pacific Islanders in relationship to health insurance. *Hawai'i Journal of Medicine & Public Health, 76*(3), 36–41.

Mossman, B. (2021). Keeping the faith. *Midweek.* Retrieved from https://www.midweek.com/dr-llewellyn-young/

Mufwene, S. (2004). Language birth and death. *Annual Review of Anthropology, 33,* 201–222.

Multilingualism. *Hawaii State Department of Education Website.* https://www.hawaiipublicschools.org/TeachingAndLearning/StudentLearning/Multilingualism/Pages/default.aspx

Myrick, C. (2019). *Language and gender ideologies in higher education: An examination of faculty discourses* (Unpublished Ph.D. Dissertation). North Carolina State University.

NACCHO (National Aboriginal Community Controlled Health Organisation). (2011). *Constitution for the National Aboriginal Community Controlled Health Organisation.* NACCHO.

Nakanaela, T. (1993). *The biography of Hon. Robert William Wilcox.* Retrieved from http://ulukau.org/chd/Texts/wilcox-intro.pdf

Nellis, A. (2016). *The color of justice: Racial and ethnic disparity in state prisons.* The Sentencing Project. Retrieved from https://www.sentencingproject.org/publications/color-of-justice-racial-and-ethnic-disparity-in-state-prisons/

NeSmith, K. (2005). Tutu's Hawaiian and the emergence of a Neo-Hawaiian language. *'Ōiwi, 3,* 68–76.

NeSmith, K. (2019). Take my word: Mahalo no i to'u matua tane. In R. Asensio (Ed.), *Old Kava in new gourds: Language revitalization and schooling in Hawaii* (pp. 93–112).

Nicholas, S. (2008). *Becoming "fully" Hopi: The role of the Hopi language in the contemporary lives of Hopi youth—A Hopi case study of language shift and vitality* (Unpublished dissertation). American Indian Studies.

Nicholas, S. (2018). Practicing living and being Hopi: Language and cultural practices of contemporary Hopi youth. In G. Wigglesworth, J. Simpson, & J. Vaughan (Eds.), *Language practices of indigenous children and youth* (pp. 303–336). Palgrave Macmillan.

Niyekawa-Howard, A. (1974). History of the Japanese language school. *Educational Perspectives, 13*, 6–14.

Nordstrom, G. (2010). Rhetoric and resistance in Hawai'i: How silenced voices speak out in a colonized context. In D. Baca & V. Villanueva (Eds.), *Rhetorics of the Americas: 114 BCE to 2012 CE* (pp. 117–141). Palgrave Macmillan.

Nordstrom, G. (2015). Pidgin as rhetorical sovereignty: Articulating indigenous and minority rhetorical practices with the language politics of place. *College English, 77*(4), 317–337.

O Murchadha, N. P., Hornsby, M., Smith-Christmas, C., & Moriarty, M. (2018). New speakers, familiar concepts. In C. Smith-Christmas, N. P. O. Murchadha, M. Hornsby, & M. Moriarty (Eds.), *New speakers of minority languages: Linguistic ideologies & practices* (pp. 1–22). Palgrave Macmillan.

Odo, C. (1975). *Phonological processes in the English dialect of Hawaii* (Ph.D. Dissertation). University of Hawai'i at Mānoa.

Odo, C. (1977). Phonological representations in Hawaiian English. *University of Hawaii Working Papers in Linguistics, 9*(3), 77–85.

Okamura, J. (2014). *From race to ethnicity: Interpreting Japanese American experiences in Hawai'i*. University of Hawai'i Press.

Okihiro, G. (1991). *Cane fires: The anti-Japanese movement in Hawaii, 1865–1945*. University of Temple Press.

Olko, J., & Sallabank, J. (2021). *Revitalizing endangered languages: A practical guide*. Cambridge University Press.

Ortega, N. (2016). *Testimony to BOE student achievement committee meeting*. Retrieved from https://boe.hawaii.gov/Meetings/Notices/Documents/2016-02-02%20SAC/2016-02-02%20SAC%20Testimony.pdf

Ortega, N. (2017). *Settler colonialism still defines power in Hawaii*. Honolulu Civil Beat. Retrieved from https://www.civilbeat.org/2017/11/settler-colonialism-still-defines-power-in-hawaii/

Osorio, J. (2006). On being Hawaiian. *Hūlili: Multidisciplinary research on Hawaiian well-being, 3*, 19–26.

Oster, R. T., Grier, A., Lightning, R., Mayan, M. J., & Toth, E. L. (2014). Cultural continuity, traditional Indigenous language, and diabetes in Alberta first nations: A mixed methods study. *International Journal for Equity in Health, 13*(1). Retrieved from https://equityhealthj.biomedcentral.com/articles/10.1186/s12939-014-0092-4

Otheguy, R., Garcia, O., & Reid, W. (2015). Clarifying translanguaging and deconstructing named languages: A perspective from linguistics. *Applied Linguistics Review, 6*, 281–307.

Otsuji, E., & Pennycook, A. (2010). Metrolingualism: Fixity, fluidity and language in flux. *International Journal of Multilingualism, 7*, 240–254.

Ovando, C. (2003). Bilingual education in the United States: Historical development and current issues. *Bilingual Research Journal, 27*(1), 1–24.

Panapasa, S. V., Mau, M. K., Williams, D. R., & McNally, J. W. (2010). Mortality patterns of Native Hawaiians across their lifespan: 1990–2000. *American Journal of Public Health, 100*(11), 2304–2310.

Patterson, W. (1988). *The Korean frontier in America: Immigration to Hawaii, 1896–1910.* University of Hawai'i Press.

Peal, E., & Lambert, W. (1962). The relationship of bilingualism to intelligence. *Psychological Monographs: General and Applied, 76*(27), 1–23.

Pennycook, A., & Otsuji, E. (2015). *Metrolingualism: Language in the city*. Routledge.

Perreira, H. K. (2011). *He Ha'i'ōlelo Ku'una: Nā Hi'ohi'ona me nā Ki'ina Ho'āla hou i ke Kākā'ōlelo* (Unpublished Ph.D. Dissertation). University of Hawai'i at Hilo.

Phillip, J., & Abbot, M. (2011). *A decade of foreign language standards: Impact, influence, and future directions. Report of Grant Project #P017A080037, Title VII, International Research Studies, U.S. Department of Education to the American Council on the Teaching of Foreign Languages.*

Piller, I. (2016). *Linguistic diversity and social justice: An introduction to applied sociolinguistics.* Oxford University Press.

Poai, A. K. (2019). *Clarabal Hawai'i Supreme court oral arguments: Clarabal v. Department of education (2018).* Retrieved from https://blog.hawaii.edu/kahuliao/ka-moae/spring-2018/clarabal/

Policing and Communities of Color in Hawai'i Webinar. (2020). Retrieved from https://www.youtube.com/watch?v=vc_1BxDdJDc

Portes, A., & Rumbaut, R. (2001). *Legacies: The story of the immigrant second generation.* University of California Press.

Preece, D. (2011). *Room service in paradise—Rap Reiplinger.* Retrieved from YouTube. https://www.youtube.com/watch?v=-nrE8zGG_P4

Pufahl, I., & Rhodes, N. (2011). Foreign language instruction in U.S. schools: Results of a national survey of elementary and secondary schools. *Foreign Language Annals, 44*(2), 255–288.

Ramirez, J. D. (1992). Executive summary. *Bilingual Research Journal, 16*(1–2), 1–62.

Ramos, T. (1996). Philippine languages in Hawai'i: Vehicles of cultural survival. *Social Processes in Hawai'i, 37*, 161–170.

Rampton, B. (2007). Neo-Hymesian linguistic ethnography in the UK. *Journal of Sociolinguistics, 11*(5), 584–607.

Rampton, B., Maybin, J., & Roberts, C. (2014). *Methodological foundations in linguistic ethnography* (Working papers in urban language & literacies).

Rampton, B., Tusting, K., Maybin, J., Barwell, R., Creese, A., & Lytra V. (2004). UK linguistic ethnography: A discussion paper. In *UK linguistic ethnography forum* (pp. 1–24).

Reagan, T. (2004). Objectification, positivism and language studies: A reconsideration. *Critical Inquiry in Language Studies: An International Journal, 1*(1), 41–60.

Reagan, T. (2019). *Linguistic legitimacy and social justice.* Palgrave.

Reagan, T., & Osborn, T. (2019). Time for a paradigm shift in U.S. foreign language education? Revising rationales, evidence, and outcomes. In D. Macedo (Ed.), *Decolonizing foreign language education* (pp. 73–110). Routledge.

Reeves, R. (2018). *How a tight-knit Pacific Island community is saving its culture.* Honolulu Civil Beat. Retrieved from https://www.civilbeat.org/2018/08/a-tight-knit-pacific-island-community-works-to-save-its-culture/

Reinecke, J. (1969). *Language and dialect in Hawai'i: A sociolinguistic history to 1935.* University of Hawai'i Press.

Reinecke, J. (1987). Appendix (Pidgin Hawaiian). In G. G. Gilbert (Ed.), *Pidgin and Creole languages: Essays in memory of John E. Reinecke* (p. 74). University of Hawaii Press.

Reyhner, J. (2010). Indigenous language immersion schools for strong indigenous identities. *Heritage Language Journal, 7*(2), 138–152.

Rice, K. (2010). The linguist's responsibilities to the community of speakers: Community-based research. In L. A. Grenoble & N. Louanna Furbee (Eds.), *Language documentation: Practice and values* (pp. 25–36). John Benjamins.

Rice, K. (2011). Ethics in fieldwork. In N. Thieberger (Ed.), *The Oxford handbook of linguistic fieldwork* (pp. 407–429). Oxford University Press.

Rickford, J. R., & King, S. (2016). Language and linguistics on trial: Hearing Rachel Jeantel (and other vernacular speakers) in the courtroom and beyond. *Language, 92*(4), 948–988.

Rickford, J. R., & Rickford, R. J. (2000). *Spoken soul: The story of Black English.* Wiley.

Roberts, S. (2004). The role of style and identity in the development of Hawaiian Creole. In G. Escure & A. Schwegler (Eds.), *Creoles, contact, and language change: Linguistic and social implications* (pp. 331–350). Benjamins.

Roche, G. (2017). Linguistic vitality, endangerment, and resilience. *Language Documentation & Conservation, 11*, 190–223.

Roche, G. (2019). Articulating language oppression: Colonialism, coloniality and the erasure of tibet's minority languages. *Patterns of Prejudice, 53*(5), 487–514.

Roche, G. (2020). Abandoning endangered languages: Ethical loneliness, language oppression, and social justice. *American Anthropologist, 122*(1), 164–169.

Rohrer, J. (2010). *Haoles in Hawai'i.* University of Hawai'i Press.

Rolstad, K., Mahoney, K., & Glass, G. V. (2005). The big picture: A meta-analysis of program effectiveness research on English language learners. *Educational Policy, 19*(4), 572–594.

Romaine, S. (1994). Hawai'i Creole English as a literary language. *Language in Society, 23*(4), 527–554.

Romaine, S. (1995). Birds of a different feather: Tok Pisin and Hawai'i Creole English as literary languages. *The Contemporary Pacific, 7*(1), 81–123.

Romaine, S. (1996). Pidgins and Creoles as literary languages: *Ausbau* and *Abstand.* In M. Hellinger & U. Ammon (Eds.), *Contrastive sociolinguistics* (pp. 271–289). Mouton de Gruyter.

Romaine, S. (1999). Changing attitudes to Hawai'i Creole English: Fo' find one good job, you gotta know how fo' talk like one haole. In J. Rickford & S. Romaine (Eds.), *Creole genesis, attitudes and discourse* (pp. 287–301). Benjamins.

Romaine, S. (2005). Orthographic practices in the standardization of Pidgins and Creoles: Pidgin in Hawai'i as anti-language and anti-standard. *Journal of Pidgin and Creole Languages, 20*(1), 101–140.

Saft, S. (2019). *Exploring multilingual Hawai'i: Language use and language ideologies in a diverse society.* Lexington Books.

Saft, S., Tebow, G., & Santos, R. (2018). Hawai'i Creole in the public domain: Humor, emphasis, and heteroglossic language practice in university commencement speeches. *Pragmatics, 28*(3), 417–438.

Sakoda, K., & Siegel, J. (2003). *Pidgin grammar: An introduction to the Creole language of Hawai'i.* Bess Press.

Salomone, R. (2010). *True American: Language, identity, and the education of immigrant children.* Harvard University Press.

Saranillio, D. I. (2013). Why Asian settler colonialism matters: A thought piece of critiques, debates, and indigenous difference. *Settler Colonial Studies, 3*(3–4), 280–294.

Saranillio, D. I. (2018). *Unsustainable empire: Alternative histories of Hawai'i statehood.* Duke University Press.

Sato, C. (1991). Sociolinguistic variation and language attitudes in Hawaii. In J. Cheshire (Ed.), *English around the world: Sociolinguistic perspectives* (pp. 647–663). Cambridge University Press.

Sato, C. (1993). Language change in a Creole continuum: Decreolization? In K. Hyltenstam & A. Viberg (Eds.), *Progression and regression in language: Sociocultural, neuropsychological and linguistic perspectives* (pp. 122–143). Cambridge University Press.

Schegloff, E. (1984). On some questions and ambiguities in conversation. In J. M. Atkinson & J. Heritage (Eds.), *Structures of social action: Studies in conversation analysis* (pp. 71–93). Cambridge University Press.

Schutz, A. J. (1994). *The voices of Eden: A history of Hawaiian language studies.* University of Hawai'i Press.

Schutz, A. J. (2020). *Hawaiian language: Past, present, future.* University of Hawai'i Press.

Seal of Biliteracy. *Hawaii State Department of Education Website.* https://www.hawaiipublicschools.org/TeachingAndLearning/StudentLearning/GraduationRequirements/Pages/Seal-of-Biliteracy.aspx

Shimada, N. (1998). Wartime dissolution and revival of the Japanese language schools in Hawai'i: Persistence of ethnic culture. *Journal of Asian American Studies, 1*(2), 121–151.

Siegel, J. (2008). Pidgin in the classroom. *Educational Perspectives, 41*(1–2), 55–65.

Silva, N. (1998). Kanaka Maoli resistance to annexation. *'Ōiwi: A Native Hawaiian Journal, 1*(1), 40–75.

Silva, N. (2004). *Aloha betrayed: Native Hawaiian resistance to American colonialism.* Duke University Press.

Silva, N. (2017). *The power of the steel-tipped pen: Reconstructing native Hawaiian intellectual history.* Duke University Press.

Sivak, L., Westhead, S., Richards, E,. Atkinson, S., Richards, J., Dare, H., Zuckerman, G., Gee, G., Wright, M., Rosen, A., Walsh, M., Brown, N., & Brown, A. (2019). "Language breathes life"—Barngarla community perspectives on the wellbeing impacts of reclaiming a Dorman Australian aboriginal language. *International Journal of Environmental Research and Public Health, 16.* Retrieved from https://www.ncbi.nlm.nih.gov/pmc/articles/PMC6843244/

Skorton, D., & Altschuler, G. (2012). America's foreign language deficit. *Forbes.* Retrieved from https://www.forbes.com/sites/collegeprose/2012/08/27/americas-foreign-language-deficit/?sh=21e3b5f44ddc

Skutnabb-Kangas, T. (2018). Language rights and revitalization. In L. Hinton, L. Huss, & G. Roche (Eds.), *The Routledge handbook of language revitalization* (pp. 13–21). Routledge.

Skutnabb-Kangas, T., & Dunbar, R. (2010). Indigenous children's education as linguistic genocide and a crime against humanity? A global view. *Galdu Cala: Journal of Indigenous Peoples Rights, 1.* Retrieved from https://www.afn.ca/uploads/files/education2/indigenouschildrenseducation.pdf

Sonoda, H. (2008). A nation incarcerated. In C. Fujikane & J. Okamura (Eds.), *Asian settler colonialism: From local governance to the habits of everyday life in Hawai'i* (pp. 99–115). University of Hawai'i Press.

Sorensen, M. J. (2008). Humor as a serious strategy of nonviolent resistance to oppression. *Peace & Change: A Journal of Peace Research, 33*(2), 167–190.

Stafford, S. (2010). Caught between "The rock" and a hard place: The native Hawaiian and Pacific Islander struggle for identity in public health. *American Journal of Public Health, 100*(5), 784–789.

Stannard, D. (1989). *Before the horror: The population of Hawaii on the eve of western contact.* University of Hawai'i Press.

Statistical Report. (2016). *Detailed language spoken at home in the state of Hawaii.* Retrieved from https://files.hawaii.gov/dbedt/census/acs/Report/Detailed_Language_March2016.pdf

Stauffer, J. (2015). *Ethical loneliness: The injustice of not being heard.* Columbia University Press.

Strani, K. (2020). Multilingualism and politics revisited: The state of the art. In K. Strani (Ed.), *Multilingual and politics: Revisiting multilingual citizenship* (pp. 17–45). Palgrave Macmillan.

Strobel, L. M. (1996). "Born-again Filipino": Filipino American identity and Asian panethnicity. *Amerasia Journal, 22*(2), 31–53.

Sullivan, M., & Bialystok, E. (2017). The importance of bilingualism for the aging brain: Current evidence and future research directions. In E. Bialystok & M. Sullivan (Eds.), *Growing old with two languages: Effects of bilingualism on cognitive aging.* John Benjamins.

Taff, A., Chee, M., Hall, J., Hall, M. Y. D., Martin, K. N., & Johnston, A. (2018). Indigenous language use impacts wellness. In K. Rehg & L. Campbell (Eds.), *The Oxford handbook of endangered languages* (pp. 862–883). Oxford University Press.

Takaki, R. (1983). *Pau Hana: Plantation life and labor in Hawai'i, 1835–1920.* University of Hawai'i Press.

Talmy, S. (2006). The other *other*: Micronesians in a Hawai'i high school. In C. Park, R. Endo, & A. L. Goodwin (Eds.), *Asian and Pacific American education: Learning, socialization, and identity* (pp. 19–49). Information Age Publishing.

Tamura, E. (1993). The English-only effort, the anti-Japanese campaign, and language acquisition in the education of Japanese Americans in Hawai'i, 1915–1940. *History of Education Quarterly, 33*(1), 37–58.

Tamura, E. (1994). *Americanization, acculturation, and ethnic identity: The Nisei generation in Hawai'i.* University of Illinois Press.

Tamura, E. (1996). Power, status, and Hawai'i Creole English: An example of linguistic intolerance in American history. *Pacific Historical Review, 65*(3), 431–454.

Tannen, D. (1995). Waiting for the mouse: Constructed dialogue in conversation. In D. Tedlock & B. Mannheim (Eds.), *The dialogic emergence of culture* (pp. 198–217). University of Illinois Press.

Teacher Shortage Crisis. (2019). *Teacher shortage crisis forces principals to hire Hawaiian immersion teachers who don't speak Hawaiian.* Retrieved from https://www.hsta.org/news/recent-stories/teacher-shortage-crisis-forces-principals-to-hire-hawaiian-immersion-teachers-who-dont-speak-hawaiian/

Teddick, D. J. (2015). United States of America: The paradoxes and possibilities of bilingual education. In P. Mehisto & F. Genesee (Eds.), *Building bilingual education systems: Forces, mechanisms and counterweights* (pp. 1–22). Cambridge University Press.

Tedick, D. J., Christian, D., & Fortune, T. W. (2011). *Immersion education: Practices, policies, possibilities.* Multilingual Matters.

Teodoro, L. (Ed.). (1981). *Out of this struggle: The Filipinos in Hawaii.* University Press of Hawaii.

The National K-12 Foreign Language Enrollment Survey. (2017). *American councils.* Retrieved from https://www.americancouncils.org/sites/default/files/FLE-report-June17.pdf

Thomas, S. L., Kana'iaupuni, S. M., Balutski, B. J. N., & Freitas, A. K. (2012). Access and success for students from indigenous populations. In J. C. Smart & M. B. Paulsen (Eds.), *Higher education of theory and research* (pp. 335–367). Springer.

Thomas, W., & Collier, V. (2012). *Dual Language education for a transformed world.* Future Press.

Tonouchi, L. (2001). *Da Word.* Bamboo Ridge Press.

Tonouchi, L. (2009). *Living Pidgin: Contemplations on Pidgin culture.* Tinfish Press.

Trask, H. K. (1999). *From a native daughter: Colonialism and sovereignty in Hawai'i.* Latitude 20 Books.

Trask, H. K. (2000). Settlers of color and "immigrant" hegemony. *Amerasia Journal, 26*(2), 1–24.

Twitchell, X. L. (2018). HAA DACHXÁ̲NX'I SÁANI KAGÉIYI YÍS: HAA YOO X̲'ATÁNGI KEI NALTSEEN. *For our little grandchildren: Language revitalization among the Tlingit* (Unpublished Ph.D. Dissertation). University of Hawai'i at Hilo.

Tymoczko, M. (2010). Translation, resistance, activism: An overview. In M. Tymoczko (Ed.), *Translation, resistance, activism* (pp. 1–22). University of Massachusetts Press.

Unvar, S., & Rahimi, A. (2013). A critical discourse analysis of discursive structures in a political text. *International Journal of Science and Advanced Technology, 3*(3), 12–20.

Van den Noort, M., Vermeire, K., Bosch, P., Staudte, H., Krajenbrink, T., Jaswetz, L., Struys, E., Yeo, S., Barisch, P., Perriard, B., Lee, S., & Lim, S. (2019). A systematic review on the possible relationship between bilingualism, cognitive decline, and the onset of dementia. *Behavioral Science, 9,* 7. Retrieved from https://www.mdpi.com/2076-328X/9/7/81

Van Dijk, T. (1993). Principles of critical discourse analysis. *Discourse & Society, 4*(2), 249–283.

Van Dijk, T. (1995). Aims of critical discourse analysis. *Japanese Discourse, 1*, 17–27.

Wagner-Seavey, S. (1980). The effect of world war i on the German community in Hawaii. *Hawaiian Journal of History, 14,* 109–140.

Walch, D. B. (1967). The historical development of the Hawaiian alphabet. *The Journal of the Polynesian Society, 76*(3), 353–366.

Warfield, S. K. (2020). *Ka Na'i Aupuni: The emergence and development of a true Hawaiian leader* (Unpublished Ph.D. Dissertation). University of Hawai'i at Hilo.

Warner, N., Luna, Q., & Butler, L. (2007). Ethics and revitalization of dormant languages: The Mutsun language. *Language Documentation & Conservation, 1*, 58–76.

Watahomigie, L. J., & McCarty, T. L. (1994). Bilingual/bicultural education at peach springs: A Hualapai way of schooling. *Peabody Journal of Education, 69*(2), 26–42.

Weaver, S. (2010). The 'other' laughts back: Humour and resistance in anti-racist comedy. *Sociology, 44*(1), 31–48.

White, L. (2015). *Free to be Mohawk: Indigenous education at the Akwesasne freedom school.* University of Oklahoma Press.

Wiener, A. (2016). America's real migrant crisis in the one you've never heard of. *Mother Jones*. Retrieved from https://www.motherjones.com/politics/2016/12/hawaii-micronesia-migration-homeless-climate-change/

Wiley, T. G., & Garcia, O. (2016). Language policy and planning in language education: Legacies, consequences, and possibilities. *The Modern Language Journal, 100*, 48–63.

Williams, R., Jr. (2009). "Aole Hoohui ia Hawaii": U.S. collegiate teams debate annexation of Hawai'i and independence prevails, 1893–1897. *The Hawaiian Journal of History, 43*, 153–179.

Williams, R., Jr. (2011). 'Ike Mōakaaka, seeing a path forward: Historiography in Hawai'i. *Hūlili: Multidisciplinary research on Hawaiian well-being* (Vol. 7, pp. 67–90).

Willig, A. C. (1985). A meta-analysis of selected studies on the effectiveness of bilingual education. *Review of Educational Research, 55*(3), 269–317.

Wilson, W.H. (1998a). The sociopolitical context of establishing Hawaiian-medium education. *Language, Culture, and Curriculum, 11*(3), 325–338.

Wilson, W. H. (1998b). I ka 'ōlelo Hawai'I ke ola, 'Life is found in the Hawaiian language.' *International Journal of the Sociology of Language, 132,* 123–137.

Wilson, W. H. (2017). Hawaiian language revitalization. In H. Sato & J. Bradshaw (Eds.), *Languages of the Pacific Islands: Introductory readings* (pp. 220–237). CreateSpace Independent Publishing Platform.

Wilson, W. H. (2018). Higher education in indigenous language revitalization. In L. Hinton, L. Huss, & G. Roche (Eds.), *The Routledge handbook of language revitalization* (pp. 83–93). Routledge.

Wilson, W., & Kamanā, K. (2001). Mai loko mai o ka 'i'ini: Proceeding from a dream, the 'Aha Pūnana Leo connection in Hawaiian language revitalization. In L. Hinton & K. Hale (Eds.), *The greenbook of language revitalization in practice* (pp. 147–176). Academic Press.

Wilson, W., & Kamanā, K. (2006). For the interest of the Hawaiians themselves: Reclaiming the benefits of Hawaiian-medium education. *Hūlili: Multidisciplinary research on Hawaiian Well-being, 3,* 153–182.

Wilson, W. H., & Kamanā, K. (2011). Insights from indigenous language immersion in Hawai'i. In D. J. Tedick, D. Christian, & T. W. Fortune (Eds.), *Immersion education: Practices, policies, possibilities* (pp. 36–57). Multilingual Matters.

Wilson, W., & Kamanā, K. (2013). E Paepae Hou 'ia Ka Pōhaku: Reset the stones of the Hawaiian house platform. In L. Hinton (Ed.), *Bringing our languages home: Language revitalization for families* (pp. 101–117). Heyday Books.

Wilson, W., & Kamanā, K. (2014). *Beyond P-20: Reviving a dying language.* YouTube Video. Accessed on June 12, 2018. https://www.youtube.com/watch?v=6Uhmj7jRvCA

Wilson, W. H., & Kamanā, K. (2017). The Hakalama: The 'Aha Pūnana Leo's syllabic Hawaiian reading program. In C. J. McLachlan & A. W. Arrow (Eds.), *Literacy in the early years: Reflections on international research and practice (pp. 133–150). Springer.*

Wilson, W. H., & Kawae'ae'a, K. (2007). I Kumu Lālā: Let there be sources; let there be branches: Teacher education in the college of Hawaiian language. *Journal of American Indian Education, 46*(3), 37–53.

Wist, B. (1940). *A century of public education in Hawai'i, 1840–1940.* Hawaii Educational Review.

Wolfram, W. (1974). *Sociolinguistic aspects of assimilation: Puerto Rican English in New York city.* Center for Applied Linguistics.

Wolfram, W., & Dunstan, S. (2021). Linguistic inequality and sociolinguistic justice in campus life: The need for programmatic intervention. In G. Clements & M. J. Petray (Eds.), *Linguistic discrimination in U.S. higher education* (pp. 156–173). Routledge.

Wong, L. (1999). Language varieties and language policy: The appreciation of Pidgin. In T. Huebner & K. Davis (Eds.), *Sociopolitical perspectives on language policy and planning in the USA* (pp. 221–237). Benjamins.

Wong, L. (2006). *Kuhi aku, Kuhi mai, Kuhi hewa ē: He mau Loina Kuhikuhi 'Ākena no ka 'Ōlelo Hawai'i* (Unpublished Ph.D. Dissertation). University of Hawai'i at Mānoa.

Wong, L. (2011). Hawaiian methodologies of indirection. In K. Davis (Ed.), *Critical qualitative research in second language studies: Agency and advocacy* (pp. 151–170). Information Age Publishing.

Woodside, O. L. L., Reyes, E. K. P., & Kim Jr., M. K. (2011). Nā Hulu Kūpuna: Living and sharing Hawaiian wisdom. *Hūlili: Multidisciplinary research on Hawaiian well-being,7,* 9–23.

Woolard, K. (1998). Simultaneity and bivalency as strategies in bilingualism. *Journal of Linguistic Anthropology, 8*(1), 3–29.

Woumans, E., Santens, P., Sieben, A., Versijpt, J., Stevens, M., & Duyck, W. (2015). Bilingualism delays clinical manifestation of Alzheimer's disease. *Bilingualism, 18,* 568–574.

Wright, W. E. (2012). Bilingual education. In W. C. Ritchie & T. Bhatia (Eds.), *Handbook of bilingualism and multilingualism.* Wiley-Blackwell.

Wroblewska, M. N. (2020). Theory, practice, activism: Gramsci as a translation theorist. In R. R. Gould & K. Tahmasebia (Eds.), *The Routledge handbook of translation and activism*. Routledge.

Yamanaka, L. A. (2000). *Heads by Harry*. Harper.

Yamanaka, L. A. (2006). *Wild meat and the bully burgers: A novel.* Picador.

Yokota, T. (2008). The 'Hawai'i Creole problem': Attitudes about Hawai'i Creole. *Educational Perspectives, 41*(1–2), 22–29.

Young, M. (2002). Standard English and student bodies: Institutionalizing race and literacy in Hawai'i. *College English, 64*(4), 405–431.

Index

S. Saft, *Language and Social Justice in Context*,
https://doi.org/10.1007/978-3-030-91251-2

T

U

The manufacturer's authorised representative in the EU is Springer Nature Customer Service Centre GmbH, Europaplatz 3, 69115 Heidelberg, Germany. If you have any concerns regarding our products, please contact ProductSafety@springernature.com

Printed and bound by CPI Group (UK) Ltd, Croydon, CR0 4YY

30/09/2026

02225502-0014